William Russell

Pulpit Elocution

Comprising remarks on the effect of manner in public discourse

William Russell

Pulpit Elocution

Comprising remarks on the effect of manner in public discourse

ISBN/EAN: 9783337082468

Printed in Europe, USA, Canada, Australia, Japan

Cover: Foto ©Suzi / pixelio.de

More available books at **www.hansebooks.com**

PULPIT ELOCUTION:

COMPRISING

REMARKS ON THE EFFECT OF MANNER IN PUBLIC DISCOURSE; THE ELEMENTS OF ELOCUTION, APPLIED TO THE READING OF THE SCRIPTURES, HYMNS, AND SERMONS; WITH OBSERVATIONS ON THE PRINCIPLES OF GESTURE; AND A SELECTION OF EXERCISES IN READING AND SPEAKING

BY

WILLIAM RUSSELL,

AUTHOR OF ORTHOPHONY, THE AMERICAN ELOCUTIONIST, THE AMERICAN SCHOOL READER, ETC.

WITH AN INTRODUCTION, BY EDWARDS A. PARK, D. D., PROFESSOR IN ANDOVER THEOLOGICAL SEMINARY; AND REV. EDWARD N. KIRK, PASTOR OF MT. VERNON CHURCH, BOSTON.

SECOND EDITION.

BOSTON:
DRAPER AND HALLIDAY.
PHILADELPHIA: SMITH, ENGLISH, AND CO.
CINCINNATI: GEO. S. BLANCHARD AND CO.
1867.

PREFACE.

The design of the present work, is, as intimated in the title, to furnish a manual of elocution, prepared with particular reference to the purposes of the pulpit.

The author's previous publications, — the American Elocutionist, and the volume on Orthophony, are intended for general use, in all literary establishments in which elocution forms a department of instruction. These two manuals furnish, it is thought, all the requisite means of acquiring a thorough knowledge of the principles of elocution, — either in a practical or a scientific form, at the option of the student.

The Orthophony prescribes the elementary discipline by which to *train the organs* to vigor and pliancy, and to *mould the voice*, in adaptation to the various modes of expressive utterance. It furnishes a series of *elementary lessons on the systematic cultivation of the voice*, — adapted to the theory and nomenclature of Dr. Rush. It includes, also, the methods of instruction, and the forms of exercise, introduced by Mr. J. E. Murdoch, in his system of "vocal gymnastics," along with those which are used by the author of the present volume, in his modes of practical training.

The Elocutionist presents, more particularly, *the correct pronunciation of words*, and the application of *the rules of elocution*, in connection with *rhetoric* and *prosody*. It comprises a course of *practical* instruction in *enunciation, inflection, emphasis, rhetorical pauses, expressive tone*, and the rudiments of *gesture*.

The general principles of elocution, however, as a science, and its practice, as an art, need particular modification, to accommodate them to the appropriate purposes of professional culture, for students of *theology*. The style of voice, adapted to the correct and impressive reading of a hymn, the Scriptures, or a sermon, requires special attention and study, and a separate course of practice. The delivery of a discourse from the pulpit, demands an appropriate training, distinct from that of popular oratory. — The materials and the suggestions for such cultivation, the present volume is designed to supply.

The plan on which the contents of the following pages, are arranged, embraces,

1st, Introductory Observations on the importance of Elocution, as a department of Theological Study.

2d, Remarks on the effect of Manner, in Voice and Gesture, as exemplified in the pulpit.

3d, A brief Summary of the most important Principles of Elocution, with particular reference to their *exemplification* in the reading of the Scriptures, hymns, and sermons.

4th, *Exercises* in these forms of reading, selected and arranged for the particular *application* of rules and principles.

5th, A brief statement of the *Principles of Gesture*.

6th, *Miscellaneous Extracts*, for practice in Reading and Speaking, intended to be analyzed by the student, and classified, in their various contents, under the points of practical elocution which they illustrate.

CONTENTS.

	PAGE
PREFACE,	3
HINTS ON THE MODES OF PRACTICE IN THE USE OF THIS VOLUME,	9
INTRODUCTORY OBSERVATIONS ON THE STUDY OF ELOCUTION,	13
The Elocution of the Pulpit. By the Rev. Dr. Edwards A. Park,	14
The Study of Elocution an important part of the Preparation required by the Public Duties of the Ministry. By the Rev. Edward N. Kirk,	21
Elocution, as a department of Preparatory Study in Theology,	29
EFFECTS OF MANNER IN THE ELOCUTION OF THE PULPIT,	56
Animation and Dulness,	56
Earnestness and Apathy,	61
Force, Feebleness,	69
Vehemence, Violence,	70
Gentleness, Spirit, Tameness,	71
Boldness, Timidity,	72
Harshness, Amenity,	74
The Cultivation of Force,	75
Modes of Cultivating Force,	75
Modes of Subduing Excessive Vehemence,	76
Freedom, Constraint, Reserve,	77
Variety, Monotony,	81
Mannerism, Adaptation, Appropriateness,	84
Individuality of Manner,	91
Dignity, Familiarity,	95
Formality, Primness, Rigidity,	99
Propriety of Manner,	104
Warmth of Manner,	107
Serenity of Manner,	113
True and Natural Manner,	116
Refinement and Gracefulness,	120
False Taste, Artificial Style,	122
Adaptation of Manner to the Different Parts of a Discourse,	124
Manner in Devotion,	126
PRINCIPLES OF ELOCUTION,	130
The Cultivation of the Voice: its Capability,	136

CONTENTS.

Neglect of Vocal Culture 134
Remedies for Defective culture, ... 135
Effects of Due Cultivation, ... 137
 on the " Quality " of the Voice, ... 140
 " Articulation, ... 141
 " Force and " Stress," 142
 " Pitch, ... 143
 " " Inflection," 147
 " " Movement," 150
 " " Rhythm " and Pausing, ... 152
 " Emphasis, ... 153
 " " Expression," 156
ELEMENTARY EXERCISES FOR THE VOICE, ... 160
Articulation, ... 160
The Fundamental Sounds of the English Language, . . 160
Combinations, ... 161
Exercises in " Quality," 164
" Pure Tone," 164
 Pathos, ... 164
 Repose, ... 165
 Placid Emotion, ... 166
 Solemnity, ... 167
" Orotund Quality," 168
 Pathos and Sublimity, ... 169
 Repose, Solemnity, and Sublimity, ... 169
 Solemnity, Sublimity, and Pathos, ... 170
 Energy and Sublimity, ... 171
 Joy and Sublimity, ... 173
 Awe and Sublimity, ... 174
EXERCISES IN FORCE, ... 175
Suppressed Force, ... 176
Subdued Force, ... 176
Moderate Force, ... 177
Declamatory Force, ... 179
Empassioned Force, ... 181
Shouting, ... 182
Calling, ... 182
EXERCISES IN " STRESS," 182
Empassioned " Radical Stress," 184
Unempassioned " Radical Stress," 185
" Median Stress," 186
" Vanishing Stress," 187
" Compound Stress," 188
" Thorough Stress," 188
EXERCISES IN PITCH, ... 190

Middle Pitch,	190
Low Pitch,	192
Lowest Pitch,	196
High Pitch,	198
EXERCISES IN INFLECTION,	202
Empassioned Inflection,	202
Vivid or Earnest Inflection,	203
Moderate Inflection,	207
Slight Inflection,	208
"Monotone,"	209
EXERCISES IN "MOVEMENT,"	211
"Slowest Movement,"	212
"Slow Movement,"	214
"Moderate Movement,"	222
"Lively Movement,"	229
EXERCISES IN RHYTHM,"	236
Verse, or Metrical Accent,	238
Prose "Rhythm,"	240
EXERCISES IN EMPHASIS,	242
Empassioned Emphasis,	243
Unempassioned Emphasis,	243
EXERCISES IN "EXPRESSION,"	244
Awe,	244
Awe and Fear,	245
Awe, Solemnity, and Tranquillity,	245
Solemnity and Reverence,	247
Praise,	247
Deep and uncontrolled Grief,	249
Deep and subdued Grief,	251
Indignation,	252
Denunciation,	254
Tenderness,	256
Patience and Contrition,	259
Regret, Repentance, and Shame,	260
Remorse, Self-reproach, Horror, and Despair,	261
Joy,	263
Happiness,	265
Composure Serenity, and Complacency,	268
EXERCISES IN "VARIATION,"	274
"Invocation of Light." — *Milton*,	275
"Soliloquy of Satan." — *Milton*,	278
"The Dying Christian." — *Pope*,	283
"The Enterprise of the Pilgrim Fathers of N. E." — *E. Everett*,	285
READING OF THE SCRIPTURES,	291
Narrative Passages,	295

CONTENTS.

Examples in Familiar Style,	296
Examples in "Middle" Style,	298
Examples in Elevated Style,	299
Didactic Passages,	303
Examples in Oral and Parabolic Style,	304
Examples from the Epistles,	306
Passages from the Prophetic Writings,	308
Lyric Passages,	311
THE READING OF HYMNS,	312
Examples of Solemnity and Awe,	319
" Grandeur, Majesty, and Power,	320
" Repose, Tranquillity, and Serenity,	324
" Joy, Praise, and Triumph,	325
" Pathos, Entreaty, and Supplication,	333
" Varied "Expression,"	337
" Didactic Sentiment,	342
PRINCIPLES OF GESTURE,	346
The Attitude of the Body, required for Public Speaking,	354
The Character of Oratorical Action,	359
MISCELLANEOUS EXERCISES IN READING AND SPEAKING,	369
English Oratory. — *Addison*,	369
Pulpit Eloquence of England. — *Sydney Smith*,	371
Eloquence of the Pulpit. — *John Quincy Adams*,	374
The Fatal Falsehood. — *Mrs. Opie*,	375
Musings on the Grave. — *Washington Irving*,	378
The Grave. — *James Montgomery*,	380
The Gallican Church, at the Period of the Revolution. — *Croly*,	382
Light. — *James Montgomery*,	384
The Land of Beulah. — *G. B. Cheever*,	385
Life's Companions. — *Charles Mackay*,	388
Henry Martyn. — *Macaulay*,	390
"Ora atque Labora!" — *Albert Pike*,	394
The Field of Battle. — *Robert Hall*,	395
"Not on the Battle Field." — *John Pierpont*,	397
Religious Principle the Vital Element of Poetry. — *Carlyle*,	399
Emblems. — *James Montgomery*,	403
The Sun's Eclipse (July 8, 1842). — *Horace Smith*,	404
On a Survey of the Heavens, before Daybreak. — *H. K. White*,	407
The Crowded Street. — *W. C. Bryant*,	409
Robert Hall. — *Anon.*,	410
The Millennium Era. — *S. T. Coleridge*,	412

PRELIMINARY HINTS

ON MODES OF PERSONAL TRAINING,

IN CONJUNCTION WITH THE USE OF THIS VOLUME.

INDIVIDUALS who have not convenient access to instruction, and are desirous of prosecuting the study and practice of elocution, as a matter of self-cultivation, may be aided by the following suggestions.

1. The preliminary condition to success in the cultivation of any branch of practical oratory, is *a healthy condition of the bodily frame*. Elocution, as the exterior part of eloquence, is altogether dependent on the vigor and flexibility of the muscular system. Flaccid, rigid, and clumsy muscles render expression by voice and action impracticable. Muscular energy and pliancy demand habits of free exposure to the open air, and the vigorous use of the arms and limbs, in daily exertions of adequate force.

No man can be effectively eloquent without energy; and the attaining of energy is, to the student and the sedentary man, a thing comparatively arduous. Several hours — not one, merely — of every day, are due to the renovation of the body; and the student who tries to evade this condition, although he may do well, apparently, for a few years, usually sinks into debility, or contracts a decided — perhaps a fatal — bronchial affection. The sedentary man who is, at the same time, a public speaker, needs a double allowance of air and exercise, to counteract the injurious tendency of the union of two modes of life naturally incompatible. The nervous excitation, and the cerebral exhilaration, arising from continued intellectual action, — by the deceptive inspiration which they impart, — often lead the student to slight physical exercise, as a thing unnecessary. A few years, — sometimes even a few months, are sufficient to undeceive the individual, and disclose all the accumulation of unsuspected injury to which he had been subjecting himself. The student is ever prone to forget that the body is a machine designed for action, and one which he is bound to keep in use, and so to keep in repair, — under a penalty not less severe than is attached to a desecration. The statistics of elocution, however, if faithfully recorded, would not show a result, usually, of one sound voice in ten, among young men who are addicted to sedentary and studious habits.

An individual who wishes to acquire or retain the power of speaking or reading with true effect, must, in the first instance, be willing to assign a considerable portion of every day to invigorating exercise and exposure.

2. It is, farther, an indispensable prerequisite to effective elocution that the student accustom himself to *activity, as a habit both of body and mind*. Expression, in elocutionary forms, is action: it is a thing utterly

incompatible with listlessness, indolence, or languor. Eloquence, — of which elocution is but the audible and visible part, — implies a tendency to perceptible effect. "*Wisdom*" may be "the *repose* of minds." But *eloquence* is not. The true orator has always defined eloquence as action. Eloquence is not — in its effective form, — the placid lake, whose charm is its serenity. It is the river "moving in majesty," or sweeping to its destination, and carrying with it whatever it encounters in its course.

The eloquence of calm thought and mild persuasion, has doubtless its time and place. But even this demands its appropriate utterance and action. Deprived of these it will lose its power. The discipline to which the student, as a scholar, so long subjects himself, — the passive and receptive state of mind to which he is habituated. — entail a tendency to inaction, as regards manifestation and expression. When he assumes, therefore, the duties of a profession which devolves on him, in frequent recurrence, the act of public speaking, he is usually unprepared for this altogether new career, in which his success depends not on his power of reception or acquisition, but of impartation and utterance. He must undergo a change of habit, as regards both mental and bodily exertion, to render him capable of accomplishing the purposes of active life and professional duty. He must become habituated to the glow of action, and the impulse of feeling; he must learn to cherish the inspiration of ardor and positive exertion, and to relish the pleasure of impelling other minds, — of compassing an object, and carrying a point. His speech must become fraught with the spirit of eloquence, in the earnestness of its tones, and the energy of its accompanying action; that he may possess the power of moving his hearers and carrying them with him. Such exertion will often demand all the spirit and enthusiasm of heroic enterprise.

The student of elocution, then, must bring to his practice a stirring ambition that shall not suffer him to subside into languor and indolence, or irresolution and inaction. His daily physical exercise must be carried to such extent as to yield the natural and healthful pleasure of exertion, and to create an earnest desire for it, and an habitual tendency towards it.

3. But the successful practice of elocution demands more than merely high-toned health and habitual activity. Expression by voice and action requires that natural result of healthful habit, which we designate, in popular language, by the phrase "high animal spirits." This is one of Nature's laws of expression. The individual in private society, not less than the public speaker, needs *animation, as a condition of oral communication*. The child, under the inspiration of vivid emotion, becomes an eloquent monitor to the man, as regards the impartation of feeling. The student of elocution, to be successful in his endeavors, needs all the aids arising from the inspiring influences of health and activity and animation. It is from the superabundant life of his own heart that he is to warm and inspire the feelings of others. Expression, in its best forms, is often something struck out in the glow of emotion. The most eloquent tones of the human voice, and the most impressive forms of attitude and action, are those which spring from the most vivid state of the soul, under a powerful inspiration.

4. A high tone of the animal spirits, and a quick sensibility of heart need, however, the associated aid of *a plastic, and*, at the same time *a powerfully active imagination*. Poetry is not such to the man who receives it into a hard or a dormant fancy. To such an individual, its no-

blest workings are but so many forms of falsehood. Let him attempt to give it voice, and his dry inexpressive tone reveals the fact that it has no power over his being. The highest expressive action of the human mind, is that in which eloquence, in its sublime inspiration, passes into the form of poetry. The art of elocution recognizes this fact, and presents to the student, as the noblest of all its exercises, the fitting recitation of sentiment embodied in verse, or in those forms of prose which bespeak the presence of the spirit, if not the letter, of poetry. To do justice to such strains, the student must bring to his work the utmost pliancy and glowing activity of imagination, to enable him to take on and give off, with correspondent effect, the "thick-coming fancies" of the poet. He must possess the power of assimilating his own mood of mind to that of the creative artist under whose inspiration he is working. Every central point of thought must be thrown out, in tone and action, in a style which clusters round it the whole investing imagery of the poet's soul and the speaker's heart. Poetic utterance requires that imagination should people the world of feeling, not less than that feeling should animate and awaken the world of fancy. Eloquence, when it is truly such, partakes largely of the character of poetry: the most eloquent passage of writing is that which is essentially the most poetical.

The student of elocution, then, if he would be successful in his art, must cherish whatever tends to impart life and power to the imaginative faculty. Nature and art, and poetry, in particular, are the great schools of imagination. But no influence is more immediate, in this respect, than the attentive practice of elocution itself. A true poetic recitation breathes into the soul, at once, the conception of the poet, the music of his verse, and the charm of a harmonized living voice, to which the heart strings are formed to thrill.

5. The effects resulting from the practice of elocution, are equally favorable, as regards *the best influence on the health and vigor and activity of the organic frame, and on the habitual tone of feeling.* The erect and expansive attitude of body, and the free and forcible action of all its parts, in the full expression of posture, motion, and gesture, tend to impart vigor and pliancy, not less than freedom and grace; while the unembarrassed and active play of heart and lungs conveys fresh life and power to all parts of the system, from the energy imparted to the muscles of the chest and throat. A highly animated condition of the whole interior of the bodily frame, is a necessary consequence of the vivid and genial emotions which inspiring sentiment and impressive utterance produce.

6. The various modes of exercise in detail, which are most conducive to healthful vigor and organic energy, may be found described in the volume on Orthophony, which is more immediately occupied with this branch of elocutionary training. The student, when he has rendered himself expert in these, or others of a similar description, may, with advantage, proceed in the course of cultivation, as developed in that work, and in the American Elocutionist. To the study of these volumes the exercises commencing with the 130th page of the present work, will form a useful sequel. Students who have not convenient access to the works now mentioned, will, it is thought, find, in the exercises presented in the following pages, a course of practice sufficient for immediate purposes.

7. The practice of the elementary exercises, should be persevered in, **till every point, successively, is mastered, and the results of cultivation**

are fully obtained in a perfectly pure, clear, round, and full Tone of voice; a perfectly distinct and well-marked, but fluent Enunciation; the power of giving forth, at pleasure, any degree of Force, from whispering to shouting and calling; every species of "Stress;" the ability to exemplify any Pitch of voice, from the lowest to the highest; a perfect command of "Inflections," in all their forms; an entire control over "Movement," from the slowest to the lively rate; an exact observance of Time and "Rhythm;" every degree of effect in Emphasis, from the most delicate to the boldest; a perfect mastery of "Expression," in all its moods, and of "Variation," through all its modifications.

8. *A separate course of practice, in the reading of the Scriptures and of hymns*, should, after the previous training, be pursued, with the aid of close analysis and frequent repetition, as exemplified in the following pages.

9. *The "miscellaneous exercises" should all be thoroughly analyzed*, previous to practising them, and the style of reading penciled, if necessary, on the margin, opposite to every passage which needs more than usual attention to "expression" and variation.

10. The next step in the student's progress, should be *the reading of passages selected from various authors*, exemplifying all the varieties of style in narrative, descriptive, didactic, and oratorical composition in prose, and of epic, lyric, and dramatic poetry.

11. The next step in preparatory training. should be *the reading of sermons*, with strict regard to the due loudness and slowness of voice required in public reading;—with a watchful attention to inflection, emphasis, and pauses, as the vehicles of distinctive thought; and to "expression" and "variation," as the means of effect in sentiment and emotion. The best security for due closeness of attention to particulars, is the preparatory use of the pencil in marking, on the margin and between the lines, every important point in the management of the voice.

12. The student should now adopt the practice of *reading matter of his own composition*, in the form of essays, lectures, and sermons.

13. As a preparation for applying the principles of *Gesture*, passages from the "ELEMENTARY" and the "MISCELLANEOUS EXERCISES," may be committed to memory, and practised in the forms of *declamation* and *recitation*.

14. The next step, in preparatory practice, should consist in *speaking on given subjects, after close and thorough premeditation*, so as to develope a train of thought in well-digested forms, leaving the language and expression, in their details, to the suggestion of the moment.

15. The last stage of elocutionary practice, may be left to *exercises in strictly extemporaneous speaking*, in the form of discourses pronounced on texts selected *ad aperturam libri*, as a preparation for the customary remarks on passages of Scripture, at prayer-meetings. When students can conveniently meet, in classes, *the practice of extemporaneous discussion and debate* may be advantageously adopted, as a means of cultivating propriety and fluency in elocution.

INTRODUCTORY OBSERVATIONS

ON THE

STUDY OF ELOCUTION.

STUDENTS of theology are not always aware of the immense importance of a perfect command of voice, and of an intimate knowledge of the rules and principles of elocution, as the only rational means to that end. A teacher in this branch of education, therefore, has often to consume much time in soliciting attention to his subject; and his arguments are not unfrequently regarded as the pleading of one whose personal interests are at stake in the question.

The author of the following treatise, labors, in common with other instructors in his department, under this disadvantage, and has found it useful to appeal, on this ground, to the testimony of individuals already engaged in the duties of the sacred profession. He was desirous, therefore, previous to commencing the task of compiling this volume, to obtain,— from those whose professional position and opportunities might give sanction to their opinions, — their views on the advantages of specific study and practice in elocution, as a part of professional training for the services of the pulpit.

Several clergymen to whom the author made application, on this subject, expressed a warm interest in the object in view, and their readiness to render it their personal aid. The urgency of professional duties, however, in some instances, and unforeseen hinderances, in others, have prevented the fulfilment of their wishes.* The author takes peculiar pleasure in acknowledging the effectual aid which, in the following instances, has been so liberally afforded to his undertaking. The sentiments of such individuals, will carry their own commendation to every mind; and in contributing them to the objects of this volume, the compiler feels assured that their authors have rendered an invaluable service to the purposes of the profession which they sustain.

---

* The late Rev. Dr. Nettleton expressed his earnest desire, in case of the restoration of his health, to give his express testimony on this subject; and, among the students attending the Theological Institute at East Windsor, during the latter years of his life, several will recollect how eloquently he urged this matter on their attention, in the counsels which he gave them, when he was lying disabled by the disease which terminated his life.

THE ELOCUTION OF THE PULPIT.

[Contributed by the Rev. Dr. Edwards A. Park, Professor in Andover Theological Seminary.]

The Author of our being has made the various organs of the body expressive of thought and emotion. The eye, the cheek, the lip, the hand, the foot, the attitude of the limbs and chest and head, may all show forth a sentiment of the soul. It is a singular fact, that the choicest selection of words will sometimes fail to exhibit a certain cast of thought, which may be indicated at once by the natural signs consisting in certain movements and appearances of the physical organs. In the person of Garrick, a mere position of the elbow or the knee, yea, a particular adjustment of the hair, has vividly portrayed a state of mind which artificial language is too inflexible to express.

Written words, even when they embody the general idea, the substantial meaning, are often unable to exhibit those evanescent shades of sentiment which are clearly expressed by tones and gestures. The inflection with which a word is uttered, conveys sometimes a delicate thought, which the word itself does not even intimate. Now this natural expressiveness of the human frame is an essential concomitant of oral language. It is the first instrument which man uses in order to communicate his thoughts, for he knows the meaning of signs before that of articulate phrases; and it is his last resort when speech fails him.

Our Creator never intended, that we should utter our words without the appropriate tones and the corroborative appearances of the body. These accompaniments of speech are as necessary to its full effect, as animal life is needful for the completeness of physical beauty. There can be no perfect speech without them. The imperfect manner in which they are frequently exhibited, results from that obtuseness of sensibility, that indolence of mind, that ignorance of the fitness of things, that want of executive power, which are remote consequences of our apostate moral condition. A complete orator must be a completely holy man; and our natural selfishness has superinduced such habits of thought and feeling as make us awkward and inexpert in our attempts to express what passes within our minds. The various developments of affectation are the result of our pride and love of display; the different forms of dullness in our speech are occasioned by that callous sensibility which the Bible denominates "hardness of heart."

The natural language of the human body, being indispensable to the full effect of arbitrary language, is, of course, an essential accompaniment of all earnest address. A proper use of this natural language, is involved in a good elocution; and such an elocution is thus a constituent part of the preaching of the gospel. A man would not be considered as preaching the word which maketh wise unto salvation, if he should proclaim it in an unknown tongue, or in any such manner as would render it unintelligible; if, for instance, he should make no pauses at the end of sentences, and should let his voice fall at those words only which cannot be understood unless uttered with a rising inflection; if he should use the interrogative tones for affirmative remarks, and the exclamatory accent for the simplest didactic phrase. This might be trifling with the gospel, or disfiguring it, but not preaching it. Now a poor elocution does make certain portions of the proclaimed word unintelligible. It fails to express those delicate shades of thought, which are elementary parts of the gospel itself. It suggests positive ideas, which the words uttered do not mean, and which are sometimes hostile to the whole spirit of divine truth. The most injurious impressions have been produced, by what are technically called "immoral tones," in the utterance of Christian doctrine.

It is evident, then, that a good elocution in the pulpit is as really important as any elocution at all. If it be useful to preach the gospel, then it is useful to preach it so that it will be understood and felt. If its truths ought to be expressed, they ought to be expressed fully and properly. To proclaim them, and yet adopt such a manner as will obscure or pervert their meaning, and blunt their force, is to do and to undo a thing at the same time. The advantages resulting from a true, natural elocution, in the pulpit, are the same with the advantages of Christian doctrine well exhibited. The evils ensuing from a false, unnatural elocution, are the same with the evils of misrepresenting the word of God. He who undervalues the right method of enunciating religious truth, undervalues also the niceties of sentiment, the delicate mouldings of thought, which are a constituent portion of that truth; and which are lost from the view, when a preacher's elocution hides behind itself the ideas which ought to be *delivered* to his hearers. An affected delivery is often a delivery of *mere* words, often words conveying a thought never intended by the speaker.

If, then, the preaching of the gospel be the appropriate enunciation of divine truth, we see why it was ordained as the chief means of impressing this truth upon the mind. The Deity might have required, that his word should be merely read in silence, or that it should be repeated in a whisper from a single individual to another, or that it should be only chanted or sung. But he chose to ordain that it should be preached, i. e. uttered in the appropriate style, by a sacred orator to a listening congregation. Long before the New Testament was committed to writing, were its truths impressed upon the public mind by the living voice of the presbyter. He who made man, knew what was in man. He knew those latent sensibilities of the soul, which can be touched by nothing so well as by truth eloquently spoken. The means for our spiritual renovation he thus wisely adapted to the principles of our nature. Hence when his word is preached, as it ought to be, in an earnest and emphatic manner, it produces a peculiar effect upon the soul. It acquires a meaning which it does not seem to possess upon the writen page. When a Whitefield utters the words, "Oh! wretched man that I am," they have an intensity of expression which a silent reader will not perceive. The power of those and of many similar phrases, is communicated, in some degree, by their conventional signs; in some degree, by the tones which are their life;—by the speaking eye, the flushed face, the whole air and mien of the impassioned orator.

Being endued with physical and spiritual susceptibilities, man is the most deeply impressed when an appeal is made to both parts of his sentient nature; when the eye and the ear are delighted, as well as the mind and heart. And such is the sympathy between the corporeal and the mental powers, that when the former are in a state of appropriate excitement, the latter act with increased vigor and success. The soul perceives the more of truth, and feels it the more keenly, when the eye traces the lineaments of this truth upon the countenance of the speaker, and the ear catches the vibrations of it from lips which have been touched as with a live coal from off the altar.

Valerius Maximus says of the Athenian orator, that "a great part of Demosthenes is wanting, for it must be heard and not read." Quintilian says of Hortensius, that "there was something in him which strangely pleased when he spoke, which those who perused his orations could not find." The younger Pitt remarked that he could never conjecture, from reading his father's speeches, where their eloquence lay hidden. And there have been thousands of preachers, who uttered truths which no stenographer could seize; which no ready writer, with a command of the most extensive vocabulary, could transfer to the silent page, for they were truths that beamed from the eye, and were breathed out in the tones of the voice, and were visible in the gesture, but could not be circumscribed within arbitrary symbols.

Conventional terms form the body of the preacher's utterance; but the soul of it is that natural language which God has made indispensable to the life-giving power of artificial speech. The ordinance of preaching, then, is no arbitrary appointment of Heaven. It was wisely chosen, as the means most philosophically adapted to impress the mind with religious truth. The more perfect the preaching is, so much the more exquisite is its adaptation to produce the intended effect. Other things being equal, that sermon will be the most efficacious which is delivered in the best manner. The very principle, on which the preaching of the gospel is more useful than the publication of it from the press, makes a natural and expressive style of preaching it more useful than a style which does not correspond with the demands of the subject. The very reason, for which God requires us to preach the word, makes it necessary to preach it well, to speak according to the best rules of elocution, which are no other than the rules prescribed by nature, by the God of nature.

Much of that which passes under the name of preaching, does not deserve the name. It may be called a poor kind of singing, a tedious method of drawling, a soporific way of reading, but it is not the living utterance of such thought as enkindles the eye, the gushing forth of those emotions which cannot be fully expressed except in the forms of eloquence. One reason why preaching is less effective than we should antecedently expect it to be, is the fact that there is *less of it* than we ordinarily suppose. All the dull, clumsy, turgid, weak, insipid, and in any way affected methods of delivery, are to be subtracted from the sum total of what is denominated preaching; and then how small is the remainder!

God will honor the laws which he has made, and will manifest his displeasure toward the violation of these laws. The true rules of elocution are established by the Author of our being, and will not be obeyed without advantage nor disobeyed without loss; and no preacher can regard himself as serving God, or doing good to man, in the act of contravening the laws of speech. He may be useful in spite of his opposition to nature and providence, but not by means of that opposition. Truth ill administered may do good; truth well administered will do more. The proprieties of the administration add a power to the truth; the improprieties of the administration take a power away from it.

It has long been a desire of good men, to make the services of the sanctuary as attractive as possible. Music, and architecture, and painting, and sculpture have all imparted of their fascinations to the exercises of worship. Every age has witnessed the invention of some new rite, or the restoration of one that had become obsolete. New measures and strange measures have made their appeal to the fancy of men, and have charmed it for a time. But the chief outward attraction of public worship has been too much overlooked. The great majority of nominal Christians have preferred the gorgeousness of a ceremonial above the eloquence of the pulpit. And yet none of the fine arts is so attractive as eloquence. The most philosophical skeptic whom the English world has seen, declared that he would travel twenty miles to hear the preaching of a certain Methodist minister.

There is something in the voice of an orator, that answers to a demand of the soul. By the flashes of his eye, the heart of an audience is inflamed; and men are sometimes spell-bound by the upraising of his hand. Whether they love or hate the truth which is addressed to them, they are enamored of the form in which it appears. Many an obnoxious doctrine of the Bible lies imbedded in a sweet historical narrative, which allures even such as dislike the doctrine. The casket may enclose a pearl, which is less highly prized than the gold in which it is encased. But thousands who come to admire the wining elocution, remain to adore the great Being whose character is so appropriately described. It is the genius of Romanism to raise the orchestra and the parade of the altar above the pulpit. Only a small proportion of its priests have cultivated the art of speaking. They have but little encouragement to do so. The forms of Christian worship most prevalent throughout the world, have tended to withdraw the mind from the proper methods of proclaiming divine truth. Men have been allured into the sanctuary by less intellectual and more artificial attractions, than those of a racy and graceful eloquence. It is, or must we say, it should be the glory of the pulpit, to restore the appropriate allurements to Christian worship; to fascinate men by thoughts well attired, well exhibited. The mind was made for thought, and will be pleased with it longer than with any external ornament. And thought expressed, is thought still. The enunciation of it increases its influence over the soul. There never was an age so intellectual as the present. Our lyceums have well nigh supplanted our theatres. It is then a great mistake to spend our time in decorating our ceremonials of worship, when the taste of the age requires something more spiritual and refined than mere pageantry. It requires a more copious supply of facts and arguments and illustrations than is now to be found, and a more interesting manner of exhibiting them.

If we would meet the demands of our time, and, indeed, of all times, we must prefer those ornaments which are the natural and appropriate dress of truth, to those which are factitious and far-fetched. The graces of elocution are those which belong to the truth itself. The expressiveness of attitudes and gestures and tones, is nature. It flows from the mind. It is the result of the inspiration of thought. Statues and pictures and robes are artificial adornings of the temple; but the apostle who "*cannot but speak* the things which he hath seen and heard," will be a permanent as well as an appropriate attraction to the sanctuary; and men who would soon be satiated with the chauntings of the matins and the vespers, will come again and again to hear the preacher who speaks like one anointed to publish glad tidings.

Let it not be said, that this mode of speaking is the result of divine grace. The gifts of the Spirit never supersede the necessity of assiduous culture. Nor let it be said, that an effective elocution must be a natural endowment. God bestows upon men the faculties, which are to be improved by laborious training. All men cannot be orators, but the majority of men may be. The majority of men *are* eloquent, when they speak for their selfish interests. It is a corrupt habit, which has made our speakers so sluggish; and now cultivation is required in order to restore the nature which has been expelled by evil practice.

The elocutionist labors not to make men artificial, but to make them cease from being so; not to mend or transform nature, but to restore and develop it. He labors to repress the intrusions of a proud, selfish spirit into the style of a preacher; to excite the dormant energies of a mind, which has been in the habit of contemplating truth with indifference; to rectify the depraved tastes of depraved men; and to teach those subordinate graces of utterance, which would never have been forgotten if man had not been sluggish, regardless of his influence over others, unmindful of his accountability to Heaven for every gift which he has received. In fine, the elocutionist labors to make the preacher natural, and therefore impressive, and thus attractive. The naturalness is to be the proper expression of the truth; the impressiveness is to be the legitimate effect of the thought fitly uttered; and the attractiveness is to be the alluring influence, which the purity and firmness and and grandeur of the word of God always exert upon a soul that is attuned to the love of holiness, or even awake to the beauties of intellect.

THE STUDY OF ELOCUTION, AN IMPORTANT PART OF THE PREPARATION REQUIRED BY THE PUBLIC DUTIES OF THE MINISTRY.

[Contributed by the Rev. Edward N. Kirk, pastor of the Mount Vernon Church, Boston.]

It is easy to recognize the difference between a speaker who is agreeable and one who is disagreeable, between one who is powerful and another who is feeble. Nor can any one entertain a doubt whether that difference is just as obvious in the pulpit as in the senate. Every preacher would desire so to deliver his sermon as that his meaning should be clearly perceived and his sentiments deeply felt, rather than to utter it in a manner unintelligible and unimpressive. Every congregation of worshippers would prefer in their pastor a good delivery, to an awkward and disagreeable style of speaking. Let two men of equal piety and scholarship be presented to any of our religious societies; the one a man of easy, becoming carriage in the pulpit, of simple, natural, and powerful utterance; the other uncouth in attitude and movement, indistinct and stammering in his enunciation, and wearisome in his drawling tones; can any man in his senses doubt, which of the two will be chosen? No; thus far the case is plain. But if we go back of this, and observe this finished speaker practising in the detail of his studies and vocal gymnasti, there we shall find some demurring. Many who admi the orator, are averse to the process of discipline whi gave him the better style. There is, in other words, a prejudice in the community, and among many excellent candidates for the gospel ministry, in regard to elocution as an art to be obtained by study and practice.

This prejudice is worthy of a candid examination and of an earnest effort to remove it. In the minds of some, he study and practice of elocution is connected, if not identified with the idea of substituting sound and emotion for sense and truth. To such persons it may be suggested that there is no necessity for this substitution. The importance of elocution presupposes the importance of other things. If a preacher have not the right things to say, and the right motives and spirit in uttering them, manner can do nothing for him nor his hearers. But for men who are morally and intellectually qualified to preach the gospel, the importance of manner can scarcely be overrated. And to overlook it is a proof neither of piety, dignity, nor wisdom. If there were some ethereal way of communicating with the mind; if the process of preaching were designed to be mesmeric; and people were to be put to sleep, instead of being aroused, in order to instruct and impress them, we might dispense with elocution and the culture it requires. But so long as men are in the body, it will be found requisite for the most effective exercise of the ministry, that a part of clerical education consist in the study and practice of oratory. That necessity is founded on these two facts, that the communication of thought and feeling depends upon the right exercise of our bodily organs; and that those organs are within the domain of that great law which requires the cultivation of the faculties. It is not sufficient for the purposes of electrical power that the battery be fully charged; a good conductor must be added. Alas! how much preaching is in the class of nonconductors. Elocution is indeed vanity and vexation of spirit in a man who has no other excellence; but it multiplies indefinitely the power of him who possesses the solid **qualities of the ministry.**

In the minds of others, elocution is identified with the ostentatious exhibition of the parts and graces of the speaker. But this is confounding the use and the abuse of a good thing. Since it is a man who is to be seen and heard, and since there is but one right way of speaking, while there are a thousand wrong ways, the man will do well to learn the right. And if the agreeable impression produced by an agreeable person and manner, can conduce to the right impression of truth, the very purity of his desire to do good, should induce him to cultivate his person and his manner. There is nothing in the study of elocution peculiarly adapted to awaken vanity. Nor is there any more inducement for an eloquent man to make display his end, than for a learned man.

Others fear that they shall be tempted to turn their attention in the pulpit, to gestures and tones; and thus infinitely degrade their high vocation. This again is a possible, but by no means a necessary consequence. It is a perversion of oratory. There is no more need of bringing the rules of oratory into the pulpit, than the rules of grammar or rhetoric. Both must be studied, and both must exercise a powerful influence in the pulpit; but neither must be seen there, for an instant diverting the current of thought or feeling in the speaker. The greatest orator, in an extemporaneous address, pays strict attention to the minutest rules of grammar. In constructing a long and complex sentence, he observes with scrupulous exactness the bearing of grammatical rules upon the inflection and position of each word; but there is no interruption in all this to the concentrated action of his understanding, no extinction of the fiery current of his feeling. The rules of elocution are designed to form the man, to correct the bad habits of attitude, speech, and gesture, to make the body, in every way, the fit instrument for a mind full of noble thoughts and powerful emotions. There may be cases of half-fledged orators or of pedantic speakers turning the rostrum or the pulpit into the platform of a school, and showing off the attitudes and tones and gestures which they admire as mere attitudes, tones, and gestures. But all this, we repeat, is perversion, equally disgusting with the parade or sholarship or any other form of pedantry in the sacred place, but no more a reason against the study of elocution than against that of Hebrew or rhetoric.

The considerations in favor of this study are so obvious, that we seem to be uttering common-places in presenting them. But since it is evident that these considerations have not yet produced their proper effect on our students of theology; since we are still compelled to witness the bodily distortions, the croakings and jerkings and screamings, the false emphasis, and the unmeaning modulations which now are, to some extent, eclipsing the brightest lights of the American pulpit, — we feel compelled to utter common-place truths.

We design, then, to show that good speaking is better than bad speaking, that propriety in speaking is more proper than impropriety. And if our chapter appears to be unworthy of a place in this work, let it be set down to the fact that men, wise men, need to be told such obvious truths, as when written, appear childish.

A preacher of the gospel is to perform the most important of his ministerial services in the pulpit. Within that sacred enclosure he spends some of the most important hours of his life. There he exhausts his physical energies; there he strikes the chord that shall vibrate in the joys or sorrows of his hearers, forever. In every view of the case, then, the best mode of occupying the pulpit, and of exercising his functions in it, cannot be unimportant. If there be a way of diminishing the weariness of the speaker; if there be a way of preventing some of the disastrous physical effects of public speaking, surely a wise man will not think the matter beneath his notice. If there be one way of standing and speaking more agreeable to an audience than another, surely a benevolent man will choose the better way. And much more if there be a way of making one's self better understood, and one's sentiments more deeply felt by an audience, no honest preacher can undervalue the instruction that will make him to know it, nor the discipline by which he may attain to it. But all these things are capable of demonstration. If we begin with the least important, the ease and health of the preacher; we may see that a speaker who has learned to stand in the pulpit on two feet, will be less fatigued, at the end of an hour, than if he has been limping and hopping on one foot, as we have seen preachers do; twining one limb around the other, as the ivy embraces the oak. By the disastrous effects of public speaking, we mean the derangement of the functions of the throat and chest. There is a mode of employing the vocal muscles, which seriously and needlessly wastes the nervous energy of the system, inflames the membrane of the throat and the delicate structure of the bronchia. All this could be avoided by learning to use the muscles that were designed for the purpose, and so to speak, that the respiration and pulsation and vocal utterance shall move in harmony; and an hour's speaking will then be, for the body, merely a healthful exercise. This is not exaggeration. The recent experience of some preachers, who, by proper exercises have totally recovered the use of their vocal powers, and have learned to speak with an ease to which they were formerly strangers in the pulpit, confirms it. A young minister will find difficulties enough in his work, to make the diminution of those which are merely physical, a matter of some moment to him.

Nor do we deem it unworthy of a preacher's attention that he should remove everything unnecessarily disagreeable from his speaking, and add to it everything that is adapted to satisfy the refined taste of his hearers. When Cowper expresses his abhorrence of the " start theatric practiced at the glass," all the world approves the censure, because all the world understands him to mean the affected and contemptible exhibition of one's self as the object of admiration to an assembly, who are waiting to hear a message from God. There certainly is neither piety nor power in clownishness. And it cannot be denied that if some speakers had practised their attitudes and starts before a glass, they would never have inflicted them on their hearers. It is true, that people of good taste will bear much from the pulpit, which, in the parlor, would seem to them offensive. But there is an evident impropriety and disadvantage in so taxing their respect for the office and its incumbent. The preacher is often called to speak unpalatable truths. There is thus a sufficient degree of offensiveness in his employment, to spare him from superadding that which may arise from uncouth positions and motions of the body, grimaces and frowns, monotony and false emphasis. An audience is often wearied under a sermon full of sound sense, distinctive remarks, and the fervent spirit of piety. They often associate with a preacher of sterling excellence some uncomfortable feelings. They know not why; for he is a good man, a sensible man, a man of true piety, and a good theologian. The true reason is, that he wearies the ear.

The mind of every hearer is so constituted, that variety pleases, and monotony wearies it. This is true of the body also. The muscles of the limbs, the organs of taste, the eye, the ear, all demand variety. And while the highest moral effect from discourse, demands unity, this law of the mind requires, at the same time, variety in unity. This principle should control alike the thought, the style, and the delivery. The unity of delivery depends upon the pitch and general current of the voice; the variety depends not only upon the occasional variation of pitch and direction, but upon another circumstance which we would briefly explain. The spoken English language contains upwards of forty distinct sounds. Some of them are very grateful to the ear; and all of them together make the music of our language. Now it generally happens that every uncultivated speaker fails to utter several of them; and usually those which are the most musical. He likewise gives those which he does employ, too much in the same mould. Indolence has made every one pronounce his words as much alike as is consistent with being understood. Hence it results that some of the most musical sounds of our language, are not heard from the lips of many speakers; and instead of more than forty, uttered in their varied combinations, we are confined to a greater or less number below this. The hearers do not know why, but their minds seldom continue aroused to the end of some discourses, when they know, at the same time, that the preacher thinks well and writes well. The monotony of sound itself is sufficient to account for it. To overcome this indolent and inelegant habit, requires the careful cultivation of the ear, to distinguish these sounds, and of the vocal organs to utter them with precision and purity.

But these considerations are still inferior to another, which is, that the perspicuity and impressiveness of a discourse require a correct delivery. The shades of thought in the mind depend for their correct expression, not merely upon words, but also upon the mode of pronouncing them. It scarcely needs to be repeated here that a bad emphasis may make a true statement become a falsehood. It is not merely the tongue that speaks; the whole frame utters a language definite and powerful. The moment a speaker rises before an audience, he makes an impression. His attitude is a language. If he be a man of true dignity, and his soul be elevated by the noblest sentiments, he may, for want of a proper cultivation of his body, produce the contrary impression on his hearers. An erect attitude is dignified, and becomes no man more than him who approaches his fellows with messages from God. And every man of true dignity should accustom his body to correspond to his mind, and not to belie it. Physical uprightness is not an unbecoming representative and expression of moral rectitude. There is more moral effect on an audience in a posture which presents the expanded front, than in the side-posture of a fencing-master. There is also more power in the gestures which are made by a body firmly sustained, than by one which reels upon its base. The voice, too, is capable of countless inflections, each one of which is itself a language to the soul. Every shade of sentiment in a discourse has an appropriate modulation of the voice; and if that modulation be not made, that sentiment must lie buried in the bosom of the speaker: the hearer fails, just so far, to participate in it. With many preachers, the exercise of reading the Scriptures and the hymns, appears to be a mere form. This is a great loss to their hearers. The reading of the Scriptures by Dr. John Mason, was said to be a commentary on them. The reading of the hymns by Mr. Nettleton, was often a sermon to the assembly.

All this may be admitted, however, and yet the conviction not be received, of the importance of cultivating elocution. Let it then be repeated, that the powers of utterance come under the great law of *education*, which pertains to the entire man. No physical function of man is capable of greater improvement than the voice. Its compass, its musical quality, its distinctness, its flexibility, its delicate utterance of sentiment. admit of indefinite improvement. The oratorical taste, too, can be cultivated to a very high degree, so that the body shall enter into the most delica e sympathy with the mind and heart, and faithfully symbolize to every other eye and ear all the wonderful workings of the spiritual man. The age of miracles is past. And since "it has pleased God, by the foolishness of preaching to save" men; and since preaching employs organs and faculties which we find to be capable of so great improvement, we must believe that God will employ a preacher who has cultivated his oratorical powers, to do a greater amount of good by preaching, than another of equal piety and learning, who has neglected this cul.ivation. From the present style of the pulpit and the senate, one might suppose that the age of eloquence is past. We believe it is yet to come. The power of a preached gos el is yet to be seen as our eyes have not seen it. And if we may still farther express our anticipations, we believe that three things are demanded for the coming of that age; a stronger faith in God and his word, a profounder knowledge of divine and human things, a thorough cultivation of the functions of speech.

ELOCUTION,

AS A

DEPARTMENT OF PREPARATORY STUDY IN THEOLOGY.

[By the Author of the present volume.]

THE preceding observations will, no doubt, be received with that full weight of effect, which justly belongs to the sources from which they come. Nor would the author feel disposed to present his own thoughts on the subject, were it not for the necessity of meeting objections such as he hears frequently offered to the systematic study of elocution, as either unnecessary or injurious.

A teacher in the department of elocution, has to communicate with minds under every variety of impression on the subject of culture. He meets, occasionally, with students whose lack of self-confidence, and even of a just self-reliance, leads them to despair of effecting anything in the way of successful cultivation, even after the most resolute and persevering exertions. He finds, sometimes, on the other hand, those whose self-esteem induces a perfect satisfaction with their habitual manner, be it what it may, and who are confident that they need little aid from any source but what is within themselves. He sees, perhaps, one individual who has formed an undue estimation of mere tuition and preparatory training, and who evidently expects too much from such aids, and subjects himself too passively to mere processes; and another who, from superficial attention to the merits of the question, or from prejudice or whim, contemns cultivation, as a thing wholly supererogatory, or necessarily artificial and false, or, at best, but mechanical and external.

An instructor has therefore to urge, on some minds, the value and importance of the processes of culture in this department of education, and to dwell on things familiar or self-evident to other minds.

The objections to systematic training in elocution, especially with reference to the purposes of the pulpit, are often founded on notions apparently just, or, certainly, quite plausible. Standing on the broad ground that the great point in expression, is the utterance of feeling, the objector maintains that nothing else is requisite, — that no rule can be required, when feeling is genuine, — that what a man feels deeply he must express strongly and truly, and therefore eloquently, — that to propose the idea of referring to a rule, when under an impulse of emotion, is absurd, — that utterance modified by rule is but an artificial mimicry of emotion, — that the idea of one man learning of another how to express his own feelings, is ridiculous, — that, if a speaker really has anything to say, he will easily find the way to say it.

But alas! the eloquent nullifier of cultivation, is, perhaps, in the meantime, uttering his very objections in the nasal tone which habit has made second nature and truth to him, but which, to one unaccustomed to hear the tones of the human voice assimilated to the twanging of a poor performer on the violin, is capable of exciting no emotions but those of the risible order: or he is emitting his voice with the guttural tones which, sometimes, make man approach the quadruped, in his utterance; he is articulating his words so imperfectly, that one syllable obliterates another; or he is marking his emphasis with a double twist of intensity, which seems to verify, on the spot, the half-malicious assertion of Dickens, that "the Americans search out every unaccented syllable in a word, to give it an accent, and every unemphatic word in a sentence, to clap an emphasis upon it;" and, — from want of natural or acquired ear for the character of vocal tone, — he is, perhaps, all the while, using a coarse violence of voice, which makes his earnestness become the vehemence of an angry dispute. The opponent of cultivation forgets, in fact, that the radical doctrine of no culture, is true only on condition that natural and acquired habits are perfect in the community in which an individual is educated, and consequently in himself.

But, even suppose such a state of things to exist, a generous and truly philosophic view of human culture, would lead to a very different conclusion, as we see in the practice of the ancient Athenians — that people so exquisitely perfect in physical organization, so quick and susceptible in ear, so delicate and true in taste, so vivid in feeling, so poetic in imagination, so subtle and refined in intellect, so intensely ardent in temperament, so expressive, so eloquent, in speech and action. It was that very people, — so endued with every grace of nature and every accomplishment of art, — that carried the systematic study of eloquence, and the artistic discipline of voice and person, tone, look, attitude, and action, to the highest point of cultivation, — that left no expedient untried, by which thought and emotion might be most efficaciously addressed to the mind, through the appointed avenues of sense.

The raw youth who is objecting to cultivation, as something that will mar the symmetry or impair the originality of his genius, forgets that the two most eloquent of men, — Demosthenes, among the Greeks, and Cicero, among the Romans, — were the most assiduous, the most rigorous, the most literal self-cultivators, in the humblest and minutest details of practical elocution.

Surely, if ever there was a community in which systematic discipline might have been dispensed with, it was that of Athens, whose humblest citizen was daily listening to the eloquence of Demosthenes, to the tragedies of Æschylus, Sophocles, and Euripides; living in the daily vision of architectural structures like the Parthenon, and of sculptures such as those of Phidias; listening to a music worthy of these sister arts, or to the recitation of the "rhapsodies" of Homer. But it was in that very community that oratory had its diversified orders of schools and seminaries, for the formation of the voice, and for the moulding of the body.

The superficial, popular objection, that the Grecian culture was fastidious, minute and fanciful, is wholly gratuitous. Men such as Demosthenes and Cicero could not have submitted to a fantastic discipline. The former stands acknowledged the strongest and manliest specimen of mind, that history has preserved to us; the latter, the most practical in tendency, and the most various in power, character, and accomplishment. The indefatigable self-culture of the former, and its sanction by the practice of the latter, — when himself in Greece, — are facts against which it is vain to dispute.

How then can we regard the presumption of him who, without study, and without practice, assumes the duties of an office which implies the power of persuasive and impressive discourse on the highest themes of thought, the noblest relations of being, and the profoundest emotions of the soul? The prince of Roman orators regarded the prelusive tremor of anxiety as an indispensable token of the earnest speaker at the judiciary tribunal, — what a reproof to the self-sufficiency which can afford to dispense with the idea of cultivation, for the loftiest purposes of speech!

But let us return, for a moment, to the actual state of the case. Whatever may have been the condition of things in ancient Greece or Rome, where a universal taste for eloquence, and the prevalent passion for distinction and renown, may have contributed much to foster the cultivation of oratory; it is a fact universally admitted, that the Anglo-Saxon constitution and temperament do not confer a predisposition to eloquence in its external relations. An instructive contrast presents itself in the case of the Irish nation. That people are, — from the noble to the peasant,—constitutionally expressive and eloquent, in attitude, action, look, and tone. The Englishman may be galled into indignant invective, he may be roused to forcible argument; but he is not spontaneously eloquent. The Scotchman may be rich in the mental materials of eloquence, in the poetry of thought, in the pathos of feeling, in the play of imagination; but he is not externally expressive — quite otherwise, — he is awkward, rather. A similar distinction obviously exists, in the United States, between the native dignity of deportment, and the eloquent expression, so generally characteristic of the people of the South, contrasted with the rigid, cold, hard, dry, angular, and reserved manner, which prevails in New England.*

The chill exterior of the Anglo-Saxon race, — although environing a world of interior and central fire, — freezes the stream of expressive feeling, and encrusts the surface of character and manner. The prevalent notion in *old* and in *New* England, alike, — that manliness demands reserve, and dignity, stiffness, — throws a morbid restraint over the tendencies of nature to communication and expression, and prematurely quenches the capability of eloquence in exterior manner. Here is one reason why, with us, the express cultivation of manner in speaking, becomes so important, as a compensation for the prevalence of counteracting habit in social and domestic life. The vivacious, the tasteful, the spirited, the graceful, ethereal Greek might, perhaps, have dispensed with the culture of manner in expressive utterance. Not so with the blunt, surly, and taciturn Englishman, or with the angular, mechanical, and constrained New Englander.

But our impediments to eloquence of manner, do not lie in constitution and habit only; they are imbedded in our systems of education. Our schools and colleges

---

* It was not a random remark in a late American divine, that the Norman, not the Saxon spirit, seemed to characterize our Southern States.

equally tend to produce a false and inexpressive style of speaking. We take a boy, at an early age, without previous moulding, and place him on the platform of the school rostrum, to speak a set speech, a formal declamation, or a political harangue, of which he knows little, and feels less. Such is our first step in oratorical training. Could the result be other than what it so generally is? Our boys early acquire an unnatural, formal, old-man-like style of speaking, which has no heart, — no truth, — no reality, — no vividness, — no genuine earnestness; although, under the exciting influence of circumstances, it may be forced, occasionally, from the monotony of the pulpit, into the hacking and jagged style of the bar, the turgid vehemence of the popular declaimer, or the unnatural violence of the partisan champion.

The unmeaning tone and manner, thus contracted in early years, become, unconsciously to the individual, the fixed habits of after life; the college declamation confirms the style acquired at school; and the professional institution stamps, with its irrevocable seal, the manner of the man in his maturity. Hence the rarity, among us, of the accomplishment of a chaste, easy, and natural style of speaking, of the power of rising gracefully and appropriately with the inspiration of a subject, — of becoming forcible, yet free from violence, — of expressing strong emotion, without turbulence.

Cultivation of manner in speaking, is rendered highly important, not only by circumstances which affect races and communities of men, but by those, also, which act upon the individual. Who is there that can say he has been duly educated, by the silent but most effective of all teaching, — that of perfect example, operating from childhood to manhood? Who is there, of whom it can be justly said, that he is free from every vice of organ and of habit, in speech or action? — The fault of misarticulating a single letter, may effectually vitiate a speaker's habit of enunciation; a single ungainly trick of gesture, may render his whole manner ridiculous. How often is a gross and glaring fault the predominating characteristic of the self-confident speaker who derides the idea of cultivation!

Objections to the study of elocution, however, are usually founded on erroneous views of its design and effect. It is thought to involve artificial processes and artifical results, — to be a fabricated attempt to imitate nature, a process of wire-pulling, by which the voice and the arms are to be mechanically moved and displayed, by rule. No view can be more false than this. Elocution is, indeed, the *art* of managing the voice and the person, in the act of speech. But, like every other form of genuine art, it is only the highest and the best, the truest forms of *nature* embodied in *practice*.

Man naturally possesses and employs all the elements of this art. The child is, in his sphere, the perfect model for the orator, — the living poet of expression. But the child, as he emerges successively into the boy, the youth the man, — just as, according to the poet, he lets the divine ray within him "fade into the common light of day," — loses this original and admirable faculty, in the dull routine of formal education. He unconsciously sacrifices nature to the lowest of all the shapes of art, — that of conventional habit, — the machinery of arbitrary form.

The human being, as he goes on from that beautiful spot in his early life, where all was truth and beauty and power, poetry and eloquence, — from the time when every look, and tone, and action was inspired with the truest and most expressive life, — would carry the atmosphere of that scene with him, and expand in power of expression, as his intellect expanded. But the expressive powers of the boy, are neglected, and left to wither. Our places of education make no provision for the culture of imagination and feeling, — the main-springs of living communication.

The young child is surrounded, in the great school of

nature, with innumerable objects which elicit expression from the heart; and his impressible imagination assimilates itself to the scene, and takes on and gives off, with ease, and with brilliant effect, the choicest forms of eloquent tone, attitude, and action. But when the period of school-life is arrived, these rich sources of influence are, in a degree, cut off, or he is debarred from them. The close room, the bench, and the book, take the place of the inspiring air, the green bank, and its alphabet of flowers. The oxygen of life is withdrawn; the lungs play feebly; the circulation lags; the spirit of communication is quenched; the brain becomes dull and inert; the mind is impoverished; the heart is quelled; the fancy languishes; the hours become irksome from the sense of weariness and restraint. Nor does an inspiring intellectual activity take the place of nature's incitements: the mental processes, on the contrary, are, principally, mechanical and insipid, — a weary round of senseless reïteration of unmeaning and unintelligible sounds, amid which the attention works with the movement of the mill-horse, in its never ending, never changing round.

But the scene is not shifted, even when ceaseless reïteration has left its mark on the memory, and the arbitrary process of spelling and syllabication, has been repeated till the mind has become expert in the mechanical operation of reading. The little student of written language, is then presented, perhaps, with a book of abstract sentences which, to him, are unintelligible, or, at most, lifeless successions of sound uninspired by feeling; in which imagination, — with its utmost stretch of inventive power, — can find no food, and amid which it gradually dies out. Add to all this neglect and privation, the effect of being drilled into the habit of duly " pausing till you can count one," at every comma, — of giving an emphasis on the model of the pedantic circumflex of the schoolmaster, and uttering the tones of emotion in the style of his stereotype utterance; and the usual consummation is attained; the power of natural, free, expressive voice, is utterly eradicated; and the transplanted scion of false habit, has taken most effectual root. The eloquent child has become a dull and mistuned reader, and is fully prepared to become, in his next stage of education, a lifeless and soulless speaker.

What elocution aims at, under these circumstances, is to restore the lost power of expression, to inspire natural life into the voice, to strip off the incrustation of mechanical habit, and leave the soul again free to utter itself in whatever mood nature prompts to the individual. Elocution prescribes no technical uniformity of manner: it, in the first place, hands to the student the implements of *scientific analysis*, and enables him to detect the complexities of tone, and to become familiar with every element, in all its varied aspects of combination; and, since the date of Dr. Rush's masterly analytic exhibition of the human voice, the requisite processes have become as definite and as tangible as those of music. Having accomplished its office as a science, elocution next presents itself as an *art*, and aids the student in reconstructing the vocal fabric; inserting every element in its due place, according to its character, — with the observant eye faithfully fixed on nature, as the only model; but carefully discriminating between the local, corrupted exhibitions of nature, in mechanical habit, and the free, general working of nature as a principle; — distinguishing the specialities of actual usage from its broad axioms and laws.

Elocution, when true to its purposes, thus emancipates the individual from the trammels of mere accidental habit and corrupted custom, and sets him out on a new career of action, in which he is guided by conscious knowledge, by intelligent preference, by recognized truth, by reflective judgment, and deliberate will, by personal organization, and individual character, — the true sources of eloquence in external manner.

Our present defective systems of education, leave this

work as a task of self-cultivation, for every student who would succeed in acquiring the power of expressive utterance; and years of assiduous endeavor are surely not too high a price to pay for such an acquirement. The eradication of the false habits which neglect and misdirected culture have accumulated, would, alone, render necessary a long and laborious course of application. The universal tone, for example, of our academic "exhibitions," displays false intonation and partial song, throughout. No student gives us, on such occasions, his own personal tone, but a certain average result of all the arbitrary effects of voice, which he has heard others use, in similar circumstances. We hear, from every speaker, but a succession of sentences, in which sound seems,— so to speak,— to have become stereotyped of old, and thence to have descended, as an inheritance, to successive generations, to be regularly assumed with the orator's academic gown.*

The false intonation thus cherished in academies and colleges, reäppears in professional life, in the dry mechanical modulation of the lawyer, the heavy and somnolent tones of the clergyman, and the "inexplicable dumb show and noise" of the popular declaimer.

The office of elocution is to enable the student to detect and avoid the various forms of error in general usage, and in the habits of the individual, — to assist him in throwing off the load of unmeaning and unnatural custom, and to give him direct access to the hearts of others, by the true and full expression of his own.

But even if there were no obstructions to progress, such

---

* The youth who desires the benefit of culture in elocution, must rely on his own diligence. The transient and imperfect aid to which our literary institutions now limit him, can effect but little. To communities such as ours, in which public speaking is so frequently the indispensable duty of individuals, an ample provision for instruction in the art of elocution, might be justly expected to exist. But its absence necessarily devolves on students individually the greater exertion, in self-culture.

as those which have been described,—did every student actually enjoy the advantage of starting on his mental career, unembarrassed by any hinderance of habit or circumstance,—the very growth and expansion of his intellectual character, would be ever making new demands for a commensurate power of expression. A mind furnished with all possible accumulations of thought,—to him who cannot give them utterance, is but "the locked coffer, without its key." — Every step up the steep of knowledge, calls forth, in the rightly constituted mind, a new fountain of emotion, a new world of association for scope to the inventive faculty, and therefore demands a new power of utterance. Fidelity to the duty of self-cultivation, requires of the student that he wrestle for the noblest achievements of self-mastery, in the acquisition of that power by which his organic constitution may become the worthy minister of his mind, and yield it a free and adequate utterance to others, of whatever sheds light on his own path, or imparts a new throb of life to his own heart. But the obligation becomes inexpressibly enhanced, when we transfer it to the highest subjects of thought, and the purest movements of benevolent feeling.

It is among the ordinations of Infinite wisdom, that, of all parts of man's organic structure, those which are employed in the functions of voice, are the most susceptible of culture and discipline. Look at the difference between the tune hummings of the little boy, and the wonderful and impressive execution of the consummate vocalist. A similar transition may be made in speech, by every human being who has sufficient force and steadfastness of will to insure the requisite diligence in practice.

The sense of duty, applied in this direction, will work its wonted wonders; and every day's observation furnishes to the elocutionist the most striking examples of individuals commencing a course of self-culture, under immense disadvantages of neglected habit and false training, yet achieving, within a few months, a complete triumph over all such obstacles, and becoming animated, correct, and impressive speakers.

The claims of liberal education, on all who have enjoyed its benefits, seem to demand the perceptible fruits of mental culture in the student's acts of communication with his fellow-men. Rudeness of speech is a venial thing in the uneducated; but it is utterly unjustifiable in those who sustain to general society the weighty responsibilities which rest upon the scholar. To him who enjoys the stores of mental wealth, Humanity says, "Be not a niggard of thy wealth: be not a niggard of thy speech, which may impart that wealth, without impoverishing thyself."

To the occupant of the pulpit, the beseeching voices of ignorance, of suffering, of degradation, all are lifted up, pleading for light, for sympathy, for renovation, in tones that would seem to make man desire the possession of angelic powers to put forth on their behalf. The offer of aid comes, too generally, from a voice that, — as far as the music of emotion is concerned, bespeaks heartless indifference, listless apathy, utter inability to assist, or entire ignorance of the facts of the case.

Aside from such considerations, however, the importance of culture and skill in address, as an indispensable qualification for the right discharge of the public duties of the profession, is a subject which, at present, demands the earnest attention of students of theology. The public voice is loud and urgent on this point: the dissatisfaction with the deplorable deficiencies of manner which are so prevalent in the pulpit, is uttered with no sparing tone. Students, if they mingled more at large with the world, would hear expressions on this subject, which might well startle them. It is a general complaint, among congregations of every denomination, that the style of pulpit elocution is miserably low and defective. To hear a sermon is not unfrequently spoken of as a matter of endurance, on the score of manner. It is not transcending the strictest limit of truth, on this subject, to say that society has become impatient and clamorous in regard to it. Elocutionists are well aware of the fact, that not a few religious societies, in various denominations, request of their ministers to put themselves under training, with a view to the remedy of defects of manner, which are so great as to prove obstacles to professional usefulnes.*

The desecrating effects of the practice, so frequent in American churches, of dismissing incumbents from their charge, are, in very many instances, to be traced to an uninteresting and unimpressive manner of preaching, as their original source. Of a hundred dismissions, not one can usually be found to have happened in the case of an earnest and eloquent preacher. No congregation considers itself as *excepting* the item of qualification for the pulpit, in their stipulations with the individual whom they receive as their pastor; and it is a prevalent impression, that no society can flourish under the charge of one who is an indifferent speaker. The world assumes due preparation for the duties of the pulpit, as a part of professional education. But, of all the theological institutions in the United States, there is not, perhaps, one, which, by adequate arrangements to that effect, enables its students to receive the benefit of an express course of training in the art of speaking.† The mere opportunity of declaiming in turn, or some other expedient not more efficacious, is all that is usually enjoyed by way of preparation for one of the most important acts that man can be called to perform in presence of his fellow-men. Theologians have slumbered over this great question : and the result is just what might be expected. The duties of the pulpit are,

---

* Speaking of reformation in modes of education, Milton says, "There would then, also, appear in pulpit other usages, or gestures, and stuff otherwise wrought, than what we now sit under, oftimes to as great a trial of our patience as any other that they preach to us."

† A similar deficiency, as to instruction and practice in elocution, exists in most of our universities.

for the most part, miserably performed; and the church and the world have to abide the consequences. Nor can the fact cease to be otherwise, while it is the fixed custom, at professional institutions, to devolve on one man the unreasonable load of labor inseparable from the double duty of teaching students to speak, as well as to write.

But, say some, why make so much of this affair of external manner? Admitting that a persuasive speaker always wins us, that an earnest one impresses us, and that a dull one wearies us, — why go through a long course of discipline to arrive at an earnest or a persuasive style of speaking? Does it not all depend on earnest feeling or affectionate interest? Is anything more than earnestness or warmth required, to produce this effect? If a man really is in earnest, he *must* make people feel; it cannot be otherwise.

So argues the merchant, who, never in his life, perhaps, wrote twenty pages of consecutive thought which he afterwards read or spoke in a public assembly: so argues, sometimes, the lawyer, who, in his busy life, is mingling continually with men in practical affairs, exciting and excited by the usual stimulants to communication, — interest, argument, professional repute; but who seldom has been subjected to the discipline of successive days of seclusion, and silence, and profound meditation on a vast theme, and then called from this life-quelling process to the life exhausting one, of public speaking, once a week, — three times, perhaps, on the same day, — on themes which, by their very depth and solemnity, exhaust the cerebral and nervous systems, and, by the deep tones which they naturally require, equally exhaust the powers of utterance.

The vicissitude which the clergyman is called to undergo, in passing from the process of the study to that of the pulpit, is one in which he makes an instantaneous transition from the sedentary and passive habits of the student, to the active and energetic exertions of the public speaker. The seclusion and stillness of the week, and the intensity of his daily mental action, have disqualified him, corporeally, for the process of vigorous and impressive utterance, on the broad scale of regular public address. To him the act of professional speaking, — or still more, that of professional reading, — is peculiarly exhausting. Hence he is more frequently subjected to an impaired state of health, than one who, like the barrister, is less confined to the act of intense thought. To him it is doubly important that he should know how to use his voice skillfully, — effectively to others, and yet with ease to himself. The sedentary form of life to which he must ever be closely limited by the nature of his professional preparation, exposes him, peculiarly, to fatigue and injury, immediately consequent on the act of speaking.

To speak extemporaneously, or from premeditation, will it is true, exempt the preacher from many of the peculiarly injurious effects of this mode of professional life. But the prevalent demand of society, for the union of two incompatible effects in pulpit speaking, — that of a carefully elaborated written discourse, and that, — at the same time, — of a well-spoken address, devolves on him a double share both of intellectual and of corporeal exertion. To give his sermon the free and natural effect of speaking, he must either lose something of the strict rhetorical character of his style of composition, in consequence of withdrawing his eye so frequently from his manuscript as to lose the details of his written expression; or he must come into the pulpit, prepared by so often repeated previous reading of his discourse, that it is virtually impressed on his memory.

The practice of systematic elocution, is, in reference to such circumstances, an important aid to facility and impressive manner in reading, and lightens effectually the burden of the task to be performed. Nor is such labor light. Few persons who have not made the experiment, can be aware of the force of impression on the mind, or of the degree of action in brain and nerve, which is necessary to produce impressive reading *aloud*, in the space usually filled by the voice of the preacher, as contrasted with that which is experienced in merely receiving the ideas of an author, by the *silent* reading of the page of a book. All that is necessary, in the latter case, is merely that the thought be passively received or felt, — up to the extent of the reader's receptive capacity; in the former, the measure of thought and emotion must not only be full but overflowing; so that the *surplus*, as it were, of feeling, may be sufficient to carry along, in its tide, the sympathies of a whole audience. The public reader not only receives but imparts, and, as it were, stamps an impression. This active state of sympathy is what alone can convey a sentiment from the heart of the reader to those of his hearers.

The practice of elocution secures the power of producing such effects easily and without fatigue. It serves, also, to render, by this means, the exercise of public speaking a salutary instead of an exhausting process. It invigorates the organs, and secures them against injury. It lightens professional labor; it tends to prolong life and protect health, while it secures an entire control over the voice, and makes it a ready and obedient instrument of the will.

The study of elocution enables the speaker to give life and effect to every sentiment which he utters, and to send it home to the heart. It gives him a comparatively unlimited control over the attention and sympathies of those whom he addresses, and secures to what he utters a deep and permanent impression on the mind; nor is it a slight consideration that it enables him to impart to all his utterance the attractions of propriety and grace. It insures, in a word, the whole benefit resulting from eloquence in manner.

All that the elocutionist, as such, pleads for, is, that the student after fifteen years, perhaps, of misdirected practice in reading, would give but the vigorous and faithful exertions of one, to the reformation of habit, or, at least, to the attempt at reformation. Half an hour, diligently employed, twice a day, for a year, on the rudiments of the art, would usually suffice for the removal of prominent faults, and for the acquisition of the most important traits of a good elocution.

The student of theology, who has yet the susceptibility of youthful life upon him, and the leisure to cultivate his powers, and form his manner, and who, whether from self-sufficiency, or ignorance, or indolence, or diffidence, deliberately prefers to neglect the consecration of his active nature, in its highest capabilities of excellence, to the function which he means to assume, — the elocutionist may well despair of moving by any argument which he can offer. The passive and lethargic pastor, who has given himself to his people, "for better, for worse," and to whom the calling, visiting, and miscellaneous jobbing of his vocation, are sufficient excuses for neglecting its nobler offices, — is still farther removed from any influence of persuasion. But to both the teacher of elocution may be allowed to say, "Look on this picture and on this," — the *uncultivated* and the *cultivated* speaker in the pulpit.

The former may, by no very improbable combination of chances, happen to exemplify all the following faults. He may have *a bad voice*. The screech of his excited tones may absolutely harrow the ear; he may have the gruff voice of the skipper of a smuggling lugger, or a hard guttural utterance, with tones which are little short of a continuous assault and battery on the ear; he may have the soft guttural tone of a voice choaked in the throat, as if every sound came from the gullet; he may have a uniform nasal twang, so strong as to provoke laughter; or he may have a thin, weak voice, with a high piping note, which, when applied to the solemn language of deep feeling creates a ludicrous incongruity. But how is he to become aware of such faults? Habit has made the sound of his voice natural and true to his ear. Culture alone can correct such faults.*

The preacher, who neglects the cultivation of his voice, suffers, sometimes, to a peculiar extent, *the penalties of violated laws of organization.* His vocal organs are the instruments of his professional action and usefulness; yet he not only omits the use of the only means of invigorating them, but employs them, perhaps, at the greatest disadvantage, from want of knowledge and skill in regard to the appropriate mode of exerting them, so as to avoid fatigue and exhaustion, and consequent loss of health. Individuals in this predicament sink, perhaps, even in early life, under the effects of wrong habits in the use of the vocal organs.

The uncultivated speaker sometimes renders himself disagreeable by his habitual violations of propriety and taste, his obvious slovenliness of style, or want of appropriate education, as regards the humble and merely rudimental attainment of correct *pronunciation*.† He may

---

* It is much to be regretted that, in many parts of the United States, education takes so little effect on outward manner, and that, in New England, particularly, a round, smooth, agreeable voice, is not invariably the characteristic of mental culture and polish. The absence of natural and acquired refinement, is unequivocally indicated in the hideous tones of voice which are not unfrequently heard from the pulpit.

† It is matter of regret, that this subject is so much neglected in early education, and that professional men, generally, do so little justice to themselves and their language, by the numerous improprieties which they habitually exemplify in speech. New England, more particularly, is marked by the extensive prevalence of local faults, in this respect; and most of these are owing to the sanction unfortunately given by Dr. Webster to such peculiarities. An obsolete and awkward style of pronunciation, has thus gained currency, even in places of learning. But some of Dr. Webster's modes are nearly a century out of date, for the present day; and not a few are absolute Scotticisms, and errors of dialect, peculiar to Yorkshire or to New England.

This defect in Dr. Webster's dictionary, was much to be regretted, as the fulness and accuracy of its definitions, render it otherwise so valua-

even fail in respect of a distinct *articulation* of syllables and sounds, so far as to obscure the sense of whatever he utters, or even to render him unintelligible. But of these evils he is unaware; he has not been accustomed to watch his own habits; he is, in this particular, the helpless victim of circumstances, which have moulded him, unconsciously to himself, into the grossest errors. An hour's practice with an elocutionist, would put it in his power to correct these faults in a few weeks, and to substitute for his errors a chaste and correct manner of pronouncing, and for his hurried and confused utterance an accurate, clear, distinct enunciation.

The undisciplined speaker frequently exhibits a displeasing *loudness or violence of voice*, or, on the other hand, *a faint and feeble utterance*, which does not allow him to be heard. He may have a uniform bawling or calling force, which indicates no variation of feeling, no softening touch of subdued emotion; or he may have nothing of that force which imparts manly energy to expression, and gives impulse to the heart. He may have, perhaps, that uniform medium of voice, which never swells or subsides with feeling, and which renders his style utterly inexpressive and uninteresting. He has never studied the working of nature in vocal habit, or watched the ebb and flow of utterance, as the tide of emotion gushes forth, or subsides, in the voice. The rising and the lulling of the wind, seem to have taught his ear no lesson. But to all such effects cultivation would have opened his ear and his heart, and imparted their power to his utterance.

The skilful *emphasis* of a good reader, which gives to the main points of his expression a sculptured prominence, and striking force of effect, the unpractised speaker has never observed. He gives little or no emphasis, at all; or, on the other hand, he *multiplies* and *crowds* his

---

ble. It is gratifying, therefore, to observe, that the Rev. Prof. Goodrich, in his revised edition of the work, has judiciously retrenched many instances of local usage, which were sanctioned in the first edition.

emphatic words, till his indiscriminate and perpetually recurring force, defeats its object, and destroys itself. He is thus compelled to give a double and exaggerated effect to all his actual emphasis, which makes him seem to be addressing an audience whose faculties were too obtuse, otherwise, to apprehend his meaning. He may even go so far with this habit of exaggeration as to make all his distinctions become epigrams in sound, and his significant expressions each one a pun, by its overcharged tone and tortuous circumflex.* But his ear has never been opened to the discriminations of kind and degree, in emphasis: he has never brought his organs under the influence of discipline, on such points: his attention, in fact, has never been turned to them. No wonder, then, that his emphasis should be so often exaggerated and disproportioned; or that his emphatic words should sometimes be thrown out with a jerk that would seem to intimate a sudden flash of impatience or ill-temper, rather than a decisive act of judgment. Culture, however, would teach such a speaker to chasten his force by due regard to moderation and dignity of manner, and to directness and simplicity of expression.

The uncultivated speaker seems, usually, either to have *no power of inflecting his voice*, so that, in reading, his sentences run on with the flat sameness of the style of an advertisment or a law-paper; or, on the other hand, he twitches and jerks his words with perpetual *double slides and circumflexes*,† so that his language seems to become a succession of verbal distinctions, quirks, or quibbles,

---

* The intellectual and argumentative tendencies of the Scotch and of New Englanders, impart this schoolmaster's tone to their current modes of colloquial emphasis, and, frequently, to their characteristic style of reading and of public address.

† Those turns of voice, which Dr. Rush, in his analysis, has termed "waves." This style forms the distinctive vocal effect of what are called "Yankee stories;" yet the prevalence of local habit causes it to be frequently heard in the pulpit.

instead of important and impressive facts, in their appropriate tone. This fault is sufficiently ridiculous to ears not indurated to it, by the effect of custom. But the speaker who makes it, has never dreamed of its existence in his personal habits; and he goes on, from year to year, announcing sacred truths in the tone and accent of a series of sly jokes. The effect of such utterance, when added to the proverbial coldness and stiffness of general manner, current, more particularly, in the pulpits of New England, is one great cause of the avowed dislike, so generally expressed in other parts of the country, to the style of preachers from that quarter. A slight attention to culture would suffice to put an end to such impediments to the legitimate influence of the pulpit.

The undisciplined speaker fails, usually, in adequate length of *pauses*. He allows no opportunity for an impressive thought to "sink down into the ear," and penetrate the heart; he hastens on, heedlessly, over the most momentous thoughts, as if they were matters of indifference; and the effects which he produces on his hearers, are correspondent to his style. Truth, uttered in such modes, is stripped of its reality, and leaves the soul callous to its power. A false current notion, that the elocution of the pulpit is to be modelled on that of the bar, or the popular assembly, induces some speakers to imagine that eloquence consists in fluency, and that the acceptable preacher is he who does not keep his people waiting for his words, but glides on, on the "*festina lente*" principle, and judiciously shortens the duration of the penance of listening to a sermon. A moderate attention to the demands of solemnity and impressiveness, as prominent features of sacred eloquence, would guard the preacher from such errors of judgment and taste, while it would equally save him and his hearers from the lagging slowness and merciless drawling, which are also among the current faults of pulpit elocution.

The preacher who neglects the cultivation of his voice,

may be congratulating himself on his exemption from hollow and artificial tones, which he detects in others. But he is, perhaps, in the habit of using *a high, thin, and squeaking pitch*, which forbids the possibility of grave, deep, or solemn emotion, on the part of his hearers;—no matter how reverential the unuttered feeling which is, all the while, latent in the bosom of the speaker.

An inevitable law of our constitution demands deep tones in the utterance of solemn emotions. The fireside tone is intolerable in the pulpit; the voice of familiar anecdote, substituted for that of grave and devout discourse, is a desecration to the ear. Yet a few hours' practice would enable most speakers to draw and observe the line which separates one pitch of voice and one mode of feeling from another. The preacher would thus obey, and coöperate with, the ordinations of Creative wisdom, and convert his voice from a hinderance into an effective aid to the purposes of his office.

But the undisciplined speaker in the pulpit, sometimes, —whether from inadvertence or erroneous impression,— allows himself to fall into the opposite fault of *a hollow, sepulchral, morbid voice*, which is a mere matter of habit, and bears no relation to his theme, for the moment. He may actually be expatiating on the joys of heaven, with a voice which has precisely the pitch of the ghost in Hamlet, when describing the horrors of hell. The effect of such intonation usually is to make the ministrations of the pulpit associate themselves, in the feelings of an audience, with a condition of gloom and repugnance. Were the themes of pulpit eloquence such as never admitted strains of animation, cheerfulness, and delight,—were love and joy necessarily debarred from the circle of sacred emotions,—the uniformly hollow, heavy voice of awe and horror, might be appropriate, as a characteristic of professional elocution. But on no other condition can it be so. Yet how often is this burden of preternatural pitch laid upon the sensibility of an audience, by the uncultivated voice of the preacher!

Fitness and beauty are the universal characteristics of organization, in all the works of God. The very analogies of man's constitution, predispose him to repeat these traits in all *his* humbler sphere of creation and effect. His nature thirsts for these, in every act of mind or body. But if false taste and erroneous habit usurp the control of the forming processes of education, the natural tendencies of mind are checked; the soul becomes callous; the eye becomes blind, and the ear deaf to propriety and grace. Perversion and evil, in every variety of shape, are the result. The mind ceases to perceive, the organs cease to execute their original purpose. Deformity is adopted as the model of grace; habit imbibes the influence, and breathes the air, which custom has prescribed. Vitiated habit and depraved taste go hand in hand, in the work of desecration and corruption.

The current style of elocution, in the pulpit, forms a striking example of this downward tendency of mind and manner. The beautiful and wondrous adaptation of the human voice to the varied functions of expressive utterance, is clearly exhibited in the vivid and eloquent tones of childhood. It forms a most exquisite page in the poetry of man's life. But neglect and perversion commence,—as formerly mentioned,—with the processes of artificial culture; and power and grace of expressive tone gradually die out; so that the man, in his maturity, has lost the faculty of adapting voice to feeling, which he possessed in his earliest years. Not only so: he has acquired mechanical and *false habits of tone*, which bury rather than give forth emotion. Of a hundred persons whom you may ask to read a vivid passage from the most natural of all writers, Shakspeare, not one, perhaps, can give the genuine tones of feeling to what he attempts to read. To do such a thing, is in fact, commonly thought to be the exercise of an art possessed only by an actor or an elocutionist, — one who has made an express business of acquiring the vivid tones of emotion.

The same experiment of reading may be made with the Bible, or the hymn book, or with a page of a sermon; and the result will, for the most part, be, that neither layman nor clergyman utters any tone of feeling with its true and appropriate character. The agonies and the ecstasies of the Psalmist, will, usually, be read with the tones of perfect decorum in a modern gentleman; the seraphic ardor of Watts will be uttered with the coolest composure; and the sermon will be read as if the ideas of God, of heaven, and of hell, were things to which the human heart had acquired a comfortable indifference.

The uncultivated reader in the pulpit, thus nullifies, to the ear, whatever may be in his heart; and what was meant to pierce the inmost soul, "plays harmless round the head." The voice of the preacher, which ought to be the living link of connection between earth and Heaven, becomes a most effectual non-conductor. The immense power which lies wrapped up in the human voice, and which is only transcended by that of the soul itself, the negligent speaker has left dormant, till he has lost faith in its existence, and actually regards the endeavor to arouse it as on a par with the infatuated search for imaginary lost treasure.

Never, from his lips, shall come the startling or the thrilling note of warning to the slumbering spirit; the tone that makes a Felix tremble at the fearful possibilities of retribution; the voice that can melt the obdurate heart to tears of contrition; the words that can inspire the despondent or soothe the sorrowing soul, or "stir the blood like the sound of a trumpet," while it summons to "glory, honor, and immortality."

To the uncultivated speaker, the natural avenues of the heart, the modes of sympathetic tone, are, comparatively, shut. His feelings may be strong and deep; but he knows not how to give them effective utterance. He is powerless from want of practice. His voice, the appointed organ of communication with the soul, has become virtually dead. It might have been an instrument of electric effect, but he has chosen to let it rust unused. His voice, however, is but what the hand of Angelo would have been, undisciplined, uninspired by his soul, — a mass of bone, flesh, ligament, and skin, as that of the laborer in the quarry, — not that wondrous instrument, which more than any other production of Divine skill, has shown how "fearfully and wonderfully" the members of the human frame are formed, in adaptation to the purposes and capacities of the soul.

The preacher who neglects the cultivation of his organs, usually subjects himself to a whole host of disadvantages, distinct from those which are connected with the unskilful use of the voice. He offends the eye, by *violating the natural laws of posture and motion*, which regulate the human frame.

Man's body was designed to depict his emotions, by its sympathetic coöperation with his mind. But the preacher has listened to the prevailing cant around him, about attitude and gesticulation, and has neglected the natural use of his bodily members, as expressive agents; so that he has lost the power of using them, and even a natural, momentary exertion of using them, has become, to him, a conscious effort. In the unperverted years of childhood, his soul beamed forth in every posture, and in every action; his very frame radiated emotion, and invested itself with the powers of a spiritual presence. Such is man's natural condition. But education steps in, and imposes on his body the same train of evils which it inflicted on his voice. It quenches the light, and steals away the warmth of his being, and moulds his susceptible nature into low and arbitrary forms, either inevitable or actually prescribed. The informing spirit withdraws itself from its original resort to the exterior frame, and ceases to actuate it: the bodily organs are soon usurped by routine and mechanism: constraint, coldness, rigidity, reserve, embarrassment, and awkwardness, take the place of freedom, warmth and life; a hard, dry, narrow, angular, mechanical gesticulation displaces the natural, free, flowing action which sprung directly from feeling. Artificial cultivation confirms all these faults into habits; judgment ceases to recognize the true and reject the false; taste becomes assimilated to style, and learns to love the arbitrary and the unnatural.

The professional speaker carries into the sphere of the pulpit, the faults which mis-directed education has made a part of himself; and unless he is willing then to assume the labor of reform and renovation, he cannot produce, in his person and action, any just effect of expression. All his traits of manner must be conventional, and, for every purpose of eloquence, untrue, and ineffectual or injurious.

A few weeks of assiduous culture, however, would remove the impediments which artificial habit has thus accumulated, and convert the awkward, ungainly, and disagreeable manner into one of genuine nature, propriety, freedom, force, and grace.*

Our sketch of the usual faults of the uncultivated speaker, has been so extended into detail, that little room remains, — in consistency with the necessary limits of this volume, — to describe the cultivated. He may be pictured, however, in imagination, as the reverse of the former, in every point. The few individuals who, as yet, have devoted their attention to the inevitable effects of manner in the pulpit, are easily distinguished: they speak with freedom, with earnestness and fervor, with impressive power, with manly force, with chaste propriety, with

---

* The Rev. Edward Irving was an impressive example of the effect of cultivation in personal manner and action. In his early professional efforts in Scotland, he exhibited a style the most awkward, constrained, and unnatural, that, perhaps, the pulpit ever exhibited. At a subsequent period, in London, his attitude and action became, by assiduous culture, most strikingly eloquent in their effect.

attractive grace. There is a living reality, a glowing life, in their utterance, a genuine refinement, a persuasive elo quence of manner, which rivet the attention, and command the whole mind and heart. They excel the preacher who is merely an eloquent writer or composer of sermons, as much as the orator does the essayist. Intellectual force, aided by scholarship and taste, will ensure all the merits of the latter. But assiduous self-culture, and resolute practice, in special and appropriate forms, are indispensable to him who would secure the power of the former; and while the young preacher may well be excused from the usurping demands on time and labor, indispensable to the attainments of a consummate orator, no unreasonable amount of exertion is required to make him an effective and successful speaker, or, in other words, to enable him to accomplish all the true objects of oratory, by uttering his thoughts earnestly, appropriately, and persuasively.

THE EFFECTS OF MANNER

IN THE

ELOCUTION OF THE PULPIT.

ANIMATION AND DULLNESS.

COMMUNICATION by speech and action, is one of the noblest functions of man's complex nature. It is the product of reason, feeling, and imagination, moulded by the expression of the countenance, the attitude of the body, the action of its members, and the modifications of the voice. It implies the activity of the whole man, in the unity of his feeling. It is the result of will; it appeals to sympathy; it is invariably a moral act; it recognizes the invisible chain which links man to man; it involves the power of choice, and the condition of responsibility, in the impartation of pleasure or of pain; it evokes, — whether by violating or observing its decisions, — the highest power within the human breast, — conscience. Its range of action is as wide as the capacities of man; it utters his conceptions of the universe and its Author, and the feelings to which these give origin; it gives language, also, to the humblest of his own daily wants, or the slightest of his transient emotions. It compasses the stars, and defines the minutest particle of dust; it breathes the winning tones, and wears the inviting aspect of love; or it utters the accents and assumes the attitude of destructive hate. Its forms and modes are as various, therefore, as its sources, its subjects, and its objects.

Regarded, however, as an act which is the result of will, it always implies life, spiritual and animal. Death seals, irrevocably, the lips of man; despair, despondency, dejection, disease, exhaustion, languor, may close them for a time. But the natural renovation of life, by joy or by repose, revives the law of sympathy and communication: animation prompts to speech and action. So uniform is this effect, that silence and reserve, in man, are recognized as the indications of illness, displeasure, depression, gloom, or dissatisfaction. The taciturn individual, in society, seems morose, dispirited, or timid.

It is a law of expression, therefore, in accordance with these facts, that life and animation are conditions of speech, both as regards the language of audible utterance, and that which exists, to the eye, in the attitudes and actions of the body. Conversation, destitute of the inspiring effect of animation, becomes dull and tedious while the spirited interchange of thought is one of the purest sources of mental and social pleasure, and, at the same time, one of the most powerful springs of intellectual action and development.

So it is in regard to the premeditated and formal communications of public address. Deprive these of life, on their wonted occasions,—and the prosing technicalities of the pleader seem but a heavy burlesque on the vaunted connection between law, eloquence, and justice; the "popular" orator, when dull, immediately becomes *un*popular,—or, in the language of Dogberry, "most tolerable, and not to be endured." Can the preacher who drones and drawls, and stands motionless and lifeless in the pulpit, reasonably hope to be exempt from the influence of the law of association which identifies dullness with stupidity?

In vain does he plead the solemnity of his themes, the gravity of his profession, and the depth of tone, and the sedateness of manner which belong to these. Profound emotion and decorous action are not dullness: they are a genuine part of living eloquence on great subjects; they are the very opposite of drawling, lagging, monotonous utterance, unemphatic expression, and lifeless, automaton-like gestures.

Want of life and animation in the preacher, extends itself, necessarily, to the congregation. Nothing is so Mesmeric in its influence as dullness. The lifeless soporific tone, like the droning hum of the bee, lulls the sense and the soul, alike, to slumber. The torpor of the preacher diffuses itself over his audience; and his own somnolent manner is soon reflected to him, in the "lack-lustre eyes" of those of the congregation, who, in such circumstances, can any longer be called *hearers*.

The chief source of dullness in the pulpit, is, no doubt, that want of tact in the handling of a subject, which makes the great themes of religion commonplace to the preacher himself, and therefore to his audience. Education, it must be acknowledged, does little to empower the preacher to breathe fresh life into old themes. The theologian enters upon his office, but little disciplined in that free, natural, original, and inspiring use of his faculties, which enables the poet to find ever new life and beauty in every component atom of the creation, and to expatiate, with an eloquence which we feel to be divine, on the common light and air of heaven, or the most ordinary plant by the wayside. The preacher seems, too often, to be consciously handling trite themes, to which it is a hopeless attempt to endeavor to impart life and interest. He speaks, accordingly, as if the utmost reach of his ambition were to invest dullness with a tolerable decency, and to get through the routine of his function, in the best way he can.

The power of taking interesting, impressive, and striking views of common things, implies, unquestionably, a higher talent than mere education can impart. But while this important acquirement remains, as at present, one of the unattempted prizes of diligence, it is certain that the obvious and palpable advantages of even a partial cultivation, are entirely overlooked, as respects the express training of preachers for the public duties of their office.

It surely is not absolutely necessary that, to want of original power, and to want of due intellectual discipline, in the occupants of the pulpit, there should invariably be added an utter want of skill in expression, as regards the use of the voice, and the appropriate accompaniments of action.

The dull and lifeless speaker may become animated, if he will resolutely set about accomplishing the task. The training prescribed in the practice of elocution, will present him with subjects of exercise, drawn from the most inspiriting passages of the most powerful writers. It will accustom him to glow over inspiring themes. It will show him the natural modes of uttering and imparting vivid emotions. It will train his organs to lively exertion. It will invigorate his tones, enhance his emphasis, sharpen his inflections, enliven his accents, breathe life into his whole expression, mould his frame into pliancy and eloquent effect, impel his arm, kindle his eye, flush his cheek with genuine emotion, and light up his whole manner with a feeling which radiates from within. All men are thus eloquent in childhood: all who have the force of resolution and the persevering diligence requsite for the endeavor, may recover "the buried talent."

The style of the pulpit, while it requires, in common with all modes of expression, the due animation of a living effect, forbids, of course, that mere animal vivacity which is incompatible with dignity and sobriety of manner, and borders on puerility, by incessant motion and gesticulation, a talkative style of utterance, with high pitch, unreserved loudness, rapid enunciation, half-mimetic tones, abrupt and startling variations, grotesque expression, and dramatic attempts at humor.

Original and eccentric characters, such as Rowland Hill and John Campbell, can be tolerated, and even occasionally relished for their native buoyancy of spirits: their exuberance of action and expression, even when it violates decorum, is pardoned, in consideration of the striking effect which, for the moment, it imparts to a thought usually uttered and received in a languid and passive mood. But mere animal spirits, in a speaker, without the depth and original force of such men, serve only to discompose and annoy the mind of the hearer who desires grave and impressive instruction on momentous subjects.

To acquire expressive power of voice and manner, the process is the same which the judicious artist adopts. Study *nature* deeply and intensely, till you imbibe its beauty, its freshness, and its power: devote ample time to the cultivation of a relish for genuine *art*, in all its varied forms; — for all the fine arts are but modifications of the one great art of expression. Above all, imbue your mind with the spirit of poetry, by the habitual studious reading of the works of the master spirits of our vernacular literature. Study, especially, the dramatists, — read them diligently aloud, with full force of feeling, — as a matter of professional culture and self-training; and the ear will inevitably open to the impressions of living emotion in tone and action; every expressive trait in your own mental character will thus be quickened, and the power of penetrating the heart and swaying the sympathies of others, be acquired, — to an indefinite extent.

Could the young preacher be but induced to bestow a tithe of the labor which is bestowed by the young player, on the acquisition of a vivid and expressive manner, in word and act, every pulpit might become comparatively a station for transmitting and diffusing the electric influence of a speaker inspired, — soul and body, — by divine truth.

EARNESTNESS AND APATHY.

The mere vividness of an emotion may lead to animated expression, in countenance, voice, and action. Such a result may be unconscious and even unintentional, as is evinced in the natural communications of childhood.

But of the deliberate and voluntary speaker, who has a definite aim in utterance, we expect more than mere vivacity. The orator, — and such, for the time, is the minister in the pulpit, — has a grave purpose to accomplish, — a specific end in view, toward which his own mind is impelled, and toward which he wishes to conduct the minds of his hearers. He has within him a deep-felt emotion, which he wishes to impart to the hearts of others. He is earnestly desirous to impress the pervading sentiment of his own soul on the sympathies of his audience. He calls imagination to his aid, to give form to his idea and figure to his language. He reasons, he argues, he persuades, he awes, he impels, he entreats, he warns, he threatens, he exhorts, he melts, he terrifies, he arouses, he subdues, he wins. His success is the reward of his earnest desire to compass his object. His triumph has been achieved, undoubtedly, by intellectual force appropriately directed, — but through what means? His glowing and irresistible eloquence was not a mere affair of the brain and the pen. These instruments have done their work well. But what would have been their effect without the aid of the living tongue and the expressive action? What gave the thoughts of the speaker an entrance to the heart, was not merely their intellectual life and power, or their ideal beauty, but the earnestness of his tone, look, and gesture.

The diffidence or the lethargic indifference of some preachers, cuts them off from all such effects. They may feel what they say; but they speak as though they felt it not. The earnest pleader might justly seem to say of them, in the expressive words of the great dramatist, "Their words come from their lips, — ours from our breast." Their own souls are not apparently aroused by what they utter; and how can it be expected that they should awaken others? If the preacher's tone is, in such cases, any index to his heart, he is indifferent as to the result. It may be, indeed, that he is one of those who disapprove of much emotion in the pulpit, and that he is an advocate of calm dignity, and manly reserve of manner. His stoic exterior is not to be disturbed by vehemence or excitement; and the slumbering soul is therefore to be left to its fatal lethargy.

But the fault of apparent apathy in the preacher, is more frequently owing to the absence of expressive facility. It sometimes, indeed, is caused by a depth of inward feeling which in vain struggles for utterance through undisciplined and unpractised organs. The suppressed and choking voice sometimes, in these circumstances, discloses, to the attentive ear, the true nature of the hinderance. But, from whatever source it springs, the fault of inexpressive utterance belies the truths which fall from the lips, and which should pierce the heart with the thrill of intense emotion.

Earnestness is the natural language of sincerity; it is the condition of persuasion. It is the security for the orator's success, — most of all, in the case of him who is not contending for palpable rights and outward interests, but who is pleading the most momentous of all causes, — that which is ever pending between the soul and God.

Earnestness is the most prominent trait of eloquence. It is a thing not to be mistaken. It depends not on science. It is a direct product of the soul. It has no halfway existence. Either it is not, or it comes "beaming from the eye, speaking on the tongue, informing every feature, and urging the whole man onward, right onward to his object." Nothing can take its place. Decorum, without it, becomes hollow formality; gravity, coldness; dignity, reserve: all expression loses life and power.

Yet earnestness is external in its character, and may be counterfeited, even, by assuming certain outward signs of tone and action. It needs but a little attention and reflection to note and discriminate its traits. Every observer perceives its characteristic glance of the eye; its energetic, warm, breathing, heart-issuing voice, its pithy emphasis, its acute and keen inflection, its vivid intonation, its animated movement; its forcible and spirited and varying action, its speaking attitude and posture; its eloquent glow of pervading inspiration. We see it manifested in all its power as the instinctive art of eloquence which nature teaches to the child, to the mother, to the loving youth, to the unconscious savage.

Earnestness, as a habit in expression, is one of those traits which education tends to quell rather than to aid. Early, in the conventional forms of school life, it gives way to reserve and morbid apathy, or to an arbitrary decorum. Inexpressive modes of action and utterance become, thus, inseparable from the prevalent habits of the student and the professional man. Resolute self-culture alone can replace the lost power in individuals. He who would recover it effectually, must watch narrowly the sources of influence on mind and character. He must frequent those mental resorts whence he may derive energetic and stirring impulses: he must learn to detect, and apply to his own being, the elements of inward life and force, to see the deep and living reality within all external forms. He must learn to deal with thoughts rather than words, and with things more than with mere thought. He who inhales the inner air of truth and reality, cannot be an indifferent spectator of life, or an indifferent pleader for its duties. The words and tones and looks and actions of the human being, are profound and instructive realities to him. He cannot be indifferent to their power: he will study them thoroughly; he will use them effectively.

One efficacious means of infusing an earnest spirit into expression, is the attentive study of the great models of eloquence, ancient and modern. It is true, that the process of verbal translation, and the routine of formal declamation, in academic exercises, have extracted much of the freshness and the life of eloquence from the best pages of classic oratory, by blunting the student's sensibility to their peculiar power and beauty. But to every true scholar there comes a time when the trammels of early association are laid aside with the other transient impressions of boyhood, and the man, in the maturity of his mind, perceives and appreciates the living force of the great masters in oratory; and then Demosthenes and Cicero and Chatham are, to his view, themselves again, in their original power and splendor.

The daily practice of reading aloud, and declaiming from these authors, cannot but rouse and impel a mind that truly feels their power. The sympathetic spirit must catch something of their glowing earnestness and breathing life of utterance. Language such as theirs it is hardly possible for the man to repeat in the cold flat tones of the school-boy's compulsory task.

The same may be said in regard to the effect produced on elocution by the reading and study of all writers whose language breathes an earnest spirit. The stirring narratives, even of the novelist, — if we take such as Scott for our illustration, — exert a similar power in awakening and impelling the feelings of the reader; and could the clergyman who pleads his incessant occupation, as an apology for neglecting the cultivation of his delivery, be induced to devote but half an hour a day to the practice of reading aloud, to his own family circle, an effective passage from such a writer, he would unavoidably acquire a vivid and earnest manner of expression, as a habit, in whatever possessed an interest to his own feelings.

The superficial impression that the habit of reading and speaking, as an affair of practice, tends to make a speaker mechanical in his style, arises from a false conception of the nature of the exercise. The practice which the elocutionist suggests is not a soulless repetition of sounds : he insists upon it that no practice is of any avail that does not carry the heart with it, or that does not bring forth sincere and earnest feeling, in tone and manner. His desire is to aid the speaker in evoking and expressing his inmost soul, as the only condition of the power to elicit the genuine sympathy of others. The elocutionist who understands his subject, can never be satisfied with a heartless, artificial style : his knowledge of his subject must prevent him from mistaking or prescribing the false for the true. His very office is to break up routine, formality, and every other trait of factitious habit.

The erroneous notion that practice and culture tend to cherish an artificial manner of expression, is owing, like many other mistakes on this subject, to our defective modes of education. The child, at school, is permitted to read sentences as merely so many words : the meaning and the spirit of a passage are not invariably associated, as they should be, with the language. The boy, the youth, and the man, accordingly, through the successive stages of education, regard reading as an arbitrary and mechanical process; and the petty instruction usually given about pausing and emphasis and the inflections of the voice, has only served to verify and confirm the impression. An education true to sentiment, to language, and to man, would render it unnatural to the ear and the voice to put asunder what God has joined, — the feeling in the heart, and its utterance in appropriate tone. Ear and voice, if trained in harmony, would always come to one result ; and the practice of reading and of speaking, would confirm, not interfere with, the tendency of nature.

The student, therefore, should see that the whole matter rests with himself. His endeavor ought to be to re-

6*

form and renovate his habits of expression, so thoroughly that his utterance shall always be true and earnest, and that he shall be incapable of executing a tone or a gesture which is not the natural and genuine result of feeling. His daily practice should have this end uniformly in view. The effects resulting from deficiencies and errors in formal education, will thus be obviated; and every exercise which he performs will be an additional security that his manner shall not be mechanical, but on the contrary, living and earnest.

One of the most valuable, in fact, of all accomplishments resulting from diligent self-culture in elocution, is the power which it imparts of entering, at once, with entire and perfect sympathy, into the mood of any sentiment which is to be read or spoken. The homely adage, that practice makes perfect, is in nothing more true than in this particular case. Nor can there be a greater mistake than that which most persons fall into, as regards the function of the elocutionist. The accomplished reader is thought to possess a certain talent of assimilation, by which he assumes or puts on the utterance of a sentiment, as if it were real. The true elocutionist, like any other sincere and earnest man, " knows not *seems;*" he either possesses by nature, or has acquired by diligence, a facility of giving up his whole being, — feeling and imagination, as well as understanding, — to the sentiment which he expresses. To him all is intense reality. In the act of reading impressively a strain of poetry, he is but exerting that receptive and expressive power which makes all things real and fresh to himself, and consequently to others, — a power which dwells in the soul and on the tongue of every child, — a power which the good reader has not lost or has only recovered. He is but performing simply and earnestly one of the truest functions of his being.

The indispensable faculty of imparting reality to thought and feeling, is, in the elocutionist, as in all other men, that, rather, of perceiving and feeling the reality of thought. He is thus enabled to impart that reality to the minds of others. But, without this condition, there can be no true use of the voice. Earnestness and eloquence, impressiveness and power, in speaking, are merely the visible and audible effects of the inspiration which emanates from this source.

The preacher, if he is more dependent than other speakers, on such influence as this, is also more largely furnished with its aid : his themes are the most inspiring and the most impressive on which the human mind can dwell. To be eloquent, he has but to be earnest. Earnestness of heart, however, does not necessarily imply earnestness of manner. The very depth and vividness of feeling, are sometimes the actual causes of silence. The preacher has to learn, like other speakers, to control and modify his emotions so that they may become capable of expression. He must learn to recognize the natural signs of earnest emotion in tone and action, and to identify these with his whole manner. He must learn to lay aside the passive habits into which he may have fallen in the silence and seclusion of his study, and enter upon the active efforts of living expression and effective communication with society. He must, if he would attain success, labor to acquire the power of imparting to others the reality which his thoughts possess to his own mind. The earnestness of his manner in speaking, is the natural gauge of this reality. The preacher, therefore, who feels the importance of this point, will not think it unworthy of his office to study and observe every effective means of imparting earnestness to his voice or his action. How often is the hearer left aware how much more the preacher might effect, were his tone more expressive, his emphasis stronger, his manner more energetic ; were he but earnest enough to secure interest in his thoughts, and sympathy with his feelings !

The quiet and placid tenor of a pastor's life, while it

favors his attainments in the contemplation of abstract and reflective truth, is not so conducive to the acquisition of the power of earnest and impressive utterance. He, as a speaker, needs, more than others, the aid of express study and practice in that art which tends to impart "action and utterance, and the power of speech to stir men's blood," for great purposes. — The player who is faithful to the duties of his vocation, gives the daily study of successive years, to the preparation for performing a great part, so as to give effective utterance to great sentiments and glowing language. He whose express business it has been to render himself expert in giving to thought and emotion their appropriate tone, look, attitude, and action, with all the earnestness of life, feels that this very process is one in which careful study and laborious practice are perpetually required to ensure success. The daily arduous study practised by such men as Kemble and Macready, might well put to the blush many a phlegmatic speaker in the pulpit, who seldom passes a thought on the only natural means of rendering his ministrations interesting or impressive.

No juster remark was ever made than that contained in the answer of the player to the preacher. "We utter fiction as if it were truth; you utter truth as if it were fiction." Nor will this observation cease to be applicable to the style of the pulpit, while a formal and ceremonious, instead of a living and earnest manner, continues to be associated with it, as a matter of habit, in preachers and hearers. No error is more general, and none is more fatal in its consequences, than that into which young preachers are so apt to fall, — that the elocution of the pulpit is a permanent fixture on which the personal habit of an individual is to make no encroachment, and that, once in the pulpit, a speaker is necessarily tied down to a certain decorous average of manner, never too earnest to disturb the repose of established routine.

FORCE, FEEBLENESS.

Force, as a trait of manner in speaking, is inseparable from earnestness. It is a natural attendant on animation. It is the invariable characteristic of the speaker who is himself awake to his subject, and whose feelings are interested in what he utters. We hear it in the vigor of his voice, in the weight of his emphasis, in the strength and fullness and impressive power of his tones of emotion; we see it in the manly energy of his action.

The property of force is not, it is true, an invariable characteristic of eloquence. There are subjects and occasions which quell and subdue force, and which forbid mere loudness of voice, or energy of action. But the public speaker who does not, on appropriate occasions, rise to impressive force of manner, falls short, not merely of eloquent effect, but of true and manly expression. Freedom, appropriateness, grace, are all inferior to this master quality. An energetic speaker will force his way to the heart, in spite of awkward and ungainly habits. Genuine force is, to sympathy, what necessity is to motive; it sweeps all before it.*

Force is the prime attribute of man; it cannot be dispensed with, in the habits of the speaker. No degree of fluency, or of mere grace, can be accepted in its stead. The feeble, florid rhetorician never affects his audience beyond the surface of fancy. The preacher whose manner is weak, never penetrates the heart, or impresses the mind. The prime characteristic of style in man address-

---

* The eloquence of the Scottish preacher Chalmers, forms a striking example in point. The uncouthness of his broad dialectic accent, and his preternatural vehemence of voice and action, were lost in the fervid force of that native enthusiasm with which he threw soul and body into his subject and his manner. His whole being was concentrated on his theme; and he held his audience, of whatever class, with the grasp of a giant.

ing man, on topics of vast concern, must be force. Culture may come in, to modulate that force into fitting and graceful forms. But where life and soul are, there must be force. Eloquence persuades; but it also impels and urges, with irresistible power.

VEHEMENCE, VIOLENCE.

Genuine force of manner in speaking, rises, indeed, on some occasions to vehemence itself. The inspiration of a strong emotion does not stop to weigh manner in "the hair-balance of propriety;" it will not wait for nice and scrupulous adaptation. The speaker who is never moved beyond a certain decorous reserve, will never move his audience to sympathy. Force will not be hedged in by arbitrary prescriptions.

It is not less true, however, that vehemence, being the offspring of enthusiasm, is, like its parent, exceedingly prone to the evils of excess. There is a bad as well as a good enthusiasm, and, consequently, a bad as well as a good vehemence. The genuine inspiration, the true vehemence, is, even in its strongest expression, like the eloquence which the great orator has so characteristically described as resembling "the outbreaking of the fountain from the earth, or the bursting forth of volcanic fire;" it has the force, but, still, the beauty or the grandeur, of nature.

The vehemence of indignation is, sometimes, one of the strongest incitements of eloquence. We trace this fact, in many instances, in the language of the sacred volume, not less distinctly than in that of Demosthenes, or Cicero, or Chatham. But true vehemence never degenerates into violence and vociferation. It is the force of inspiration,—not of frenzy. It is not manifested in the screaming and foaming, the stamping and the contortions, of vulgar excess. It is ever manly and noble, in its intensest excitement: it elevates, — it does not degrade. It never descends to the bawling voice, the guttural coarseness, the shrieking emphasis, the hysteric ecstasy of tone, the bullying attitude, and the clinched fist of extravagant passion.

GENTLENESS, SPIRIT, TAMENESS.

The excesses of improper vehemence in delivery, however, while they are utterly revolting to humanity and taste, are no excuse for the habitual weakness of manner, which is betrayed by speakers of the opposite character. Gentleness, it is true, is one of the most efficacious of all the means of persuasion; and it is nowhere more successful or more becoming, than in the pulpit. But, as force is not violence, so neither is gentleness tameness. "He is gentle, and not fearful," is one of the truest of those just and beautiful discriminations which are the charm of the great dramatist, in his exquisite delineations of the various shades of human character.

The act of expression, whether it is performed by the voice, the eye, or the hand, or by the natural union of them all, demands a living force. It may be moderate; but it must be spirited. It requires that easy and skilful, perhaps gentle, exercise of force, which characterizes the decisive touches of the artist, and which gives prominence and life to the figures of his canvas. It is the farthest thing possible from tameness and feebleness. Power of expressive utterance, is the positive electricity of the soul; it implies a percussive force of will on the organic frame; its natural language is energy of voice and gesture.

The tame speaker wearies his audience, and sends

them away indifferent to any effect; — their minds a mere blank. The feeble speaker excites the pity of his hearers; they sympathize with the organic weakness under which he seems to labor, and leave the place of assembly, utterly unimpressed with any feeling but of compassion for the preacher personally. Had he but exerted his organs sufficiently to fill with his voice the building in which he spoke; had he but given a hearty emphasis to his utterance, or a manly energy to his tones; had he not allowed himself to "mutter like the wizard behind the wall;" had he permitted himself the just force and decision of a messenger empowered to deliver an authoritative message; — how different might have been the result! His subject might then have penetrated every mind, and impressed every heart: his audience might have departed lamenting, if anything, their own lack of spiritual life, not the feeble style of the preacher.

BOLDNESS, TIMIDITY.

A reckless boldness of manner, is repulsive in any speaker, and, most of all, in him who addresses his fellow-men on sacred themes. It is utterly at variance with the spirit of gentleness and tenderness which was manifested by the preacher's great Exemplar. Yet, owing to the absence of the moulding influence of true culture, how often is an audience harangued from the pulpit in a style of address which implies no respect for the speaker's fellow-beings.

This style is usually characterized by an ungoverned loudness of voice, a violent emphasis, an unmitigated vehemence of tone, a perpetual sweeping and jerking of the arm, and a frequent clinching of the fist. It is true that such a style is often the unconscious result of the speaker's force of conviction and fullness of feeling, in regard to his subject rather than the persons whom he is addressing; and that the idea of a bullying effect in his style, never, probably, occurred to him. But one seasonable suggestion from his teacher at school, would have sufficed to guard him against this obstacle to his usefulness, by leading him to recognize the difference between a manner which merely expresses the excitement of the speaker himself, and that which moulds this very excitement into an eloquent effect on others.

The timid or the diffident speaker, on the contrary, who has not, apparently, the courage, or the self-possession to lift up his voice in an audible sound, and whose hand seems glued to his side, and his whole body paralyzed,— so that he appears a statue-like personification of constraint,— unavoidably imparts to the feelings of those whom he addresses a degree of the irksomeness and misery under which he himself is laboring. Whatever he would attempt to say, becomes, as it were, frozen in the act of issuing from the mouth. His arm, if it ever rises to an action, makes but an approach to gesture, and only leaves the eye more sensitive to the want of it.

The embarrassed speaker, with his suppressed and imperfect utterance, and cowed, hesitating action, does not even fulfil the organic conditions of address; he falls equally short of reaching ear, eye, and heart. His matter may be rich and strong,— his composition eloquent; but all is lost for want of that courage which a little training and practice might easily impart, and which would inspire the due boldness that becomes a man addressing his fellow-beings.

There is, undoubtedly, a good as well as a faulty boldness. The preacher, if true to his subject and his hear~~ will often have occasion to exert the former. It the~ decomes an element of appropriate manner and jus~esture, It is, in such circumstances, indispensable to since~ professing and true eloquence, not less than to good elo~

† Ibid.

HARSHNESS, AMENITY.

The too bold speaker is apt to add to the bad effects of apparent indifference to the presence of his hearers, that of a repulsive harshness of voice and aspect, — a fault at variance with everything like persuasive or genial effect. Sternness and asperity of expression preclude the speaker from access to the heart, and seal the mind to his influence. Yet inadvertent habit, in the absence of culture, has sometimes stamped such a manner on the preacher.

The energy of such speakers soon becomes vehemence, and their vehemence, apparent anger. No wonder that they should displease, rather than win their hearers. Faults of this description are usually matters of utter unconsciousness to the individuals who commit them. They are often the results of mere constitutional austerity and ill-regulated force of expression. Ten minutes of the so much derided practice before the looking-glass, would reflect so faithfully to such speakers the visible image which they present, that they could not tolerate its associations; and the reform of mien and aspect would unavoidably extend its softening influence to the voice.

An insipid, simpering, blandness of manner, is certainly a very undesirable trait in any speaker. It is peculiarly silly or ridiculous in a preacher; he is the ambassador of Divine truth; and, if he understands his office, is clothed with a higher dignity than can be conferred by man. His office entitles him to speak as one having authority.

But the spirit of love which should breathe from the preacher's lips, will diffuse its genial amenity over his whole manner. His tones, his features, his action, will ⸱te, will intreat, will persuade, will win his hearers, lou⸱ ⸱tract them to his subject. The humane and benevⱽᵉʰᵉ ⸱irit of his office, will be legible in every trait of the aᶦ⸱ₑₛₛ₎ that st⸱

THE CULTIVATION OF FORCE.

Modes of cultivating Force.

The cultivation of elocution with a view to the acquisition of due force of manner, — a style free from all the faults of feebleness and tameness, — requires a proper attention to health and vigor of body, as an indispensable condition of energetic expression in utterance and action. The weak and constrained speaker may become effective and free, by due exposure and exercise. The flaccid muscle, and the enfeebled nerve, will thus acquire tone; the voice will become sonorous; the arm energetic; the attitude firm; the whole manner impressive.

The sedentary life of the student and the preacher, subjects them to weakness of body and languor of spirits, and predisposes them to feebleness in voice and action. They need double care and diligence, for the preservation of that healthy tone of feeling, which alone can ensure energy of habit in expressive utterance.

To such measures should be added a constant resort to all the genuine sources of mental vigor; the attentive study of the effects of force in all its natural forms, in the outward phenomena of the universe; in the varied shapes which it assumes in all the expressive arts, — particularly in music, sculpture, and painting, and, most of all, in written language.

The express discipline of the voice, with a view to the acquisition of organic force and vocal power, in the modes prescribed in the volume on Orthophony,* will fully reward the student, by the command which it will give him over his organs. and the fullness and energy which it will impart to his tones. The daily practice of vigorous declamation, aided by the study of the principles of gesture, as laid down in the Elocutionist,† will enable the profes-

---

* See preface to the present work. † Ibid.

sional speaker to acquire that force in action, which is an indispensable part of effective and impressive delivery.

Modes of subduing excessive Vehemence.

The only effectual means of correcting faults of excessive force, such as violence, undue boldness, harshness of manner, and similar qualities, must be sought in an entire revolution of taste and habits. The speaker whose style is marked by such blemishes, must learn to perceive the appropriateness and moral beauty of gentleness, dignity, calmness and composure of mien and action, moderation of voice, and amenity of manner, in him whose office is sacred in all its associations, and whose habitual expression should breathe the spirit of humanity and love.

The unseemly vehemence which degrades the pulpit to the level of the popular arena, implies a grievous error of judgment not less than of taste. It involves a fatal defect in the whole mental structure and character of the speaker himself. The sense of fitness and of beauty, must, to such individuals, be a matter of acquisition: it can be attained only by means of attentive study and close observation. Discipline must, in such instances, be applied as a corrective to taste and tendency; eloquence should be studied in its power to soften and subdue; the heart should be subjected to the calm and gentle influence of nature, the tranquil beauty of art, and the tender breathings of such poetry as that of Cowper; the spirit should be moulded by the softening touch of refining intercourse in elevated social life; a genial sympathy with humanity should be acquired by habitual benevolent communication with its sufferings and depressions. The speaker's whole manner may thus be formed anew, and acquire that moderation and that mildness which are the characteristics of genuine eloquence.

FREEDOM, CONSTRAINT, RESERVE.

An indispensable trait of manliness, not less than of eloquence, is entire freedom of manner, arising from due self-reliance, and, at the same time, that self-forgetfulness which is naturally caused by a speaker's interest in his subject. A modest estimation of his own powers, a proper respect for others, and a profound feeling of the importance of his subject, are not incompatible with perfect ease and self-possession. Embarrassment and constraint, indeed, are not unfrequently owing to that vacillation of attention, which allows the speaker's mind to vibrate between the duty before him, and the consciousness of his personal relation to it. The unity of his mental and bodily action, would remain unimpaired, were his whole mind absorbed in his theme: the disturbing self-conscious reference would thus be precluded; and his manner would be concentrated in earnest, impressive utterance.

Freedom, self-possession, and ease of manner, would seem to be the natural condition of man addressing man; and these traits would be the spontaneous concomitants of public discourse, if education in early life, were properly regulated. But this advantage is not enjoyed, in the present forms of school routine. The exercise of declamation, which is the only training prescribed for boys, is too formal and ceremonious in its style, to lead to free, unembarrassed manner in address. The subject of his declamation is usually too abstract and general, or of too conventional a character, to permit the young speaker to identify it with the workings of his own mind. The exercise is accordingly performed in the spirit of mechanical routine, as a task to be undergone,—as an unmeaning ceremony.

The unnatural position of the juvenile speaker, embarrasses him; and his whole style is constrained and awkward. His voice is smothered by his conscious inability to utter aright the sentiments which he is expressing: his emphasis is quelled by the conviction that his feelings are unnatural to him: his tones, uninspired by genuine emotion, deviate into an arbitrary chant: his action becomes, — from the consciousness that he is performing a part, — forced and unnatural. The inevitable result of such processes, is, that the habits of the boy are moulded into forms which indicate constraint as inseparably associated with the act of declaiming. At no subsequent stage of education is this association broken up; and it continues to hang, as a visible load, on the habitual manner of the professional speaker.

The injurious effects of misdirected education, in this particular, are frequently perceptible in the elocution of the pulpit. The preacher often seems, in consequence of these, to be going through an irksome process, from which it would be a grateful relief to be set free. His suppressed voice, his imperfect utterance, his reserved tones, his constrained mien and posture, his confined, angular, hesitating, awkward, half-executed gestures, all seem to indicate the prisoner of restraint, rather than the voluntary speaker.

A little preparatory training would save the young preacher from this process of suffering and exposure, and enable him to deliver his message with, at least, the due degree of composure and self-possession. The reserve which diffidence throws over the speaker's manner, is utterly at variance with that spirit of sympathy and communication, which is the true source of speech. Earnest and impressive address is incompatible with a manner which seems to withhold rather than impart the thoughts and feelings of the speaker, — to suppress rather than to give utterance to his emotions. The preacher then becomes the messenger who keeps back rather than delivers his message: the man is virtually unfaithful to his trust. His audience leave him unimpressed with the spirit of the communication which it was his office to make, and to which all his energies should have been devoted.

The easy, self-possessed speaker, on the contrary, imparts composure by his very manner. His flowing speech, and unconstrained action, cause his thoughts to glide easily into the mind. His unembarrassed and natural utterance finds its way immediately to the sympathies of his audience: persuasion dwells on the very accents of his voice: he seems to mould the mind at will: he secures the attention by winning both ear and eye: his hearers follow the strain of his remarks without effort: their complacency with the speaker predisposes them to receive the truths which he inculcates.

An easy, unconstrained style, in speaking, is more dependent on culture and practice, than is any other trait of elocution. Attention and diligence, however, are the only conditions on which a speaker can become effectually master of himself, as to outward manner. Early education, if it were what it should be, would mould all cultivated men into habitual ease in expression, from their first attempts at speaking, in boyhood. But our present arrangements at school and college, do not call the individual into practice often enough to allow him to feel at home in the act. The process of criticising, too, whether it is performed by the teacher, or devolved on the speaker's class-fellows, is customarily limited to the indication of some prominent faults, after the exercise is over. This practice may prune and repress and chill; but it never can inspire and guide and develop and warm and invigorate. Its usual effect is to restrain and embarrass. The student feels, in the exercise of declamation, that he is speaking before critics, for the express purpose of being criticised. He knows he is not uttering his personal feelings to sympathetic listeners; and his reserve of manner betrays the fact of his conscious condition. He studies coolness and correctness, rather than earnestness and warmth. He shuns the natural glow of feeling and expression, and quenches rather than cherishes the spirit of eloquence.*

Early education ought to exhibit and implant principles which would anticipate and preclude the growth of false habits. A preventive regimen should be adopted in this, as in every other branch of culture. The office of instruction is to preöcupy the mind, and infuse truth, rather than to eradicate error, — to form and mould and strengthen the power of expression, rather than to trim excrescences, — to inspire genuine emotion, and to infuse true grace, rather than to correct the petty errors of judgment, or check the transient excesses of feeling, and castigate the venial errors of immature taste. These offices, it is true, form a part of the duties of the faithful teacher. But they are the mere " mint, anise, and cummin," compared to " the weightier matters of the law."

The spirit of finical criticism invariably turns away the speaker's attention from his subject to himself. It troubles his mind with an embarrassing self-consciousness, which constrains his manner, and cools his emotion.

The professional speaker has to labor under the disadvantage of a long course of such training. No wonder, therefore, that his style should be unnatural and constrained, as a result of habit and association. Against such evils the student who would form his manner to a free, expressive character, must necessarily watch, and zealously guard himself by constant practice. His chief aids will lie in the attentive study of the freest and most natural of all the forms of expression, those which are presented in the perfect products of art, — more particularly those of sculpture and painting. He will be assisted by the daily practice of reading and reciting from the

---

* The easy and fluent manner of students from the South, forms an obvious contrast to the prevalent stiffness and reserve of the local manner at our Eastern colleges. The difference, in this case, is owing, largely, to the unrestrained freedom of style, which results from the modes of Southern education, during the early period of life.

freest and most flowing language of poetry. He will derive still more benefit from accustoming himself to the vivid recitation of the most natural and expressive passages of the drama. No exercise in elocution is so conducive to freedom of manner as this.*

The general effect on the preacher's style of address in the pulpit, as regards due freedom and facility, is, no doubt, dependent on the extent to which he accustoms himself to mingle with society, and contract that familiarity with man which renders the office of communicating with him easy and spontaneous. The secluded student is little prepared for one main office of the ministry, — that of free, unembarrassed utterance. Like every other art worth mastering, it requires of every individual, culture and practice, as the only conditions on which he can attain skill and facility.

VARIETY, MONOTONY.

Sentiments which possess force and interest to the mind, though they sometimes run comparatively long in one channel of feeling and expression, do not pursue an undeviating, unvarying course. The natural tendency of impressive thought, is to call up varied emotions and diversified forms of imagination. The appropriate communication of such thought, implies, therefore, a varying tone, aspect, and action. Trite thoughts may justify a monotonous manner of expressing them. But public address, especially from the pulpit, forbids the presentation of thread-bare topics and insignificant ideas. We pardon these in the aimless movement of unpremeditated con-

---

* The ancient practice of acting plays at school and college, and even at professional institutions, was founded on a true impression of the importance of free and natural manner in speaking.

versation, but not on occasions when numbers are assembled to hear important and impressive truths.

The popular complaint, therefore, that preachers are deficient in variety of manner in their speaking, — although sometimes an arbitrary objection, founded on a vague and general impression, regardless of particular circumstances which may happen to forbid variety, — is by no means destitute of foundation. Sermons are too commonly written after the fashion of academic themes on prescribed common-place topics. The mind of the writer pursues, in such cases, an unexciting, mechanical routine of thought; his pen betrays the fact in its trite language; and his tones, — his very looks and gestures, — repeat the effect to ear and eye, in flat and wearisome monotony.

The defects of early education, which, in other points, are so injurious to manner and so destructive to eloquence, reveal themselves distinctly here. The speaker in the pulpit carries with him the deadening influence of years of false habit and lifeless utterance, contracted from the neglect of his style in youth; from the custom of declaiming, in an unmeaning and inexpressive way, passages either unintelligible or uninteresting to him; and, sometimes, from the stiffening effect of the arbitrary directions which he has received in the shape of formal instruction. The lifeless tones of school reading, are still haunting his ear, as an unconscious standard; and he consequently observes the beaten round of a uniform force, a uniform pitch, and a uniform gait of voice, destitute of expression, — the primitive tone of no meaning and no feeling, which he instinctively and very justly applied in childhood, to what he could neither understand nor feel, — but a tone which inveterate habit has made natural to his ear. To such modes of voice the preacher not unfrequently adds a lifeless stillness of body, and an insipid sameness of gesture, which produce a similar effect on the eye to that which his utterance exerts on the ear.

The fault of monotony is, if anywhere, unpardonable in the pulpit, where the speaker has the range of the universe, for his subjects, and the topics of spiritual and eternal life for his habitual themes. Why should the elocution of the preacher be almost proverbially monotonous? Why should it so often furnish just ground for the sleepy hearer to devolve the fault of his condition on the preacher's voice?

The easy remedy for this state of matters, lies in the study of elocution, and the cultivation of expressive tone and action. A knowledge of the principles of audible and visible expression, will enable the student to trace the natural and appropriate difference of tones, and to identify every mode of utterance with its peculiar characteristic emotion. It will be impossible for him, afterwards, to mistake a dead level of voice for expressive variation. The discipline which the study of elocution prescribes, will enable him to acquire that command over his organs by which he may easily execute every transition and change of expression, which appropriate utterance or action requires. He will thus learn to substitute, for his pipe with one note, or his harp with one string, the natural, varied and powerful effect of man's living voice, inspired by varied emotion. He will be enabled to resume something of that vivid effect of bodily attitude and motion, which made him, in childhood, the envied model of the orator, in the freedom, variety, and efficacy of his expressive action. The ever-varying style of Scripture will, thenceforth, no longer be misrepresented by his flat sameness of voice; the inspiring hymn will not have its appropriate effect quenched by the morbid dullness of his heavy style of reading; nor will his discourse any longer operate, by its "sleepy tune," as a soothing soporific.

The diligent cultivation of his manner, will enable the preacher to breathe life and freshness into all its aspects, and infuse a corresponding effect into his ministrations. The subjects which he presents, will naturally assume their appropriate and most striking lights, and fall upon the mind with their full force of effect. His hearers instead of reiterating the old complaint regarding the Sabbath, " What a weariness is it!" will leave the sanctuary with hearts refreshed and reinvigorated, and minds " stirred up " anew to every good work and every noble purpose.

MANNERISM, ADAPTATION, APPROPRIATENESS.

One of the common results of inadequate or misdirected early culture, in regard to elocution, is, that the style of young speakers, is so soon permitted to settle into fixed mannerism. An observer who has opportunity of tracing the successive stages of development in individuals subjected to the customary routine of education, will perceive that the preacher in the pulpit bears, upon his style of delivery, the stamp of the same characteristics by which he was distinguished as a youth at college, and as a boy at school. This fact, were it the natural consequence of the growth and evolution of individual character and original tendency, — were it a spontaneous product of genius, — would be not only tolerable but positively agreeable, as a trait of elocution. The objection lies in the obvious fact, that the manner is arbitrary and conventional, — a mere matter of acquired habit, — a compound result of the influence of academic precedent and example, blending with a few accidental peculiarities of personal tendency. For the speaker in the pulpit is often found reading his sermon with precisely the same tones and inflections, and the same gestures, with which he declaimed at school, when doing his best to play the juvenile representative of Cicero pleading against Verres, or Chatham rebuking the inhumanity of Lord Suffolk. **The preacher may be discoursing on the worth of the** soul, and the vastness of eternal interests, and the danger of tampering with them; but habit has set so irrevocably the key of his voice, that the whole sermon sounds, — sentence for sentence, cadence for cadence, — an exact copy of the utterance with which, when a candidate for college honors, he read his essay on the rhetorical traits of eminent writers.

The habit of reading and declaiming sentences as such, which results from the uniformity of custom at school, converts every paragraph into a succession of detached sentiments, each marked by an identical "beginning, middle and end" of tone in the voice: — no matter what the difference of style or of subject. A similar effect is produced on gesture. Action is limited to two or three forms, — perhaps, not even more than one, — perpetually recurring, whether the natural emotion connected with the language of the sentence be joy or grief, complacency or aversion, courage or fear.

An early culture adapted to the purposes of expression, would make the young pupil sensitively alive to the difference of character and effect in the feelings of the heart, as expressed in the various tones of the voice, and the diversified language of mien and action, in the body. It would convert the human organs into so many instruments obedient to the skilful touch; uttering, with unerring certainty, the exact music of each emotion, as it rose in the soul of the speaker. It would impart pliancy and grace and power to every member of the corporeal frame, in the act of executing the forms in which imagination naturally embodies the thoughts and feelings of the mind, when animated by the spirit of communication.

Eloquence, in its external shape, would thus resemble the natural effect of the shifting lights and shades and the changing colors of the mental scene.

Elocution, were it duly cultivated, would teach the student that the perpetual recurrence of one tone, one pitch, one force, one inflection, one uniform melody, and one sing-song cadence, is as untrue to nature, and to the facts of language and sentiment, as it is false to feeling, and to the ear. The study of elocution would teach the indispensable lesson, that one sentiment inspires one look and action, and another, another, — that there is no more truth or consistency in using one movement of the arm, or one attitude of the body, for every sentiment and every sentence, than there would be in using one form of words, for the structure of every period in a discourse. The natural shadings of emotion and sympathy, are, in fact, infinitely more diversified in the aspect and expression of the countenance and the person of the speaker, than they can ever become in the most pliant phrases of speech.

The negligent speaker often justifies his mannerism, on the ground of personality. Speaking of his prominent faults, he will say, " This is my natural manner: I like to see individuality of style in delivery, as in all other forms of expression; and this trait constitutes mine. I cannot change it for another; because that other, though perhaps better in itself, would not be natural to me." This reasoning would be as sound as it is plausible in itself and comforting to indolence, were habit and nature invariably the same in individuals, and were manner inevitable and immutable, like Richter's cast-metal king. But manner in expression is the most plastic of all things: it can be moulded, at will, to whatever shape a decisive resolution and a persevering spirit determine. Attentive cultivation will reform, renovate, and re-create, here, as extensively as elsewhere. It will enable the individual to shake off the old and put on the new vesture of habit, and to wear it, too, with perfect ease, as the true and the natural garb of expression. For all genuine culture is but the cherishing or the resuscitating of nature.

A good writer is recognized by that perfect command of his pen, which enables him to vary his language with his subject; and he is the most successful in written expression, who can most easily and effectually give the changing aspect of thought its shifting hue of style. So it is with the good speaker: his manner ever varies with his subject: with him, every passing emotion has its appropriate mode of utterance. He is like the skilful and accomplished performer who ranges over the whole compass of his instrument, and forever draws forth new echoes of sympathy from the heart, in response to its changing tones. The natural and effective speaker, by the eloquence of his varying utterance, infuses fresh life into thought, and affects the soul of his hearers as the breath of morning or of spring. The factitious style of the mannerist, when it is strongly marked, attracts our attention to itself, and obscures our impression of his thought; but, even when it is comparatively weak, it still hangs as a veil between the subject and the hearer's mind: its tendency is not to add but subtract effect; it deducts something from the impression which would otherwise have been made. A manner well adapted to matter, is not merely a transparent medium: it sheds light on the objects of the mental scene: it has the kindling effect of sunlight on the landscape; it brings out into distinct and impressive effect, the form, color, and character of whatever it touches.

To remove the defects of mannerism, and to secure the advantages of adaptation and appropriateness in delivery, the speaker's great aim should be to lose himself in his subject, and in every successive part of it, as it is developed in the progress of his discourse. His style will thus acquire its proper analogy to the sunlight and the shade, the life and the repose, the alternate brilliancy and the depth of effect, which nature gives when sun and shadow are shifting over the field, in correspondence with the passing cloud. The mannerist holds to himself, and to his accidents of personal habit, — and these perhaps quite artificial, — rather than to the current of his thoughts and their natural accompaniment of emotion.

The speaker who is desirous of possessing the charm

of fitting manner, will train his voice to the genuine utterance of every tone of emotion; he will endeavor to acquire all that depth which the most impressive of his themes demand, in those tones which are the natural expression of solemnity and awe; he will cultivate the power of giving voice to those thrilling notes of joy and rapture, in which the lofty strains of sacred lyrics so frequently abound; he will study the effect of force and grandeur and sublimity in swelling the tones of praise and triumph; he will watch the transition to the subdued and softened strains of penitence and contrition; he will distinguish the slow movement of pathetic and solemn emotion from the accelerated utterance of cheerful and lively expression. His outward manner, in attitude and action, will be as various as his voice: he will evince the inspiration of appropriate feeling in the very posture of his frame; in uttering the language of adoration, the slow-moving, uplifted hand will bespeak the awe and solemnity which pervade his soul; in addressing his fellow-men in the spirit of an ambassador of Christ, the gentle yet earnest spirit of persuasive action, will be evinced in the pleading hand and aspect; he will know, also, how to pass to the stern and authoritative mien of the reprover of sin; he will, on due occasions, indicate, in his kindling look and rousing gesture, the mood of him who is empowered and commanded to summon forth all the energies of the human soul; his subdued and chastened address will carry the sympathy of his spirit into the bosom of the mourner; his moistening eye and his gentle action will manifest his tenderness for the suffering: his whole soul will, in a word, become legible in his features, in his attitude, in the expressive eloquence of his hand; his whole style will be felt to be that of heart communing with heart.

The mannerist in speaking is often cut off from the possibility of attaining to the effects of genuine eloquence, by the inappropriateness of his fixed habit to the language and the sentiment which he is uttering. Mannerism is usually the predominance of one trait, which has more or less exclusive character attached to it. The vehement mannerist, accordingly, when addressing the sufferer whose heart is well-nigh crushed under the weight of calamity, jars the whole sympathetic nature of his hearer, by the inappropriate and revolting violence of his tone and action. His very consolations may assume the expression of scolding. The feeble mannerist, when employed to arouse an assembly from spiritual supineness, soothes them to sleep by his lifeless humming tone, and the sway of his waving, spiritless action.

One of the most obvious traits of mannerism, and one which nothing but the assiduous practice of elocution can do away, is that mode of utterance which is, in popular phrase, called "a tone." The fault implied by this term, consists in the continual recurrence of a particular mode of voice, in emphasis, inflection, cadence, or "expression,"* but, more frequently, in the "melody,"† or peculiar notes, which characterize a speaker's vocal habits.

This species of mannerism in speech, has been expressly designated by Dr. Rush, the great analyst of elocution, as a "drift" or obvious tendency of voice, in the effect of one repeated trait of utterance, on the ear. Every passion, or strain of emotion, has a distinctive "drift,"—a tendency to repeat certain qualities of expression; and the effect arising from change of direction in "drift," by the natural shifting of the vocal current, with every new emotion, in successive passages, consti-

---

* The peculiar effect of *feeling*, or *emotion*, on the voice; as when we speak of the *tone of anger*, or *of pity*.

† The effect of sound as depending on the succession of *notes* which the voice executes in a given strain, clause, or phrase. Thus, *awe* is characterized by the recurrence of low notes, and inclines to *monotony;* joy, traverses the scale, from *low* to *high*, and from *high* to *low*, and is marked by *variety;* *interrogation* slides *up* the scale; and the *cadence* of a sentence glides *downward*.

tutes a marked peculiarity of animated, true, and expresive style,—alike in conversation, in reading, and i public speaking.

The fault of mannerism in utterance, substitutes, fc this appropriate variation of voice, an arbitrary recurrenc of sound, not authorized or required by the nature of th emotion which, in a given passage, ought to set the key and guide the style. The reader, in consequence of ths fault, utters not the meaning and spirit of his authors language, but the song of his own arbitrary and accidental habit. He does not change the character of his utterance, with the varying sentiments of the composition; but while the most striking changes of feeling are obviously indicated in the phrases which he is enunciating, he continues to repeat his identical melody, with no attempt at variation. He goes on executing, with undeviating precision, one and the same inflection at every comma, and one and the same cadence at every period,—be the sense or the feeling of the sentence what it may. His voice is like a hand-organ set to but one tune: it may be kept going by the hour, the day, or the year; yet it will give out but the same succession of sounds.

A ready ear may catch a preventive lesson, as regards this fault, by listening to the natural variations of voice, in conversation, and thus enable the reader to mould his utterance to diversity of effect. But empiric methods imply no definite and certain aims, and consequently no sure results. The reader or the speaker who aims at the style of conversation, as his model, if he succeeds in bringing his vocal habits out of mechanical and unmeaning "drift,"—if he frees himself from the formalities of a mere "reading tone,"—is apt, on the other hand, to acquire that characteristic "drift" of mere conversational style, which is, literally, a "talking tone,"—too versatile, too vivacious for the dignity of public reading or speaking,—and fit only for easy and careless communication by the fireside.

The power of applying musical distinctions to the varying sounds of the voice, will be of great service to the reader, by rendering his ear discriminating as to vocal effect. But the modes of voice which come under the special cognizance of elocution, must be studied by themselves, in exact detail, by all who wish to acquit themselves thoroughly to the duty of public speaking. The close analysis which Dr. Rush has exemplified in his Philosophy of the Voice,* enables every student who is willing to take the pains, to become expert in the discrimination and execution of every point of vocal expresssion. The application of the elementary distinctions exhibited in that treatise, will effectually remove every trait of factitious manner from vocal habit in elocution.

INDIVIDUALITY OF MANNER.

Mannerism in delivery not unfrequently passes for the real excellence of individuality in style, — a trait which, so far from possessing any artificial character, is the expression of spontaneous life and eloquence. But this feature of expressive power, is, like many others, depressed by the deadening influence of formality and routine in education. Boys at school are left to sink into one uniform mould, in their habits of utterance and action : their exercises possess so little life and interest to their minds, that to perform such tasks with natural spirit, and as a part of their own mental action and experience, is impossible. Juvenile declamation, accordingly, wears, in most instances, the second-hand air of a thing done as others do it, and *because* others do it. It is allowed to

---

* The manual of Orthophony, mentioned in the preface to the present volume, contains a practical exposition of Dr. Rush's system.

consist of a certain unmeaning loudness of voice, a singing and swelling utterance, and a given upraising of the hand,—all bearing the stamp of prescription, and habit, and average style. The formality, indeed, of the usual staple of language in declamation, seems, of itself, to prescribe just such uniform manner in every speaker: there is nothing in it which speaks to the heart of the individual, and brings out the inner man, with his own peculiar tones, and looks, and actions.

Could teachers and parents be content to let boys utter their own sentiments in their own language, the result of exercises in speaking would be very different from what it is. Boys would, in that case, speak as boys, not as "potent, grave, and reverend" *seniors*. Every juvenile speaker would give his heart to his work, and would bring out his own manner. The teacher would then take his true place as a friendly guide, prompter, and aid, not as a cool critic and *ex-post-facto* executioner: he would assist the pupil in bringing out his native impulses of thought and feeling, in forms adapted to his own nature. Speaking would thus become a spontaneous and pleasurable function of the individual; habit would grow into natural and accordant forms, revealing the genuine mental life that lay under them.

The prevalence of neglect and perversion, in our customary modes of education, suffers every youth, as he enters a place of instruction, to be cast into the academic mould, and come out precisely like the rest. He carries with him, accordingly, into subsequent stages of life, the impress which he has thus received: the school tone, somewhat deepened and amplified, and the school gesture, somewhat strengthened, may clearly be traced in the man, even at the bar and in the pulpit.

The effects of neglect and of erroneous training, are conspicuous in the prevalence of uniformity of manner among clergymen. The act of delivering a discourse is apparently, in many cases, a process of repeating certain prescribed tones and gestures which every individual is expected to go through very much like all others. The natural diversity of temperament and character, is not,— to judge by appearances, — considered an appropriate element of effect.

A good speaker, it is true, will always merge himself in his subject, and never obtrude himself at its expense. But thought, even the most abstract, when it passes into expression, is, like the purest water, naturally subjected to the tinge of the channel through which it flows. The individuality of the man should never be lost in the formal function of the speaker. There is no law of necessity that every sermon should be a succession of low and hollow tones, false inflections, mechanical cadences, and stereotype gestures ; — the whole manner so proverbially unnatural, that, among juvenile classes at school, when one pupil would sum up, in one expressive word, his criticism on a fellow-pupil who has spoken in a heavy, uniform style, he says of him, " He does not speak, he *preaches*."

The study of elocution, if it were duly attended to, as a part of early education, would enable the young speaker to recognize and trace the natural differences of manner, which ought to exist in individuals, in their modes of applying the same general principles. The genuine characteristics of expression, are so numerous and varied, that they afford vast scope for the natural diversity of action, in different mental and physical constitutions. The elements of effect, blended in one expressive tone, amount sometimes to more than six or eight, even in the unstudied utterance of a person utterly illiterate. The temperament and tendency of an individual, therefore, may well be expected to cause him to lean to one more than others among these elements.

The enunciation, for example, of the phrase in devotional address, " O Lord !" may receive its reverential effect in the utterance of one speaker, from its deep and solemn *pitch*, chiefly ; in that of another, from its majestic *fullness* and *swell;* in that of a third, from its *prolongation* and *slowness* of sound ; whilst all these properties may still be traced united in the style of each ; with this distinction, only, that while one quality preponderates in one speaker, another may in another. A similar remark applies to gesture. Constitution and temperament may incline one speaker to one shade of difference in the line or the force of an action, and another to another; and yet both may coincide in the general style and effect.

Our prevalent modes of education permit all individual tendencies to be swallowed up in one engulfing routine of neglect or prescription. The preacher, therefore, under the influence of such early training, comes before us divested of that native originality of manner, which is so distinctly felt as the eloquence of private communication. To recover his individuality, he must reform and renovate his whole style of speaking, so as to let his own nature shine through it. In address, *heart* " only is the loan for " *heart.* But how seldom can its throb be felt through the enveloping folds of false and formal habit !

The preacher who would successfully discharge the duty of his office, must acquire the power of throwing his personal character into his manner. Mere elocution is a poor substitute for the living sympathy of soul in the man who addresses us. The former, even when it is perfect, gains only admiration : the latter wins the whole heart, and convinces the mind, at once, of the speaker's sincerity, and of the truth of what he utters.

We hear, sometimes, a just complaint of the influence and tendency of ceremony in religion. But no robing or costume so effectually enwraps the soul, as a ceremonious tone, which offers to the ear the language of the office and not of the man.

DIGNITY, FAMILIARITY.

Man's upright form and noble stature are naturally attended by dignity in movement and action. An erect attitude, a lofty carriage, a commanding air, are characteristic even of the savage who spends his days in little else than asserting his dominion over the brutes, or communicating with his fellows whose habits are but a little more elevated than those of the animals which they hunt. Civilized life, by its enervating influence, brings down the erect and heroic mien, and the fearless demeanor, which are natural to man, while consciously sufficient to himself, and independent of factitious support. The courtesy and the condescensions of refinement, bring along with them tameness and feebleness in manner and in character: a bland and flexible exterior takes, in the forms of conventional habit, the place of the manly and majestic port of nature.

The transition from childhood to manhood, is attended with similar effects on the aspect and deportment of the human being. The unconscious, unabashed child exhibits, often, the noblest forms of attitude and action. The school-boy loses his self-possession, and shrinks and cowers, in the consciousness of being observed: he lacks the decision, the firmness, and the dignity of manner, which he possessed in earlier life, when mingling with his equals and companions. The bearing of the youth gives still stronger evidence of being vitiated by self-consciousness, and overweening regard for the estimation of others. The speaker, who, in the maturity of manhood, addresses his fellow-beings, manifests, not unfrequently, in his crest-fallen air, in his hesitating utterance and embarrassed actions, his want of conscious elevation and power, and betrays the fact that he does not approach the task with a manly reliance on himself and his subject. **Self-respect** seems to desert him, when subjected to observation: his nature appears to shrink, rather than to expand, with the circumstances in which he is placed.

Eloquence, the result of expressive power, is a thing unattainable in such a situation; for eloquence implies freedom, manly firmness, and force, a genuine moral courage, a conscious elevation of soul, a positive inspiration of mind. It presupposes that the speaker stands, for the moment, above those whom he addresses, for the very purpose of lifting them up to the level of his own views and inspiring them with his own feelings. The persuasive condescension of the orator is never incompatible with the native majesty of man.

The preacher, more than any other speaker, should evince a just consciousness of the noble nature of his commission. Haughtiness, undoubtedly, or arrogance of manner, is utterly incompatible with the meek spirit of the Christian minister. But a due sense of the dignity of his office, should breathe an air of genuine nobleness into all his expression. It should equally forbid a disturbing and degrading consciousness of the presence of his fellow-men, and an unbecoming remissness or familiarity of manner, on his own part, by which he might seem to let down his just self-respect, or his regard for the sacred office which he is called to fill.

One mode of address by which the pulpit is lowered in the estimation of the world, is that undignified familiarity of tone, which some preachers assume, under the impression that such a manner is the proper way to be easy and natural in utterance, and thus to gain access to the minds of their hearers. The line, in such cases, is not drawn between conversation and mere talk,—much less between private and public conversation. Simplicity, naturalness, and directness of style, all demand an analogy to serious and elevated conversation, in the utterance of the preacher But the dignity of the pulpit forbids all talking familiarity and slipshod ease which border on carelessness of air and manner. The sacredness of association with which the place and the man are invested, should be felt by the preacher, not less than the people, as a barrier of sanctity against every freedom which tends to desecrate the pulpit.

The leaning and lounging attitudes, and the slack, familiar gestures in which some preachers permit themselves to indulge, bear more resemblance to the air of the toil-worn rustic, resting his wearied frame on the fence-rail, as he chats with his neighbor at the close of the day, than to the deportment of one who is or should be fulfilling a nobler function than was ever imagined in the highest conceptions of the ancient orator. It is true that dignity is not stiffness, nor decorum constraint. But some speakers in the pulpit seem never to have drawn the line that separates freedom from negligence and slovenliness of manner, ease and self-possession from low familiarity and nonchalance. If there is one spot on earth where the stamp of vulgar habit and association is disgusting, it is the pulpit, which even the grossest minds are inclined to regard with veneration. Nor is it going too far, to assert, that nothing has so strong a tendency to diminish the proper influence of the pulpit, as the remissness of its occupant, regarding the first requirements of personal dignity in him who conducts the office of public worship, and presents, for the time, the living impersonation of religious sentiment.*

---

* The slovenly habit of former years, of allowing the hand to repose in the pocket, used to extend itself to some pulpits. A negative rule of attitude is, in all forms of address, that the speaker's right hand should be by his side, when not raised in gesture, as the very dropping and the stillness of the hand are properly parts of the effect of gesture. The act of addressing a public assembly, implies that the speaker is in possession of sufficient health and strength to stand on his feet, and to support his own weight. It forbids, therefore, the sluggish habit of leaning on surrounding objects. Dignity of carriage forbids equally the indolent air produced by resting one hand on the side, on the back, or anywhere on the speaker's person. Convenience and freedom of manner allow the left hand to repose on or near the speaker's notes, so

A few hours' attention to the subject would enable the preacher to recognize the appropriate traits of becoming dignity and elevation of manner, and to avoid habits which are offensive to the general sense of propriety, not less than to refined taste. A single glance at the mirror in his room, while the speaker was at practice, would be the most effectual admonition to guard against those writhings of the body, noddings of the head, and jerkings of the arm, which degrade the preacher into the free and easy debater at a club-meeting. A few weeks' study of the principles of gesture, would open up to the mind a whole world of association, and of law and principle, regarding attitude and action. It would mould the speaker's whole outward man anew, and, at least, cut off the glaring errors of habit, if it did not inspire appropriateness and grace.

The stately dignity of deportment, which, in former years, was the distinguishing trait of the Christian gentleman and accomplished scholar, in the pulpit, has passed away with the noble race of men who exemplified its effects. The polish of private life from which it sprung, has, to say the least, obviously declined. But the change leaves something wanting to the heart. The authoritative mien of the old divine, had, perhaps, something in it of the arrogance of office. But in taking away the conventional elevation of manner, we have removed with it, a portion of genuine dignity. The reformation which has "popularized" the pulpit, has lowered its tone, and limited its influence on the preacher as well as on the people.

---

as to execute, when needful, the indispensable act of turning the leaves. But nothing can warrant the unseemly, uncouth, and awkward habit of supporting the body with each hand resting on one side of the cushion, or that of reposing with one elbow embedded in it. The former trick leads, unavoidably, to the consummation of ungainly appearance, by rendering it necessary that, when the speaker becomes earnest, he should manifest it by wriggling his vertebral column, instead of obeying nature's law, and using his hand in gesture.

FORMALITY, PRIMNESS, RIGIDITY.

One effect of manner, which impairs the life of pulpit eloquence, is formality of style. A professional, ceremonious intonation, and a technical, measured solemnity of mien and action, are the characteristics of this mode of delivery. The speaker's whole aspect, his voice, and his gestures, are, in consequence of this fault, thrown, apparently, into a mechanical mould which has left its impress on the whole man, and prevents the possibility of his expressing himself with a natural, life-like effect.

Preachers of this class are distinguished by a marble fixedness of features, an habitual upturned eye, a heavy, hollow, and uniform tone, a rigid and laborious style of movement and action. This stereotype manner precludes everything like adaptation to change of circumstances or of subject. The man becomes, in such cases, too much of an automaton, to impart spiritual or intellectual life to others. He kills rather than awakens sympathy: he renders himself incapable of arousing or interesting the mind. His fixed formality of manner converts devotion into ceremony, and worship into soulless routine: it renders preaching an unmeaning and unprofitable piece of custom.

Solemnity and decorum are, undoubtedly, the aim of the speaker, in all such instances of manner. But the mechanical and labored style, and the literal character of the whole affair, produce, unavoidably, an exterior rather than an interior effect. The origin of the fault of formality, seems to be the general impression, stamped in early life, that the pulpit is necessarily associated with certain looks and tones. The preacher himself yields unconsciously to the influence of such impressions, and complies with it, in his manner of speaking. The result is that he moulds his style into a decorous gravity, or a deep solemnity, more than into an earnest and living expression of his personal sentiments. He assumes, unintentionally, an air and an utterance which are not, properly, his own, but part and parcel of his profession.

The study of elocution prescribes the easy and certain remedy for such habits, by accustoming the speaker to analyze his tones, and trace distinctly the difference between the mode of voice which betrays a factitious utterance, and that which comes warm and true from the heart, with the inspiration of the moment fresh upon it. The preparatory discipline in elocution would enable the student to awaken and vivify his voice, and modulate its expression into the natural variations of personal feeling, without which there can neither be life nor eloquence in speech.

Formality, in the case of some speakers, assumes the feeble form of primness of manner, with its sparing voice, precise articulation, nice emphasis, fastidious inflection, meagre tone, and mincing gesture. This prudery of style is not unfrequently exemplified in the pulpits of New England, in consequence of the anxious precision and exactness of habit which are so general as local traits. The speaker's whole manner seems, in consequence of this cadency, to be weighed and given out with the most scrupulous and cautious regard to rigorous accuracy of effect in petty detail. Elocution becomes, in such cases, a parallel to the transplanted tree, trimmed of all its natural life and beauty, and, for the time, resembling, in its quaintnes and rigidity, rather a bare pole, than a product of vegetable nature.

The result of such a manner is to anatomize and kill feeling, — not to inspire it: the head is, in this way, allowed to take the place of the heart. Exact discrimination and subtle nicety of intellect, preponderate, usually, in the effect of such speaking on the hearer: his affections are left unmoved : he is unconscious, throughout the discourse, of one manly impulse or strong impression. The prim, guarded, neutralizing manner of the preacher, seems, in such instances, the appropriate style of coldness and scepticism, rather than of a warm and living faith. The fault of undue precision of manner, may be traced partly to the influence of undue anxiety about mere literal exactness, partly to the absence of manly force and independence of character, and partly to faulty education, which has led the speaker to pay more regard to the effect which he produces on the understanding and the judgment, than that which he exerts on the moral sympathies of his audience.* The last of these influences accustoms the school-boy to precision and point of emphasis, and speciality of inflection, more than to earnest energy of utterance and impressive emotion. Early habit, thus directed, leads the student and the preacher to a corresponding mode of address, and involves all the defects of an over-pruned manner, with its unavoidable results of cool and fastidious preciseness, which offers nothing to the heart, and therefore leaves undone the great business for which the preacher addresses mankind.

Formality of manner in speaking, is sometimes caused, in part, by an unbending rigidity of habit, which is plainly legible in the unyielding features, stiff postures, and stiff gestures, of some preachers. These faults of habit in address, are partly owing to false impressions regarding manly firmness and dignity, partly to the want of free and genial and extensive intercourse with the world, and partly to an early culture deficient in the means of imparting flexibility and grace to the mental and bodily faculties.

It is a matter of frequent observation among the people

---

* An impressive lesson on the futility of mere preciseness, used to be given by a popular lecturer on local peculiarities of character, to his audiences at the West, in a humorous delineation, in which two worthy Eastern deacons were represented as discussing, at great length, and with much earnestness, the comparative significance of the synonymous terms *rules* and *regulations*. The parties, after much expenditure of logic, "concluded upon the whole, that '*rules*' would best apply to a *canal*, and '*regulations*' to a *railroad*."

of other countries, and a fact noted also by English writers, themselves, that the characteristic manner of the English, is ungainly and rigid, in comparison with that of other nations. A sullen taciturnity of habit, a surly brevity of reply, a constrained stiffness of posture and motion, and a confined, reluctant gesture, are the predominating national traits in daily intercourse. The New Englander seems to inherit a full share of the hereditary stiffness and constraint, though not of the taciturnity and bluffness of the family stock. This feature of the common lineage, becomes haughtiness in the Englishman. But in the New Englander it degenerates into mere rigidity and unmeaning stiffness.

A genial early culture, and a wide intercourse with mankind, tend equally to render the human being plastic and flexible: they give him the power and the spirit of self-adaptation; they give him ease and fluency in address, and the power of eliciting sympathy from others. But the general defect of established modes of education, is that, from the absence of due provision for the development of man's social and moral nature, youth is left destitute of appropriate aids to the formation of exterior manner in the daily communications of private life, and in the act of public speaking.

Hence it happens that we so often see the juvenile speaker on the academic stage, rigid in posture, and awkward in movement and action. The want of early training leaves him utterly deficient in the natural case and grace of a cultivated and polished youth. His body seems nailed to the floor, his members galvanized into metallic stiffness, his head glued to his neck, his eye motionless in its socket, his arm pinioned to his side. His whole visible mien and movement are those of an ill-adjusted machine. His voice, too, possesses the same inflexible character, in its monotonous utterance.

A degree of this style continues to exert its injurious **influence on the college student and the professional man.**

A rigid, inflexible air, and a mechanical stiffness in gesture, are, accordingly, in many instances, the habitual style of the speaker in the pulpit. These faults unavoidably attract the attention of the audience to the preacher's personal manner, more than to his subject; as a messenger of ungainly, rigid manner and aspect, presents himself, rather than his message, to those whom he accosts. And, even when the mind has become somewhat enured to the fault of manner, there is still a hinderance caused by it, in regard to any effectual access to the feelings. Men naturally refuse to yield the sympathy of the heart to a speaker whose manner is so inappropriate in point of judgment and taste. The stiff attitude and inflexible features do not solicit and win attention; and the rigid arm and rigid hand are incapable of executing a motion which shall come as an appeal to the heart.

The correctives for rigid habit in a speaker's manner, are, in part, to be sought in the cultivation and refinement of taste, by which the mind is guarded against every uncouth and repulsive effect in expression. An excellent remedial influence will always be derived from habitual contact with the ease and polish of elevated society. The meliorating influence of the fine arts should ever be solicited by the student whose purpose is to addict himself to public speaking. But the express study of gesture, as a part of elocution, will exert the most direct influence on manner and habit. It will lead the student to discern the character and effect of every attitude and action of the body. It will teach him that there is no escape from the impression which external manner produces; that the speaker who neglects this part of elocution, incurs the effects of inappropriateness and awkwardness, and, sometimes, of self-contradiction, in the discrepance between the style of his gesture and the language of his tongue; that he who flatters himself with the hope of escaping inappropriate manner by avoiding action, gives, by his statue-like and motionless posture, the lie to any earnestness betrayed in his voice. Earnestness warms and impels the heart; and, by the law of our constitution, the same nerve which glows and quivers at the fountain head thrills along the arm to the expressive hand, and solicits its action. The rigid speaker who attempts to counteract this effect, kills, equally, his own emotions and those of his audience: he destroys the natural character of communication, and defeats its purposes.

PROPRIETY OF MANNER.

Nothing so effectually prevents the existence of eloquence in a speaker's manner, as a fastidious primness in his style of utterance and action, which hems him in on every side, and allows him no latitude of tone or scope of expressive action. There can be no interest felt in the address of a preacher whose whole elocution is so pruned and pared that it is utterly destitute of the natural freedom and flow of life.

It is not less true, however, that if there is any form of public speaking, in which a strict regard to propriety is demanded, it is that of a discourse delivered from the pulpit. The comparative freedom of manner, in the accustomed forms of general society, among us, ought to inspire a noble dignity of address, in our public speakers. Its actual effect, however, on individuals, is often to create an indifference, or even recklessness of deportment, which is anything but appropriate, in connection with sacred oratory.

The following is as literal a delineation as the writer's command of words enables him to give of impressions received by him, from the manner of an eminent preacher. At the appointed hour for commencing services, the minister came bustling along the aisle, — ran rapidly up the pulpit steps, and, on entering the pulpit began rubbing his hands in compliment to the cold air of the wintry morning, — dashed open the leaves of the Bible, — rattled off a few verses in the style of the most violent hurry, calling out the words in rapid succession, — implored a blessing on the services in nearly the same style of voice, — read the hymn after the fashion of a lively paragraph in a newspaper, — called out a prayer in which every portion — adoration, confession, thanksgiving, and petition, *all alike*, had no slight resemblance to the style of military command, or of popular harangue. The sermon, in its bold, rapid, and vehement style, was eloquent with the tones of the most indignant invective, accompanied by the effects of the most arrogant and dogmatic expression of head, eye, and person. The speaker's whole manner embodied the language of natural signs, in a style so marked and fierce, that a phrenologist would have found his eye instinctively wandering over the surface of the preacher's head to trace its associated indications in the regions of "combativeness" and "self-esteem," in confirmation of his theory of human tendencies.

The moral proprieties of the pulpit, are not, it is true, very often violated to this extent. Yet we frequently hear tones, in the exercise of devotion, which the ear is accustomed to recognize as those of deciding, ordering, and commanding, rather than of supplicating. We hear, sometimes, a strain, in prayer, which reminds us rather of familiar talking than of devotion ; we hear, sometimes, in a sermon, the tone of domestic scolding ; and we see, occasionally, in the speaker's manner, the frown of personal anger, and the clinched fist of the popular partisan.

All these undeniable indications of misdirected and unmodified habit, are unintentional, — in effect, at least. They are the natural results of unrestrained and undisciplined violence of personal tendency in the individual: they are, to him, but the expressions of earnest feeling. **Yet could a friendly hand present to the speaker's eye,** in one of his paroxysms of excitement, the reflection of his own countenance and figure in a mirror, he would need no other monitor to remind him, that how natural soever these results of emotion might have become in his own habits, or innocuous to himself personally, they are grossly immoral in their effect on others.

A very moderate degree of attention to the study and practice of elocution, would assist speakers of this stamp to subdue the voice to the tones of decency, and the person to the aspect of decorum, and to win the hearers whom they otherwise disgust and repel. The discipline of elocution, in its connection with the pulpit, if it is true to its purposes, suggests to the speaker, that, in sacred oratory, the chastening spirit of Christian meekness, is ever a most eloquent though silent effect.

Many preachers, whose temperament and habit secure them from the moral improprieties of manner, fail in the due observance of that species of propriety, which has been termed obedience to the code of minor morals. The legion of negligent, not to say low, personal habits, which defective early education, at home, leaves so generally prevalent among us, as a people, are by no means excluded from the pulpit. It may be sufficient, here, to allude to the Scottish preacher stopping, in the midst of his discourse, to regale his nostrils with their wonted portion of snuff, as finding his "pendant" in the picture of our own Southern preacher attending, in the face of his congregation, to the nauseating process which necessity or habit entails on the chewing of tobacco. We forbear, likewise, to enlarge on the gross offences committed against decency, in the not unusual act of combing the hair with the fingers, during the intervals of active duty; — the public exhibition and display of the handkerchief which has just been employed to prove its very serviceable character in cases of catarrh; — the tooth-pickings and nail-cleanings, which are sometimes deferred to be done in the pulpit; — the copious indulgence in coughing and expectoration, which is often more a necessity of habit than of disease; the lollings, and loungings, and leanings, and multiform free and easy postures occasionally exhibited.

When, amid sights of this description, the hearer happens to advert to the fact, that the preacher is, for the moment, the ambassador of Infinite Majesty, the shock of incongruous feeling is too much to be endured. The preacher's standard of personal manner ought certainly to be at least as high as any that the highest elevation of genuine taste and refinement has ever established.

The study of elocution would, in relation to propriety of effect in aspect and bearing, suggest, in a single lesson of a few minutes' duration, the few practical rules which are requisite to mould the outward man in habit. Even a very slight attention to the preliminary rules of posture and movement, would exert such an influence on the associations of the mind, as would insure a tendency to becoming style in personal carriage and demeanor. The preacher might thus be saved from habitually committing revolting offences against taste and propriety, and so avoid the barrier which, otherwise, he builds up, with his own hands, between himself and his hearers.

WARMTH OF MANNER.

Feeling, when it is earnest and vivid, rises naturally to those stages which we designate by the terms "warmth" and "fervor." These qualities bear the same relation to eloquence, that the "lyric fire" does to the higher species of poetry. The element of "passion" is indispensable to all the transcendent effects of expression, in whatever form or in whatever art they are exemplified. Homer and Horace, among the poets of antiquity, and Milton and Watts, in modern times, display, in high perfection, this genuine trait of excellence in expression.

Empassioned utterance, or that which rises to the full height of inspired and inspiring emotion, and attains to a vivid eloquence, is indebted, for its characteristic effect, to the "celestial fire" with which it glows. Intensity and ardor in the desires and aspirations of the soul,—the very fervor of its highest devotional feeling,—all are evinced by the "burning words" which seem to issue direct from the heart.

This highest form of emotion demands a correspondent intensity and empassioned power of utterance. We hear it in the voice of the orator, when kindled by vivid personal feeling transcending the formal limits of art. We hear it in the recitation of poetry, when the speaker gives forth the poetic fire of genuine, intense emotion. We hear it in the true and appropriate reading of the rapturous strains of the prophets and the psalmist, in the sacred Scriptures. It belongs, also, to the empassioned aspirations and devout ecstasies of the soul, in the language of the higher species of hymns. Its effect may be heard in the utterance of the preacher whose lips have been touched with the "live coal from the altar," and whose soul is aglow with those emotions which spring from near intercourse with God and fervent feeling for man.

The inspiring thrill of genuine passion pervades all earnest eloquence, in whatever form it kindles the heart and fires the imagination of man. As a mood of emotion, it exists, in degree, even in the humbler forms of public address on ordinary occasions, if these imply life and spirit in expression. Its effect is, in all cases, analogous, more or less, to the communicative heat which imparts itself from object to object, till all are enveloped in the common flame. The electric spark from the vivid and eloquent speaker, is thus transmitted to the sympathies of his audience, till all are thrilled by the common impulse, and fired with the common glow.

The speaker who never rises to warmth and fervor of feeling, falls short of the highest and noblest purposes of eloquence. To the preacher in the pulpit there is an impressive lesson to be caught from the spirit of the poet's phrase, when he speaks of "the seraph that adores and burns." A noble zeal cannot exist without ardor; devotion cannot inspire the soul, without fervor; the heart cannot beat for man's highest good, without warmth.

Some preachers, it is true, give themselves up too exclusively to the influence of this element of eloquence: their fire degenerates into frenzy: excessive passion is, with them, allowed to usurp the whole man: their manner becomes that of animal excitement, and deviates into extravagance and excess. Hence the ungovernable violence of voice, in such speakers, and their frenzied vehemence of gesture.

Other preachers, however, err on the other extreme, and by their uniform coldness of utterance and frigidity of gesture, chill the feelings of their hearers. The special office of sacred eloquence, is to incite and inspire and enkindle the soul. But the effect of the too common style of the pulpit, is to cool and to benumb. How can the preacher cause the heart to glow with the sacred fire of love or joy, whose accents "freeze as they fall," and whose torpid frame seems to have been transmuted to marble?

Questions of intense interest are justly expected to excite ardor of feeling and glow of expression. Men, in relation to such subjects, are generally more willing to pardon something to the spirit of warm emotion, than to be content with deliberate coolness. Heartfelt and earnest conviction will not stop short at ordinary manifestations; it will incline rather to a fervor of utterance and action, at which fastidiousness might be apt to take offence. There is, occasionally, something irrepressible in genuine emotion. He who speaks from the inmost soul, is himself sometimes carried away in the common rush of feeling which his own eloquence has caused. The preacher who deeply feels the worth of the human soul, the brevity and uncertainty of life, and man's proneness to callous indifference regarding his eternal wellbeing, cannot contemplate the case coolly, and treat of it in well-ordered sentences, and quiet tones, and remonstrate upon it with tranquil mien and composed action. The deeper sources of feeling must, in such circumstances, necessarily be stirred within him: the inner fire of the soul must be kindled: his whole being will glow with intense emotion: his tones, if true to his heart, will be fired with a sacred fervor: his features will beam with empassioned expression: his whole frame will be inspired, his arm impelled, by the zeal and ardor of his spirit.

Coldness of manner is, in some speakers, a fault of habit which originates partly in constitution and temperament. But, in most, it is the consequence of imperfect or ill-directed culture. Faults of the former description are by no means so obdurate as is sometimes imagined. The testimony of the physiologist is clear and decisive on the point that, with adequate attention and care, we can, by processes of cultivation, change the temperament of individuals from the muscular to the nervous character. The discipline of education, in ancient Greece, was conducted so as to blend and unite these temperaments, in every individual, by a high-toned physical training, accompanied by the most elevated forms of intellectual culture, and an intense incitement applied to the sentiments and passions. The magnificent ideal of human excellence which Grecian education set up as its standard, was fully attained in the personal and mental character of such men as Xenophon and Epaminondas,—instances in which the attainments of the philosopher, the statesman, the general, the scholar, the poet, the orator, the artist, the athlete, the moral enthusiast, were all blended in the individual man.

Modern education aims principally at the development of a few of the intellectual faculties. It leaves the general character cold and feeble, from the absence of healthful vigor of body, and inspiring energy of heart and will. It represses emulation, and limits ambition, but substitutes no inciting motives of equal force and of higher character. Its tendency to excite the cerebral organ, by too great intensity of action, causes, by its morbid excess, a correspondent depression of genial emotion and ennobling sentiment: it leaves feeling and fancy, — the main sources of expression, — to languish and subside. It furnishes no adequate instruction in the art of speaking, but rather quenches or cools the spirit of eloquence, by inappropriate influences.

Few, accordingly, among our youth, retain the natural glow of utterance, through the various stages of education, so as to come out warm, energetic, and effective speakers. The young minister in the pulpit, commences his career of public duty, disabled, to a great extent, for the discharge of its functions. He has, in his academic life, lost, not gained, tone and power, as a living man, whose office it is to exert, by eloquent address, the most momentous of all influences on his fellow-men. The cold and powerless being who rises to address us from the pulpit, bears, not unfrequently, on his very frame, and in his voice and aspect, the traces of infirmity — not of strength. His words fall lifeless on the ear: his sentiments take no effect on the heart.

The introduction of elocution into our means of education, would do much to obviate the impediments to effective speaking, under which professional men generally labor. The systematic practice of elocution, as an art, involves a healthful preparatory training in muscular exercise and in the energetic, varied, and graceful forms of oratorical action. It prescribes an extensive course of daily practice in all the modes of voice which tend to invigorate and enliven the organs of respiration and of speech. It imparts the inspiring influence of eloquent emotion, in the themes with which it makes the student conversant.

It incites his whole mental being to vivid and glowing activity.

These invaluable results may all be secured, to a great extent, by whatever individual has the requisite decision of purpose and perseverence in resolution, to commence and prosecute the business of self-cultivation. The theological student who feels the importance of elocution to the purposes of his profession, will not shrink from the toil which a thorough renovation of habit demands for this purpose. His own progress will open to him, continually, new objects to be accomplished, — both as regards an intimate knowledge of his own corporeal structure, and a distinct perception of the nature of expression, in all its manifold relations to man. It will disclose to him more fully the sympathetic influences by which the heart is actuated, as well as those outward analogies and effects which eloquence implies. He will allow himself the full benefits of a regenerating physical and æsthetic discipline, to compensate for the defects of formal education. He will resort to the instructive lessons furnished by all the expressive arts. Music, in particular, he will cultivate, as one of the most effective and inspiring of all influences that operate on the human soul, as the best adapted to create the expressive mood and the glow of utterance.* He will omit no means of cherishing the life and activity of imagination, — that faculty which, in our prevalent modes of culture, is left nearly dormant, but which, by its tendencies, decides the character of the orator, not less than of the poet; the power of expression, in every man, being as his ability to find a vehicle or a mould for his thought, which must otherwise be "without form and void."

Elocution, in its details of exercise and of tuition, fur-

---

* The exhibitions of dramatic art are, by far, the most instructive of all schools of eloquence; and it is much to be regretted that their usual accompaniments, and the general impression of society, debar any class of public speakers from resorting to them.

nishes, in ample abundance, to the diligent student, the means of acquiring and cherishing expressive power in voice and action. It enables him, by analysis, to detect the peculiar nature of every tone of feeling, — to trace the effect of life and warmth in every element, to sympathize with these, and to acquire them as habits of utterance and gesture. A few exercises, attentively performed, will enable him to recognize the breathing warmth of a full-hearted utterance, the vivid force and fire of genuine emotion, the flash of the kindled eye, the sweep and energy of a gesture which springs from the inmost soul.

SERENITY OF MANNER.

The tendencies of constitution and habit, in some individuals, incline them to speak, on all occasions, under a strong impulse of emotion; so that their manner never possesses the dignity of repose. Speakers of this class seem to demand excitement, as a condition of eloquence, and, when interested in their subject, are apt to flash out abruptly into intensity of utterance and action: they do not possess the power of holding emotion in check, and of rising equably, from the ordinary level of their subject to the higher strains of empassioned style: their delivery is consequently irregular, abrupt and unequal. The beautiful symmetry and perfect unity of manner, which tranquility and self-possession impart, are wanting in the delivery of such speakers; and their effect on their hearers is correspondent: it resembles that of the fitful gleams of lightning between successive clouds, rather than the growing brightness which "shineth more and more unto the perfect day." When the flash and the peal are over, there remains "but the cold pattering of rain."

A general composure and serenity of manner are by no

means incompatible with the natural vicissitudes of emotion and expression. But abrupt changes are comparatively rare, in the natural progress of thought and feeling: they are the exceptions,—not the rule of speaking. Some preachers, however, whether from impulsive habit or incorrect ear, incline to sudden wrenchings of the voice and jerkings of the arm, which startle rather than impress an audience.

Others destroy the repose and dignity of their manner by perpetual restlessness of body, and hacking reïteration of gesture: they seem to mistake excitement for earnestness, and mere animal vivacity for the inspiration of genuine emotion. A due restraint on personal tendencies, and a just reserve of manner, are the basis of all true effect in elocution.

Mere liveliness of tone and action possesses, at the best, but the humble merit of the wakeful talker. It may, in fact, serve to dissipate rather than to deepen impression. The appropriate effects, even of earnestness, vehemence, and fervor, are dependent on the relief which they derive from a prevalent repose. Arbitrary and abrupt variation disturbs the current of attention, on the part of the hearer. The equable speaker leaves the mind of the audience unruffled and calm, reflecting distinctly every thought which his eloquence calls up: the abrupt speaker breaks and shivers every successive mental image, by the agitation attending his abruptness of manner. The serene and tranquil effect of appropriate expression, as a characteristic habit, gives the preacher easy access to the mind, and enables him to hold up steadily before the attention the mental objects on which he would have his hearers dwell.

There are, indeed, many subjects and many occasions on which a quiet, unexcited utterance, breathes the genuine spirit of expressive eloquence. The themes of pulpit discourse are not unfrequently of this character; and, in the management of some, an unequal irregular, and restless manner in the speaker, would jar upon the ear, with the disturbing effect of discord in music.

The preacher may ever derive impressive lessons from the study of symmetry and harmony, as they reveal themselves in the beautiful and majestic forms and aspects of nature, and in the graceful proportions of every masterpiece of art.

Different subjects require a difference of style in elocution, as in all other arts. But the prevalent mood and spirit of sacred eloquence, should be calmness and serenity. Force and fire of manner will then have their value, in their place. But the transition, even to such effects, is not necessarily violent or abrupt.

A prevalent serenity of manner leaves the speaker at liberty so to modulate his voice and control his action, that his very transitions are felt to be as appropriate as they are striking; while an agitated and hurried utterance, jerking incessantly into unnatural changes of pitch and force, added, perhaps, to ceaseless motion and gesticulation,— destroys even the effect of variation itself, and ends in discomposing rather than impressing the mind.

The manly composure of manner which properly belongs to all forms of public address, but especially to the style of the pulpit, is quite incompatible with a very common fault into which some preachers are habitually betrayed by nervous excitement. This fault evinces itself in an overstrained expression on the features, and is legible in the wrinkling or knitting of the brow, in the upraising of the eye-brows, and in the staring projection of the eye. Such effects are unavoidably associated, in the mind of those who are addressed, with a feeling of pain or repulsion. Habitual serenity of mien and aspect, does not forbid the occasional expression of even the strongest emotion. But it cannot be reconciled with a continued stare or frown, which seems incompatible with decorum or self-possession. Offences of this description might all be easily put down by an occasional glance at a mirror, when the student is at practice. Without such recourse, or the admonition of a friend, the unconscious habit must continue an obstacle to the speaker's success in attaining to persuasive manner.

TRUE AND NATURAL MANNER.

Eloquence, in whatever form, and, most of all, in addresses from the pulpit, demands, as a condition of its effect, a conviction, on the part of the hearer, of the perfect sincerity of the speaker. The slightest indication of artifice, or, even, of mere art, becomes an effectual barrier between the orator and his audience; as it betrays the fact that he is not in earnest in his communication, or, at all events, that he is not expressing himself with the directness and simplicity which a deep conviction of his sentiments ought to inspire.

Artifice and affectation are utterly incompatible with the "simplicity and godly sincerity" which the Scriptures ascribe to the preacher. But the fact of having been accustomed, during the period of early training, to utter sentiment by rote, in the unmeaning and uninteresting routine of school declamation, has, in most instances, untuned the ear for the genuine effects of voice, and reconciled it to false intonation, just as it has misled the eye, and accustomed it to a mechanical and artificial style of gesture. The living effect of tone and natural manner, is thus irrecoverably lost, and, with it, the speaker's power over the heart: his conventional tone, attitude, and action, all plainly indicate that it is the clergyman, not the individual, who is addressing us. The style, in such cases, is, at best, too obviously of that secondary gradation of art, which knows not how to "conceal art."

We can trace the absence of single-minded purpose, in every speaker whose voice evidently assumes a new and factitious character, when he begins to read or speak in public; we feel the fact in the false hollowness and affected swell of utterance, which some preachers always assume in the pulpit; we perceive it in their studied precision of enunciation, forced emphasis, mechanical inflection, chanting tone, and arbitrary variations of voice, and in their premeditated and elaborate motions of the arm. The whole machinery of effect is thus, as it were, perpetually thrust on ear and eye, at the expense of the great business of the hour. It is impossible, under such circumstances, for the hearer to derive the proper impression from the subject, or to enter into sympathy with the speaker; and it is well if the result of the whole discourse is not, unavoidably, a state of dissatisfaction and disgust with the manner of the preacher, rather than any just influence from his sentiments.

Earnest and warm feeling will not allow the speaker to wait for niceties of elocution, in the act of speech. The preacher who feels that the decision of a soul may be hanging, for the moment, on the accents that fall from his lips, will not be found stopping to adjust his inflections, and mould his gestures. It is quite a false impression, which is current regarding the practice of elocution, that it consists in acquiring certain fixed modes of voice, putting on a certain air, or practising set actions, which, after a given time, will become natural by habituation, but which must necessarily be awkward, at first. There is no such thing as speaking naturally by rule and study, applied during the act of speech. All, then, must be left to the guidance of feeling and intuitive perception, and the influence of unconscious tendencies of taste, previously disciplined by critical and reflective judgment.

True elocution allows no artificial processes of expression: it cuts off all false habit. The operation bears no analogy to that of the dentist, who extracts the natural implements and substitutes artificial ones. It is a process of retrenching acquired faults, and recovering original and natural tendencies, which had been lost, through neglect or misdirection. Elocution, as a science, enables the student to analyze, and become familiar with, all the modifications of voice and gesture. It defines their nature and relations. It teaches him to discriminate, among them, and to select and apply those which natural emotion, in every instance, requires. It guards him against artificial effects of every kind, with as strict care as it does against other faults of manner. It rejects all spurious tones, as counterfeits offered instead of the current coin of the heart. It points out every tendency to dwell on sound rather than on sense and feeling. A false manner, in any particular, it denounces as the worst of all faults, — as an unpardonable violation at once of manliness, truth, propriety, and taste.

Elocution, however, insists, with equal earnestness, on the student's drawing a firm and decided line of distinction between natural and acquired habit, as regards the local accidents of usage, and the general principles of expression. It allows no servile spirit of accommodation to some trick of custom which happens to prevail around the speaker. It requires peremptorily of the New England student, that he lay aside his unique nasal tones and circumflex accents, and frigid, diminutive action, — of the Southern student, that he lay aside his broad drawl, and mouthing tone, and exaggerated gesture. It demands of the man of education, everywhere, that he do not descend to the standard which uncultivated taste exemplifies and prescribes, but that he adopt a manner which shall bear the stamp of dignity and propriety, in enlightened judgment, wherever exercised.

Affectation of manner, though apparently originating in insincerity and art, is often the result of a perception of common errors, and a desire to avoid them. It proceeds, sometimes, from the wish to be correct or graceful. It is the natural product of the prevalent neglect of manner and deportment, which characterizes our modes of education. The moulding influence of taste, if applied, as it ought to be, to the formation of habit, would anticipate and cut off this reäction of the mind against the consequences of early neglect. A sound judgment and a manly taste are the only possible security against faults of affectation; and the cultivation of these traits of mind ought to form a prominent part of intellectual training. The systematic study and practice of elocution, may do much to form and direct the mental tendencies, in regard to modes and habits of expression; as the principles of the art involve a recognition of all the distinctive features of chaste and correct style, not merely in this, but also in every other art which gives form to thought and feeling.

Simplicity, as the grand characteristic of truth and nature, holds as high a place in elocution as in any other mode of expressive art; and directness of tone and emphasis it enjoins as the straight road to the heart: it forbids all attempts at arbitrary modulations of voice, — all merely mechanical variations for effect. The simplest and the truest manner it holds up as the most eloquent and the most effective. The studied changes in which the speaker passes arbitrarily from soft to loud, from high to low, and the opposites to these, it condemns as false to the subject, and destructive to every effect of genuine and earnest address.

A just view of elocution, while it would cherish every natural trait of grace in utterance and action, would lead the student to avoid every trace of manner which indicates a distinct and separate attention to gracefulness. Every modification of the voice, and every movement of the arm, which is executed merely because it is graceful, is untrue to the higher demands of truth and manly energy. It is something deducted from the weight of a sentiment and its power over the mind and heart. It can be compared only to the juvenile messenger's loitering by the wayside, to pluck flowers, when urgent business demands speed.

All true grace is inherent in the sentiment which the speaker utters. It is not a thing which he can superadd in tone or action. It requires no attention, apart from that which is due to the thought and the language of the composition. To linger on poetic tones, or to delay for studied graces of action, on occasions demanding earnest and direct speech, betrays an utter ignorance of the first principles of expression. Beauty itself must, in such circumstances, lose its character, and become deformity. A single gratuitous flourish of voice or hand, seals the doom of the speaker, as to any effect on intelligent and cultivated minds. The only effect of such obtrusions of manner, is to lower the hearer's estimation of the speaker, and to mar the impression made by his subject.

REFINEMENT AND GRACEFULNESS.

Elocution, as an art, while it rejects all spurious beauty of ornament in manner, as a hinderance to effect, cherishes a just regard for that refinement which is the natural accompaniment of a cultivated taste. Education is ineffectual, if it does not extend to the whole mental character. Classical learning has fallen short of its design, if it has not left its graceful impress on the imagination, and moulded the expressive powers into habits of symmetrical and harmonious action. Its office, in the formation of the intellectual character, is to quicken the sensibility to beauty and elegance, by the admirable perfection of the models which it presents for imitation, and which ought to exert a silent but enduring influence on the associations and tendencies of the mind.

Society has a right to demand, in the educated speaker,

the fruits of the highest culture, and, among these, a true elegance and a genuine refinement of manner. The educated clergyman owes to society the results of scholarship, embodied in an oratory which is, at least, correct and graceful. There are, no doubt, qualities and accomplishments which are of vastly higher value than mere gracefulness of elocution. No degree of elegance can atone for the absence of natural, manly, free, and appropriate manner. But if there is any form of eloquence which naturally and justly invests itself with the associations and the language of the highest beauty, it is that of the pulpit. The wonted themes of sacred oratory, are themselves the highest species of poetry; and the preacher who does not cause this truth to be felt, loses his hold of one of the most powerful influences on the human soul. The transcendent beauty of the language of the Scriptures, seems to haunt the ear of all men, as a charm equally powerful in all stages of life, from childhood to old age; and the preacher who drinks deepest at the sacred fount, will ever be found the most eloquent in expression;—his whole manner will evince the influence of the discipline of that school in which he has trained himself.

Nothing can be further from the accustomed associations of every mind, than the remotest idea of anything odd, blundering, awkward, or coarse, in the language of the sacred writers. The principle which causes us to revolt from such effects in the style and manner of the preacher, is of the same nature : it is the shrinking of the mind from the thought of desecration. Yet how often are our pulpits occupied by men on whom all the beauties of nature, of art, and even of revealed truth, seem to have fallen without one perceptible effect on the soul, and who apparently address themselves to the delivery of a sermon, in the spirit of a laborer setting about a coarse job of work!

How often we hear from the pulpit the tones of the

lowest passions and of the vilest associations, the coarse bawling of utter rudeness, or the harsh guttural sounds of the "malignant emotions," which cause the voice of man to approach that of the lower animals! How frequently we hear the pulpit, which should be looked up to, as the model of intellectual refinement and of true culture, degraded by an utterance which, in the very pronunciation of words, bespeaks the ascendancy of low associations in the personal habits of the speaker! The elocution of the pulpit should, in the simplicity and chastened dignity of its inflection, and in the well attempered moderation of its tones, furnish lessons of true eloquence to every other form of address. The impression is utterly false, that the way to bring religion home to "the business and bosoms" of men, is to discourse in the dialect of the market-place, and to use the tones and gesture of the street. Lessons of directness and earnestnes, may, it is true, be gathered from these. But the literal transference of them to the pulpit, can be suggested only by a taste which relishes what is low, and a judgment utterly blind to the fitness of things. The preacher's office is not to bring down his subject to the level of his hearers, but to assist them in rising to that of his subject. Neither is the rudest mind at all insensible to the becoming grace of refinement, as the natural attendant of eloquence, on themes which are sacred and spiritual in their relations.

FALSE TASTE, ARTIFICIAL STYLE.

But while a coarse and low style of address, is revolting to every one's natural sense of propriety, the manner which betrays artificial and studied elegance, seems to solicit attention to the speaker rather than to his subject. All merely arbitrary and conventional forms of grace, seem ridiculous, when brought into contact with those vast conceptions of the soul to which it is the preacher's business to give utterance. The speaker who adopts them, incurs all the degradation of "voluntary humiliation," and "worshipping the angels," of vitiated custom, — a thing directly opposite to the idea of the service of God.

The world justly shrinks from the preacher who, in the delivery of his discourse, serves up some choice delicacy of finical manner, some fantasy of ultra pronunciation, some elegance of mere elocution, when he ought to be dealing out the bread of life. A mincing, affected manner, in the tone or action of a preacher, can excite only the feeling of deep disgust. Nor can the prevalence of coarseness or awkwardness in others, form any plea for the individual who betrays an artificial and affected manner, which pleases only his own fancy, but disgusts the taste of every body else. The coarse and vehement speaker may justly claim that we pardon something to his earnestness and rough force. But the affected speaker can do nothing to redeem the littleness to which he voluntarily descends.

A spurious elegance of manner, it is true, is, not unfrequently, the result of false notions of grace, and of a misguided desire to obey the indications of taste. It is not always an intentional fault: it is contracted, perhaps, from the unconscious imitation of an esteemed model: it is a vice inculcated, in many instances, by false instruction. But, from whatever source it springs, its effect on delivery is that of insincerity and artifice, or of display: it is not merely an obstacle but a positive nuisance. No matter how studiously it aims at grace, it proves but labored deformity.

The only effectual corrective for false taste in elocution, consists in the attentive study of genuine beauty, as it embodies itself in the simple forms of nature and of true art. **Perfect simplicity is perfect grace.** Elegance, if it would not degenerate into fantasy, must not deviate from simplicity. The highest ornaments of eloquence, are the truest touches of nature, in utterance and action. Elocution, as the art which moulds the exterior of eloquence, necessarily recognizes and obeys the laws which regulate the higher art to which it is tributary. The best elocution, therefore, is that which preserves a perfectly simple and natural manner.

ADAPTATION OF MANNER TO THE DIFFERENT PARTS OF A DISCOURSE.

One of the common results of defective early instruction in reading, is the habit of uttering all the portions of a discourse, — particularly when it is read and not spoken, — in nearly the same tone; and along with this fault usually goes that of using, throughout, the same style and form of action. Appropriate manner would, on the contrary, exhibit an obvious change of voice, in passing from the explanatory and quiet utterance of the opening paragraphs to the argument and illustration by which the subject is exhibited and sustained, and a still more impressive variation of tone, in the closing application, or direct address, which appeals immediately to the feelings of the audience. The whole discourse, (if constructed on the plan now implied,) would exhibit a progressive force of voice, from the quiet to the earnest, and thence to the vivid, effects of utterance. Appropriate elocution thus renders the reading of a sermon one continuous climax of effect to the ear, by which the hearer becomes more and more deeply interested or forcibly impressed, till the close.

A similar remark would apply to the proper style of action in the successive parts of a discourse. The merely explanatory statements addressed to the understanding, would produce little or no gesture, the argumentative and descriptive passages would elicit a growing freedom and force of action, as the speaker's own feelings and those of his hearers became more deeply interested in the train of thought and the attendant emotions, developed in the progress of the discourse; and, in the concluding address, the full eloquence of earnest and impressive gesture, would naturally be brought out by the heightened interest of the speaker's mind, in his subject and his audience. The whole man would now be alive with the spirit of expressive utterance: the hand would render its full tribute of aid to tongue and eye, in stamping the impress of the speaker's soul on the sympathies of his hearers.

All sermons, it is true, do not admit of a regular and systematic progression of effect like what has just been described. But the consequence of speaking, for an hour, on one subject, ought naturally to be that of drawing out more and more of the natural resources of eloquence, which continuous thought should always have the power to develope. There ought, perhaps, to be more regard paid, in rhetorical training, to such modes of treating subjects as would ensure the eloquence of progressive effect. The lawyer who arranges his pleading so as to bring out his arguments in successive stages of accumulating force, and the player who never willingly leaves the stage without a strong effect of voice or action, might afford an instructive lesson to the preacher; for it is now too often the fact that his last point would weigh no more than his first, and that, at the very close of his discourse, he seems to have made no progress, reached no conclusion, gained no position, by what he has read or spoken. The lawyer who should so wind up his pleading, or the player who should thus tamely go off the stage, would be justly deemed to have made an utter failure in his part. The professional phrase which one barrister sometimes uses, when speaking of the professional efforts of another, that "his learned brother took nothing by his motion," would very often apply most justly to the vague and immethodical, and consequently ineffective speaker in the pulpit.

The principle of climax, or growing force and effect, should be distinctly perceptible not only in the successive stages of a discourse, but in every paragraph and in every sentence which it contains. The preacher's voice and whole manner should perpetually indicate, in progressive intensity, that he is consciously drawing nearer and nearer to the consummation of his train of associated thought and feeling. The aim of the preacher's mind, as indicated in the increasing earnestness of his manner, should, during every successive paragraph of his discourse, be growing clearer and more impressive to his audience, till his object is fully effected, at the close.

MANNER IN DEVOTION.

The prevalent inattention, in our community, to the effects of manner and address, are in nothing more perceptible than in the customary tones and attitudes of the devotional exercises in public worship. Some preachers cannot, even in such circumstances, abstain from an irregular and revolting violence of voice: their earnestness seems to know no controlling power of reverence and decency: their empassioned vehemence of manner seems to recognize no difference between the tones which might justly be used in importuning a fellow-being, and those which are appropriate in entreaty addressed to God. It is no unusual thing to hear a whole prayer thundered out, in the accents of imperious command.

What a lesson might such speakers learn of the docile and respectful child, that proffers its request in subdued though earnest tones! The child, wiser instinctively than the man, is aware that, in such cases, violence shuts, but does not open, the heart. It adopts, therefore, the irresistible eloquence taught it by nature, and urges its request in pleading tones, piercing by their very suppression: and its suit is, in such circumstances, seldom refused.

Some preachers adopt a style which forms the extreme opposite to the fault of voice mentioned above, and uniformly employ a high, feeble whine, in their devotional utterance; as if an audience with God were a scene of servile humiliation and abject timidity; as if the act of communing with the Father of spirits were a powerless prostration of the soul, and an occasion of mere wailing and lamentation. The appropriate fervor and sublimity of devotion, which, not less than humility and self-abasement, are its just characteristics, are thus entirely lost sight of; and the effect of the whole exercise, is to impress upon the mind the meanness of man, rather than the grandeur and majesty of God.

A voice moulded by appropriate emotion, would impart to the tones of prayer a degree of the manifold power which characterizes the grandest of all the instruments of music, — that which we term emphatically *the organ*, and which from its majestic compass and effect, we consecrate to the office of worship. The deep, full, and solemn strains of adoration, would then pour themselves forth on the ear, with a strength but softness of effect allied to the deep tones of the wind, when breathing low through the forest, or with something of their ample swell, when raising the sublime hymn of nature to the power and glory of the Creator. The pleading and pathetic voice of penitence would be recognized by its plaintive notes. The low murmur and broken whisperings of contrition, the earnest and thrilling intensity of the soul's aspiration after pardon, purity and peace, the fervent breathings of heartfelt gratitude, the rapture of devout joy, would all, in turn, be felt, as they rose or fell upon the ear, in the successive outpourings of the heart.

The inexpressive, level, mechanical, "recitative" strain, which is so often heard in the utterance of the language of devotion, is the most efficacious of all means of quenching the spirit of the exercise, and reducing worship to a hollow ceremony.

Vividness and fervor of feeling are, in no respect, incompatible with the softened tones of subdued and reverential emotion. The chastened expression of earnestness is the most eloquent of all the moods of the human voice: suppressed intensity of tone penetrates the heart more deeply than the strongest utterance. The study of the natural language of expression, with a view to the discrimination of vocal effects, and the acquisition of true and natural modulation, cannot be too earnestly urged on the student of theology. The voice is the instrument of his usefulness; and surely the ability to use it justly, to use it skillfully and impressively, well deserves the most assiduous application of his powers. The measure of devotional feeling, in an assembly, must ever be in accordance with the depth and fullness of heart imparted by the tones of the minister. The cold and dry manner in which the exercise of devotion is often conducted, sufficiently accounts for the slight sympathy which it excites. Yet it would demand no great amount of time, from the minister, to acquire the power of giving true and effectual utterance to his inward feelings, and of bringing his congregation into accordant sympathy. The existing evil consists obviously in the habit of unmeaning and inexpressive tone on his part,—a habit which neglect or perversion has allowed to become a portion of his self-education, but which a moderate degree of study and application would enable him to correct.

The attitudes into which the pastor suffers himself to fall, in the act of devotion, are not unfrequently a cause of inharmonious and discordant impression on the feelings of his people. His lounging posture, his sleepily folded hands, his hanging head, added to his drowsy voice, may all interfere with the spiritual tendency of the exercise, by causing the natural law of sympathy with given signs and effects, to transcend the speaker's power of raising and exalting the soul; so that a pervading dullness and apathy, instead of a vivid emotion, shall be the predominating mood of the audience.

The error, however, lies, in some cases, at the opposite extreme: the mere ardor of the speaker is suffered to carry him into vehement contortions of body, and, sometimes, even into violent gestures, in the act of prayer. A most impressive rebuke to this animal turbulence, might be derived from the touching Scripture representation of the seraphim, in the act of adoration, veiling their faces with their wings. The stillness of awe is one of the most obvious traits of tendency in expression. The submissive mien of reverence; the erect attitude of praise, the uplifted hands of gratitude, blessing, adoration, joy, and ardent aspiration; the humble posture of penitence and contrition; the clasped hands of supplication and entreaty; the folded hands of resignation and submission; the imploring outstretched arms;—all speak a natural language, and have their meaning in the heart of man. Devotion, destitute of these, may be pronounced decorous and chaste, and well-bred; but it is false to the great law of the Creator, that man's soul should find a language in his frame.

PRINCIPLES OF ELOCUTION.

THE preceding brief remarks on manner, were designed to lead the reader to the study and practice of the prominent rules and principles of elocution. These will be found laid down, in detail, in the two volumes formerly mentioned, — the manual of Orthophony and the American Elocutionist, — the former designed to furnish the modes and means of cultivating the voice, on the system of Dr. James Rush; and the latter, the rules and principles of elocution, in connection with orthoëpy, rhetoric, and prosody, and the practice of gesture. To these works, therefore, the reader is referred for the full systematic study of elocution, as a science, and as an art.

The design of the following synopsis, is to present those principles of elocution, which are immediately applicable to the purposes of the pulpit. Persons who had not paid attention, previously, to the art of reading, will thus be furnished with an outline of its most useful parts; and those who have become versed in its theory, will be provided with a special course of practice for professional purposes.

THE CULTIVATION OF THE VOICE.

Capability.

The voice, like every other endowment or capacity of man, is a gift which bespeaks, at once, the power, the wisdom, and the beneficence of the Creator. It is an organ of wondrous power, of exquisite flexibility, of vast compass, of the most extensive range, of inexhaustible expression. Its capability of intense force is such as to render it clearly audible, at a distance, on some occasions, of several miles.* It is capable, also, of executing the "sound so fine, that nothing lives 'twixt it and silence." It traverses, with ease, from notes allied, in depth, to the mutterings of distant thunder, up to those which pierce the ear with the shrillness of the horn. Its mellow tones, its softened breathings, and gentle undulations, are the charm of power to melt the heart to love: its yell of rage strikes terror into the fiercest of the brutes. Its plaintive wailings cause the arm of the warrior to fall powerless: its rousing and thrilling tone of courage, impels "the mass of living valor" to the cannon's mouth. Its moral and spiritual effect varies from the soul-subduing reverence of the strain of devotion, to the revolting violence of the curse of vindictive wrath. It passes, in a moment, perhaps, from the whisper of fear, to the shriek of terror, or from the groan of despair to the ecstatic shout of joy.

The natural powers, and capacities of the voice, are scarcely more wonderful than its susceptibility of cultivation by the processes of human art. It becomes, even in the humble culture which it receives, under the training of maternal care, capable of executing all the varied functions of speech, which are demanded by the daily communications of life. It attains, thus, to the power of giving utterance to every form of thought or mood of feeling, as prompting the language of seriousness and gravity, or of fancy, humor, and wit. The conventional forms of speech, embodied in articulate utterance, enable it, to a certain extent, to keep up with the innumerable and ever shifting movements of the mind.

---

* The literal exactness of the above statement, can probably be avouched, as having been personally verified by other elocutionists as well as the author. Strong and clear voices, exerted in the form of a well-vocalized or perfectly musical call, may be easily heard, at a distance of from one to three miles, over water, or other level surfaces.

The systematic and regulated culture which the voice receives, under adequate training, empowers the orator to sway the minds of men, at will, by the consummate mastery of eloquence. It enables the actor to enchain the attention, and entrance the imagination and feelings of his fellow-men, in a mental illusion which, for the moment, catches the very hue of reality. Such is man's vocal progress, from the helpless wailings of his infancy, to the triumphs which artistic genius enables him to achieve by the disciplined utterance of his maturity.

That wisdom of the ancient world, which was derived from the faithful observation of nature, led to the assiduous cultivation of the vocal powers. The Greeks considered elocution as a part of the proper education of man as an expressive being; but they regarded it as an indispensable preparation for the functions of the orator. The Athenian mode of discipline for the formation of the voice, was so extensive as to comprehend a range of practice requiring the professional superintendence of three different classes of instructors, enumerated, by Roman writers, under the designation of *"phonasci," "vociferarii,"* and *"vocales."* The office of the first named class, seems to have been that of moulding the voice as to "quality," — the effect of vocal sound, as true, full, and agreeable, or otherwise, — that of the second, to impart force and compass by rigorous practical training in set exercises, — that of the third, to regulate the vocal habits in regard to intonation and inflection. To the effect of this strictly vocal discipline was added that of special athletic and gymnastic exercises, which were likewise arranged and classified in separate schools, established for the purpose of securing health and vigor, each by a form of muscular practice peculiar to itself. Five such schools have been distinctly enumerated by writers curious on such subjects; and to all of these it was deemed the duty of the rhetorician to recommend his pupils.

The slight regard paid, in modern times, to the development, either of the physical or the expressive powers of the human being, disposes us to look with an eye of suspicion and distrust, equally, on the athletic and the rhetorical discipline adopted by the ancient Greeks. We are prone to ascribe the one to their passionate love of external beauty, and the other to their fastidious regard to intellectual grace and polish: we condemn the whole process of their culture, as artificial and fantastic; or we refer their rigor of preparatory training to the necessity of the case, in the fact that their orators were accustomed to speak in the open air, and hence required a species of voice as little applicable to our purposes of speech, as would be that of a public crier.

The stern character of Demosthenes, — the most diligent and indefatigable in training, of all the orators of antiquity, — forbids, (as was mentioned before,) the very idea of his submitting to a discipline artificial or fanciful in its prescriptions; and Cicero himself has borne eloquent testimony to the value of the vocal training to which he subjected himself, when in Greece.

The cultivation of the voice is required on grounds quite distinct from those of anticipated professional duties. The vocal muscles and the nerves of expression, (the great instruments of utterance,) are not only susceptible of cultivation to an equal degree with the other portions of the muscular and nervous systems of the human body, but to a much higher. — The spiritual vividness of their action, — so important to their power of rendering instant obedience to the ever-varying requisitions of the mind, — renders these portions of the human frame the most plastic and the most docile of all. There is no form of muscular or of nervous action in which so entire a revolution can be speedily effected, as that which is exemplified in the production of vocal sound. A few weeks' daily practice are, usually, sufficient to produce an utter change of circumstances, as regards the ability to execute the prominent effects of voice, in "force" and "pitch," — the main characteristics of utterance, in impressive speaking. The whole style of voice, as to "quality," is often changed from bad to good, within as short a period.

Neglect of Vocal Culture.

Our established modes of education, were they adequate to the purpose of a thorough cultivation of the various powers and capacities of man, would furnish ample provision for the development of the organ of voice, as the exponent of heart and mind, the connecting link of man's mental and social being. No exertion would then be spared by which it could be rendered vigorous, pliant, expressive, and, at the same time, agreeable to the ear, by its natural and appropriate music, as a portion and a most effective one, of the great system of universal harmony, which reigns among the works of God.

The prevalent neglect of this divine instrument, designed to contribute its share to the symmetry and the grace, as well as to the immediate uses, of life, not only leaves many even of those whose professional duties render an agreeable and skilful use of it indispensable, disqualified for their proper occupation, by inability to exert it aright, but subjects them to pain and suffering and exhaustion, and consequent loss of health, or even, ultimately, of life, from unskilful and inappropriate modes of exerting the voice; and, as not unfrequently happens to speakers of this description, it renders, from the same causes, their whole utterance disagreeable and even painful to others.

Elocutionists often have occasion, in their professional capacity, to see instances of the noblest powers of mind rendered unavailing for the purposes of public speaking, by neglected habit, or erroneous cultivation, in early life. A little daily attention to the subject, would have easily secured, in season, a clear, agreeable, melodious tone to many speakers who now habitually exert their organs in such a manner as to thwart the purposes of speaking, and even to produce pain or disgust in the hearer. Persuasion must ever be up-hill work, where a harsh and grating effect of voice is incessantly jarring the nerves, and undoing the harmonious effect of sentiment.

The preacher, more than any other speaker, needs all available aids of culture, in the use of the voice. His duties, — as was mentioned before, — require that he spend a large part of every day in strictly sedentary and intellectual occupation, — a condition extremely unfavorable to the free and energetic use of the organs of speech. Close study constrains the body, checks the circulation, impedes equally the functions of respiration and digestion, and is necessarily followed by languor and weakness. A strong, full, and smooth voice, must, to one subjected daily to such experience, be the result of a rare original force of constitution and vivacity of function, which unfriendly influences have not had the power to impair. Rigorous application of mind is injurious to the character of the voice; as, by impairing, through impeded and imperfect respiration, the vigor of the larynx, the glottis, and the vocal ligaments, as well as the bronchial tubes and the air-cells of the lungs, it generates what musicians designate as "impure tone," — that imperfectly vocalized sound, which bespeaks a mode of forming the voice more or less painful and exhausting, as well as disagreeable to the ear. Frequent access to the open air, an habitually cheerful mood, and the genial influence of social feeling, are all essential to the free and agreeable exercise of the voice. The physiologist can very easily account for the feeble, thin, hollow, dry, unmusical voices which are so often heard in our pulpits.

Remedies for Defective Culture.

The preacher, more than any other public speaker, requires the physical and mental influences of **muscular** exercise, recreation, repose, change of scene and occupation, vocal practice in singing, reciting, declaiming, reading, and whatever else tends to exhilarate the spirits, promote health, or impart power to the voice.* He should possess a perfect knowledge of the structure of the human frame, that he may use his vocal organs intelligently and effectively, spare himself fatigue and pain and injury, and be able to sustain long and vigorously the exercise of the voice in public speaking. Due practice soon renders an hour's reading or speaking an invigorating and inspiring rather than an exhausting process. The true and skilful use of the voice, in these forms of action, is similar, in effect, to the easy and pleasurable practice of an hour's singing. A well vocalized tone is, in any case, the same thing in its nature and formation, and consequently in its effects, both on the vocal organs of him who produces it, and on the ear of those who hear it: its character is that of a sound pure, easy, and agreeable, even in its utmost energy.

The prevalent opinion, that the study and practice of elocution lead to the formation of an artificial style of voice, is founded on one of those false impressions which ignorance and indolence are so prone to foster as pleas for error and defect. The elocutionist would say to the student, Select, for study, the most natural, smooth, and pleasing voice that you hear in others, and observe its peculiar properties;—select the corresponding tones in your own: cultivate these, and cherish them into habits: watch the sound of the human voice as it is affected by ennobling and bland emotions, by courage, joy, love, admiration, tranquility;—dwell on such tones till your ear has acquired a relish and a thirst for them: your voice will then become instinctively genial, as a matter of predilection and tendency. No one whose ear is unperverted,

---

* The volume entitled Orthophony, or Vocal Culture in Elocution, contains directions, in detail, for the appropriate discipline of the organs of voice.

utters a joyous emotion in a hollow, sepulchral tone, which habit seems to have fixed irretrievably on some speakers in the pulpit: no one naturally utters the warm and tender notes of love or admiration, in the cold and hard voice which so often falls from the mouth of the preacher: the language of a serene and tranquil spirit cannot be uttered in the harsh and hacking accents of a controversial dispute; — the calm expanse of the ocean or the heavens, and the quiet flow of the stream, suggest a very different lesson to the discerning ear, and prompt the voice to the placid, smooth, and full yet gentle sounds of entire repose.

Elocution enjoins on the preacher no false depth or artificial hollowness of voice. It reminds him only of the natural effect of solemnity, awe, and reverence, in at once deepening and enlarging and gently filling every vocal sound, and converting it to a natural and perfect unison with all those tones of majesty and grandeur, which nature is ever breathing into the ear of man, from ocean and river and forest, from the tempest and the thunder; and which flow from the noblest of all the instruments of music. The practice of elocution leads the minister, in his acts of devotion, to attune his utterance to the great laws which the Creator has written on the human ear. It forbids him to belittle and degrade a solemn and sacred act by the high, light, and trivial effect of a pitch appropriate only to what is trite and familiar and insignificant. It enables him to select, from the natural range of his own voice, those notes which even the intuitive perceptions of childhood recognize as intimations of the overshadowing presence of a great thought, or as the swell of a vast emotion, rising from the heart to the lips.

Effects of due Cultivation.

The cultivation of elocution will enable the preacher to discriminate, with perfect precision, and to execute, with natural freedom, all the varying modes of voice, as they come and go in successive utterance. His expression will be adapted to each, in all its fullness and peculiarity of effect. His whole mode of voice will be inspired with life and truth and power. The native dignity of man, stamped on the noble and eloquent accents which assign him his rank in the creation, will be audible in every word that falls from his lips.

It would be impossible for an individual whose ear was once opened to discriminate the quality and character of sound, to give forth those muttering and grumbling effects of voice, those guttural and croaking notes, those snuffling nasal, and wiry twangings, those barking explosions of unmitigated abruptness, those "softly sweet," effeminate mincings, by which the pulpit is so often degraded.

To man regarded as an intelligent and gregarious animal merely, there is something attractive and interesting in the very sound of the human voice. The awful desolation of utter solitude is never more impressively felt than when the forlorn being becomes fully conscious of his forsaken condition, by the oppressive weight of unbroken silence. This truth the poet Cowper has imaged most strikingly in his supposed soliloquy of Selkirk, when he represents him as deploring the doom which condemns him never more to "hear the sweet music of speech."

The attainments of distinguished vocalists serve to show what, in corresponding degree, might be effected by the due cultivation of the voice, for the various purposes of reading, recitation, and speaking. Not that a merely artificial culture can ever be desirable, either for the useful purposes of speech, or the tasteful enjoyment of elocution. But let us select, from the private circle, the example of voice which best pleases the ear, and most vividly affects our sympathy, whether in the appropriate and impressive reading of a page of literature, or in the freer and simpler form of intelligent conversation in the social circle, and affectionate communication by the fireside. Let us select the public speaker whose voice perfectly true, easy, natural, chaste, yet vivid and impressive, seems to spring directly from the heart of the man, and to dwell equally on the ear and in the heart of his hearers, as a perfect embodying of the whole soul whence it sprung. Let the instance be one in which the human organ is felt to be no unworthy channel of the messages of peace and love from on high: let it even be one in which the beauty of perfect excellence seems realized; so that, — as sometimes happens, even in our own day, — "a world lying in wickedness" is induced to listen to the prophet, as to "one that playeth skilfully on an instrument," and to sit, for a time, rapt in admiration of the music of his voice. Let the supposed example be carried even so high, it will still be, in most cases, but a specimen of what intuitive observation and undisciplined skill may accomplish. — Suppose, on the other hand, an individual trained under advantages no more than equal to those which every vocal musician confers upon himself, who allows himself the customary opportunities of systematic and scientific cultivation for successive years. What might not a speaker so trained accomplish, with the genius, especially, which insures distinction in other pursuits, and with a soul absorbed in the spirit of his vocation?

Training to such extent, (thanks to the philosophic spirit and enthusiastic application of the great American analyst, Dr. James Rush!)* has now become a thing easily practicable to the spirit of diligence and perseverance. The means of attaining to high excellence, — to comparative perfection, — are now offered to every student of elocution, and exhibited with a perspicuity, precision, and certainty, which leave no excuse for skepticism or ignorance.

---

* See his Philosophy of the Human Voice, *passim.*

Effects of Cultivation on the "Quality"* of the Voice.

The student who will faithfully apply his powers to the mastering of Dr. Rush's system, will be enabled so to use his voice that every truth which he utters, every emotion which he endeavors to impart, will be carried home to the minds and hearts of his hearers, " clothed in fitting sound." Every mode of vocality which is essential to expression, will be fully at his command. We shall hear, in his utterance, an entire exemption from all those vulgarisms of voice which degrade the pulpit, when uttered within its precincts: we shall recognize, in his tones, the perfect " purity "† and subdued manner, which pathos, tranquility, and solemnity impart: — the ample and noble effect of grandeur and sublimity, in the appropriate style of a voice trained to roundness, smoothness, and fullness, the characteristic qualities demanded by the larger dimensions of space, and the stronger incitement of feeling, in public speaking, as it differs from private conversation.‡

---

* The effect produced on the ear by the mere sound of the voice, as agreeable or otherwise. Thus, we recognize one voice as harsh, another as smooth; one as thin, another as full.

† What the musician denominates " pure tone," or " head tone," — from its resonance in the head, — is nothing else than that perfectly liquid quality of voice, which is its natural perfection, — as is evinced in the untutored utterance of early childhood, — and which corresponds to the sound of a flute, when played on by a skilful performer, as contrasted with the mere learner, whose manner is recognized in consequence of its harsh and hissing sound.

‡ The perfect voice of the accomplished elocutionist, Dr. Rush has designated by the introduction of a new but expressive term, — " *orotund*," — in allusion not only to the rotundity of its sound, but, also, the actual position of the interior and back part of the mouth, by which it is produced.

Articulation.

The well-trained speaker will be distinguished, moreover, by the perfect exactness yet perfect ease of his articulation, and even by its brilliancy of effect and positive beauty of sound, in consequence of the exact adjustment and free play of the organs of speech, in every function which they perform, and in every sound which they execute.

A distinct and perfect enunciation is of the utmost service to the public reader or speaker; as it not only secures to him the indispensable condition of intelligible communication, and gives an intellectual clearness and finish to his style of expression, but, by the definite and precise character which it imparts to every sound of his voice, it enables him to dispense with that mere loudness which would otherwise exhaust his own strength, and annoy the ears of his audience. Pure tone and distinct articulation enable a speaker of comparatively limited vocal power to convey his words, with perfect ease, through a large extent of space. The result is similar to that which attends the performance of the softest strains of vocal music, by a skilful singer: the ear loses neither his notes nor his syllables; as he delivers every tone with perfect clearness and purity of sound, and every letter with exact though delicate execution, in its articulation.

The faulty character of early education, however, in very many instances, leaves the professional speaker quite deficient in correct habit as to enunciation. Not a few preachers are, in this respect, inaccurate and remiss, to an extent which hinders their usefulness, and degrades their address.

The same remark applies to the habitual accent and pronunciation of many speakers in the pulpit, who, instead of exhibiting the appropriate refinement of good education, descend to the style of vulgar negligence and slovenliness.

The discipline of the vocal organs which is prescribed by the art of elocution, while it would guard the speaker against all such faults, would save him from the opposite ones of finical nicety and affectation.*

Force and " Stress."

The cultivated speaker will be felt, in his power of producing, on the requisite occasions, any effect of force and volume of voice, — from the approach to whispering, which extreme earnestness produces, to the full body of tone thrown out in warm and powerful exclamations, resembling, perhaps, the style even of a hearty shout or piercing call. The thorough-going cultivation of the voice will impart to every word uttered by the speaker its peculiar modification of force, as regards the characteristic commencement and termination of sounds expressive of emotion.† His tones of command will be marked by the boldness and decision with which the accented sound of every emphatic word commences,‡ — his tones of entreaty by sounds commencing softly, but swelling out earnestly, and afterwards diminishing :§ his utterance in the mood of stern and determined resolve, will be marked, on the contrary, by the abrupt explosive termination of characteristic sounds ;‖ and his tones of surprise will exhibit the

---

* An extensive course of practice in orthoëpy, is contained in the American Elocutionist.

† The modes of force above referred to, are termed, by Dr. Rush, the "stress," (the *maximum*, or sometimes, the *ictus*,) of the voice, in a given sound ; as in the gentle "swell" of *pity*, or the abrupt "explosion" of *anger*.

‡ "*Radical*" (initial) "*Stress*."

§ "*Median Stress*," — force attaining its *maximum* at the middle of a sound.

‖ "*Vanishing*" (final) "*Stress*."

peculiar intensity of this emotion in its characteristic tendency to mark, with special force, both the opening and the closing of emphatic sounds :* his exclamations of empassioned excitement will be distinguished not merely by vague and general loudness, or by an ordinary swell of voice, but by a well-marked and highly characterized utterance which lays an obvious stress on the beginning, the middle, and the end of every emphatic sound.† It is thus that the language of emotion is rendered intelligible by nature's distinct alphabet of sound being preserved specifically to heart and ear, while the unpractised speaker, whose voice has not been disciplined on these distinctions, utters his words with the "uncertain sound" of the trumpet unskilfully blown, — at which "no man armeth himself for the battle."

Pitch.

The discipline of the voice imparts to the practised speaker an indescribable power over the feelings of his audience, not merely by his command over every mood and form of force by which the soul may be roused or tranquillized, impelled or subdued, but not less by the range which it gives to his voice over all the keys of expressive utterance, as high or low-pitched, lively or grave, gay or sombre, brisk or solemn. The unpractised reader or speaker has but little compass of utterance, and clings to the same unvaried notes. The disciplined voice traverses, with the utmost facility, and with electric effect, from pole to pole of the scale of expressive tones, touches every point with perfect precision and definite meaning, and throws out, at pleasure, the most impressive effects of contrast, whenever the sudden shifting of the current

---

* "*Compound Stress,*" — combining the effects of both "Radical" and "Vanishing" "Stress."

† "*Thorough*" (pervading) "*Stress.*"

of language and emotion, requires a marked transition of vocal effect.

It is such reading only which can present the tones of the heart, in the language of the Psalmist, as he passes from the lowest depths of despondency and remorse, to the highest strains of joy and praise. Many of the hymns so commonly read with a dead level of voice, require similar variations of utterance, to give anything like true and soul-felt effect to the emotions which they were designed to express. The habitual tones of many readers of hymns, are so cold, so lifeless, and inexpressive, so flatly prosaic and mechanical, that the whole style is virtually a desecration of the sacred lyrics, which were composed for the express purpose of breathing a higher and purer life into the exercise of devotion. — The miserable defectiveness of education as it is, never appears more striking than when the minister who has spent a large part of life, the whole period from the commencement of his academic career to the close of his professional course, — in professed preparation for the right discharge of the duties of the pulpit, "goes through the ceremony" of reading a hymn, as if it were a page of an almanac, with a perpetually returning clink of voice, that seems to resemble nothing so much as the never varying sound of the hammer on the anvil.

No reader needs so complete a control over the pitch and range of the voice as the preacher. The deepest notes of profound awe, solemnity, and reverence, are indispensable to his utterance, not as an occasional resort for variety and effect, but as the prevalent strain of devout expression, whether in the reading of the Scriptures and of hymns, or in the appropriate effect of a sermon which happens to exemplify, with more or less frequency, the language of profound emotion. None but a practised speaker can sustain long the peculiar organic action requisite for the production of deep-toned utterance. It is, of all modes of voice, the most exhausting to organs no .

expanded and invigorated by special exercise. The case is analogous to that of a vocalist whose natural "register" and habitual practice are "tenor," changing, for an hour, to the exercise of singing "bass." The effect is usually felt, in such cases, to be altogether enfeebling. Yet the same individual will sustain, without fatigue, his wonted form of vocal exertion, for a whole evening. The average voice of conversation and unempassioned reading or speaking, is in the "tenor" or middle range of notes; that of solemn and deep emotion, in public address, is relatively as low as "bass." The latter is properly the prevalent style of the pulpit, which demands the strong and impressive utterance of passages naturally pitched on a low key; while conversation, in consequence of the limited space which it requires the voice to fill, admits the easier task of vocal exertion on a low pitch, united with a softened force.

Persons conversant, to any extent, with the nature of the process of "phonation,"* will at once perceive the peculiar necessity of vocal training for the preacher, as it arises from the special form of utterance connected with his professional functions. Any ear, however, can readily detect the helpless and inexpressive hollowness into which the preacher's voice so often falls in the strains of deep feeling, — a fault against which due cultivation and practice would be an infallible safeguard.

The dreaded reaction of nature, on Monday, after the excessive exertions of the Sabbath, — a thing which preachers of delicate or susceptible organization so often anticipate with a sense of coming misery, is, no doubt, caused, in part, by the unreasonable extent of exertion encountered in repeating the effort of public speaking twice, or even thrice, on the same day. But the chief cause of exhaustion is usually to be traced to the state of the larynx and the bronchial tubes, induced by the fre-

---

* The formation of vocal sound.

quent repetition and long continued use of the lowest notes of the voice, which of necessity cause the expenditure of a comparatively large supply of breath, in their production and formation.

A rigorous course of vocal exercise, serving, for the organs of speech, the same purpose with powerful gymnastic discipline for the limbs, is the only security for the long continued possession of strength of utterance, especially if exerted on low notes. The parts so severely taxed must be protected by exercise adapted both to indurate and supple the muscular apparatus, so as to impart, at once, vigor and flexibility to the voice.

The unreflecting observer often contents himself, in view of the professional difficulty now referred to, with prescribing to the preacher the habitual use of a higher key of voice, in his public performances, as a sufficient security against injurious effects. But it is forgotten, in these instances, that the preacher, if true to his office, must habitually use the natural and proper tones of deep and solemn emotion; and, although it is certain, that evils not unfrequently arise from the undue prevalence of one strain of feeling and of utterance, yet it is not less so, that the very themes on which the preacher discourses, require, for the most part, a deepened note of voice.

There is, in fact, no alternative, in most cases, but due practice and training, as a security against those fatal inroads of disability and disease, which are so frequent among the members of the clerical profession. Powerful constitutions and cheerful tempers enable individuals to bear much injury without sinking under it. The cerebral and nervous systems (not to speak of the muscular frame) of some men, enable them even to bid defiance to the effects of habitual intemperance, and to attain, in spite of these, to a vigorous old age, — as in the case of the Scottish highlander, whose daily potations would destroy most Americans, in a few years, or even months. But no sound-minded person thinks of quoting such cases as authority for indulging in such practices. The case is similar, as regards the tear and wear of vocal exertion: if not counteracted by rational preventives, it cuts off, silently but surely, its annual multitudes of victims. The seasonable precautions which a proper early education would prescribe, might obviate all such evils. But, as matters are, this result is left to the choice of the adult student, at a stage when the remedy, if not speedily applied, may prove too late.

"*Inflection.*"

The systematic cultivation of the voice, is in no respect more important to true and effective expression, than in its proper inflection, or, in other words, its transits upward and downward on the scale, in accommodation to the variations of thought and feeling, whether in emphatic words, or the successive clauses of a sentence. The utterance of unpractised and unskilful readers, is usually marked by the absence of inflection, and, consequently, a prevailing monotony; or by mechanical inflections, which never rise or fall beyond a certain note, and which necessarily give a measured correspondence of parts to all sentences, alike; gliding up at one clause and down at another, in a regularly alternating see-saw of sound, which destroys the natural variety of thought and emotion. This uniformly recurring verbal melody, resembles, in effect, the singing of all the hymns in a book to the same tune. Another common fault in inflection, is that of overdoing it; so that the upward and downward slides are rendered mechanically and disagreeable prominent, projecting themselves upon the ear, as the jagged rocks of wild scenery upon the eye; or that of exaggerating every inflection into a double form, comprising both slides in every distinctive or emphatic accent. This style destroys all repose and dignity of voice, by its jerking turns and reduplications, and its over anxious emphasis. Another error, still, converts all poetry into prose by substituting the pointed and marked inflections of common discourse, for the reduced and melodious ones of verse. This fault seems to extract the appropriate feeling from a hymn, and to bring it down from devotional elevation to mere practical associations of utility, such as are appreciated by the understanding, rather than felt in the heart. But the most prevalent of all faults in inflection, is that of varying the voice by a certain personal melody of tone, habitual to the reader alone; sliding upward or downward or waving and undulating, at the dictate of a false ear, without any regard to the expression of thought or feeling, and in obedience to no law but the accustomed gait of the individual's peculiar style of utterance, contracted at school. This fault constitutes what is termed, in popular language, "a tone." It marks the man, but does not express his meaning. Its effect resembles that of singing "out of tune," and adding to false intonation a vitiated melody. Whatever may be the sentiment which such a speaker utters, its effect is neutralized, more or less, by this trick of habit. Yet it is a fault from which few speakers comparatively are exempt. Some exemplify it more conspicuously; others, less so: but it is an error in elocution which holds possession of the pulpit, to the exclusion of the genuine expressive utterance that nature prompts, and which alone can elicit a true personal sympathy.

A degree of attention, no greater than is usually given, in the cultivation of vocal music, to the mastering of the gamut, would cure all the faults which usually disfigure the inflections of pulpit elocution, and would enable the preacher to speak with effect both to head and heart, in the appropriate language of inflection. The simple and complex* slides of the voice upward and downward on the scale, are the only proper means of drawing intellec-

---

* The complex or double slide of the voice, Dr. Rush terms the "*wave.*"

tual distinctions, of indicating the constituent and relative parts of a sentiment, as these are subdivided and arranged in the consecutive clauses of a sentence, or of conveying those emotions which predominate in the heart of the speaker, and which he wishes to transfer to those of his audience.

"Inflection," whether it is exemplified in the form of the "slide" or the "wave," may be analyzed scientifically, in the manner exhibited in Dr. Rush's work on the voice, by the application of the musical scale; or it may be studied practically, by attentive observation of the actual turns of voice, in the exercises of reading and speaking. But, in either case, it requires a close and penetrating application of the attention to nice and exact distinctions of sound. It cannot be mastered by ordinary inspection or transient notice. But the due study and practice of this part of elocution will be richly rewarded, in the acquisition of a skilful and effective control over the true "melody" of speech and reading, and, consequently, over that music of the voice which plays, at the will of the orator, the tune of thought or that of feeling. Inflections are, always, the vocal exposition of a sentence: they are the interpreters of speech and enforce its meaning; without them, reading is but the senseless syllabication of the juvenile learner, in his unpractised steps, when the spirit of a passage is merged in the mere sound of words as such. The voice of the skillful reader, aided by appropriate inflections, strikes a thought home to both head and heart, and awakes in the soul every kindred association. Inflection is, in all cases, one of the most useful and effectual instruments of true eloquence. It is the purest and most brilliant of all the ornaments which a consummate elocution confers on the voice. It is the appropriate language of a cultivated intellect and a discerning spirit; and it is, not less distinctively, the melody into which emotion breathes the life and power of expression.*

---

* The various forms of inflection will be found scientifically arranged

PULPIT ELOCUTION.

"Movement."

Another distinguishing trait of a cultivated voice, and one which is of the utmost moment to the preacher, is the complete control which it ensures over the "movement," or rate of time observed in utterance, as adapted to different emotions. A slight observation is sufficient to enable any ear to detect the common faults, in this particular, which are exhibited in the pulpit. Some preachers, desiring to secure a plain, familiar style of expression, resembling that of conversation, run into the error of too great rapidity. A similar result is produced by the constitutional vivacity of others. In either case, dignity and impressiveness, and even distinctness, are, more or less, sacrificed to impulse and velocity.

The audience which the minister of religion usually addresses, is of a mixed character, as to intellectual discipline and ability, and is largely made up of persons who are daily engaged in the practical pursuits of active business. Minds addicted to habits of this description, do not usually prove rapid in the formation of strictly intellectual associations: they need a comparatively full allowance of time to aid the development of a train of thought. An audience formed of students and professional men, accustomed to facility and rapidity of mental action, can more easily keep up with the succession of ideas created by a reader whose gait of voice inclines to velocity. The habit of silent reading enables the practised student to follow the succession of thought with the utmost rapidity; and his discipline of intellect renders him competent even to foresee a speaker's drift of thought, and anticipate his train of argument. But the man of

---

and designated in Dr. Rush's Philosophy of the Voice. They are exemplified in technical detail, in the volume on Orthophony, formerly mentioned, and practically applied to an appropriate selection of passages in the American Elocutionist.

merely operative and practical habit, must move deliberately, and follow, rather than accompany, a speaker. The aged hearer, who has little intellectual facility, often complains of the preacher's rapidity and confusion of utterance. Complaints such as this, are not always well grounded; and the waning faculties of age are, too often in these cases, the chief source of apparent feebleness and indistinctness in the voice of the preacher. No speaker, however, who addresses a mixed audience, should suffer himself to fall into the rapidity of utterance which leaves any passage unintelligible to any individual among his hearers.

Deliberateness of manner is not only an indispensable requisite to intelligible address, but a powerful and natural aid to impressive utterance. Without a moderate rate of "movement" in the voice, there can be no association of grave or grand effect on the ear: the style of utterance is, in such instances, unavoidably rendered light and trivial. Solemnity, in particular, demands the utmost slowness of utterance. The uncultivated reader is always prone to celerity of enunciation, and thus hinders repose and reverence, and every other form of deep and tranquil impression. A style like this, is peculiarly ill-suited to the purposes of reading and speaking, as connected with the duties of the sacred office.

The cultivated reader is taught to appreciate the becoming effect and moral beauty of due slowness, as an attribute of sacred eloquence. He gives, accordingly, ample scope to sound, lengthens the duration of every prominent vowel, and thus makes it the fit vehicle of deep and full emotion: he avoids a crowded utterance as the very bane of serious and grave feeling; he cultivates the habit of moderation in the succession of sounds; and his pauses all naturally receive a proportioned length, by which they become deeply impressive to the ear. These traits of utterance are indispensable to the majesty of style prevalent in all the sublime descriptions of the Old

Testament, and are required, not unfrequently, in the New.

But while taste and feeling demand due slowness in uttering whatever is deeply impressive to the mind; they forbid equally all lagging and drawling, as wholly destructive of every good effect, — as only irksome or ridiculous, bespeaking a feeble temperament and habit, and an utter inability to create any deep or powerful effect. This style, however, is proverbially current in pulpit elocution, and forms one of the distinctive and prominent features of its mechanically solemn and exaggerated manner. The discipline of elocution dispels such effects, by the light which it sheds on the nature of "movement," as an element of vocal effect; and, just as the musician obeys, with instinctive readiness, the direction which accelerates or retards his voice, with the most definite precision, and vivid effect on the ear, so does the instructed reader produce the characteristic expression of every sentiment by the instantaneous adaptation of his rate of utterance to the spirit of the language which falls from his lips. Truth, and nature, and propriety, preside, thus, over his whole manner, and render it living and eloquent.

"Rhythm" and Pausing.

The discipline of the voice offers to the public speaker a great facility, as regards the proper vocal effect required for his purposes, in the regularity of "rhythm," or the equable succession of sound, and the due length of pauses. "Rhythm," as a part of elocution, enables the reader to maintain an equal and symmetrical flow of voice, while it guards him, not less carefully, against a mechanical prominence of rhythmical accent, which is attended with a hammering effect on the ear.

A true rhythm has been demonstrated by Steel to constitute, as distinctly, a trait of appropriate reading and speaking, as of music. It serves, in the former, the same purposes as in the latter: it imparts a smooth, agreeable, and symmetrical effect to the voice: it prescribes and facilitates a regular and easy style of breathing: it enables the reader or speaker to pronounce the successive clauses of every sentence with a regulated, easy, fluent style of accent, which renders the effort of full utterance comparatively light, promotes the tranquillity of his emotions, saves his own organic strength, and gives forth his language with an harmonious and pleasing effect to the ear of others.

The uncultivated reader wastes breath and strength, and disturbs his utterance, by want of regularity in the alternate successions of sound and pause. His whole style of voice is like that of a person who, in singing, pays no regard to "time," — the very foundation of music.*

Emphasis.

Nothing, perhaps, displays so strikingly the benefit of systematic practice in elocution, as the force, the spirit, and the efficacy which it imparts to emphasis.† The dull routine of school reading, in its customary forms, deadens the distinctive character of all prominent phrases, and reduces all the words of a sentence to one flat, monotonous level, in which there are no projecting and salient points to arrest the attention; the voice gliding on from beginning to end of a period, as if every clause were of exactly equal weight, and every word of precisely the same significance.

The influence of early habit is so strong with most persons, that few, even among professional readers, seem to

---

* For exercises in "rhythm," see the manual on Orthophony.

† Dr. Rush has justly given to the word "emphasis" a wider application than that which restricts it to mere *comparative force*. He comprehends under it, in accordance with its etymology, all the phenomena of voice which render a word significant or impressive.

have the power of throwing into a significant word, or an expressive phrase, that force which an energetic and distinctive effect of sense or emotion demands. A proper emphasis adds a heightened coloring of passion, or gives a bolder prominence of meaning, to the most energetic style, and is capable even of concealing the deficiencies of expression comparatively tame. But most public readers have accustomed themselves to a certain medium of ordinary effect in emphasis, which forbids the possibility of their imparting weight, or significance, or vivid force to distinctive expressions. Hence their mode of reading is so far from lending a powerful aid to written composition, that it serves rather to weaken and impair it.

The actor who is distinguished in his art, studies his emphasis with the most assiduous attention, and uses every endeavor which professional ambition can prompt, or professional skill can suggest, to give the most prominent relief and the boldest effect to emphatic turns of expression. He will sometimes devote successive hours to the most laborious reïteration of vocal effort, to give life and pungency to a single passage. Nor is this the practice of mere drudges in their vocation, endeavoring to work up dull conceptions to a vivid effect: it was the daily self-discipline of men whose expressive genius the world has always acknowledged and admired.

A disciplined voice may be recognized in its emphasis as readily as in any other point, notwithstanding the current notion that, to give a true emphasis, nothing more is needed than a right understanding of the language which requires it. Force and skill are, in this as in all other things, the fruit of practice. The violent blow of the angry rustic may fall with little harm to him at whom it is aimed: the skilful one of the scientific athlete, tells with a direct and concentrated force, which renders it as effective as it is inevitable. A similar result is exhibited in the use of the voice, when the practised reader throws into the emphasis of a single word a whole world of meaning, condensed into one energetic sound; while the unskilful voice, with its vague loudness and aimless noise, fights "as one that beateth the air."

The study of elocution not only prescribes this due discipline of the voice for positive force of emphasis, but for that not less valuable means of impressive effect, the power and the habit of withholding force, in anticipation of emphasis or subsequently to its occurrence, so as to give it the due relief arising from the comparative reduction of preceding and following words. In this mode of managing the voice lies the main effect of expressive and distinctive force. The unpractised reader is prone to follow the negligent habit of conversational utterance, which throws out a more frequent but a feebler emphasis than impressive public reading demands. He is addicted, perhaps, to those habits of false emphasis which lead him to give unnecessary prominence to insignificant and inexpressive words, and, consequently, to mar the whole effect of what emphasis he chiefly intends. He forces into emphatic style the auxiliaries and particles of a sentence, to the utter subversion of meaning and emotion.* The elocutionary training of the voice in emphasis, leads to the observance of a principle directly contrary to such practice, and accustoms the reader, by the use of a few obvious rules, to reserve his force for the prominent points of meaning, and always to husband his emphasis so as to make it tell.

Another very important effect of the due discipline of the voice, as to emphasis, is the security which it gives that the student shall avoid those sharp and jagged turns of voice which indicate a species of nervous fastidiousness about emphasis. This fault was described, in a preceding part of the present work, as an error of inflec-

---

* The ecstatic joy of the father, at the return of the prodigal son, is, in this style, converted from a burst of grateful and glad feeling, into the recitation of a lesson in etymology; thus, "For this my son *was* lost, and *is* found!"

tion, as well as emphasis, and as subverting all simplicity, directness, and dignity of utterance. It can be effectually cured in no way but by the faithful and rigorous analysis of intonation and expression, which systematic elocution prescribes. The gradations of inflection, in the slides and waves of the voice, are all distinctly classified and illustrated in the successive steps of elocutionary training in this department; and to the practice of these, as laid down in the manuals before mentioned, the student who is desirous of attaining a correct and genuine emphasis, is, for the present, referred.

"*Expression.*"

The discipline of the voice, in the expression of feeling and emotion, is a part of elocution which, to the preacher, is of vast moment. The imperfect utterance which characterizes the ordinary style of reading formed at school, — the period when habit is generally fixed, — predisposes even the clergyman, in the pulpit, to an inexpressive mode of voice, which belies rather than manifests whatever emotion may exist in his soul. The voice of most persons in adult life needs a thorough renovation of habit, to enable it to utter truly the vivid language of the Scriptures, of sacred poetry, or even of expressive prose. The unfriendly influences of neglect and perversion of vocal habit, in early years, and the equally unfavorable effect of a conventional coldness of utterance, current in society, have been frequently, in our preceding remarks, referred to, as the sources of prevalent defects in reading and speaking. Elocution, as a remedial art, offers to the student the means and the methods of self-reformation in expression. It prescribes an extensive and varied course of practice on the most vivid passages of the most effective writers, with a view to awaken emotion and keep it alive, in the exercise of reading. The materials for practice it draws largely from poetry, as the natural language of feeling, and as the most inspiring source of empassioned utterance. To the theological student, in particular, it suggests the earnest reading of the Scriptures, — the most vivid and the most poetic of all books, — as one of the most influential in imparting expressive character to the habits of the voice. The reading of sacred poetry, especially in the lyric form, as the most inspiring of all, it prescribes as another means of forming vocal habit to a true and living style. It suggests, also, the frequent practice of reading essays, lectures, and discourses in the form of sermons, with a view to rendering the last of these modes of exercise an easy and natural and habitual exertion, instead of leaving it to prove an unattempted, unfamiliar, and unnatural performance, inducing mechanical and artificial manner, and conscious awkwardness and embarrassment.

The preparatory discipline of elocution, by the familiarity which it produces with the genuine style of true reading, brings this exercise to an identity with speaking, in its manner and effect, and imparts to the varying tones of emotion a distinctness and a force of character, which make them pass with power from the heart of the reader to that of the hearer. It thus takes off the coldness and formality of the conventional style of sermonizing, and substitutes for it that of actual personal communication between man and man. It enjoins, accordingly, such a frequency of repetition in the preparatory reading of a discourse, as shall stamp the substance of it on the mind, and enable the preacher to deliver it as virtually a spoken address, rather than the school-boy reading of a prescribed task. This frequency of repetition, in previous reading, it requires, farther, to such an extent as shall leave the preacher free to direct his eye, principally, to his audience rather than his paper; as the language of the eye is nature's primary effect in expression, whether as the means of securing the attention and sympathy of those to whom a discourse is addressed, or as the most efficacious mode of securing, by reäctive effect on the reader himself, the tones of genuine personal feeling in his voice.*

The study of elocution leads to a thorough-going analysis of all the component elements of expressive effect of voice, and to an intimate knowledge of their character. It provides an extensive course of practice on each singly, and, also, in their combinations, till all can be executed with unerring precision, fullness, and effect. The bad results of cold and inexpressive manner, have been already described in this volume. On these, therefore, it is unnecessary at present, to dwell. The opposite style, of false, excessive warmth, and of studied, artificial variety of intonation, has also been described. The analysis which practical elocution presents of all the constituents of vocal expression, makes familiar to the student the exact character and value of each; so that he is secured against the tendency, otherwise, to slight or exaggerate any. He becomes accustomed, accordingly, to observe closely the proper effect of every point by which the expression of emotion is naturally heightened or reduced: he acquires an intuitive readiness and exactness of judgment, and a critical refinement of taste, which guide him instinctively to the vivid, full, and true utterance of every characteristic tone of feeling. He preserves thus, the quiet, chaste, unimpassioned, didactic style of exposition and discussion, in the essay, the lecture, and the doctrinal discourse; while, in the treatment of subjects that naturally call forth intensity of feeling, his utterance adapts itself, with no less propriety and certainty of effect, to the language of

---

* Preachers, if they would observe how easy it is for an audience to hold at arm's length the man who merely *reads at them*, (with his head down, and his eye on his manuscript,) compared to the man who *speaks to them*, (with the natural eloquence of his eye directed to theirs,) would understand better how easy it is to listen with indifference to the one, and how difficult to escape from the influence of the other. Prudence might, in such cases, be excused for whispering the half-worldly suggestion, how easy it may be, in given circumstances, to "dismiss" the one and how difficult to part with the other.

vivid emotion. His voice takes, in a word, the hue of every subject over which it passes, and tinges his whole utterance with the coloring of the heart. He knows how to restrain expression, and how to give it free scope, how to call home the energy of the voice, and how to throw it out. His extensive and varied discipline on expressive tone, renders it easy for him to pass from the level and tranquil moods of utterance to those which are imbued with passion. His tones, therefore, spring directly from feeling, and are as free from any arbitrary trait as they are from morbid chill and reserve.

The diligent student of elocution recovers, in short, that power of instantaneous sympathy and of vivid expression, which characterized him at that early stage of life, when the freshness and fullness of his tones indicated a heart unmodified by conventional and arbitrary influence. The power which he has thus recovered, his mature mind and reflective judgment enable him to apply to those deeper and richer sources of thought, which his intellectual culture has opened up to him. The still higher sphere of thought and feeling to which the preacher's vocation transfers him, he enters with a preparatory training, which, if it does nothing else, frees him, at least, from the embarrassing consciousness that he has not acquitted himself fully and honorably, as far as human abilities may go, to a part of the peculiar duties which are to be devolved upon him, by his professional relation.

ELEMENTARY EXERCISES FOR THE VOICE.

The following exercises are designed for the practical application of the principles discussed in the foregoing remarks: they consist, accordingly, of examples selected with reference to those parts of elocution which are immediately applicable to the training of the voice for the purposes of the pulpit. To students who had already acquired a knowledge of the general principles of elocution, from the manuals formerly mentioned, or from any similar source, the exercises now presented will suit the purpose of special application to professional uses; and to persons who had not previously made elocution a particular study, they will serve as a partial substitute for a more extended course of elementary discipline.

ARTICULATION.

The Fundamental Sounds of the English Language.*
" Tonic " Elements.
[So classed by Dr. Rush, from their susceptibility of "intonation."]
Simple.

†*A*-ll, *A*-rm, *A*-n, *Ai*-r, *E*-rr, *E*-nd, *I*-n, *E*-ve, *O*-r, *O*-n, *U*-p, *Oo*-ze, L-*oo*-k.

---

* The inadvertency of attention, or the ascendency of erroneous habit, being the principal causes of indistinct enunciation, the rigorous practice of the above elements, becomes, even to professional speakers, a useful exercise, as a means of securing attention to details.

† The Italic letters contain, in each instance, the element of sound, which is the object of direct attention. Each element should be repeated after the pronunciation of the word in which it occurs.

ELEMENTARY EXERCISES. — ARTICULATION.

Compound.

A-le, *I*-ce, *O*-ld, *Ou*-r, *Oi*-l, *U*-se (the verb,) *U*-se (the noun).*

"Subtonics."

[So denominated by Dr. Rush, because of their inferior susceptibility of intonation, when compared with the "tonic" elements.]

L-u-*ll*, *M*-ai-*m*, *N*-u-*n*, *R*-ap, Fa-*r*,† Si-*ng*, *B*-a-be, *D*-i-*d*, *G*-a-*g*, *V*-al-*ve*, *Z*-one, A-*z*-ure, *Y*-e, *W*-oo, *Th*-ine, *J*-oy.

"Atonics."

[So called from their deficiency as to capacity for intonation.]

P-i-*pe*, *T*-en-*t*, *C*-a-*ke*, *F*-i-*fe*, *C*-ea-*se*, *H*-e, *Th*-in, Pu-*sh*, *Ch*-ur-*ch*.

Combinations.

‡*Bl*-ame, *Cl*-aim, *Fl*-ame, *Gl*-are, *Pl*-ace, *Sl*-ay, *Spl*-ay, *Br*-ave, *Cr*-ave, *Dr*-ain, *Fr*-ame, *Gr*-ain, *Pr*-ay, *Spr*-ay, *Tr*-ace, *Str*-ay, *Shr*-ine, *Sm*-all, *Sn*-arl, *Sp*-ace, *St*-ay, Bo-*ld*, E-*lf*, E-*lk*, E-*lm*, He-*lp*, Fal-*ls*, Fau-*lt*, E-*lve*, Mai-*m'd*, Glea-*ms*, A-*nd*, Gai-*ns*, Ba-*nk*, Da-*nce*, A-*nt*, Ba-*rb*, Ba-*rb'd*, Ha-*rd*, Ha-*rk*, Ma-*rk'd*, A-*rm*, A-*rm'd*, Ea-*rn*, Ea-*rn'd*, Hea-*rse*, Du-*rst*, Ba-*rs*, Ma-*rt*, Ca-*rve*, Ca-*rv'd*, Cha-*sm*, Rea-*s'n*, A-*sp*, Va-*st*, Pa-*ss'd*, Ma-*kes*, A-*ct*, Wa-*k'd*, Wa-*ft*, Qua-*ff'd*, A-*pt*, Su-*pp'd*, O-*p'n*, Ta-*k'n*, Sad-*d'n*, Gra-*v'n*, Brigh-*t'n*, Ca-*ll'st*, A-*rm'st*, Ca-*nst*, Du-*rst*, Mi-*dst*, Hea-*rd'st*, A-*rm'dst*, Lea-*rn'dst*, A-*ble*, Trou-*bl'd*, Am-*ple*, Top-*pl'd*, Cra-*dle*, Bri-*dl'd*, Ma-*rl*, Wo-*rld*, Ri-*ngs*, Ha-*ng'st*, Wro-*ng'd*, Wro-*ng'dst*.§

---

* For explanation of the few points of difference in arrangement, between the above table and that of Dr. Rush, see statements in the volume on Orthophony.

† The five elements at the beginning of the above table, may, from their comparative approach to vocality, be termed, "pure subtonics."

‡ The combination of elements is, in every case, indicated by italics. Every combination should be repeated separately, after pronouncing the word in which it occurs.

§ For a list of common errors in articulation, see American Elocutionist.

14*

The elementary sounds and combinations contained in the preceding tables, should be repeated till they can be enunciated with perfect exactness and well-defined character, in the full style of public speaking.

Distinctness of enunciation will be much promoted by a careful, slow, exact, syllabic and literal analysis of selected words, read with special precision and force, for the purpose of practising a clear, firm, well-marked articulation. This exercise is rendered still more conducive to its intended effect, if lines or sentences are read in inverted order, so as to detach them from their ordinary associations of sound.

A useful exercise for the purpose of securing a critical knowledge of orthoëpy, and a strict accuracy of habit in pronouncing, is to read aloud several columns, daily, from Worcester's edition of Johnson and Walker's dictionaries, as combined by Todd, and by Smart,* while close attention is paid to observe whether the sounds of the voice correspond precisely to the notation of the orthoëpy.

A copious list of words commonly mispronounced, even in the pulpit, formed a part in the original plan of the present work. But the extent of the list rendered it impracticable to introduce it without swelling the size of the volume beyond its limited extent. It may be sufficient, perhaps, to refer here to the tables presented in the Elocutionist, as a specimen of the classes of words which are most liable to mispronunciation, and as an indication of the importance of the exercise suggested in regard to the use of the dictionary.

The pulpit, in our day, and in this country, is so generally regarded as the standard of accuracy in pronunciation, that more than usual attention to this branch of elocution is justly required of ministers. But some young preachers, in particular, are too prone to shrink from their

---

* Worcester's Universal and Critical Dictionary, published by Hickling, Swan, & Brewer.

proper responsibleness as scholars, and to accommodate their own style to mere popular usage, while others, from a fastidious anxiety about bare exactness, adhere to the letter of the law of nicety, and even transcend its requirements. Hence we hear, in some American pulpits, the pronunciations — *air*th, *mair*cy, *pair*fect, from speakers who follow literally Walker's notation of orthoëpy, but do not pay attention to his own qualification of it. The former class of errors, however, — that which arises from accommodation to mere negligent common usage, — is the more prevalent, and particularly in New England. Hence the many broad and obsolete and peculiar sounds which characterize the pulpit pronunciation of this region.

It would seem to be an axiom of education, that in an extensive country like the United States, all young persons should be everywhere trained to do their part in preserving the unity of language and the refinement of custom. A liberal education should enable every young man to fill with propriety the office of public speaker, in any part of his native country. But the fact is quite otherwise. Our young New England clergy usually carry with them their marked local peculiarities of usage in pronouncing, and throw an unnecessary impediment in the way of their own acceptance as speakers elsewhere. A few months or years, it is true, usually suffice to rub off such points. But a seasonable attention would prevent their existence.

The pulpit orators of our Middle and Western States, are very generally chargeable with gross negligence and improprieties in pronunciation, which a little study in early years would have sufficed to correct. The pulpit cannot command the respect of any but the illiterate, while it tolerates a slovenly inaccuracy and low taste, in the use of language, or in the manner of pronouncing the most ordinary forms of expression. The minister, as an educated, or, at least, a reading man, should ever feel that he is looked to as a model in this particular, and that his influence in this, as in other things, is either upward or downward.

EXERCISES IN QUALITY.

"*Pure or Head Tone.*"*

This quality of voice belongs to *moderate, soft, and subdued* utterance, as in the expression of *pathos, repose,* and *solemnity, when not accompanied by grandeur or sublimity.* The object in view, in the practice of such passages as the following, is, to secure the power of moulding the voice into perfectly clear, pure, and smooth sound, as the true and proper habit of utterance, but particularly important in all passages of tender and softened effect. This mode of voice characterizes the appropiate reading of some of the Psalms, many of the most affecting hymns, and all the subdued appeals of direct address, in discourses from the pulpit. Pure head tone is of as much service to the public reader and speaker as to the singer. It renders the emission of vocal sound at once clear, easy, natural, and agreeable, and enables the performer to exert his organs without fatigue.

The following, and all other exercises, should be repeated till a perfect vocal execution is attained. To secure fully the quality in view, the "tonic" elements should be repeated in the same style. The ear and the voice will thus become perfectly attuned to the effect.

Pathos.

Ode to Peace.— Cowper.

" Come, peace of mind, delightful guest!
Return, and make thy downy nest,
Once more, in this sad heart!

---

* Properly, pure "head tone," — the "quality," or *resonance*, which is naturally inseparable from the upper "register," or range of notes uttered by the human voice. This species of quality is the opposite to "pectoral," — the resonance of the *chest*, in the execution of the deep, bass notes which form the lower "register."

Nor riches I nor power pursue,
Nor hold forbidden joys in view:
   We therefore need not part.

"Where wilt thou dwell, if not with me,
From avarice and ambition free,
   And pleasure's fatal wiles? —
For whom, alas! dost thou prepare
The sweets that I was wont to share,
   The banquet of thy smiles?

"The great, the gay, shall they partake
The heaven that thou alone canst make?
   And wilt thou quit the stream
That murmurs through the dewy mead,
The grove and the sequestered shed,
   To be a guest with them?

"For thee I panted; thee I prized;
For thee I gladly sacrificed
   Whate'er I loved before; —
And shall I see thee start away,
And helpless, hopeless, hear thee say —
   'Farewell! — we meet no more?'"

Repose.

Invocation to Evening. — Cowper.

"Come, Evening, once again, season of peace;
Return, sweet Evening, and continue long!
Methinks I see thee in the streaky west,
With matron step slow moving, while the night
Treads on thy sweeping train; one hand employed
In letting fall the curtain of repose
On bird and beast, the other, charged for man
With sweet oblivion of the cares of day:
Not sumptuously adorned, nor needing aid,
Like homely-featured Night, of clustering gems;

A star or two, just twinkling on thy brow,
Suffices thee; save that the moon is thine
Not less than hers, not worn, indeed, on high,
With ostentatious pageantry, but set
With modest grandeur in thy purple zone,
Resplendent less, but of an ampler round. —
Come, then; and thou shalt find thy votary calm,
Or make me so. Composure is thy gift."

Placid Emotion *

Books. — Addison.

"Aristotle tells us, that the world is a copy, or transcript, of those ideas which are in the mind of the First Being, and that those ideas which are in the mind of man, are a transcript of the world. To this we may add, that words are the transcript of those ideas which are in the mind of man, and that writing or printing is the transcript of words. As the Supreme Being has expressed, and, as it were, printed his ideas in the creation, men express their ideas in books, which, by this great invention of these latter ages, may last as long as the sun and moon, and perish only in the general wreck of nature.

"There is no other method of fixing those thoughts which arise and disappear in the mind of man, and transmitting them to the last periods of time; no other method of giving a permanency to our ideas, and preserving the knowledge of any particular person, when his body is mixed with the common mass of matter, and his soul retired into the world of spirits. Books are the legacies

---

* Conversational passages, essays, lectures, and discourses, when read in the study or the parlor, the conference or the lecture-room, may, particularly when composed in moderate and unimpassioned style, be properly read in merely pure "head" tone. But the public reading of the same may, from the larger demands of space, and, consequently, the fuller tone of voice, be carried to the extent of moderate "orotund" utterance. See page 168.

that a great genius leaves to mankind, which are delivered down from generation to generation, as presents to the posterity of those who are yet unborn.

"All other arts of perpetuating our ideas, continue but a short time. Statues can last but a few thousands of years, edifices fewer, and colors still fewer than edifices. Michael Angelo, Fontana, and Raffaelle, will, hereafter, be what Phidias, Vitruvius, and Appelles, are at present; the names of great statuaries, architects, and painters, whose works are lost. The several arts are expressed in mouldering materials. Nature sinks under them, and is not able to support the ideas which are impressed upon it.

"The circumstance which gives authors an advantage above all these great masters, is this, that they can multiply their originals, or, rather, can make copies of their works, to what number they please, which shall be as valuable as the originals themselves. This gives a great author a prospect of something like eternity. — If writings are thus durable, and may pass from age to age, throughout the whole course of time, how careful should an author be of committing anything to print, that may corrupt posterity, and poison the minds of men with vice and error!"

Solemnity.

Funeral Hymn.

"How still and peaceful is the grave,
　Where, — life's vain tumults past, —
The appointed house, by Heaven's decree,
　Receives us all at last!

"The wicked there from troubling cease, —
　Their passions rage no more;
And there the weary pilgrim rests
　From all the toils he bore.

"All, levelled by the hand of death,
Lie sleeping in the tomb,
Till God in judgment call them forth
To meet their final doom."

"*Orotund Quality.*"*

This mode of voice is characterized by peculiar *roundness, fullness*, and *resonance*, combining the "purity" of the "head tone" with the reverberation of the chest. It has a deeper effect than mere purity of tone, and usually ranges with the upper *bass* notes of the male voice; while the head tone has a lighter character, and seldom extends below the tenor level. Orotund quality is the natural mode of utterance in all *deep, powerful*, and *sublime* emotions. It belongs, accordingly, to *oratory*, and to the *bolder* forms of *poetry*.

Orotund utterance is, like pure tone, a most effective aid to easy and full voice. It serves to diminish the fatigue of vocal exertion, and, at the same time, to give out clear and agreeable sound: it renders the utmost force of energetic utterance easily practicable; and, by throwing vigor into the voice, it spares the lungs.

The remarks on frequency of practice in pure tone, apply also to orotund quality. Every exercise should be perfectly mastered before proceeding to another; and the

---

* The term "orotund" Dr. Rush has adopted from a modification of the Latin phrase "*ore rotundo.*" The word, as was mentioned before, is a good technical designation in elocution; as it not only intimates the peculiar *rotundity* of the proper voice for public speaking, but the special condition of the interior and back parts of the mouth, which its production requires. As a "quality" of voice, it is the natural resonance of notes of the middle and lower tenor and upper bass "register," when uttered in a round, full, and bold style, with the glottis freely opened, and all the circumjacent parts of the throat and mouth well expanded. An ample "laryngial" effect is thus produced: to this effect the technical term "orotund" is applied. See Orthophony.

practice should not cease till all the "tonic elements" can be easily and exactly executed in orotund style.

Pathos* and Sublimity.
Rome. — Byron.

"O Rome! my country! city of the soul!
  The orphans of the heart must turn to thee,
  Lone mother of dead empires! and control
  In their shut breasts, their petty misery.
  What are our woes and sufferance? — Come and see
  The cypress, hear the owl, and plod your way
  O'er steps of broken thrones and temples, Ye!
  Whose agonies are evils of a day: —
A world is at our feet as fragile as our clay.

"The Niobe of nations! there she stands,
  Childless and crownless, in her voiceless woe;
  An empty urn within her withered hands,
  Whose holy dust was scattered long ago; —
  The Scipios' tomb contains no ashes now;
  The very sepulchres lie tenantless
  Of their heroic dwellers: — dost thou flow,
  Old Tiber! through a marble wilderness?
Rise, with thy yellow waves, and mantle her distress!"

Repose, Solemnity, and Sublimity.
Evening. — Milton.

"Now came still evening on; and twilight gray
  Had in her sober livery all things clad:
  Silence accompanied; for beast and bird,
  They to their grassy couch, — these to their nests

---

* *Pathos, repose,* and *solemnity,* if united with *grandeur,* assume the orotund voice, although, without this union, they do not transcend the comparatively moderate limits of pure tone. The orotund is the distinctive quality of grandeur and power.

Were slunk, all but the wakeful nightingale; —
She, all night long, her amorous descant sung:
Silence was pleased. Now glowed the firmament
With living sapphires. Hesperus that led
The starry host, rode brightest, till the moon,
Rising in clouded majesty, at length,
Apparent queen, unveiled her peerless light,
And o'er the dark her silver mantle threw."

- Solemnity, Sublimity, and Pathos.

The Treasures of the Deep. — Mrs. Hemans.

" What hid'st thou in thy treasure-caves and cells,
Thou hollow-sounding and mysterious Main? —
Pale glistening pearls, and rain-bow colored shells,
Bright things which gleam unrecked of, and in vain. —
Keep, keep thy riches, melancholy Sea!
    We ask not such from thee.

" Yet more, the depths have more! — What wealth untold
Far down, and shining through their stillness lies!
Thou hast the starry gems, the burning gold,
Won from ten thousand royal argosies. —
Sweep o'er thy spoils, thou wild and wrathful main:
    Earth claims not these again.

" Yet more, the depths have more! — Thy waves have rolled
Above the cities of a world gone by!
Sand hath filled up the palaces of old,
Sea-weed o'ergrown the halls of revelry! —
Dash o'er them, Ocean, in thy scornful play:
    Man yields them to decay.

" Yet more, the billows and the depths have more:
High hearts and brave are gathered to thy breast.
They hear not now the booming waters roar;
The battle thunders will not break their rest. —

Keep thy red gold and gems, thou stormy grave : —
    Give back the true and brave!

" Give back the lost and lovely! those for whom
The place was kept at board and hearth so long,
The prayer went up, through midnight's breathless
    gloom,
And the vain yearnings woke 'mid festal song! —
Hold fast thy buried isles, thy towers o'erthrown, —
    But all is not thine own!

" To thee the love of woman hath gone down :
Dark flow thy tides o'er manhood's noble head,
O'er youth's bright locks, and beauty's flowery crown,—
Yet must thou hear a voice, — ' Restore the dead!' —
Earth shall reclaim her precious things from thee, —
    ' Restore the dead, thou Sea!' "

      Energy and Sublimity.

    Hallowed Ground. — Campbell.

" What's hallowed ground? — Has earth a clod
Its Maker meant not should be trod
By man, the image of his God, —
    Erect and free, —
Unscourged by Superstition's rod
    To bow the knee?

" That's hallowed ground, where, mourned and missed,
The lips repose our love has kissed;
But where's their memory's mansion? — Is 't
    Yon churchyard's bowers?
No : in ourselves their souls exist, —
    A part of ours.

" What hallows ground where heroes sleep? —
'T is not the sculptured piles you heap; —
In dews that heavens far distant weep

Their turf may bloom,
Or genii twine beneath the deep
Their coral tomb.

"But strew his ashes to the wind
Whose sword or voice has served mankind, —
And is he dead, whose glorious mind
Lifts thine, on high?
To live in hearts we leave behind,
Is not to die.

"Is 't death to fall for Freedom's right? —
He's dead alone, that lacks her light,
And murder sullies, in Heaven's sight,
The sword he draws.
What can alone ennoble fight? —
A noble cause!

"Give that! and welcome War to brace
Her drums, and rend heaven's reeking space: —
The colors planted face to face,
The charging cheer, —
Though death's pale horse lead on the chase, —
Shall still be dear; —

"And place our trophies where men kneel
To Heaven! — But Heaven rebukes my zeal. —
The cause of Truth and Human Weal,
O God above!
Transfer it from the sword's appeal
·To Peace and Love!

"Peace, Love! — the cherubim that twine
Their spread wings o'er Devotion's shrine, —
Prayers sound, in vain, and temples shine,
Where they are not. —
The heart alone can make divine
Religion's spot."

Joy and Sublimity.

Prophetic Anticipations. — Cowper.

" O scenes surpassing fable, and yet true,
Scenes of accomplished bliss; which who can see,
Though but in distant prospect, and not feel
His soul refreshed with foretaste of the joy?
Rivers of gladness water all the earth,
And clothe all climes with beauty: the reproach
Of barrenness is past. The fruitful field
Laughs with abundance; and the land, once lean,
Or fertile only in its own disgrace,
Exults to see its thirsty curse repealed.
The various seasons woven into one,
And that one season an eternal spring:
The garden fears no blight, and needs no fence;
For there is none to covet, — all are full.
The lion, and the libbard, and the bear,
Graze with the fearless flocks; all bask at noon
Together, or all gambol in the shade
Of the same grove, and drink one common stream.
Antipathies are none. No foe to man
Lurks in the serpent now: the mother sees,
And smiles to see, her infant's playful hand
Stretched forth to dally with the crested worm,
To stroke its azure neck, or to receive
The lambent homage of his arrowy tongue.
All creatures worship man, and all mankind
One Lord, one Father. Error has no place:
That creeping pestilence is driven away;
The breath of heaven has chased it. In the heart
No passion touches a discordant string;
But all is harmony and love. Disease
Is not: the pure and uncontaminated blood
Holds its due course, nor fears the frost of age.
One song employs all nations; and all cry,
 ' Worthy the Lamb! for he was slain for us.'

>   The dwellers in the vales and on the rocks
>   Shout to each other; and the mountain tops
>   From distant mountains catch the flying joy;
>   Till, — nation after nation taught the strain, —
>   Earth rolls the rapturous hosanna round."

Awe and Sublimity.

The Final Judgment. — Horsley.

"God hath warned us, — and let them, who dare to extenuate the warning, ponder the dreadful curse with which the Book of Prophecy is sealed, — 'If any man shall take away from the words of the book of this prophecy; God shall take away his part out of the book of life:' — God hath warned us, that the inquiry into every man's conduct will be public; — Christ himself the Judge, — the whole race of man, and the whole angelic host, spectators of the awful scene.

"Before that assembly, every man's good deeds will be declared, and his most secret sins disclosed. As no elevation of rank will then give a title to respect, no obscurity of condition shall exclude the just from public honor, or screen the guilty from public shame. Opulence will find itself no longer powerful; — poverty will be no longer weak; — birth will no longer be distinguished; — meanness will no longer pass unnoticed. The rich and poor will indeed strangely meet together, when all the inequalities of the present life shall disappear; and the conqueror and his captive, — the monarch and his subject, — the lord and his vassal, — the statesman and the peasant, — the philosopher and the unlettered hind, — shall find their distinctions to have been mere illusions. The characters and actions of the greatest and the meanest have, in truth, been equally important, and equally public; while the eye of the omniscient God has been equally upon them all, — while all are at last equally brought to answer to their common Judge, and the angels stand around spectators, equally interested in the dooms of all.

"The sentence of every man will be pronounced by him who cannot be merciful to those who shall have willingly sold themselves to that abject bondage from which he died to purchase their redemption, — who, nevertheless, having felt the power of temptation, knows to pity them that have been tempted; by him on whose mercy contrite frailty may rely, — whose anger hardened impenitence must dread.

"To heighten the solemnity and terror of the business, the Judge will visibly descend from heaven, — the shout of the archangels and the trumpet of the Lord will thunder through the deep, — the dead will awake, — the glorified saints will be caught up to meet the Lord in the air; while the wicked will in vain call upon the mountains and the rocks to cover them.

"Of the day and hour when these things shall be, knoweth no man; but the day and hour for these things are fixed in the eternal Father's counsels. Our Lord will come, — he will come unlooked for, and may come sooner than we think."

EXERCISES IN FORCE.

The thorough discipline of the voice, for the purposes of public speaking, extends from whispering to shouting, — not with a view, in the case of these extremes, to the actual use of them, in the exercise of reading but for the purpose of reaching the natural limits of capability, and securing a perfect command over every degree of force, whether for acquiring organic power, and pliancy of voice, or ensuring command of expression as dependent on any degree of loudness.

The following exercises, and the elements, of all three classes, tonic, subtonic, and atonic, should be repeated several times, daily, for months, till their effect is fully felt in strengthening and compacting the sounds of the voice, and rendering the production of any degree of force an easy and agreeable exercise. Diligent cultivation in this department of elocution, for even a few weeks, will impart a stentorian power of vocal effort to persons whose volume of voice was previously insufficient, and whose degree of organic vigor, as well as their expressive power, in actual utterance, was very low.

Suppressed Force. (Whisper and half whisper.)*
Awe and Tenderness.
Evening Prayer at a Girls' School. — Mrs. Hemans.
" Hush ! 'tis a holy hour : — the quiet room
  Seems like a temple, while yon soft lamp sheds
A faint and starry radiance, through the gloom
  And the sweet stillness, down on young bright heads,
With all their clustering locks, untouched by care,
And bowed,— as flowers are bowed with night,— in prayer.

" Gaze on, — 't is lovely ! — childhood's lip and cheek,
  Mantling beneath its earnest brow of thought :
Gaze — yet what seest thou in those fair and meek
  And fragile things, as but for sunshine wrought ? —
Thou seest what grief must nurture for the sky,
What death must fashion for eternity !"

Subdued Force. (Softened Utterance : " Pure Tone.")
Pathos.
The Death of Reynolds. — J. Montgomery.
" Behold the bed of death, —
  This pale and lovely clay !
Heard ye the sob of parting breath ?
  Marked ye the eye's last ray ?

---

* All passages of deep awe, require a degree of suppression, and hence of "aspiration," or breathing effect, which always produces more or less impurity of tone, in consequence of the restraining effect of awe upon the organs, and the unavoidable escape of unvocalized breath, along with the sound of the voice.

No; — life so sweetly ceased to be,
It lapsed in immortality.

" Could tears revive the dead,
    Rivers should swell our eyes;
Could sighs recall the spirit fled,
    We would not quench our sighs,
Till love relumed this altered mien,
And all the embodied soul were seen.

" Bury the dead; — and weep
    In stillness o'er the loss;
Bury the dead; — *[in Christ *they* sleep,
    Who bore on earth his cross;
And from the grave their dust shall rise,
In his own image to the skies."]

Moderate Force.†

Serenity. [Exemplified in Verse.]
Scene after a Tempest. — Bryant.

" It was a scene of peace; — and like a spell
    Did that serene and golden sunlight fall
Upon the motionless wood that clothed the fell,
    And precipice upspringing like a wall,
    And glassy river and white waterfall,
And happy living things that trod the bright
    And beauteous scene; while far beyond them all,
On many a lovely valley, out of sight,   [light.
Was poured from the blue heavens the same soft golden

" I looked, and thought the quiet of the scene
    An emblem of the peace that yet shall be,
When, o'er earth's continents and isles between,
    The noise of war shall cease from sea to sea,

---

  * The lines within brackets exemplify a change of expression from the *subdued* voice of *pathos* to the *moderate* and *cheerful* tones of *serenity* and *hope*.

  † The usual degree of force in the unempassioned style of **sentiment**.

And married nations dwell in harmony;
When millions crouching in the dust to one,
    No more shall beg their lives on bended knee,
Nor the black stake be dressed, nor in the sun
The o'erlabored captive toil, and wish his life were done.

" Too long, at clash of arms, amid her bowers,
    And pools of blood, the earth has stood aghast, —
The fair earth that should only blush with flowers
    And ruddy fruits; but not for aye can last
The storm, — and sweet the sunshine when 't is past.
Lo! the clouds roll away; they break, — they fly;
    And, like the glorious light of summer, cast
O'er the wide landscape from the embracing sky,
On all the peaceful world the smile of heaven shall lie."

Serenity. [Exemplified in Prose.]*

Good Intention. — Addison.

" If we apply a good intention to all our actions, we make our very existence one continued act of obedience; we turn even our diversions and amusements to our eternal advantage, and are pleasing Him whom we are made to please, in all the circumstances and occurrences of life.

† " It is this excellent frame of mind, this holy officiousness, (if I may be allowed to call it such,) which is recommended to us by the apostle, in that uncommon precept wherein he directs us to propose to ourselves the glory of our Creator, in all our most indifferent actions, 'whether we eat, or drink, or whatsoever we do.'

---

* The usual style of essays, lectures, expository and practical discourses, and other forms of didactic address.

† The ordinary rule of elocution prescribes a *diminishing* of the force of the voice at the opening of a new paragraph. But when, as in the text, there is a vivid turn of thought introduced, the opposite rule prevails, and the force increases with the momentum of the additional mental impulse.

*" A person who is possessed with an habitual good intention, enters upon no single circumstance of life, without considering it as well pleasing to the great Author of his being, conformable to the dictates of reason, suitable to human nature in general, or to that particular station in which Providence has placed him. He lives in the perpetual sense of the Divine presence, regards himself as acting, in the whole course of his existence, under the observation and inspection of that Being who is privy to all his emotions and all his thoughts, who knows his 'downsitting and his uprising, who is about his path and about his bed, and spieth out all his ways.' In a word, he remembers that the eye of his Judge is always upon him; and, in every action, he reflects that he is doing what is commanded or allowed by Him who will hereafter either reward or punish it. This was the character of those holy men of old, who, in the beautiful phrase of Scripture, are said to have 'walked with God.'"

Declamatory Force.†

Energetic Emotion.

The Slave Trade. — Webster.

"I deem it my duty, on this occasion, to suggest, that the land is not yet wholly free from the contamination of a traffic at which every feeling of humanity must revolt, — I mean the African slave trade. Neither public senti-

---

* The usual rule of slackening the tension of voice at the opening of a new paragraph, is exemplified here; as, in such cases, the train of thought is either resumed, or commenced anew. The force, therefore, is progressive in the sentence. All well composed sentences are naturally read with the growing force of climax. The same remark applies to paragraphs and larger portions of a discourse.

† The word "declamatory" is used, in elocution, as the designation of the full, bold style of oratory, in warm and forcible address. The sense thus attached to the word, it will be perceived, is special and technical, merely, and implies no imputation on the character of the sentiment or the language, as in the rhetorical and popular uses of the term.

ment nor the law has yet been able entirely to put an end to this odious and abominable traffic. At the moment when God, in his mercy, has blessed the world with a universal peace, there is reason to fear, that, to the disgrace of the Christian name and character, new efforts are making for the extension of this trade, by subjects and citizens of Christian States, in whose hearts no sentiment of justice inhabits, and over whom neither the fear of God nor the fear of man exercises a control. In the sight of our law, the African slave trader is a pirate and a felon; and in the sight of Heaven, an offender far beyond the ordinary depth of human guilt. There is no brighter part of our history, than that which records the measures which have been adopted by the government, at an early day, and at different times since, for the suppression of this traffic; and I would call upon all the true sons of New England, to coöperate with the laws of man and the justice of Heaven.

"If there be, within the extent of our knowledge or influence, any participation of this traffic, let us pledge ourselves here, upon the Rock of Plymouth, to extirpate and destroy it. It is not fit that the land of the pilgrims should bear the shame longer. — I hear the sound of the hammer — I see the smoke of the furnaces where manacles and fetters are still forged for human limbs. I see the visages of those who, by stealth, and at midnight, labor in this work of hell, foul and dark, as may become the artificers of such instruments of misery and torture. Let that spot be purified, or let it cease to be of New England. Let it be purified, or let it be set aside from the Christian world; let it be put out of the circle of human sympathies and human regards; and let civilized man henceforth have no communion with it.

"I would invoke those who fill the seats of justice, and all who minister at her altar, that they execute the wholesome and necessary severity of the law. I invoke the ministers of our religion, that they proclaim its denunciation of these crimes, and add its solemn sanctions, to the authority of human law. If the pulpit be silent, whenever or wherever there may be a sinner, bloody with this guilt, within the hearing of its voice, the pulpit is false to its trust."

Empassioned Force.*

Imprecation.

Faliero's Dying Curse on Venice. — Byron.

" Ye elements! in which to be resolved
I hasten, let my voice be as a spirit
Upon you! — Ye blue waves! which bore my banner, —
Ye winds! which fluttered o'er as if ye loved it,
And filled my swelling sails, as they were wafted
To many a triumph! Thou, my native earth,
Which I have bled for! and thou foreign earth,
Which drank this willing blood from many a wound!
Ye stones, in which my gore will not sink, but
Reek up to heaven! Ye skies, which will receive it!
Thou sun! which shinest on these things, and Thou!
Who kindlest and who quenchest suns! — attest!
I am not innocent — but are these guiltless?
I perish, but not unavenged: far ages
Float up from the abyss of time to be,
And show these eyes, before they close, the doom
Of this proud city; and I leave my curse
On her and hers forever. ———

" Then, in the last gasp of thine agony,
Amidst thy many murders, think of *mine!*
Thou den of drunkards with the blood of princes!
Gehenna of the waters! thou sea Sodom!

---

* The style in which utterance becomes intense, and greatly transcends even the usual energy or vehemence of declamation. This degree of force is, generally speaking, restricted to poetry, or to prose of the highest character as to emotion.

Thus I devote thee to the infernal gods
Thee and thy serpent seed!"

*Shouting.**
Exultation.
The Exclamations of Tell, on his Escape. — Knowles.
" Ye crags and peaks, I'm with you once again!
I hold to you the hands you first beheld,
To show they still are free!

" Ye guards of liberty,
I'm with you once again! — I call to you
With all my voice! — I hold my hands to you,
To show they still are free!"

Calling.†
[As in the case of the greatest distance between the speaker and the hearers.]
Command.
The Herald's Message. — Shakspeare.
" Rejoice ye men of Angiers! Ring your bells!
Open your gates, and give the victors way!"

EXERCISES IN "STRESS."

" Stress" may be briefly defined as the term used in elocution to designate the mode and the place of forming

---

* This form of voice, although seldom exemplified in actual oratory, unless in vehement address in the open air. is of immense value, as an exercise for invigorating the organs and strengthening the voice. in orotund quality. Its effects, when practiced a few times daily, for even a few weeks, are such as to impart great volume and power of utterance to persons who commence the exercise with weak organs and imperfect tone.

† The effect of this exercise is to give compactness, and clearness, and purity of tone, to the utmost extent of voice. The call, although rising to a high note, with great loudness, should always be kept perfectly vocal or musical in its sound, resembling the easy, smooth effect of the loudest singing, in its gradual and skilful swell. It is nothing else than the *maximum* of "*pure*" or "*head* tone."

the *maximum* of force in a single sound. Thus, in the appropriate utterance of some emotions, the force of the voice bursts out suddenly, with a percussive *explosion;* as in angry command, in which vocal sound is intended to vent the passion of the speaker, and to startle and terrify the hearer. An example occurs in the burst of *fierceness* and *wrath* with which Death replies to Satan : " *Back* to thy punishment, false fugitive!" We may contrast with this form of stress the *gentle swell* of *reverence* and *adoration*, in the devotional language of Adam and Eve in their morning hymn, in paradise: " *Hail!* universal Lord!" The utterance of the word "*Back*," in the former instance, exemplifies "explosive" "radical" (initial) "stress," which bursts out, with percussive abruptness, on the initial or first part of the sound; that of the word " *Hail*," in the latter, "median," (middle,) as gently swelling out to its maximum on the *middle* of the sound, whence it diminishes to the end or "vanish." Another mode of stress,— termed "vanishing,"— withholds the abrupt explosion till the last particle (so to speak) of the empassioned sound, and then throws it out with a wrenching and jerking violence on the very "vanish," or last audible point of voice. This form of stress occurs in the tones of *ungovernable impatience, deep, determined will,* and *excessive* or *inconsolable grief.* Of the first of these emotions we have an example in the mad impatience of Queen Constance, when protesting against the peace between France and England, which was to sacrifice the rights of her son. " War! war!— no peace! Peace is to me a war!" Of the second we have an instance in the reply of the Swiss deputy to Charles the Bold, when he is announcing to the Duke the final determination of the cantons to resist, to the last, the invasion of their rights. " Sooner than submit we will *starve* in the icy wastes of the glaciers!" Of the third, in the Psalmist's exclamation, " My God! my God! why hast thou forsaken me?"

A fourth mode of stress unites the "radical **and the**

vanishing" on the same syllable, by an *abrupt jerk* of force on the *first* and *last* portions of the empassioned sound. This is the natural expression of *astonishment*, and is displayed with peculiar vividness, when the speaker reïterates the words of another person. An example occurs in the exclamation of Queen Constance, when she hears, for the first time, of the conditions of the peace between France and England, and repeats the words of the messenger. "*Gone* to be *married!*—*gone* to swear a *peace!*"

A fifth form of stress,—peculiar to intense emotions,—throws out the voice, with the utmost force, on all the points of a sound which admit of being rendered conspicuous or prominent,—the *beginning*, the *middle*, and the *end*. This mode of utterance in emphatic syllables, is, from its pervading effect, termed "thorough" stress. It is exemplified in the shout of *defiance*, with which Fitz-James addresses the band of Roderic Dhu,

"Come one, come *all!* This rock shall fly
From its firm base as soon as I."*

Empassioned " Radical Stress."
Bold, angry, and threatening Command.
[Abrupt, explosive style of utterance.]
Satan's Address to Death.—Milton.

" Whence, and what art thou? execrable shape!
That dar'st, though grim and terrible, advance
Thy miscreated front athwart my way
To yonder gates? Through them I mean to pass,
That be assured,—without leave asked of thee.
Retire, or taste thy folly, and learn by proof,
Hell-born! not to contend with spirits of heaven!"

---

* The explanations and examples given in the text, will, it is thought, serve to render the requisite distinctions plain. But fuller statements may be referred to in Dr. Rush's Philosophy of the Voice, or in the manual of Orthophony.

Courageous Sentiment and Eloquent Address.

[Energetic expulsive style.]*

Supposed Speech of John Adams. — Webster.

" Read the declaration of our independence at the head of the army, — every sword will be drawn from its scabbard, and the solemn vow uttered, to maintain it, or to perish on the bed of honor. Publish it from the pulpit, — religion will approve it; and the love of religious liberty will cling round it, resolved to stand with it, or fall with it. Send it to the public halls, — proclaim it there, — let them hear it, who heard the first roar of the enemy's cannon, — let them see it, who saw their brothers and their sons fall on the field of Bunker Hill, and in the streets of Lexington and Concord; — and the very walls will cry out in its support!"

Unempassioned " Radical Stress." †

Earnestness and elevation of Thought.

The Progress of Discovery. — Anon.

" Are the properties of matter all discovered? — its laws all found out? — the uses to which they may be applied, all detected? I cannot believe it. — The progress which has been made in art and science, is, indeed, vast. We are ready to think that a pause must follow, that the goal must be at hand. But there is no goal, and there can be no pause; for art and science are in themselves progressive. They are moving powers, animated principles: they are instinct with life; they are themselves the intellectual life of man. Nothing can arrest them, which

---

* A vivid initial force, without abruptness or violence.

† This style, though utterly free from empassioned vehemence, preserves the abrupt explosive opening of sound, to the extent required by distinct articulation, for vivid intellectual impression. The effect to the ear is like that, comparatively, of the clear tinkle of the falling icicle, or of the drop of rain, — a moderate, but remarkably clear sound.

does not plunge the entire order of society into barbarism. There is no end to truth, no bound to its discovery and application; and a man might as well think to build a tower, from the top of which he could grasp Sirius in his hand, as prescribe a limit to discovery and invention."

"*Median Stress.*"
Solemnity and Reverence.
Adoration offered by the Angels.— Milton.

" Thee, Father, first they sung, omnipotent,
Immutable, immortal, infinite,
Eternal King; thee, Author of all being,
Fountain of light, thyself invisible
Amidst the glorious brightness where thou sitt'st,
Throned inaccessible, but when thou shad'st,
The full blaze of thy beams, and through a cloud,
Drawn round about thee, like a radiant shrine,
Dark with excessive bright, thy skirts appear,
Yet dazzle heaven, that brightest seraphim
Approach not, but with both wings veil their eyes"

Pathos.
Extract from Psalm CIII.

V. 13. "Like as a father pitieth his children, so the Lord pitieth them that fear him. 14. For he knoweth our frame; he remembereth that we are dust. 15. As for man, his days are as grass: as a flower of the field so he flourisheth. 16. For the wind passeth over it, and it is gone; and the place thereof shall know it no more."

Tranquility.
Psalm XXIII.

V. 1. "The Lord is my shepherd: I shall not want. 2. He maketh me to lie down in green pastures: he leadeth me beside the still waters. 3. He restoreth my soul; he leadeth me in the paths of righteousness, for his name's sake. 4. Yea, though I walk through the valley of the shadow of death, I will fear no evil: for thou art with me; thy rod and thy staff they comfort me. 5. Thou preparest a table before me in the presence of mine enemies: thou anointest my head with oil; my cup runneth over. 6. Surely goodness and mercy shall follow me, all the days of my life; and I will dwell in the house of the Lord forever."

"*Vanishing Stress.*"
Complaint.
Job's Reply to his Friends. — Job XIX.

V. 2. "How long will ye vex my soul, and break me in pieces with words? 3. These ten times have ye reproached me: ye are not ashamed that ye make yourselves strange to me.

6. "Know, now, that God hath overthrown me, and hath compassed me with his net. 7. Behold, I cry out of wrong, but I am not heard: I cry aloud, but there is no judgment. 8. He hath fenced up my way that I cannot pass, and he hath set darkness in my paths. 9. He hath stripped me of my glory, and taken the crown from my head. 10. He hath destroyed me, on every side, and I am gone; and my hope hath he removed like a tree."

Denunciation.
Extract from Isaiah XXXIV.

V. 5. "My sword shall be bathed in heaven: behold, it shall come down upon Idumea, and upon the people of my curse to judgment." "9. And the streams thereof shall be turned into pitch, and the dust thereof into brimstone, and the land thereof shall become burning pitch. 10. It shall not be quenched night nor day; the smoke thereof shall go up forever: from generation to generation it shall be waste; none shall pass through it forever and ever."

"*Compound Stress.*"
Interrogation.
Extract from Job XLI.

V. 1. " Canst thou draw out leviathan with a hook? or his tongue with a cord which thou lettest down? 2. Canst thou put a hook into his nose? or bore his jaw through with a thorn? 3. Will he make many supplications unto thee? will he speak soft words unto thee? 4. Will he make a covenant with thee? wilt thou take him for a servant forever? 5. Wilt thou play with him as with a bird? or wilt thou bind him for thy maidens?"

Extracts from I. *Corinthians* XII. *Chapter.*

V. 15. " If the foot shall say, Because I am not the hand, I am not of the body; is it therefore not of the body? 16. And if the ear shall say, Because I am not the eye, I am not of the body; is it therefore not of the body?"

29. " Are all apostles? are all prophets? are all teachers? are all workers of miracles? 30. Have all the gifts of healing? do all speak with tongues? do all interpret?"

" *Thorough Stress.*"
Vehement Denunciation.
Extract from Isaiah XXVIII.

V. 1. " Wo to the crown of pride, to the drunkards of Ephraim, whose glorious beauty is a fading flower, which are on the head of the fat valleys of them that are overcome with wine! 2. Behold, the Lord hath a mighty and strong one, which, as a tempest of hail and a destroying storm, as a flood of mighty waters overflowing, shall cast down to the earth with the hand. 3. The crown of pride, the drunkards of Ephraim, shall be trodden under feet."

Joyous Command.
Extract from Isaiah LII.

V. 1. "Awake, awake, put on thy strength, O Zion; put on thy beautiful garments, O Jerusalem, the holy city: for henceforth there shall no more come into thee the uncircumcised and the unclean. 2. Shake thyself from the dust; arise, and sit down, O Jerusalem: loose thyself from the bands of thy neck, O captive daughter of Zion."

Indignant Rebuke.
Extract from Isaiah I.

V. 10. "Hear the word of the Lord, ye rulers of Sodom: give ear unto the law of our God, ye people of Gomorrah. 11. To what purpose is the multitude of your sacrifices unto me? saith the Lord: I am full of the burnt-offerings of rams, and the fat of fed beasts; and I delight not in the blood of bullocks, or of lambs, or of he-goats. 12. When ye come to appear before me, who hath required this at your hand, to tread my courts? 13. Bring no more vain oblations: incense is an abomination unto me: the new-moons and sabbaths, the calling of assemblies, I cannot away with; it is iniquity, even the solemn meeting. 14. Your new-moons and your appointed feasts my soul hateth: they are a trouble unto me; I am weary to bear them. 15. And when ye spread forth your hands, I will hide mine eyes from you; yea, when ye make many prayers, I will not hear: your hands are full of blood."

Courage and Energy.
Stanzas of a hortatory Hymn.

"Awake, my soul! — stretch every nerve,
    And press with vigor on:
A heavenly race demands thy zeal,
    A bright, immortal crown.

"'T is God's all-animating voice
That calls thee from on high;
'T is his own hand presents the prize
To thine aspiring eye."

EXERCISES IN PITCH.

*Middle Pitch.**

Emotion progressive from Seriousness to Cheerfulness and Animation.

Hope. — Addison.

" No life is so happy as that which is full of hope, especially when the hope is well-grounded, and when the object of it is of an exalted kind, and in its nature proper to make the person happy, who enjoys it. This proposition must be self-evident to those who consider how few are the present enjoyments of the most happy man, and how insufficient to give him an entire satisfaction and acquiescence in them.

†" My next observation is this; that a religious life is

---

* The average level of the voice in public reading or speaking, — in the form of lectures, practical and doctrinal discourses, and unempassioned address, — a pitch somewhat lower than the middle notes of conversation; as the former implies graver tone.

† The new pitch with which every new paragraph properly commences, is a point of the greatest moment in elocution, as deciding the natural and appropriate style of reading, and distinguishing it from that which is mechanical and unimpressive. True reading causes the paragraphs of a piece, and the heads of a discourse, to indicate the change which is taking place in the current and direction of the thought. Every new topic, subordinate, as well as principal, requires a new shade of voice, in pitch, as higher or lower than the average tone of the preceding paragraph. The same remark applies to single sentences. The common fault, derived from school habits, is to rise to a new and higher pitch, at the beginning of every sentence or paragraph, and gradually fall in the successive clauses or sentences. Correct reading varies the pitch according to the connection existing between sentences, and commences on the low note of the cadence of the preceding sentence or par-

that which most abounds in a well-grounded hope, and such a one as is fixed on objects that are capable of making us entirely happy. This hope, in a religious man, is much more sure and certain than the hope of any temporal blessing; as it is strengthened not only by reason but by faith. It has, at the same time, its eye perpetually fixed on that state which implies, in the very notion of it, the most full and the most complete happiness.

*" Religious hope does not only bear up the mind, under sufferings, but makes her rejoice in them, as they may be the instruments of procuring her the great and ultimate end of all her hope. Religious hope has likewise this advantage above any other kind of hope, that it is able to revive the *dying* man, and to fill his mind not only with comfort, but with rapture and transport. He triumphs in his agonies, while the soul springs forward with delight to the great object which she has always had in view, and leaves the body with an expectation of being re-united to it in a glorious and joyful resurrection."

---

agraph, when the sense is continuous or analogous, but rises to a new and a higher strain, only when there is a new, a distinct, or an opposite thought in the new sentence or paragraph. On the other hand, a new sentence or paragraph, opening with a graver mood of sentiment, begins, properly, with a lower pitch than, perhaps, even the cadence of the preceding context.

The opening of a new paragraph should, generally, be lower in pitch than the strain of utterance in the preceding part of a discourse. But when, as in the example to which the present note refers, the speaker intimates, in the beginning of a paragraph, the plan or order of his discourse, the voice is higher in pitch, as well as slacker in force; so as to keep the main subject of address distinct from the parenthetical allusions to the speaker's train of thought for the time. The practical rule of elocution, for the commencing pitch of paragraphs is, usually, Begin anew; i. e., Slacken the force, lower the pitch, and retard the rate of the voice. This rule is founded on the obvious principle that it is not till progress has been made in a sentence or paragraph, that the new impulse of thought is felt in the force, pitch, and movement of the voice.

* An example of the usual lower pitch of a new paragraph.

Low Pitch.

Grave Emotion.

Man is born to Trouble. — Finlayson.

"That no man can promise to himself perpetual exemption from suffering, is a truth obvious to daily observation. Nay, amid the shiftings of the scene in which we are placed, who can say that, for one hour, his happiness is secure? The openings through which we may be assailed, are so numerous and unguarded, that the very next moment may see some message of pain piercing the bulwarks of our peace. Our body may become the seat of incurable disease. Our mind may become a prey to unaccountable and imaginary fears. Our fortune may sink in some of those revolutionary tempests which overwhelm so often the treasures of the wealthy. Our honors may wither on our brow, blasted by the slanderous breath of an enemy. Our friends may prove faithless in the hour of need, or they may be separated from us forever. Our children, the fondest hope of our hearts, may be torn from us in their prime; or they may wound us still more deeply by their undutifulness and misconduct.

"Alas! my brother of the dust, in this uncertainty of worldly blessings, where is the joy on earth, in which thou canst repose thy confidence? or what defence canst thou rear against the inroads of adversity? Dost thou hope that by rising to power, or by increasing thy goods, thou wilt insure the continuance of thy comfort? Vain man! hast thou not seen that the loftiest mountain meets first the lightnings of the sky, and that the spreading tree, when loaded with the glories of its foliage and fruit, is most easily broken by the fury of the blast? In this manner, the children of this world, by multiplying their stores and extending their connections, furnish a broader mark to the arrows of misfortune, and with **the greater certainty suffer disappointment and sorrow.**"

Sublime Emotion.

The Works and Attributes of God. — Moodie.

"All vast and unmeasurable objects are fitted to impress the soul with awe. The mountain which rises above the neighboring hills, and hides its head in the sky, — the sounding, unfathomed, boundless deep, — the expanse of Heaven, where, above and around, no limit checks the wandering eye; — these objects fill and elevate the mind, — they produce a solemn frame of spirit, which accords with the sentiment of religion.

"From the contemplation of what is great and magnificent in nature, the soul rises to the Author of all. We think of the time which preceded the birth of the universe, when no being existed but God alone. While unnumbered systems arise in order before us, created by his power, arranged by his wisdom, and filled with his presence, — the earth and the sea, with all that they contain, are hardly beheld amidst the immensity of his works. In the boundless subject the soul is lost. It is he who 'sitteth on the circle of the earth, and the inhabitants thereof are as grasshoppers. He weigheth the mountains in scales. He taketh up the isles as a very little thing.' 'Lord, what is man that thou art mindful of him!'

"The face of nature is sometimes clothed with terror. The tempest overturns the cedars of Lebanon, or discloses the secrets of the deep. The pestilence wastes, — the lightning consumes, — the voice of the thunder is heard on high. Let these appearances be connected with the power of God. These are the awful ministers of his kingdom. 'The Lord reigneth, let the people tremble. Who would not fear thee, O King of nations! By the greatness of thy power thine enemies are constrained to bow.'"

Pathetic Emotion.

Autumnal Meditation instructive to the Aged. — Alison.

"There is an eventide in human life, a season when the eye becomes dim, and the strength decays, and when the winter of age begins to shed upon the human head its prophetic snow. It is the season of life to which autumn is most analogous; and much it becomes, and much it would profit you, to mark the instructions which the season brings. The spring and the summer of your days are gone, and with them, not only the joys they knew, but many of the friends who gave them. You have entered upon the autumn of your being; and whatever may have been the profusion of your spring, or the warm intemperance of your summer, there is yet a season of stillness and of solitude, which the benificence of Heaven affords you, in which you may meditate upon the past and the future, and prepare yourselves for the mighty change which you are soon to undergo.

"If it be thus you have the wisdom to use the decaying season of nature, it brings with it consolations more valuable than all the enjoyments of former days. In the long retrospect of your journey, you have seen every day the shades of the evening fall, and every year the clouds of winter gather. But you have seen also, every succeeding day, the morning arise in its brightness, and in every succeeding year, the spring return to renovate the winter of nature. It is now you may understand the magnificent language of Heaven, — it mingles its voice with that of revelation, — it summons you, in these hours when the leaves fall, and the winter is gathering, to that evening study which the mercy of Heaven has provided in the book of salvation; and while the shadowy valley opens which leads to the abode of death, it speaks of that Hand which can comfort and can save, and which can conduct to those 'green pastures, and those still waters,' where there is an eternal spring for the children of God."

Grave, Sublime, and Pathetic Emotions.
Marathon and Athens. — Byron.

"Where'er we tread, 't is haunted holy ground;
No earth of thine is lost in vulgar mould!
But one vast realm of wonder spreads around;
And all the Muse's tales seem truly told,
Till the sense aches with gazing to behold
The scenes our earliest dreams have dwelt upon:
Each hill and dale, each deepening glen and wold,
Defies the power which crushed thy temples gone:
Age shakes Athena's tower, but spares gray Marathon.

"Yet to the remnants of thy splendor past,
Shall pilgrims, pensive, but unwearied, throng;
Long shall the voyager, with the Ionian blast,
Hail the bright clime of battle and of song;
Long shall thine annals and immortal tongue
Fill with thy fame the youth of many a shore;
Boast of the aged! lesson of the young!
Which sages venerate and bards adore,
As Pallas and the Muse unveil their awful lore.

"Ancient of days! august Athena! where,
Where are thy men of might? thy grand in soul?
Gone — glimmering through the dream of things that
First in the race that led to Glory's goal,   [were!
They won, and passed away — Is this the whole?
A schoolboy's tale, the wonder of an hour!
The warrior's weapon and the sophist's stole
Are sought in vain; and o'er each mouldering tower,
Dim with the mist of years, gray flits the shade of power."

Lowest Pitch.*

Solemnity, Awe, and Reverence.

Devotion.— Young.

" O thou great Arbiter of life and death!
Nature's immortal, immaterial sun!
Whose all-prolific beam late called me forth
From darkness, teeming darkness, where I lay
The worm's inferior; and, in rank, beneath
The dust I tread on; high to bear my brow,
To drink the spirit of the golden day,
And triumph in existence; and couldst know
No motive but my bliss; and hast ordained
A rise in blessing! with the Patriarch's joy
Thy call I follow to the land unknown:
I trust in thee, and know in whom I trust:
Or life or death is equal: neither weighs;
All weight in this — Oh! let me live to thee!"

Meditation.— Id.

" How is night's sable mantle labored o'er,
How richly wrought, with attributes divine!
What wisdom shines! what love! This midnight pomp,
This gorgeous arch with golden worlds inlaid!
Built with divine ambition! — nought to Thee, —
For others this profusion. — Thou, apart,
Above, beyond, Oh! tell me, mighty Mind!
Where art thou? — shall I dive into the deep?
Call to the sun? or ask the roaring winds
For their Creator? Shall I question loud
The thunder, if in that the Almighty dwells?

---

* The lowest notes of the voice are naturally accompanied by "pectoral quality," since the extremely wide opening of the glottis, inseparable from their formation, is necessarily attended by resonance in the chest, as may be observed in the act of singing deep-toned bass strains.

Or holds He furious storms in straitened reins,
And bids fierce whirlwinds wheel his rapid car?
What mean these questions? — Trembling I retract:
My prostrate soul adores the present God!

very deep   Sublimity and Awe.

Extract from Psalm XVIII.

V. 7. "Then the earth shook and trembled; the foundations also of the hills moved and were shaken, because He was wroth. 8. There went up a smoke out of his nostrils, and fire out of his mouth devoured: coals were kindled by it. 9. He bowed the heavens also, and came down; and darkness was under his feet. 10. And he rode upon a cherub and did fly: yea, he did fly upon the wings of the wind. 11. He made darkness his secret place; his pavilion round about him were dark waters and thick clouds of the skies. 12. At the brightness that was before him his thick clouds passed, hailstones and coals of fire. 13. The Lord also thundered in the heavens, and the Highest gave his voice; hailstones and coals ot fire. 14. Yea, he sent out his arrows, and scattered them; and he shot out lightnings, and discomfited them. 15. Then the channels of waters were seen, and the foundations of the world were discovered at thy rebuke, O Lord, at the blast of the breath of thy nostrils."

Deep Grief.

Extract from Jeremiah. IX. CHAP.

V. 1. "Oh! that my head were waters, and mine eyes a fountain of tears, that I might weep day and night for the slain of the daughter of my people! 2. Oh! that I had in the wilderness a lodging-place of way-faring men, that I might leave my people and go from them! for they be all adulterers, an assembly of treacherous men."

Despondency and Despair.

Extract from Job. XVII. Chap.

V. 11. "My days are past; my purposes are broken off, even the thoughts of my heart. 12. They change the night into day; the light is short because of the darkness. 13. If I wait, the grave is my house: I have made my bed in darkness. 14. I have said to corruption, Thou art my father: to the worm, Thou art my mother and my sister. 15. And where is now my hope? as for my hope who shall see it? 16. They shall go down to the bars of the pit, when our rest together is in the dust."

Awe and Horror.

Stanzas of a Death Hymn. — Scott.

" That day of wrath! that dreadful day,
When heaven and earth shall pass away!
What power shall be the sinner's stay?
How shall he meet that dreadful day, —

" When, shrivelling like a parched scroll,
The flaming heavens together roll;
And louder yet, and yet more dread,
Swells the high trump that wakes the dead?"

*High Pitch.**

Joy.

Sympathy of Departed Spirits with Humanity. — Finlayson.

" What a delightful subject of contemplation does the thought of such sympathy open to the pious and benevo-

---

* The "high" pitch of sacred eloquence is, from the solemnity of association, lower in its note, than that of ordinary oratorical style. It rises but little above the middle tones of the voice. It requires, however, on this account, to be the more carefully observed, that the proper distinctions of utterance may not be lost.

lent mind! What a spring does it give to all the better energies of the heart! Your labors of love, your plans of beneficence, your swellings of satisfaction in the rising reputation of those whose virtues you have cherished, will not, we have reason to hope, be terminated by the stroke of death. No! your spirits will still linger around the objects of their former attachment. They will behold with rapture even the distant effects of those beneficent institutions which they once delighted to rear; they will watch, with a pious satisfaction, over the growing prosperity of the country which they loved; with a parent's fondness, and a parent's exultation, they will share in the fame of their virtuous posterity; and, by the permission of God, they may descend, at times, as guardian angels, to shield them from danger, and to conduct them to glory.

"Of all the thoughts that can enter the human mind, this is one of the most animating and consolatory. It scatters flowers around the bed of death. It enables us who are left behind, to support with firmness the departure of our best beloved friends; because it teaches us that they are not lost to us forever. They are still our friends. Though they be now gone to another apartment in our Father's house, they have carried with them the remembrance and the feeling of their former attachments. Though invisible to us, they bend from their dwelling on high to cheer us in our pilgrimage of duty, to rejoice with us in our prosperity, and, in the hour of virtuous exertion, to shed through our souls the blessedness of heaven."

Joy.
Extracts from Isaiah LX.

V. 1. "Arise, shine; for thy light is come, and the glory of the Lord is risen upon thee. 2. For, behold, the darkness shall cover the earth, and gross darkness the people: but the Lord shall arise upon thee, and his glory shall be seen upon thee. 3. And the Gentiles shall come to thy light, and kings to the brightness of thy rising. 4.

Lift up thine eyes round about, and see: all they gather themselves together, they come to thee: thy sons shall come from far, and thy daughters shall be nursed at thy side."

13. "The glory of Lebanon shall come unto thee, the fir-tree, the pine-tree, and the box together, to beautify the place of my sanctuary; and I will make the place of my feet glorious. 14. The sons also of them that afflicted thee shall come bending unto thee; and all they that despised thee shall bow themselves down at the soles of thy feet; and they shall call thee the city of the Lord, The Zion of the Holy One of Israel. 15. Whereas thou hast been forsaken and hated, so that no man went through thee, I will make thee an eternal excellency, a joy of many generations."

Consolation.

Extracts from Isaiah LXI.

V. 1. "The Spirit of the Lord God is upon me; because the Lord hath anointed me to preach good tidings unto the meek; he hath sent me to bind up the brokenhearted, to proclaim liberty to the captives, and the opening of the prison to them that are bound; 2. To proclaim the acceptable year of the Lord, and the day of vengeance of our God; to comfort all that mourn; 3. To appoint unto them that mourn in Zion, to give unto them beauty for ashes, the oil of joy for mourning, the garment of praise for the spirit of heaviness; that they might be called Trees of righteousness, The planting of the Lord, that he might be glorified."

Triumph.

Stanzas from a Hymn on the Advent.

"Hark! — the herald angels sing,
' Glory to the new-born king!
Peace on earth and mercy mild,
God and sinners reconciled!'

"Joyful all ye nations, rise,
Join the triumph of the skies;
With the angelic host proclaim,
'Christ is born in Bethlehem!'

"Hail the heaven-born Prince of Peace!
Hail the Son of Righteousness!
Light and life to all he brings,
Risen with healing in his wings!"

Earnest and Tender Emotion.*
Hymn of Invitation.— Collyer.

"Return, O wanderer — now return!
 And seek thy Father's face!
Those new desires which in thee burn,
 Were kindled by his grace.

"Return, O wanderer — now return!
 He hears thy humble sigh:
He sees thy softened spirit mourn,
 When no one else is nigh.

"Return, O wanderer — now return!
 Thy Saviour bids thee live:
Go to his feet, — and grateful learn
 How freely he 'll forgive.

"Return, O wanderer — now return!
 And wipe the falling tear:
Thy Father calls — no longer mourn!
 'T is love invites thee near."

---

* Pathos and Tenderness are expressed by a high though softened tone.

EXERCISES IN "INFLECTION."*

Empassioned Inflection.

Interrogation. (Admitting of a positive or a negative Answer.)
Indignation and Astonishment.
[Highest accent of Rising Inflection, or Upward Slide.]†
" Shall the work say of him that made it, He made me nót? or shall the thing framed say of him that framed it, He had no understánding?"
" Can a man be profitable unto Gód, as he that is wise may be profitable to himsélf? Is it any pleasure to the Almighty that thou art ríghteous? or is it gain to him, that thou makest thy way pérfect? Will he reprove thee for féar of thee? will he enter with thee into júdgment?"
"Jesus! and shall it ever be —
A mortal man ashamed of thée?
Ashamed of thée, — whom angels praise?
Whose glories shine through endless dáys?"

Apostrophe.
Indignant Appeal.
[Lowest descent of Falling Inflection, or Downward Slide.]‡
" Hear, O hèavens, and give ear, O èarth: for the Lòrd hath spoken, I have nourished and brought up children, and they have rebèlled against me. —'Ah! sìnful nation, a people laden with iniquity, a seed of evil dòers, children that are corrùpters!"

Vehement Denunciation.

" Wò unto them that call evil good, and good evil; that put darkness for light, and light for darkness; that put

---

* The analysis of inflection may, at the option of individuals, be studied in practical forms, as laid down in the Elocutionist, or scientifically, as in the Orthophony. The exercises in the present volume, are restricted to the application of prominent principles.

† "Upward Concrete" of an Octave, — on the system of Dr. Rush.

‡ "Downward Concrete" of an Octave, — on the system of Dr. Rush.

bitter for sweet, and sweet for bitter! Wò unto them that are wise in their own eyes, and prudent in their own sight! Wò unto them that are mighty to drink wine, and men of strength to mingle strong drink!"

Remonstrance and Expostulation.
Indignant Address.
[Example of boldest Upward and Downward Slides.]

" Is it súch a fast that I have chosen? a day for a man to afflict his sóul? Is it to bow down his head as a búlrush, and to spread sackcloth and áshes under him? wilt thou call thís a fast and an acceptable day unto the Lord? — Is not thìs* the fast that I have chosen? to loose the bands of wìckednes, to undo the heavy bùrdens, and to let the oppressed go frèe, and that ye break every yòke? Is it not to deal thy bread to the hùngry, and that thou bring the poor that are cast out to thy hòuse? when thou seest the naked, that thou còver him; and that thou hide not thyself from thine own flèsh?"

Vivid or Earnest Inflection.
Argumentation.
Discussion.
High ascent of Rising Inflection, or Upward Slide.†

" Know ye not, brethren, (for I speak to them that know the law,) how that the law hath dominion over a man as long as he líveth?

" What then? shall we sín, because we are not under the law, but under grace? God forbid. Know ye not, that to whom ye yield yourselves servants to obey, his servants ye are to whóm ye obey; whether of sin unto déath, or of obedience unto ríghteousness?"

---

* Interrogation, in the form of remonstrance or expostulation, adopts the downward slide, as do all other emphatic forms of language.

† "Upward Concrete" of a "Fifth,"— in the nomenclature of Dr. **Rush**.

Exclamation.
Admiration.
[Low descent of Falling Inflections, or Downward Slide.]*

"Oh! the depth of the riches both of the wisdom and knowledge of Gòd! how unsèarchable are his judgments, and his ways past finding òut! For who hath known the mind of the Lord, or who hath been his còunsellor? Or who hath first given to him, and it shall be recompensed unto him agàin? For òf him, and thròugh him, and tò him are all things: to whom be glory forèver. Amèn!"

Hortatory Injunction or Command.
Earnest and Authoritative Address.
[Inflection as in the preceding examples.]

"If it be pòssible, as much as lieth in you, live peaceably with all men. Dearly beloved, avènge not yourselves, but rather give plàce unto wrath: for it is written Vengeance is mìne: 'I will repay, saith the Lord. Therefore, if thine enemy hunger, feed him; if he thirst, give him drìnk: for in so doing thou shalt heap coals of fìre on his head. — Let every soul be subject unto the higher powers. For there is no power but of God: the powers that be are ordained of God."

Assurance.
Emphatic Assertion.
[Inflection as before.]

"I am persuaded that neither death nor life, nor angels, nor principalities, nor pòwers, nor things present, nor things to còme, nor height nor dèpth, nor any other crèature, shall be able to separate us from the love of God which is in Christ Jesus our Lord."

---

* "Downward Concrete" of a "Fifth."

Exclamation. — *Gratitude.*

[Inflection as before.]

" Father of mercies, in thy word
What endless glory shìnes!
Forever be thy name adored
For these celestial lìnes!

" Here may the wretched sons of want
Exhaustless riches find, —
Riches beyond what earth can grant,
And lasting as the mìnd."

Exclamation. — *Exultation.*

[Inflection as before.]

" Sìng, O ye hèavens; for the Lord hath dòne it: shòut, ye lower parts of the èarth: break forth into sìnging, ye mòuntains, O fòrest, and every trèe therein: for the Lord hath redèemed Jacob, and glòrified himself in Israel!"

Scorn.

Extract from Isaiah XLIV.

V. 9. " They that make a graven image are all of them vànity; and their delectable things shall not pròfit; and they are their own wìtnesses they sèe not, nor knòw, that they may be ashàmed. 10. Who hath formed a gòd, or molten a graven ìmage, that is profitable for nòthing? 11. Behold, all his fellows shall be ashàmed: and the workmen, they are of mèn: let them all be gathered togèther, let them stand ùp; yet they shall fèar, and they shall be ashàmed togèther. 12. The smith with the tongs both worketh in the coals, and fashioneth it with hàmmers, and worketh it with the strength of his àrms: yea, he is hùngry, and his strength fàileth: he drinketh no water, and is fàint. 13. The carpenter stretcheth out his rùle: he marketh it out with a lìne; he fitteth it out with plànes, and he marketh it out with a còmpass, and maketh it after the figure of a màn, according to the bèauty of a man; that it may remain in the house. 14. He heweth him down cèdars, and taketh the cypress and the òak, which he strengtheneth for himself among the trees of the fòrest: he planteth an òak, and the rain doth nourish it. 15. Then shall it be for a man to bùrn: for he will take thereof, and wàrm himself; yea, he kìndleth it, and baketh brèad; yea, he maketh a gòd, and wòrshippeth it; he maketh it a graven image, and falleth dòwn thereto. 16. He burneth part thereof in the fìre; with part thereof he eateth flèsh; he roasteth roast, and is sàtisfied; yea, he wàrmeth himself, and saith, Ahà! I am wàrm, I have seen the fìre: 17. And the residue thereof he maketh a gòd, even his graven ìmage: he falleth down unto it, and wòrshippeth it, and pràyeth unto it, and saith, Delìver me, for thou art my gòd. 18. They have not known nor understòod: for he hath shùt their eyes that they cannot see; and their hearts, that they cannot understànd. 19. And none considereth in his hèart, neither is there knowledge nor understànding to say, I have bùrned part of it in the fìre; yea, also, I have baked bread upon the còals thereof; I have roasted flèsh, and èaten it: and shall I make the residue thereof an abominàtion? shall I fall down to the stock of a trée? 20. He feedeth on àshes: a deceived heart hath turned him asìde, that he cannot deliver his soul, nor say, Is there not a lìe* in my right hand?"

Contrasted Interrogation.

[Inflections exemplifying both Slides.]

" And thinkest thou this, O man, that judgest them which do such things, and doest the same, that thou shalt escape the judgment of Gód? Or despìsest thou the riches of his goodness, and forbearance, and long-suffering; not knowing that the goodness of God leadeth thee to repèntance?"

---

* Downward slide of emphatic expression.

*Moderate Inflection.**

[Rising Inflection, or Upward Slide.]

Unempassioned or Unemphatic Interrogation.

" Have ye understóod all these things?"
" Knów ye what I have done to you?"
" Is it well with thée? Is it well with thy húsband? Is it well with the chíld?"

Suspended, or Incomplete sense.

" And if some of the branches be broken off, and thou, being a wild olive-tree, wert graffed in among them, and with them partakest of the root and fatness of the ólive-tree; boast not against the branches."

" Inconstant service we repay,
And treacherous vóws renew,
As false as morning's scattering cloud,
And transient as the dew."

[Falling Inflection, or Downward Slide.]

Complete Sense.

" All things are lawful unto me; but all things are not expèdient: all things are lawful for me; but I will not be brought under the domìnion of any."

" Render therefore to all their dùes: tribute to whom trìbute is due; custom to whom cùstom; fear to whom fèar; honor to whom hònor.

" Having, then, gifts, differing according to the grace that is given to us, whether prophecy, let us prophesy according to the proportion of fàith: or ministry, let us wait on our mìnistering; or he that teacheth, on tèaching; or he that exhorteth, on exhortàtion; he that giveth, let him do it with simplìcity; he that ruleth, with dìligence; he that sheweth mercy, with chèerfulness."

---

* Upward or Downward " Concrete," or slide, of a " Third."

"Great God, thy penetrating eye
Pervades my inmost pòwers:
With awe profound my wondering soul
Falls prostrate, and adores!"

[Inflections exemplifying both Slides.]
Correspondence and Contrast.

"Professing themselves to be wíse, they became fòols."*
"Now if we be déad with Christ, we bẹlieve that we shall also lìve with him."
"For if we have been planted together in the likeness of his déath, we shall be also in the likeness of his resur‑rèction."
"To be carnally minded is déath; but to be spiritually minded is life and pèace."
"We are fóols for Christ's sake, but ye are wìse in Christ; we are wéak, but ye are stròng; ye are hónorable, but we are despìsed."
"Now to him that wórketh, is the reward not reckoned of gráce, but of debt. But to him that worketh nòt, but believeth on him that justifieth the ungódly, his fàith is counted for righteousness."

Slight Inflections.†

Upward Slide.
Interrupted Sense.

——— "Oh! bind this héart —
This ròving héart — to thee!"

"Oh! may his lóve — immòrtal fláme! —
Tune every heart and tongue!"

---

* The common error, in contrasts, is that of a double slide, or circum‑flex, instead of the single upward or downward transit.

† These extend no farther on the scale than the interval of a "Sec‑ond," — a single tone, or the space occupied by the transit of the voice from one note to the next above or below. Pathetic expression reduces them to the "semitone."

Poetic Effect.*

"Nor áir, nor éarth, nor skíes, nor séas,
Deny the tribute of their praise."

"Eternal Wisdom, thee we praise,
Thee all thy creatures sing;
While with thy name, rócks, hílls, and séas,
And heaven's high pàlace ring.

"Thy glories blaze all nature round,
And strike the gazing sight,
Through skíes, and séas, and solid gróund,
With terror and delight."

"Foolish féars, and fond desíres,
Vain regrets for things as váin,
Lips too seldom taught to práise,
Oft to murmur and complain;—

"These,—and every secret fault,
Filled with grief and shame, we own."

"Monotone."†

Sublimity and Awe.

Extract from Revelation XX.

V. 11. "And I saw a grēat whīte thrōne, and hīm that sāt on it, from whose fāce the ēarth and the hēaven flēd

---

* Verse, and even poetic prose, require the comparatively melodious effect of the "slight" inflection, in unemphatic "series" or sequences, of words and clauses which are comprehended under one and the same rule of syntax.

† Rigorous analysis may enable an attentive ear to detect the "Second," in the "monotone," so called. But the characteristic effect on the ear, by the recurrence of the same note, is that of strict monotone or sameness of sound,—as in the successive sounds of a bell, compared with those of any other instrument of music.

awāy; and there was fŏund nō place for them. 12. And I sāw the dĕad, smāll and grēat, stănd before Gōd; and the bōoks were ōpened: and anŏther book was ōpened, which is the bōok of life: and the dĕad were jŭdged out of thōse things which were wrītten in the bōoks, according to their works. 13. And the sēa gāve ŭp the dĕad which were in it; and dĕath and hĕll delīvered ŭp the dĕad which were in thĕm: and they were jūdged ēvery mān accōrding to their works."

Stanzas.

" His voice is heard the earth around,
 When through the hĕavens his thŭnders rōll;
The trŏubled ōcean hĕars the sōund,
 And yields itself to his control.

" Whĕn hē upon the līghtning rīdes,
 His vōice in lōudest thūnder spēaks;
The fīery ēlement divīdes,
 And earth to its deep centre shakes."

" *Double Slide*," "*Circumflex*" or "*Wave.*"

Mockery.

" And Elijah mocked the priests of Baal, and said, Cry aloud;* for he is a gŏ́d:† either he is tâlking, or he is pur-sûing, or he is in a jŏurney, or peradventure he slēepeth, and must be awâked."‡

---

* " Falling Circumflex," or " Direct Wave," in which there is first an " Upward," then a " Downward Slide."

† " Rising Circumflex," or " Indirect Wave," in which there is first a " Downward " then an " Upward " slide of voice.

‡ The exemplifications of inflection, in detail, may be found in either of the manuals before mentioned. Those which are presented in the present work, are such as are most frequently required in the reading of the Scriptures and of hymns, or of pulpit discourses.

EXERCISES IN "MOVEMENT."

The word "movement" has properly the same application in elocution as in music. It designates the rate of utterance, as slow, fast, or moderate, and implies the recognition of "time," as an element of effect, in the modifications of the voice. "Movement," in elocution, has not the strict gradations of music; and, in its applications to reading and speaking in the pulpit, is usually limited to the following degrees, — "slowest," "slow," "moderate," "lively."

The first mentioned of these distinctions, is exemplified in the style of awe and deep solemnity, which prevails in the utterance of the profoundest emotions of the soul. It occurs in many passages of the Old Testament, in which the language is of a marked poetic character, as in the book of Job, the Psalms, and portions of the prophetic writings. It pervades, also, the peculiar style of the Book of Revelation, in the New Testament. The "slowest movement" characterizes likewise the poetry of Milton and of Young, and, sometimes, that of Cowper and of Thomson. It belongs appropriately to the reading of those hymns which describe the awful majesty of Jehovah, and to those which embody the ideas of death, retribution, and eternity. It is the peculiarly distinctive point of style in funeral discourses.

The full command over the movement of the voice, is an indispensable requisite to the proper effect of the utterance of devotion, whether in the reading of psalms and hymns, or in the act of prayer. The following exercises should be frequently practised till the full solemnity of the slowest enunciation is attained, in that prolonged, though not drawling style, which gives ample scope and majestic effect to every sound of the voice, and causes every element of speech to succeed another in the most impressive and deliberate style.

The language of reverence and awe, demands space for feeling and imagination, in every characteristic sound. A single devotional exclamation ought, sometimes, to convey the whole heart and soul of the speaker, in one element of sound.

"*Slowest Movement.*"

Awe.

Immortality. — Young.

"Thou! whose all-providential eye surveys,
Whose hand directs, whose spirit fills and warms
Creation, and holds empire far beyond!
Eternity's Inhabitant august!
Of two eternities amazing Lord! —
One past, ere man's or angel's had begun;
Aid! while I rescue from the foe's assault
Thy glorious immortality in man:
A theme forever, and for all, of weight,
Of moment infinite!"

Profound Solemnity.

Midnight. — Thomson.

"As yet 'tis midnight deep. The weary clouds,
Slow-meeting, mingle into solid gloom.
Now, while the drowsy world lies lost in sleep,
Let me associate with the serious Night,
And Contemplation, her sedate compeer."

"Father of light and life, thou Good supreme!
Oh! teach me what is good! teach me Thyself!
Save me from folly, vanity, and vice,
From every low pursuit; and feed my soul
With knowledge, conscious peace, and virtue pure;
Sacred, substantial, never-fading bliss!"

Reverence and Awe.
Stanzas. — Needham.

" Holy and reverend is the name
Of our eternal King;
' Thrice holy Lord,' the angels cry —
' Thrice holy,' let us sing!

" The deepest reverence of the mind,
Pay, O my soul, to God;
Lift, with thy hands, a holy heart,
To his sublime abode!"

Awe.
Extract from Psalm XC.

V. 2. "Before the mountains were brought forth, or ever thou hadst formed the earth and the world, even from everlasting to everlasting, thou art God. 3. Thou turnest man to destruction; and sayest, Return, ye children of men. 4. For a thousand years, in thy sight, are but as yesterday when it is past, and as a watch in the night. 5. Thou carriest them away as with a flood; they are as a sleep; in the morning they are like grass which groweth up. 6. In the morning it flourisheth, and groweth up; in the evening it is cut down, and withereth."

Pathos and Sublimity.
Address of the pastor La Roche. — M'Kenzie.

"You behold the mourner of his only child! the last earthly stay and blessing of his declining years! Such a child, too! — It becomes not me to speak of her virtues! yet it is but gratitude to mention them, because they were exerted towards myself! — Not many days ago, you saw her young, beautiful, virtuous and happy! — Ye who are parents will judge of my affliction now! But I look towards Him who struck me! I see the hand of a father, amidst the chastenings of my God! Oh! could I make you feel what it is to pour out the heart, when it is pressed down with many sorrows! to pour it out, with confidence, to Him in whose hands are life and death! on whose power awaits all that the former enjoys, and in contemplation of whom disappears all that the latter can inflict! — For we are not as those who die without *hope!* We know that our Redeemer liveth! —

"Go, then: mourn not for me! I have not lost my child! But a little while, and we shall meet again, never to be separated!"

." *Slow Movement.*"

This style is exemplified in the ordinary forms of solemn and pathetic language, in description, narration, and sentiment. It pervades the elocution of the more impressive passages of Scripture, generally, of most hymns, and of all discourses adapted to the excitement of profound emotion.

The main object of practice in this mode of voice, is to preserve it from a lagging, drawling, formal, or heavy effect, on the one hand, and from a tone too dry and unimpressive, on the other.

Solemnity.

Extract from the Thanatopsis. — Bryant.

"All that tread
The globe are but a handful to the tribes
That slumber in its bosom. — Take the wings
Of morning, and the Barcan desert pierce,
Or lose thyself in the continuous woods
Where rolls the Oregon, and hears no sound
Save his own dashings; — yet — the dead are there;
And millions in those solitudes, since first
The flight of years began, have laid them down
To their last sleep : — the dead reign there alone. —

So shalt thou rest; — and what if thou withdraw
Unheeded by the living, and no friend
Take note of thy departure? All that breathe
Will share thy destiny. The gay will laugh
When thou art gone, the solemn brood of care
Plod on, and each one as before will chase
His favorite phantom; yet all these shall leave
Their mirth and their employments, and shall come
And make their bed with thee. As the long train
Of ages glides away, the sons of men,
The youth, in life's green spring, and he who goes
In the full strength of years, matron and maid,
The bowed with age, the infant, in the smiles
And beauty of its innocent age cut off, —
Shall, one by one, be gathered to thy side
By those who, in their turn, shall follow them.
 " So live, that when thy summons comes to join
The innumerable caravan, that moves
To the pale realms of shade, where each shall take
His chamber in the silent halls of death,
Thou go not, like the quarry slave at night,
Scourged to his dungeon, but sustained and soothed
By an unfaltering trust, approach thy grave,
Like one who wraps the drapery of his couch
About him, and lies down to pleasant dreams."

Solemnity and Sublimity.

Extract from the Hymn of the Seasons. — Thomson.

" Nature, attend! join, every living soul:
Beneath the spacious temple of the sky,
In adoration join; and, ardent, raise
One general song! To Him, ye vocal gales,
Breathe soft; whose Spirit in your freshness breathes:
Oh! talk of Him in solitary glooms,
Where o'er the rock, the scarcely waving pine
Fills the brown shade with a religious awe.

And ye, whose bolder note is heard afar,
Who shake the astonished world, lift high to heaven
The impetuous song, and say from whom you rage.
His praise, ye brooks, attune, ye trembling rills;
And let me catch it, as I muse along.
Ye headlong torrents, rapid, and profound;
Ye softer floods, that lead the humid maze
Along the vale; and thou, majestic main,
A secret world of wonders in thyself,
Sound His stupendous praise: whose greater voice
Or bids you roar, or bids your roarings fall.
Soft roll your incense, herbs, and fruits, and flowers,
In mingled clouds to Him; whose sun exalts,
Whose breath perfumes you, and whose pencil paints.
Ye forests bend, ye harvests wave, to Him;
Breathe your still song into the reaper's heart,
As home he goes beneath the joyous moon.
Ye that keep watch in heaven, as earth asleep
Unconscious lies, effuse your mildest beams,
Ye constellations, while your angels strike,
Amid the spangled sky, the silver lyre.
Great source of day! best image, here below,
Of thy Creator, ever pouring wide,
From world to world, the vital ocean round;
On nature write with every beam His praise.
The thunder rolls: be hushed the prostrate world;
While cloud to cloud repeats the solemn hymn."

Solemnity and Tranquility.
The Antidote to Adversity. — Wordsworth.

" One adequate support
For the calamities of mortal life
Exists, — one only; — an assured belief
That the procession of our fate, howe'er
Sad or disturbed, is ordered by a Being
Of infinite benevolence and power,

Whose everlasting purposes embrace
All accidents, converting them to Good. —
" The darts of anguish fix not where the seat
Of suffering hath been thoroughly fortified
By acquiescence in the Will Supreme,
For Time and for Eternity; by faith,
Faith absolute in God, including hope,
And the defence that lies in boundless love
Of his perfections; with habitual dread
Of aught unworthily conceived, endured
Impatiently, ill-done, or left undone,
To the dishonor of His holy name. —
" Soul of our souls, and safeguard of the world'
Sustain, — Thou only canst, — the sick of heart;
Restore their languid spirits, and recall
Their lost affections unto Thee and Thine!"

Pathos.

Extract from Kirk White's " Prospect of Death."

" Sad, solitary Thought! who keep'st thy vigils,
Thy solemn vigils, in the sick man's mind;
Communing lonely with his sinking soul,
And musing on the dubious glooms that lie
In dim obscurity before him, — thee
Wrapt in thy dark magnificence, I call
At this still midnight hour, this awful season,
When on my bed in wakeful restlessness,
I turn me wearisome: while, all around,
All, all, save me, sink in forgetfulness;
I only wake to watch the sickly taper
Which lights me to my tomb. — Yes, 't is the hand
Of Death I feel press heavy on my vitals,
Slow-sapping the warm current of existence.
My moments now are few; — the sand of life
Ebbs swiftly to its finish. — Yet a little,
And the last fleeting particle will fall,

Silent, unseen, unnoticed, unlamented. —
"On my grassy grave
The men of future times will careless tread,
And read my name upon the sculptured stone;
Nor will the sound, familiar to their ears,
Recall my vanished memory."

Solemnity, Sublimity, and Awe.
Extract from Job XXVI.

V. 4. "To whom hast thou uttered words? and whose spirit came from thee? 5. Dead things are formed from under the waters, and the inhabitants thereof. 6. Hell is naked before him, and destruction hath no covering. 7. He stretcheth out the north over the empty place, and hangeth the earth upon nothing. 8. He bindeth up the waters in his thick clouds; and the cloud is not rent under them. 9. He holdeth back the face of his throne, and spreadeth his cloud upon it. 10. He hath compassed the waters with bounds, until the day and night come to an end. 11. The pillars of heaven tremble, and are astonished at his reproof. 12. He divideth the sea with his power; and by his understanding he smiteth through the proud. 13. By his spirit he hath garnished the heavens; his hand hath formed the crooked serpent. 14. Lo! these are parts of his ways; but how little a portion is heard of him! But the thunder of his power who can understand?"

Pathos.
Extract from Lamentations, V.

V. 15. "The joy of our heart is ceased: our dance is turned into mourning. 16. The crown is fallen from our head: wo unto us that we have sinned! 17. For this our heart is faint; for these things our eyes are dim; 18. Because of the mountain of Zion, which is desolate: the foxes walk upon it. 19. Thou, O Lord, remainest forever;

thy throne from generation to generation. 20. Wherefore dost thou forget us forever, and forsake us so long time? 21. Turn thou us unto thee, O Lord, and we shall be turned; renew our days as of old."

Consolation.

Stanzas. — Doddridge.

"Peace! humbled soul, whose plaintive moan
   Hath taught these rocks the notes of wo;
Cease thy complaint, — suppress thy groan,
   And let thy tears forget to flow:
Behold, the precious balm is found,
To lull thy pain, to heal thy wound!"

Pathos and Solemnity.

The Strangers' Nook in the Burial-ground. — R. Chambers.

"The graves of the strangers! — what tales are told by every undistinguished heap, — what eloquence in this utter absence of epitaphs!" — "Here, we may suppose, rests the weary old man, to whom, after many bitter shifts, all bitterly disappointed, wandering and mendicancy had become a trade. His snow-white head, which had suffered the inclemency of many winters, was here, at last, laid low forever. Here, also, the homeless youth, who had trusted himself to the wide world in search of fortune, was arrested in his wanderings; and whether his heart was as light and buoyant as his purse, or weighed down with many privations and disappointments, the end was the same, — only, in the one case, a blight; in the other, a bliss. The prodigal, who had wandered far, and fared still worse and worse, at length returning, was here cut short in his better purpose, far from those friends to whom he looked forward as a consolation for all his wretchedness. Perhaps, when stretched in mortal sickness in a homely lodging, in the neighboring village, where, though kindness was rendered, it was still the kindness of strangers, his mind wandered in repentant fondness to that mother whom he had parted with in scorn, but for whose hand to present his cup, and whose eye to melt him with its tenderness, he would now gladly give the miserable remains of his life. Perhaps he thought of a brother, also parted with in rage and distrust, but who, in their early years, had played with him, a fond and innocent child, over the summer leas, and to whom that recollection forgave everything. No one of these friends to soothe the last moments of his wayward and unhappy life — scarcely even to hear of his death when it had taken place. Far from every remembered scene, every remembered face, he was doomed here to take his place amidst the noteless dead, and be as if he had never been.

"Perhaps one of these graves contains the shipwrecked mariner, hither transferred from the neighboring beach. A cry was heard by night through the storm which dashed the waves upon the rocky coast; deliverance was impossible; and next morning, the only memorial of what had taken place, was the lifeless body of a sailor, stretched on the sand. No trace of name or kin; not even the name of the vessel, was learned; but, no doubt, as the villagers would remark in conveying him to the Strangers' Nook, he left *some* heart to pine for his absence, *some* eyes to mourn for him, if his loss should ever be ascertained. There are few so desolate on earth as not to have one friend or associate. There must either be a wife to be widowed, or a child to be made an orphan, or a mother to suffer her own not less grevious bereavement. Perhaps the sole beloved object of some humble domestic circle, whose incomings and outgoings were ever pleasant, is here laid low; while neither can the bereaved learn aught of the fate and final resting-place of their favorite, nor can those who kindly, but without mourning, performed his last offices, reach their ears with the intelligence, — grateful even in its pain, — of what had been done to his remains here the energies which had battled with the waves in their hour of might, and the despair whose expression had been wasted upon the black tempest, are all stilled into rest, and forgotten. The storm is done; its work has been accomplished; and here lies the strange mariner, where no storms shall ever again trouble him." —

"To the other graves there was also some one to resort afterwards, to lament the departure of those who lay below. The spot was always cherished and marked by at least one generation of kind ones; and, whether distinguished by a monument or not, there was always a greater or less interval before the memory of the deceased entirely perished from its place. Still, as each holy day came round, and the living flocked to the house of prayer, there was always some one to send a kind eye aside towards that little mound, and be for a moment moved with a pensive feeling, as the heart recalled a departed parent, or child, or friend. But the graves of the strangers! all regard was shut out from them as soon as the sod had closed over them. The decent few who had affected mourning over the strangers, had no sooner turned away, than they were at once forgotten. That ceremony over, their kind had done with them forever. And so, there they lie, distinguished from the rest only by the melancholy mark that they are themselves undistinguished from each other; no eye to weep over them now or hereafter, and no regard whatsoever to be paid to them till they stand forth, with their fellow-men, at the Great and Final Day."

Awe and Pathos.

The Death of the Wicked. — Massillon.

"The remembrance of the past, and the view of the present, would be little to the expiring sinner: could he confine himself to these, he would not be so completely miserable; but the thoughts of a futurity convulse him with horror and despair. That futurity, that incomprehensible region of darkness, which he now approaches, —

conscience his only companion; that futurity, that unknown land from which no traveller has ever returned, where he knows not whom he shall find, nor what awaits him; that futurity, that fathomless abyss, in which his mind is lost and bewildered, and into which he must now plunge, ignorant of his destiny; that futurity, that tomb, that residence of horror, where he must now occupy his place amongst the ashes and the carcasses of his ancestors; that futurity, that incomprehensible eternity, even the aspect of which he cannot support; that futurity,— in a word, that dreadful judgment, at which, before the wrath of God, he must now appear, and render account of a life, of which every moment almost has been occupied by crimes.

"Alas! while he only looked forward to this terrible futurity at a distance, he made an infamous boast of not dreading it; he continually demanded, with a tone of blasphemy and derision, Who is returned from it? He ridiculed the vulgar apprehensions, and piqued himself upon his undaunted courage. But from the moment that the hand of God is upon him; from the moment that death approaches near, that the gates of eternity open to receive him, and that he touches upon that terrible futurity, against which he seemed so fortified — ah! he then becomes either weak, trembling, dissolved in tears, raising up suppliant hands to heaven, or gloomy, silent, agitated, revolving within himself the most dreadful thoughts, and no longer expecting more consolation or mercy, from his weak tears and lamentations, than from his frenzies and despair."

"*Moderate Movement.*"

This modification of the "time" of utterance, occurs in the style of the epistles in the New Testament, of hymns of sentiment, essays, lectures, practical and doctrinal discourses, — whatever, in a word, falls under the customary rhetorical designation of "didactic" composition. The character of the "movement," or rate of voice, in the elocution of pieces of this description, is adapted to the comparatively moderate emotions, and, consequently, the unempassioned tones, which pervade their language.

The practice of the following exercises, demands attention to that proper medium of utterance which avoids equally slowness and hurry. Deliberateness and composure are the states of feeling to be expressed in the formation and succession of the sounds of the voice.

Elevated Sentiment.

The Enlargement of our Intellectual Powers. — Savile.

"From the right exercise of our intellectual powers arises one of the chief sources of our happiness. The light of the sun is not so pleasant to the eye as the light of knowledge to the mind. The gratifications of sense yield but a delusive charm, compared with the intellectual joys of which we are susceptible. But these intellectual joys, however refined, are at present much interrupted. However wide the extent of human knowledge, however deep the researches of human wisdom, still it must be confessed, that, in this life, our faculties are exceedingly limited, and our views exceedingly confined. Light, to us, is everywhere mixed with darkness. Wherever we cast our eyes, or turn our thoughts, we are reminded of our ignorance, are liable to perpetual mistakes, and often fall into them even in our wisest pursuits. But when the day of immortality dawns, all this shall vanish; the encumbrance of flesh and blood shall no longer grieve us, nor the thick shades of ignorance ever more surround us. The happy spirit emancipated, and having left the spoils of mortality behind it, shall be able to comprehend, fully and at once, all the truths and objects which now either come but very partially within, or entirely escape, its observation. — Here we are only children, but in heaven we shall arrive at the manhood of our being; and therefore we justly infer, that the strength and manhood of our intellectual powers *then*, will surpass, at least, as much what they are *now*, as the reason and judgment of a man exceed those of a child.

"But however this may be, certain we are, that the faculties with which we are at present blessed, and which are essential to our nature, shall be to a wonderful degree invigorated and improved. They shall be capable of taking in far more copious views, and abundantly larger emanations of God's excellence, nay, of tracing the hidden springs of his mysterious operations. — The volumes of nature, of providence, and of redemption, shall be revealed: all the records both of time and eternity shall be opened and explained.

"We already know, in some measure, the charms of novelty, and feel the delight which arises from the contemplation of objects new, grand, and beautiful. Let us imagine then, if we can, the pleasing sensations we shall experience, the high transports we shall feel, when other and unseen worlds shall be disclosed to our view, and all the glories of the celestial paradise beam on our wondering eyes. — Such a felicity, even in prospect, enlarges the mind, and fills it with emotions which, while it feels, it cannot express.

"That our intellectual powers, in a future state, shall really be thus amazingly enlarged, is not a matter of mere conjecture; it is what experience, and reason, and revelation, lend their combined aid to confirm. Experience teaches us, that activity is essential to mind, and necessary to true enjoyment. Reason tells us, that the acquisition of knowledge, particularly that which respects the works and ways of the Most High, is the noblest exercise in which the active powers of the mind can be employed, and a source of the most refined enjoyment of which an intellectual being is capable. And to confirm the dictates of reason, revelation assures us, that 'now we know only in part; but that hereafter that which is in part shall be done away; — that now we see through a glass darkly; but that then we shall see God face to face, and know him even as also we are known.' — Blissful perfection! most amazing exaltation! While the men of the world walk in a vain show, and tire themselves in folly, — Oh! let us expatiate wide in the fields of wisdom, explore the traces of infinite beauty, the impressions of celestial majesty, — lose ourselves in the depths of unutterable grace, — the knowledge of the adorable Jesus, and thus taste in time the pleasures of eternity."

Mercy. — Shakspeare.

" The quality of mercy is not strained;
It droppeth as the gentle rain from heaven
Upon the place beneath: it is twice bless'd,
It blesseth him that gives and him that takes.
'T is mightiest in the mightiest: it becomes
The throned monarch better than his crown:
His sceptre shows the force of temporal power,
The attribute to awe and majesty,
Wherein doth sit the dread and fear of kings;
But mercy is above the sceptered sway, —
It is enthroned in the hearts of kings, —
It is an attribute to God himself;
And earthly power doth then show likest God's
When mercy seasons justice."

Argument.
Reasons against Anger. — Holland.

" However manly and vigorous anger may sometimes be thought, as a defensive instinct, it is, in fact, but a weak principle, compared with the sedate resolution of a wise and virtuous man. The one is uniform and permanent, like the strength of a person in perfect health; the other, like a force which proceedeth from a fever, is violent for a time, but it soon leaves the mind more feeble than before. To him, therefore, who is armed with a proper firmness of soul, no degree of passion can be useful in any respect. And to say it can ever be laudable and virtuous, is indeed a very bold assertion. For the most part, we blame it in others; and, though we are apt to be indulgent enough to our own faults, we are often ashamed of it even in ourselves. Hence, it is common to hear men excusing themselves, and seriously declaring they were not angry, when they gave unquestionable proofs to the contrary.

" But do we not commend him who resents the injuries done to a friend or innocent person! Yes, we commend him; yet not for passion, but for that generosity and friendship of which it is the evidence. For, let any one impartially consider which of these characters he esteems the better; — his, who interests himself in the injuries of his friend, and zealously defends him with perfect calmness and serenity of temper; or his, who pursues the same conduct under the influence of resentment.

" If anger, then, is neither useful nor commendable, it is certainly the part of wisdom to suppress it entirely. We should rather confine it, you tell us, within certain bounds. But how shall we ascertain the limits, to which it may, and beyond which it ought not to pass? When we receive a manifest injury, it seems we may resent it, provided we do it with moderation. When we suffer a worse abuse, our anger, I suppose, may rise somewhat higher. Now, as the degrees of injustice are infinite, if our anger must always be proportioned to the occasion, it may possibly proceed to the utmost extravagance. Shall we set bounds to our resentment, while we are yet calm? How can we be assured, that being once let loose, it will not carry us beyond them? or shall we give passion the reins, imagining we can resume them at pleasure, or trusting it will tire or stop of itself, as soon as it has run to its proper length.? As well might we think of giving laws to a tempest; as well might we endeavor to run mad by **rule and method.**

"In reality, it is much easier to keep ourselves free from resentment, than to restrain it from going to excess, when it has gained admission; for if reason, while her strength is yet entire, is not able to preserve her dominion, what can she do when her enemy has in part prevailed, and weakened her force? To use the illustration of an excellent author: we can prevent the beginnings of some things, whose progress afterwards we cannot hinder. We can forbear to cast ourselves down from a precipice: but, if once we have taken the fatal leap, we must descend, whether we will or not. Thus, the mind, if duly cautious, may stand firm upon the rock of tranquility; but if she rashly forsake the summit, she can scarcely recover herself, but is hurried away downwards by her own passion, with increasing violence"

Explanatory Instruction.

II. *Corinthians. Chap.* IV.

V. 1. " Seeing we have this ministry, as we have received mercy, we faint not; 2. But have renounced the hidden things of dishonesty; not walking in craftiness, nor handling the word of God deceitfully; but by manifestation of the truth, commending ourselves to every man's conscience in the sight of God.

3. "But if our gospel be hid, it is hid to them that are lost: 4. In whom the god of this world hath blinded the minds of them which believe not, lest the light of the glorious gospel of Christ, who is the image of God, should shine unto them.

5. "For we preach not ourselves, but Christ Jesus the Lord; and ourselves your servants for Jesus' sake. 6. For God, who commanded the light to shine out of darkness, hath shined in our hearts, to give the light of the knowledge of the glory of God in the face of Jesus Christ.

7. "But we have this treasure in earthen vessels, that the excellency of the power may be of God, and not of

us. 8. We are troubled on every side, yet not distressed, we are perplexed, but not in despair; 9. Persecuted, but not forsaken; cast down, but not destroyed; 10. Always bearing about in the body the dying of the Lord Jesus, that the life also of Jesus might be made manifest in our body. 11. For we which live are always delivered unto death for Jesus' sake, that the life also of Jesus might be made manifest in our mortal flesh. 12. So then death worketh in us, but life in you.

13. " We having the same spirit of faith, according as it is written, I believed, and therefore have I spoken; we also believe, and therefore speak; 14. Knowing, that he which raised up the Lord Jesus, shall raise up us also by Jesus, and shall present us with you. 15. For all things are for your sakes, that the abundant grace might, through the thanksgiving of many, redound to the glory of God.

16. " For which cause we faint not; but though our outward man perish, yet the inward man is renewed day by day. 17. For our light affliction, which is but for a moment, worketh for us a far more exceeding and eternal weight of glory; 18. While we look not at the things which are seen, but at the things which are not seen: for the things which are seen are temporal; but the things hich are not seen are eternal."

Humane Sentiment.

Hymn. — Mrs. Barbauld.

" Blest is the man whose softening **heart**
  Feels all another's pain;
To whom the supplicating eye
  Is never raised in vain; —

" Whose breast expands with generous **warmth,**
  A brother's woes to feel,
And bleeds in pity o'er the wound
  He wants the power to heal.

" He spreads his kind supporting arms
 To every child of grief:
His secret bounty largely flows,
 And brings unasked relief.

" To gentle offices of love
 His feet are never slow:
He views, through mercy's melting eye,
 A brother in a foe."

"*Lively Movement.*"

This modification of utterance belongs to all animated composition, whether narrative, descriptive, or didactic. It implies vivid emotion or sentiment, as the prompting cause of a quicker movement of voice, than belongs to merely moderate feeling and expression. The frequent practice of the subjoined examples, will serve to impart animation to the voice, in appropriate passages. The error to be guarded against, in these exercises, is that of not coming fully up to the standard of animated movement, as regards its liveliness and brisk effect. A common fault which deadens the character of utterance, is that of using "median" instead of "radical stress," in conjunction with the proper acceleration of movement. The pungent and piercing effect of awakening and kindling emotion, is thus lost to the ear. The proper union of lively movement and radical stress, has the pointed effect of what are termed "staccato" notes, in music,—or that of the distinct touch of the harp, compared to the gliding sound produced by the bow on the violin.

Animation and Courage.
Stanzas.— Watts.

" Awake, our souls,—away, our fears,
 Let every trembling thought be gone!
Awake, and run the heavenly race,
 And put a cheerful courage on!

"Swift as an eagle cuts the air,
  We'll mount aloft to Thine abode;
On wings of love our souls shall fly,
  Nor tire amid the heavenly road."

Joy.

Hymn. — Doddridge.

"Sing, all ye ransomed of the Lord,
  Your great Deliverer sing:
Ye pilgrims, now for Zion bound,
  Be joyful in your King!

"His hand divine shall lead you on
  Through all the blissful road,
Till to the sacred mount you rise,
  And see your gracious God.

"Bright garlands of immortal joy
  Shall bloom on every head;
While sorrow, sighing, and distress,
  Like shadows all are fled.

"March on; in your Redeemer's strength
  Pursue his footsteps still;
With joyful hope still fix your eye
  On Zion's heavenly hill!"

Triumph.

Extract from Psalm LXVIII.

V. 1. "Let God arise, let his enemies be scattered: let them also that hate him flee before him. 2. As smoke is driven away, so drive them away. as wax melteth before the fire, so let the wicked perish at the presence of God. 4. But let the righteous be glad; let them rejoice before God: yea, let them exceedingly rejoice. 4. Sing unto God, sing praises to his name."

15. "The hill of God is as the hill of Bashan; a high hill as the hill of Bashan. 16. Why leap ye, ye high hills? this is the hill which God desireth to dwell in; yea, the Lord will dwell in it forever. 17. The chariots of God are twenty thousand, even thousands of angels: the Lord is among them, as in Sinai, in the holy place. 18. Thou hast ascended on high, thou hast led captivity captive: thou hast received gifts for men; yea, for the rebellious also, that the Lord God may dwell among them."

Animated Exhortation.

Christian Courage.—Moodie.

"The heathen, unsupported by those prospects which the Gospel opens, might be supposed to have sunk under every trial; yet, even among them, was sometimes displayed an exalted virtue,—a virtue, which no interest, no danger, could shake; a virtue, which could triumph amidst tortures and death,—a virtue, which, rather than forfeit its conscious integrity, could be content to resign its consciousness forever. And shall not the Christian blush to repine? the Christian from before whom the veil is removed? to whose eyes are revealed the glories of heaven?

"Your indulgent Ruler doth not call you to run in vain, or to labor in vain.—Every difficulty, and every trial, that occurs in your path, is a fresh opportunity presented by his kindness, of improving the happiness after which he hath taught you to aspire. By every hardship which you sustain in the wilderness, you secure an additional portion of the promised land. What though the combat be severe? A kingdom, an everlasting kingdom is the prize of victory. Look forward to the triumph which awaits you, and your courage will revive.—Fight the good fight, finish your course, keep the faith: there is laid up for you a crown of righteousness, which the Lord, the righteous Judge, shall give unto you at that day. What though, in the navigation of life, you have sometimes to encounter the war of elements? What though the winds rage, though the waters roar, and danger threatens around? Behold, at a distance, the mountains appear. — Your friends are impatient for your arrival; already the feast is prepared; and the rage of the storm shall serve only to waft you sooner to the haven of rest. — No tempests assail those blissful regions which approach to view, — all is peaceful and serene; — there you shall enjoy eternal comfort; and the recollection of the hardships which you now encounter, shall heighten the felicity of better days."

Joy.

The Happiness of those who have extended Human Knowledge.—
Brougham.

" The more widely knowledge is spread, the more will they be prized whose happy lot it is to extend its bounds by discovering new truths, or multiply its uses by inventing new modes of applying it in practice. Their numbers will, indeed, be increased. But the order of discoverers and inventors will still be a select few; and the only material variation in their proportion to the bulk of mankind, will be, that the mass of the ignorant multitude being progressively diminished, the body of those will be incalculably increased, who are worthy to admire genius, and able to bestow upon its possessors an immortal fame.

" And if the benefactors of mankind, when they rest from their pious labors, shall be permitted to enjoy hereafter, as an appropriate reward of their virtue, the privilege of looking down upon the blessings with which their toils and sufferings have clothed the scene of their former existence; do not vainly imagine that, in a state of exalted purity and wisdom, the founders of mighty dynasties, the conquerors of new empires, or the more vulgar crowd of evil-doers, who have sacrificed to their own aggrandizement the good of their fellow-creatures, will be gratified by contemplating the monuments of their inglorious fame : *theirs* will be the delight, — theirs the triumph, — who can trace the remote effects of their enlightened benevolence in the improved condition of their species, and exult in the reflection, that the prodigious changes they now survey, — with eyes that age and sorrow can make dim no more, — of knowledge become power, virtue sharing in the dominion, superstition trampled under foot, tyranny driven from the world, — are the fruits, — precious though costly, and though late reaped, yet long enduring, — of all the hardships and all the hazards they encountered here below!"

Vivid Personification.

Happiness. — Colton.

" She is deceitful as the calm that precedes the hurricane, smooth as the water on the verge of the cataract, and beautiful as the rainbow, that smiling daughter of the storm; but, like the mirage in the desert, she tantalizes us with a delusion that distance creates, and that contiguity destroys. Yet, when unsought, she is often found, and when unexpected, often obtained; while those who seek for her the most diligently, fail the most, because they seek her where she is not. Anthony sought her in love; Brutus, in glory; Caesar, in dominion; — the first found disgrace, the second disgust, the last ingratitude, and each destruction. To some she is more kind, but not less cruel; she hands them her cup; and they drink even to stupefaction, until they doubt whether they are men, with Philip, or dream that they are gods, with Alexander. On some she smiles, as on Napoleon, with an aspect more bewitching than an Italian sun; but it is only to make her frown the more terrible, and by one short caress to embitter the pangs of separation. Yet is she, by universal homage and consent, a queen; and the passions are the vassal lords that crowd her court, await her mandate, and move at her control. But, like other mighty sovereigns, she is so surrounded by her envoys, her officers, and her ministers of state, that it is extremely difficult to be admitted to her presence chamber, or to have any immediate communication with herself. Ambition, Avarice, Love, Revenge, all these seek her, and her alone; alas! they are neither presented to her, nor will she come to them. She despatches, however, her envoys unto them, — mean and poor representatives of their queen. To Ambition, she sends Power; to Avarice, Wealth; to Love, Jealousy; to Revenge, Remorse: alas! what are these, but so many other names for vexation or disappointment? Neither is she to be won by flatteries or by bribes: she is to be gained by waging war against her *enemies*, much sooner than by paying any particular court to herself. Those that conquer her adversaries, will find that they need not go to her, for she will come unto them. None bid so high for her as kings; few are more willing, none more able, to purchase her alliance at the fullest price. But she has no more respect for kings than for their subjects; she mocks them, indeed, with the empty show of a visit, by sending to their palaces all her equipage, her pomp, and her train; but she comes not herself. What detains her? She is travelling incognita to keep a private appointment with Contentment, and to partake of a dinner of herbs in a cottage."

Graphic Conversational Description.

Rebuke of Flippancy. — Cumberland.

" Hear the crude opinions that are let loose upon society in our table conversations; mark the wild and wandering arguments that are launched at random, without ever hitting the mark they should be levelled at: what does all this noise and nonsense prove, but that the talker has indeed acquired the fluency of words, but never known **the exercise of** thought, or attended to the development of a single proposition? Tell him that he ought to hear what may be said on the other side of the question — he agrees to it, and either begs leave to wind up with a few words more, which he winds and wire-draws without end; or, having paused to hear, hears with impatience a very little, foreknows everything you had farther to say, cuts short your argument, and bolts in upon you with — an answer to that argument — ? No; with a continuation of his own babble; and, having stifled you with the torrent of his talk, places your contempt to the credit of his own capacity, and foolishly conceives he speaks with reason, because he has not patience to attend to any reasoning but his own.

"There are also others, whose vivacity of imagination has never felt the trammels of a syllogism.

"To attempt at hedging in these sciolists, is but lost labor. These talkers are very entertaining, as long as novelties with no meaning can entertain you; they have a great variety of opinions, which, if you oppose, they do not defend, and if you agree with, they desert. Their talk is like the wild notes of birds, amongst which you shall distinguish some of pleasant tone, but out of which you compose no tune or harmony of song. These men would have set down Archimedes for a fool, when he danced for joy at the solution of a proposition, and mistaken Newton for a madman, when, in the surplice which he put on for chapel over night, he was found the next morning, in the same place and posture, fixed in profound meditation on his theory of the prismatic colors. So great is their distaste for demonstration, they think no truth is worth the waiting for: the mountain must come to them: they are not by half so complaisant as Mohammed. They are not easily reconciled to truisms, but have no particular objection to impossibilities. For argument they have no ear; it does not touch them; it fetters fancy, and dulls the edge of repartee. If by chance they find themselves in an untenable position, and wit is not at hand to help them out of it, they will take up with a pun, and ride home upon a horse laugh: if they cannot keep their ground, they will not wait to be attacked and driven out of it. Whilst a reasoning man will be picking his way out of a dilemma, they, who never reason at all, jump over it, and land themselves at once upon new ground, where they take an imposing attitude, and escape pursuit. Whatever these men do, whether they talk, or write, or act, it is without deliberation, without consistency, without plan. Having no expanse of mind, they can comprehend only in part; they will promise an epic poem, and produce an epigram. In short they glitter, pass away, and are forgotten; their outset makes a show of mighty things; they stray out of their course into byways and obliquities; and, when out of sight of their contemporaries, are forever lost to posterity."

EXERCISES IN "RHYTHM."*

"Rhythm" is, in elocution, the result of that regular and symmetrical movement of the voice, which is caused by the comparatively measured style of rhetorical composition. It implies, also, a just observance of those pauses, whether marked in the punctuation or not, which the sense of a passage demands; and these pauses thus become, like rests in music, portions of the measure and rhythm It is this last mentioned effect which renders rhythm so important to an easy, fluent, and natural use of the voice, in reading and speaking; suggesting the practice of frequent, slight, but well-timed breathing, instead of the common faulty mode of drawing breath at distant and irregular intervals, and with painful effort. The former of these habits renders public reading and speaking easy, even to persons of feeble health; the latter wears away the organic strength of the most vigorous. The former mode preserves the smooth, even

---

* The word "rhythm" is used, in elocution, to designate that regulated movement of voice, which exists, in its fully marked form, in the combined effect of the metre and pauses of verse, but which belongs, in degree, to all well-written and well-spoken language, in prose,—in the **forms, particularly,** of declamation and discourse.

flow of voice; the latter breaks the continuity both of sound and sense.

Rhythm is, in detail, the regular recurrence of accent, at definite and measured intervals, and may be beat and marked as strictly as in music, if attention is paid to the suspensions of sound by pauses, so as to include them, as well as the actual sounds of the voice, between the beats, as in the bars of music. Every accented syllable is, in elocution, equivalent to the beginning of a bar in music, and may be so marked; thus, | *Muse* | *music* | *musical* | *un-* | *musical* | ; or, if read with pauses | *Muse* | , | or | ♩ | *music* | , | or | ♩ | *musical* | , | or | ♩ | ♩ | *un-* | *musical* | .*

The subjoined exercises should be practised with the aid, at first, of beating time at the commencement of every bar, as in music. The rhythm should be, for some time, marked quite strongly with the voice; the beat and the decided marking may be gradually laid aside, as the ear becomes competent to direct itself. But the actual time should never cease to be carefully observed in reading, speaking, and reciting, any more than in music itself. The fact, however, should never be forgotten, that an habitual strong marking of rhythm, is the same fault in elocution as in music. It protrudes what should be a barely perceptible property, and turns an excellence into a defect. A delicate marking of rhythm, is a genuine grace of cultivated elocution, in the reading of verse, and in the language of oratory or of sentiment. The great object of practice, as regards "time," is *truth*, not *force*.

The student of elocution would do well to score numerous passages, for himself, in the manner exemplified as follows.

---

* Every accented monosyllable, in elocutionary rhythm, constitutes a bar; all the unaccented syllables, in a polysyllable, are grouped in th same bar, with the accented syllable, or pause preceding. The rule marking is simply, Place a bar before every accented syllable, where found, and before every pause. — One or more unaccented syllables ar sometimes grouped into the same bar with a pause. For the convenience of marking, a bar is assumed as composed of one quarter or two eighth notes.

Half or secondary accents, wherever they occur, commence a new bar; thus, the syllable *man-*, in the word | *manifes-* | *tation*, or the syllable *con-*, in the word *in-* | *contro-* | *vertible*.

Verse, or Metrical Accent.

Iambic Metre.

Blank Verse.

* | ⁊ "Be | wise | ⁊ to- | day | ; | ⁊⁊ | ⁊ t is | madness | ⁊ to de- | fer | ; | ⁊⁊ |
Next	day	⁊ the	fatal	precedent	⁊ will	plead	;	⁊⁊
Thus	on	,	⁊ till	wisdom	⁊ is	pushed	out of	life	.	⁊⁊	⁊⁊
⁊ Pro-	crasti-	nation	⁊ is the	thief	⁊ of	time	.	⁊⁊	⁊⁊
Year	⁊	after	year	⁊ it	steals	,	⁊ till	all	⁊ are	fled	,
⁊ And to the	mercies of a	moment	⁊⁊	leaves
⁊ The	vast con-	cerns	⁊ of an e-	ternal	scene	."	⁊⁊	⁊⁊	⁊⁊

Heroic Couplets.

" Hope	⁊⁊	springs e-	ternal	⁊ in the	human	breast	;	⁊⁊
Man	⁊⁊	never	is	⁊ but	always	⁊ to	be	blest	;	⁊⁊	⁊⁊
⁊ The	soul	,	⁊ un-	easy	⁊ and con-	fined from	home	,
Rests	⁊ and ex-	patiates	⁊ in a	life	⁊ to	come."

Octosyllabic Couplets.

⁊ " There's	nothing	bright	,	⁊ a-	bove	,	⁊ be-	low	,	⁊⁊
⁊ From	flowers	⁊ that	bloom	⁊ to	stars	⁊ that	glow	,	⁊⁊
But in its	light	⁊ my	soul	⁊ can	see
⁊ Some	feature	⁊ of	thy	Deity	!"	⁊⁊	⁊⁊	⁊⁊

Octosyllabic Quatrain Stanza (Long Metre).

" Dear	⁊ is the	hallowed	morn	⁊ to	me	;
⁊ When	village	bells	⁊ a-	wake the	day	;	⁊⁊
⁊ And	⁊ by their	sacred	minstrelsy	,
Call me	⁊ from	earthly	cares	⁊ a-	way."

---

* The rests are usually "rhetorical" pauses, or prolongations added to the grammatical pauses indicated by the punctuation. The initial rest represents the slight interval between the first bar and the preceding utterance, whatever that may be.

Common Metre Stanza.

| ♩ " Like | children | ♩ for some | bauble | fair
| ♩ That | weep them- | selves to | rest | ; | ♩♩ |
| ♩ We | part with | life | — | ♩♩ | ♩ a- | wake | ! | ♩♩ | ♩ and | there
| ♩ The | jewel | — | ♩♩ | ♩ in our | breast!"

Short Metre Stanza.

| " Sweet | ♩ at the | dawning | light | , |
| ♩ Thy | boundless | love | ♩ to | tell | ; | ♩♩
| And when ap- | proach | ♩ the | shades of | night | , |
| Still | ♩ on the | theme to | dwell!"

Trochaic Measure.

| " Now be- | gin the | heavenly | theme | , |
| Sing of | mercy's | healing | stream | : | ♩♩ | ♩♩
| Ye | , | ♩ who | Jesus' | kindness | prove | . |
| Sing of | his re- | deeming love | !" | ♩♩ | ♩♩ | ♩♩ |

| " Teach me | some me- | lodious | measure | , |
| Sung | ♩ by | raptured | saints ♩ | ♩ a- | bove;
| Fill my | soul | ♩ with | sacred | pleasure | , |
| ♩ While I | sing re- | deeming | love!"

Anapæstic Measure.

| ♩ " Re- | ligion | ! | ♩ what | treasure | ♩ un- | told
| ♩ Re- | sides | ♩ in that | heavenly | word | ! | ♩♩ |
| ♩ More | precious | ♩ than | silver | ♩ and | gold | , |
| ♩ Or | all | ♩ that this | earth | ♩ can af- | ford!"*

---

* From the analysis which has been given of rhythm, in conjunction with metrical accent in its principal forms, it may be perceived that, in reading, the prosodial grouping of syllables is subordinate — not predominant — in the audible effect. The common fault in reading verse is caused by inverting this rule; and, when to this defect is added that of omitting the rhythmical pauses, nothing is left to the ear but the mere jingle of the scanning.

Prose Rhythm.

Extract from Psalm XXXIII.

V. 1. "Re- | joice in the | Lord | , | O ye | righteous | : | ⌐⌐ | ⌐⌐ | ⌐ for | praise | ⌐ is | comely | ⌐ for the up- | right | . | ⌐⌐ | ⌐⌐ | 2. | Praise the | Lord | ⌐ with | harp | : | ⌐⌐ | ⌐⌐ | sing un- | to him | ⌐ with the | psaltery | ⌐ and an | instrument of | ten | strings | . | ⌐⌐ | ⌐⌐ | ⌐⌐ | 3. Sing | unto him a | new | song | : | ⌐⌐ | ⌐ and | play | skilfully | ⌐ with a | loud | noise | . | ⌐⌐ | ⌐⌐ | ⌐⌐ | 4. | ⌐ For the | word of the | Lord | ⌐ is | right | ; | ⌐⌐ | and | all his | works | ⌐ are | done | ⌐ in truth | . | ⌐⌐ | ⌐⌐ | ⌐⌐ | 5. ⌐ He | love'h | righteousness | ⌐ and | judgment | : | ⌐⌐ | ⌐⌐ | ⌐ the | earth | ⌐ is | full | ⌐ of the | goodness | ⌐ of the | Lord | . | ⌐⌐ | ⌐⌐ | ⌐⌐ | 6. ⌐ By the | word of the | Lord | ⌐ were the | heavens | made | ; | ⌐⌐ | ⌐ and | all the | host of them | ⌐ by the | breath of his | mouth | . | ⌐⌐ | ⌐⌐ | ⌐⌐ | 7. ⌐ He | gathereth the | waters of the | sea | ⌐ to- | gether | ⌐ as a | heap | : | ⌐⌐ | ⌐⌐ | ⌐ he | layeth up the | depth | ⌐ in | store-houses | . | ⌐⌐ | ⌐⌐ | ⌐⌐ | 8. | ⌐ Let | all the earth | fear the | Lord | : | ⌐⌐ | ⌐⌐ | ⌐ let | all the in- | habitants of the | world | ⌐ stand in | awe of him | . | ⌐⌐ | ⌐⌐ | ⌐⌐ | 9. | ⌐ For he | spake, | ⌐ and it was | done | ; | ⌐⌐ | ⌐ he com- | manded, | ⌐ and it | stood | fast | ." | ⌐⌐ | ⌐⌐ | ⌐⌐ |

Didactic Style.

Reflections in Westminster Abbey. — Addison.

| ⌐ " Though I am | always | serious | , | ⌐ I do not | know what it | is | ⌐ to be | melancholy | ; | ⌐⌐ | ⌐ and can | therefore | take a | view of | Nature | ⌐ in her | deep | ⌐ and | solemn | scenes | , | ⌐ with the | same | pleasure | ⌐ as in her | most | gay | ⌐ and de- | lightful ones | . | ⌐⌐ | ⌐⌐ | ⌐⌐ | ⌐ By | this | means | ⌐ I can im- | prove myself | ⌐ with | those | objects | ⌐ which | others | ⌐ con- | sider with | terror | . | ⌐⌐ | ⌐⌐ | ⌐⌐ | ⌐ When I | look upon the | tombs of the | great | , | every e- | motion of | envy | ⌐ dies in me | ; | ⌐⌐ | ⌐ when I | read the | epitaphs | ⌐ of the | beautiful | , | every in- | ordinate de- | sire | ⌐ goes | out | ; | ⌐⌐ | ⌐ when I | meet with the | grief of | parents | ⌐ upon a | tomb- stone | , | ⌐ my | heart | ⌐⌐ | melts | ⌐ with com- | passion | ; | ⌐ | ⌐ when I | see the | tomb of the | parents | ⌐ them- | selves | , |

ELEMENTARY EXERCISES. — "RHYTHM." 241

' I con- | sider the | vanity of | grieving | ' for | those | '' | whom we must | quickly | follow | : | '' | '' | '' | ' when I | see | kings | '' | lying by | those who de- | posed them | , | ' when I con- | sider | rival | wits | , | placed | '' | side by | side | , | ' or the | holy | men | ' that di- | vided the | world | ' with their | contests | ' dis- | putes | , | ' I re- | flect | , | ' with | sorrow | ' and as- | tonishment | , | ' on the | little | ' compe- | titions | , | factions | , | ' and debates | ' of man- | kind | . | '' | '' | '' | ' When I | read the | several | dates of the | tombs | , | ' of | some | ' that | died | yesterday | , | ' and | some | '' | six | hundred | years a- | go | , | ' I con- | sider | that | great | day | ' when we shall | '' | all of us | '' | ' be con- | temporaries | , | ' and | make our ap- | pearance to- | gether."

Oratorical Apostrophe.

Anticipation. — Webster.

| " They | ' are in the | distant | regions | ' of fu- | turity | , | — | they | ' ex- | ist | '' | only in the | all-cre- | ating | power | ' of | God | , | — | ' who shall | stand | here | , | ' a | hundred | years | hence | , | ' to | trace | , | ' through | us | , | ' their de- | scent from the | Pilgrims | , | ' and to sur- | vey | , | ' as | we have | now sur- | veyed | , | ' the | progress of their | country | , | during the | lapse of a | century | ." | '' | '' | '' | ' " On the | morning of | that | day | , | ' al- | though it | will not dis- | turb | us | ' in our re- | pose | , | ' the | voice | ' of | accla- | mation | ' and | gratitude | , | ' com- | mencing | ' on the | Rock | ' of | Plymouth | , | ' shall be trans- | mitted | ' through | millions | ' of the | sons | of the | Pilgrims | , | ' till it | lose itself | ' in the | murmur | ' of the Pa- | cific | seas | ." | '' | '' | '' | ' | '' |

| ' " Ad- | vance | , | ' ye | future | *gener- | ations | ! | '' | '' | ' We would | hail you | , | ' as you | rise | ' in your | long suc- | cession | , | ' to | fill the | places | ' which | we | now | fill | , | ' and to | taste the | blessings | ' of ex- | istence | , | ' where | we | ' are | passing | , | ' and | soon | ' shall have | passed • | , | ' our | human du- | ration | . | '' | '' | '' | ' We

---

* The initial half accent, in words analogous to the above, is assumed as the equivalent of a full accent; — the *time* of half accent being equal to that of accent, although the *force* is not.

| bid you | welcome | ⌐ to | this | pleasant | land | ⌐ of the | Fathers | . | ⌐⌐ | ⌐⌐ | ⌐ We | bid you | welcome | ⌐ to the | healthful | skies | , | ⌐ and the | verdant | fields | ⌐ of | New England | . | ⌐⌐ | ⌐⌐ | ⌐ We | greet your ac- | cession | ⌐ to the | great in- | heritance | ⌐ which | we | ⌐ have en- | joyed | . | ⌐⌐ | ⌐⌐ | ⌐ We | welcome you | ⌐ to the | blessings | ⌐ of | good | government | ⌐ and re- | ligious | liberty | . | ⌐⌐ | ⌐⌐ | ⌐ We | welcome you | ⌐ to the | treasures of | science | , | and the de- | lights of | learning | . | ⌐⌐ | ⌐⌐ | ⌐ We | welcome you | ⌐ to the tran- | scendant | sweets | ⌐ of do- | mestic | life | , | ⌐ to the | happiness | ⌐ of | kindred | , | ⌐ and | parents | , | ⌐ and | children | . | ⌐⌐ | ⌐ ⌐ | ⌐ We | welcome you | ⌐ to the im- | measurable | blessings | ⌐ of rational ex- | istence | , | ⌐ the im- | mortal | hope | ⌐ of | Christi- | anity | , | ⌐ and the | light | ⌐ of | ever- | lasting | Truth | !" | ⌐⌐ | ⌐⌐ | ⌐⌐ | ⌐⌐ | ⌐⌐ | ⌐⌐ | ⌐⌐ | *

EXERCISES IN EMPHASIS.

Emphasis, as properly defined by Dr. Rush, in his Philosophy of the Voice, and, indeed, as is implied in the very etymology of the term, is not a mere comparative force of accent only, but a concentration of several or of many expressive elements of vocal sound, upon one element or syllable. The comparative force does, no doubt, exist; but its use is to embody and impress the effect of the rest. Thus, if we select, as an example, the reply of Death to Satan, " *Back* to thy *punishment!* false fugitive," we shall find that the first of the emphatic words, while

---

* True rhythm extends itself not only from clause to clause, but from sentence to sentence, and from paragraph to paragraph, and even to the long quadruple pause which follows the close of a piece or discourse. One of the faults in elocution by which the pulpit is sometimes degraded, is the business-like dispatch with which the minister passes from the last word of his sermon to the formula that follows. — as if his purpose were to obliterate, as quickly as possible, the effect of his discourse. — Paragraph pauses are usually double the length of those of periods. Double paragraph pauses are the proper distinctions of the heads of discourse; and *these* ought to be doubled, if referred to as a definite measure for the pause which should follow an entire discourse.

it is intensely forcible, derives much of its effect from "explosive" utterance and "radical stress," from "aspirated pectoral and guttural quality," from "low pitch," "falling inflection," or "downward slide," and "rapid movement," or "brief time;" and that if we subtract some or even any one of these properties, the exclamation sounds as if divested, more or less, of emphasis.

Emphasis may be regarded as classed under the following designations: "empassioned," or "absolute," as in the above example, — "unempassioned" or "intellectual," as in "designation," "distinction," or "discrimination," "correspondence," "contrast," and "preference," or "choice."

Examples.

Empassioned Emphasis.

"*Wò* is me! for I dwell among a people of unclean lips."

"*Gràce!* 'tis a *chàrming* sound" —

"In the day that thou eatest thereof, thou shalt surely *dìe.*"*

Unempassioned Emphasis.

Designation. "The supreme love of *Gòd* is the duty enjoined in the text."

Contrast. "The *fòrmer* is a *blìnd* and *nóisy* applause, — the *làtter*, a more *sìlent* and *intèrnal* homage."

Correspondence. "As ye *sów*, so shall ye *réap.*" "As the *hàrt* panteth after the *wáter brooks*, so panteth *my sóul* after *thèe*, O God!"

Preference. "Better is a dinner of *hèrbs*, where *lóve* is, than a *stalled óx*, and *hàtred* therewith."†

---

* Additional examples, in large numbers, may be selected from any or all of the preceding exercises which express strong emotion.

† More examples may be found for practice, in the exercises on "inflection." The emphasis will, in these cases, be found coincident with the accent indicating the slides of the voice.

EXERCISES IN "EXPRESSION."

"Expression," in elocution, as in music, is the term used to indicate the effect of *feeling*, in utterance. Thus, the learner enunciates words without "expression," when endeavoring to read, and still laboring under the difficulty of combining the sounds of syllables: the finished reader gives "expression," or throws feeling into what he reads. "Expression," therefore, in elocution, implies the utterance of emotion in all its characteristic properties of "quality," of voice, "force," "stress," "pitch," "inflection," "melody," "movement," "time," — or "quantity," "rhythm," and "pause," — "emphasis."

When "expression" is regarded in consecutive passages, it is termed "variation," or, arbitrarily, — but not correctly, — "modulation." *

The following exercises should be assiduously practised, till every property of utterance, mentioned in each designation, is combined, in full effect, on its example.

Awe.

"Pectoral Quality," "Aspirated" Utterance,† "Suppressed" Force, "Median Stress," "Lowest" Pitch, "Monotone," "Slowest Movement," Long Pauses.

Stanza. — Translated by Bowring.

"Thou breathest; — and the obedient storm is still:
Thou speakest; — silent the submissive wave:
Man's shattered ship the rushing waters fill,
And the hushed billows roll across his grave!

---

* The terms "key" and "modulation," though in frequent use with reference to elocution, belong exclusively to music; as there are no correspondent facts, in speech and reading, to those which justify these designations in music. See Dr. Rush's just observations on this point.

† The deep *resonance* of the voice in the *chest*, and an "impure" or breathing quality of voice, in which we hear the whispering effect of the breath mingling, more or less, with the sounds which are uttered.

Sourceless and endless God! compared with Thee,
Life is a shadowy, momentary dream:
And time, when viewed through thy eternity,
Less than the mote of morning's golden beam!"

Awe and Fear.

"Expression" as before, but with more "aspiration," and extremely low note.

Extract from Job IV.

V. 13. " In thoughts from the visions of the night, when deep sleep falleth on men, (14.) Fear came upon me, and trembling, which made all my bones to shake. 15. Then a spirit passed before my face: the hair of my flesh stood up: 16. It stood still: but I could not discern the form thereof: an image was before mine eyes; there was silence; and I heard a voice, saying, (17.) Shall mortal man be more just than God? shall a man be more pure than his Maker?"*

Awe, Solemnity, and Tranquillity.

" Orotund and Pectoral Quality."

Evening in the Grave-yard. — Anon.

" The moon is up; the evening star
  Shines lovely, from its home of blue;—
The fox howl's heard on the fell afar,
  And the earth is robed in a sombre hue;
From the shores of light the beams come down
On the river's brink and cold grave-stone.

" The kindling fires o'er heaven so bright,
  Look sweetly out from yon azure sea;
While the glittering pearls of the dewy night,
  Seem trying to mimic their brilliancy;—

---

* For farther practice on examples of *awe*, selections may be made from previous exercises under the same designation of emotion.

Yet all these charms no joy can bring
To the dead, in the cold grave slumbering.

" To numbers wild, yet sweet withal,
    Should the harp be struck o'er the sleepy pillow;
Soft as the murmuring breezy fall
    Of sighing winds on the foaming billow; —
For who would disturb, in their silent bed,
The fancied dreams of the lowly dead?

" Oh! is there one in this world can say
    That the soul exists not after death?
That the powers which illumine this mould of clay
    Are but a puff of common breath?
Oh! come this night to the grave, and see
The sleepy sloth of your destiny.

" The night's soft voice, in breathings low,
    Imparts a calm to the breast of the weeper: —
The water's dash and murmuring flow
    No more shall soothe the ear of the sleeper,
Till He who slept on Judah's plains,
Shall burst death's cold and icy chains.

" I've seen the moon climb the mountain's brow,
    I've watched the mists o'er the river stealing;
But ne'er did I feel in my breast, till now,
    So deep, so calm, and so holy a feeling:
'T is soft as the thrill which memory throws
Athwart the soul in the hour of repose.

" Thou Father of all! in the worlds of light,
    Fain would my spirit aspire to Thee;
And, through the scenes of this gentle night,
    Behold the dawn of eternity:
For this is the path which thou hast given,
The only path to the bliss of heaven."

Solemnity and Reverence.

"Orotund Quality," "Subdued" Force, "Median Stress," "Low" Pitch, Prevalent "Monotone," "Slow Movement," Long Pauses.

Extract from the Forest Hymn. — Bryant.

"Father, thy hand
Hath reared these venerable columns, thou
Didst weave this verdant roof. Thou didst look down
Upon the naked earth, and, forthwith, rose
All these fair ranks of trees. They, in thy sun,
Budded, and shook their green leaves in thy breeze,
And shot towards heaven. The century-living crow,
Whose birth was in their tops, grew old and died
Among their branches ; till, at last, they stood,
As now they stand, massy, and tall, and dark, —
Fit shrine for humble worshipper to hold
Communion with his Maker. —

"Thou art here — thou fill'st
The solitude. Thou art in the soft winds
That run along the summits of these trees
In music; thou art in the cooler breath,
That from the inmost darkness of the place,
Comes scarcely felt; — the barky trunks, the ground,
The fresh, moist ground, are all instinct with thee.
Here is continual worship; — nature, here,
In the tranquility that thou dost love,
Enjoys thy presence."

Praise.

"Orotund Quality," Full Force, "Thorough" and "Median Stress," Moderately Low Pitch, Prevalent "Falling Inflection," Moderate "Wave," or "Monotone," Moderately Slow "Movement," Moderate Pauses.

Psalm CXLVIII.

V. 1. "Praise ye the Lord. Praise ye the Lord from the heavens: praise him in the heights 2. Praise ye him, all his angels: praise ye him, all his hosts. 3. Praise ye him, sun and moon: praise him, all ye stars of light. 4. Praise him, ye heavens of heavens, and ye waters that be above the heavens. 5. Let them praise the name of the Lord: for he commanded, and they were created. 6. He hath also established them forever and ever: he hath made a decree which they shall not pass. 7. Praise the Lord from the earth, ye dragons and all deeps: (8.) fire, and hail; snow and vapor; stormy wind, fulfilling his word: (9.) mountains, and all hills; fruitful trees, and all cedars: (10.) beasts, and all cattle; creeping things, and flying fowls: (11.) kings of the earth, and all people; princes, and all judges of the earth: (12.) both young men, and maidens; old men, and children. 13. Let them praise the name of the Lord: for his name alone is excellent; his glory is above the earth and heaven."

"Expression" as in the preceding example, but with softer Force, greater prevalence of "Median Stress," and slower "Movement," with longer Pauses.

Morning Hymn in Paradise. — Milton.

" Speak, ye who best can tell, ye sons of light,
Angels; for ye behold him, and with songs
And choral symphonies, day without night,
Circle his throne, rejoicing; ye in heaven:
On earth, join all ye creatures to extol
Him first, him last, him midst, and without end.
Fairest of stars, last in the train of night,
If better thou belong not to the dawn,
Sure pledge of day, that crown'st the smiling morn
With thy bright circlet, praise him in thy sphere,
While day arises, that sweet hour of prime.
Thou sun, of this great world both eye and soul,
Acknowledge him thy greater; sound his praise
In thy eternal course, both when thou climb'st,
And when high noon hast gained, and when thou fall'st.

Moon, that now meetst the orient sun, now fliest,
With the fixed stars, fixed in their orb that flies;
And ye five other wandering fires, that move
In mystic dance, not without song, resound
His praise, who out of darkness called up light.
Air, and ye elements, the eldest birth
Of Nature's womb, that in quaternion run
Perpetual circle multiform; and mix,
And nourish all things; let your ceaseless change
Vary to our great Maker still new praise." —
" His praise, ye winds, that from four quarters blow,
Breathe soft or loud; and wave your tops, ye pines,
With every plant, in sign of worship, wave.
Fountains, and ye that warble, as ye flow,
Melodious murmurs, warbling tune his praise.
Join voices. all ye living souls; ye birds,
That singing up to heaven-gate ascend,
Bear on your wings, and in your notes, his praise."*

Deep and uncontrolled Grief.

" Aspirated " " Orotund " and " Pectoral Quality," " Full and Subdued " Force, alternating, " Vanishing Stress," " Lowest " Pitch, Prevalent " Monotone," " Slowest Movement," Very long Pauses.

Extract from the Complaint. Night VI. — Young.

" Oh! the long dark approach, through years of pain,
Death's gallery! (might I dare call it so,)
With dismal doubt and sable terror hung,
Sick Hope's pale lamp its only glimmering ray:
There Fate my melancholy walk ordained, —
Forbid Self-love itself to flatter, there.
How oft I gazed prophetically sad!
How oft I saw her dead, while yet in smiles! —
In smiles she sunk her grief to lessen mine:

---

* Farther practice may be found in the repetition of previous exercises of the same class, introduced for the illustration of different principles.

She spoke me comfort, and increased my pain.
Like powerful armies, trenching at a town,
By slow and silent, but resistless sap,
In his pale progress gently gaining ground,
Death urged his deadly siege; in spite of art, —
Of all the balmy blessings Nature lends
To succor frail humanity. Ye stars!
(Not now made first familiar to my sight,)
And thou, O Moon! bear witness: many a night
He tore the pillow from beneath my head,
Tied down my sore attention to the shock
By ceaseless depredations on a life
Dearer than that he left me. — Dreadful post
Of observation! darker every hour!
Less dread the day that drove me to the brink,
And pointed at eternity below,
When my soul shuddered at futurity;
When, on a moment's point the important die
Of life and death spun doubtful, ere it fell,
And turned up life, my title to more wo!"

Extract from Job III.

V. 3. "Let the day perish wherein I was born.—4. Let that day be darkness; let not God regard it from above, neither let the light shine upon it. 5. Let darkness and the shadow of death stain it; let a cloud dwell upon it; let the blackness of the day terrify it. 6. As for that night, let darkness seize upon it; let it not be joined unto the days of the year; let it not come into the number of the months. 7. Lo! let that night be solitary; let no joyful voice come therein. 8. Let them curse it, that curse the day, who are ready to raise up their mourning. 9. Let the stars of the twilight thereof be be dark; let it look for light, but have none; neither let it see the dawning of the day."*

---

* Repeat previous examples of the same emotion.

Deep and subdued Grief.

"Orotund" and "Pectoral Quality," "Subdued" Force, Prevalent "Median," with occasional "Vanishing," and "Radical Stress," Low Pitch, Level Voice, "Slow Movement," Long Pauses.

Extract from Burke's Allusion to the Death of his Son.

"Had it pleased God to continue to me the hopes of succession, I should have been, according to my mediocrity and the mediocrity of the age I live in, a sort of founder of a family; I should have left a son, who, in all the points in which personal merit can be viewed in science, in erudition, in genius, in taste, in honor, in generosity, in humanity, in every liberal sentiment, and every liberal accomplishment, would not have shown himself inferior to the duke of Bedford, or to any of those whom he traces in his line. His grace very soon would have wanted all plausibility in his attack upon that provision which belonged more to mine than to me. He would soon have supplied every deficiency, and symmetrized every disproportion. It would not have been for that successor to resort to any stagnant wasting reservoir of merit in me, or in any ancestry. He had in himself a salient, living spring, of generous and manly action. Every day he lived he would have re-purchased the bounty of the crown, and ten times more, if ten times more he had received. He was made a public creature; and had no enjoyment whatever but in the performance of some duty. — At this exigent moment, the loss of a finished man is not easily supplied.

"But a Disposer whose power we are little able to resist, and whose wisdom it behooves us not at all to dispute, has ordained it in another manner, and, (whatever my querulous weakness might suggest,) a far better. — The storm has gone over me; and I lie like one of those old oaks which the late hurricane has scattered about me. I am stripped of all my honors; I am torn up by the roots, and lie prostrate on the earth! There, and prostrate there, I most unfeignedly recognize the divine justice, and in some degree submit to it. — I am alone. I have none to meet my enemies in the gate. — Indeed, I greatly deceive myself, if, in this hard season, I would give a peck of refuse wheat for all that is called fame and honor in the world. — I live in an inverted order. They who ought to have succeeded me, are gone before me. They who should have been to me as posterity, are in the place of ancestors. I owe to the dearest relation, (which ever must subsist in memory,) that act of piety, which he would have performed to me."*

Indignation.

"Orotund" "Pectoral Quality," somewhat "aspirated,"— Full Force, sometimes "Empassioned,"— "Vanishing Stress," "Low" Pitch, Prevalent "Falling Inflection," "Slow Movement," Pauses long, Strong Emphasis

Extracts from Fears in Solitude. (Writen in 1798). — Coleridge.

" From east to west
A groan of accusation pierces heaven!
The wretched plead against us; multitudes,
Countless and vehement, the sons of God,
Our brethren! Like a cloud that travels on,
Steamed up from Cairo's swamps of pestilence,
Even so, my countrymen, have we gone forth,
And borne to distant tribes slavery and pangs,
And, deadlier far, our vices, whose deep taint,
With slow perdition murders the whole man,
His body and his soul!
" Thankless, too, for peace,
(Peace long preserved by fleets and perilous seas,)
Secure from actual warfare, we have loved
Too well the war-whoop, passionate for war!

---

* Repeat previous examples of the same emotion.

Alas! for ages ignorant of all
Its ghastly workings, (famine, or blue plague,
Battle, or siege, or flight through wintry snows,)
We, this whole people, have been clamorous
For war and bloodshed; — animating sports!
The which we pay for, as a thing to talk of,
Spectators, and not combatants! — No guess
Anticipative of a wrong unfelt,
No speculation or contingency,
However dim and vague, too vague and dim
To yield a justifying cause; and forth
(Stuffed out with big preamble, holy names,
And adjurations of the God in heaven,)
We send our mandates for the certain death
Of thousands and ten thousands! — Boys and girls,
And women that would groan to see a child
Pull off an insect's leg, all read of war, —
The best amusement for our morning meal!
The poor wretch who has learned his only prayers
From curses, who knows scarcely words enough
To ask a blessing from his heavenly Father,
Becomes a fluent phrase-man, absolute
And technical in victories and defeats,
And all our dainty terms for fratricide;
Terms which we trundle smoothly o'er our tongues,
Like mere abstractions, empty sounds to which
We join no feeling, and attach no form!
As if the soldier died without a wound;
As if the fibres of this godlike frame
Were gored without a pang; as if the wretch
Who fell in battle, doing bloody deeds,
Passed off to heaven translated, and not killed;
As though he had no wife to pine for him, —
No God to judge him! Therefore, evil days
Are coming on us, O my countrymen!
And what if all-avenging Providence,
Strongly retributive, should make us know

The meaning of our words, force us to feel
The desolation and the agony
Of our fierce doings?"

Extracts from Isaiah IX.

V. 13. "The people turneth not unto him that smiteth them, neither do they seek the Lord of hosts. 14. Therefore the Lord will cut off from Israel head and tail, branch and rush, in one day. 15. The ancient and honorable, he is the head; and the prophet that teacheth lies, he is the tail. 16. For the leaders of this people cause them to err; and they that are led of them are destroyed. 17. Therefore the Lord shall have no joy in their young men, neither shall have mercy on their fatherless and widows: for every one is a hypocrite and an evil doer, and every mouth speaketh folly. For all this his anger is not turned away; but his hand is stretched out still. 18. For wickedness burneth as the fire; it shall devour the briers and thorns, and shall kindle in the thickets of the forest, and they shall mount up like the lifting up of smoke. 19. Through the wrath of the Lord of hosts is the land darkened; and the people shall be as the fuel of the fire; no man shall spare his brother." — 21. "For all this his anger is not turned away; but his hand is stretched out still."

Denunciation.

"Expression" as before, but moderated to a more restrained and calmer mood, by the influence of Solemnity and Regret.

Extract from Matthew VIII.

V. 21. "Wo unto thee, Chorazin! wo unto thee, Bethsaida! for if the mighty works which were done in you, had been done in Tyre and Sidon, they would have repented long ago, in sackcloth and ashes. 22. But I say unto you, It shall be more tolerable for Tyre and Sidon, at the day of judgment, than for you. 23. And thou Capernaum, which art exalted unto heaven, shalt be thrust down to hell: for if the mighty works which have been done in thee, had been done in Sodom, it would have remained until this day. 24. But I say unto you, that it shall be more tolerable for the land of Sodom, in the day of judgment, than for thee."

The Slave-Trade. — Dewey.

"The world is full of wrongs and evils, and full of wronged and suffering men. But still I do say that of all wrongs, slavery is the greatest. It denies to man his humanity, and all its highest and holiest rights. And of all slavery, the African is the most monstrous. Other men have fallen under this doom by the fate of war. They have bought life at the price of bondage. With Africa there has been no war but that of the prowling man-stealer! He has gone up among the river-glades of that ill-fated land; he has torn men and women and children, from their country and their homes, who never did him any wrong; he has hurried them to his prison-ship; he has plunged them into the dungeon of "the middle passage," — *middle passage!* — phrase that passes in universal speech for all the atrocities that human nature can inflict or endure, — he has thrust them down into that dark, unbreathing confine, in mingling and writhing agony and despair and disease and corruption and death; he has borne them away, regardless of their tears and entreaties, and sold them into hopeless bondage in a strange land; forty millions, — it is calculated, — forty millions of human beings have suffered this awful fate! Oh! it is the great felon act in humanity! Oh! it is the monster crime of the world!"

Tenderness.

"Pure Tone," "Subdued" Force, "Median Stress," "Middle" Pitch, Prevalent "Semitone," "Slow Movement," Long Pauses, Gentle Emphasis.

Extract from Lines to an Infant. — Coleridge.

" Poor stumbler on the rocky coast of wo,
Tutored by pain each source of pain to know!
Alike the foodful fruit and scorching fire
Awake thy eager grasp and young desire;
Alike the good, the ill, offend thy sight,
And rouse the stormy sense of shrill affright.
Untaught, yet wise! mid all thy brief alarms
Thou closely clingest to thy mother's arms,
Nestling thy little face in that fond breast
Whose anxious heavings lull thee to thy rest!

" Man's breathing miniature! thou mak'st me sigh,—
A babe art thou — and such a thing am I!
To anger rapid, and as soon appeased,
For trifles mourning, and by trifles pleased,
Break Friendship's mirror with a tetchy blow,
Yet snatch what coals of fire on Pleasure's altar glow!

' O Thou that rearest, with celestial aim,
The future seraph in my mortal frame,
Thrice holy Faith! whatever thorns I meet,
As on I totter with unpractised feet,
Still let me stretch my arms and cling to thee,
Meek nurse of souls through their long infancy!'"

"Expression" as before, but moderated in its characteristics.

Extract from Matthew, XI.

V. 28. " Come unto me, all ye that labor, and are heavy laden; and I will give you rest. 29. Take my yoke upon you, and learn of me: for I am meek and lowly of heart; and ye shall find rest unto your souls. 30. For my yoke is easy, and my burden is light."

"Expression" as before, but more vivid.
Extract from Genesis, XLIV.
V. 13. " Then they rent their clothes, and laded every man his ass, and returned to the city. 14. And Judah and his brethren came to Joseph's house, (for he was yet there :) and they fell before him on the ground. 15. And Joseph said unto them, ' What deed is this that ye have done? wot ye not that such a man as I can certainly divine?' 16. And Judah said, ' What shall we say unto my lord? what shall we speak? or how shall we clear ourselves? God hath found out the iniquity of thy servants : behold we are my lord's servants, both we, and he also with whom the cup is found.' 17. And he said, ' God forbid that I should do so: but the man in whose hand the cup is found, he shall be my servant; and as for you, get you up in peace unto your father.' 18. Then Judah came near unto him, and said, ' O my lord, let thy servant, I pray thee, speak a word in my lord's ears; and let not thine anger burn against thy servant: for thou art even as Pharaoh. 19. My lord asked his servants, saying, Have ye a father, or a brother? 20. And we said unto my lord, We have a father, an old man, and a child of his old age, a little one; and his brother is dead, and he alone is left of his mother, and his father loveth him. 21. And thou saidst unto thy servants, Bring him down unto me, that I may set mine eyes upon him. 22. And we said unto my lord, ' The lad cannot leave his father: for if he should leave his father, his father would die.' 23. And thou saidst unto thy servants, ' Except your youngest brother come down with you, ye shall see my face no more.' 24. And it came to pass, when we came up unto thy servant my father, we told him the words of my lord. 25. And our father said, ' Go again, and buy us a little food.' 26. And we said, ' We cannot go down: if our youngest brother be with us, then will we go down; for we may not see the man's face, except our youngest

brother be with us.' 27. and thy servant my father said unto us, 'Ye know that my wife bare me two sons: 28. And the one went out from me, and I said, 'Surely he is torn in pieces;' and I saw him not since: 29. And if ye take this also from me, and mischief befall him, ye shall bring down my gray hairs with sorrow to the grave.' 30· Now therefore when I come to thy servant my father, and the lad be not with us; (seeing that his life is bound up in the lad's life;) 31. It shall come to pass, when he seeth that the lad is not with us, that he will die: and thy servants shall bring down the gray hairs of thy servant our father with sorrow to the grave. 32. For thy servant became surety for the lad unto my father; saying, 'If I bring him not unto thee, then I shall bear the blame to my father forever.' 33. Now therefore, I pray thee, let thy servant abide instead of the lad a bondman to my lord; and let the lad go up with his brethren. 34. For how shall I go up to my father, and the lad be not with me? lest peradventure I see the evil that shall come on my father.'"

"Expression" as before, but more solemn.

Consolation. — Finlayson.

" Hast thou, with weeping eyes, committed to the grave the child of thy affections, the virtuous friend of thy youth, or the tender partner, whose pious attachment lightened the load of life? Behold they are not dead. Thou knowest that they live in a better region, with their Saviour and their God; that still thou holdest thy place in their remembrance; and that thou shalt soon meet them again to part no more. Dost thou look forward with trembling to the days of darkness that are to fall on thyself, when thou shalt lie on the bed of sickness, when thy pulse shall have become low, — when the cold damps have gathered on thy brow, — and the mournful looks of thy attendants have told thee that the hour of thy departure has come? To the mere natural man this scene is awful and alarming; but if thou art a Christian, — if thou knowest and obeyest the truth, thou needest fear no evil. The shadows which hang over the valley of death shall retire at thy approach; and thou shalt see beyond it the spirits of the just, and an innumerable company of angels, the future companions of thy bliss, bending from their thrones to cheer thy departing soul, and to welcome thee into everlasting habitations."

Penitence and Contrition.

" Pure Tone," " Subdued " Force, " Median " and " Vanishing Stress," " High " Pitch, Prevalent " Semitone," " Slowest Movement," Long Pauses, Earnest Emphasis.

Hymn. — Mrs. Steele.

" O Thou, whose tender mercy hears
 Contrition's humble sigh;
Whose hand indulgent wipes the tears
 From sorrow's weeping eye; —

" See, Lord, before thy throne of grace,
 A wretched wanderer mourn:
Hast thou not bid me seek thy face?
 Hast thou not said — ' Return?'

" And shall my guilty fears prevail
 To drive me from thy feet?
Oh! let not this dear refuge fail,
 This only safe retreat.

" Absent from thee, my Guide! my light!
 Without one cheering ray,
Through dangers, fears, and gloomy night,
 How desolate my way!

" Oh! shine on this benighted heart,
 With beams of mercy shine!
And let thy healing voice impart
 A taste of joy divine."

Regret, Repentance, and Shame.

"Aspirated Orotund Quality," "Suppressed" Force, "Vanishing Stress," "Low" Pitch, Prevalent "Falling Inflection," "Slow Movement," Long Pauses, Strong Emphasis.

Adam's Confusion, on awakening to the sense of Guilt.

" How shall I behold the face,
Henceforth, of God or angel, erst with joy
And rapture so oft beheld? Those heavenly shapes
Will dazzle now this earthly with their blaze
Insufferably bright. Oh! might I here
In solitude live savage, in some glade
Obscured, where highest woods, impenetrable
To star or sun light, spread their umbrage broad
And brown as evening. Cover me ye pines,
Ye cedars, with innumerable boughs
Hide me, where I may never see them more!"

"Expression," as in the preceding example.

Job's Confession. XLII. Chap.

V. 2. "I know that thou canst do everything, and that no thought can be withholden from thee. 3. Who is he that hideth counsel without knowledge? therefore have I uttered that I understood not; things too wonderful for me, which I knew not. 4. Hear, I beseech thee; and I will speak: I will demand of thee, and declare thou unto me. 5. I have heard of thee by the hearing of the ear: but now mine eye seeth thee: 6. Wherefore I abhor myself, and repent in dust and ashes."

Stanzas.—Watts.

"Oh! wash my soul from every sin,
And make my guilty conscience clean;
Here, on my heart, the burden lies,
And past offences pain mine eyes.

"My lips, with shame, my sins confess,
Against thy law — against thy grace:
Lord, should thy judgment grow severe,
I am condemned, — but thou art clear."

Remorse, Self-reproach, Horror, and Despair.
"Aspirated Pectoral Quality," "Vanishing Stress," "Low" Pitch, Prevalent "Falling Inflection," "Slowest Movement," Long Pauses, Strong Emphasis.
Adam's Emotions, in Retrospection and Anticipation. — Milton.

"But say
That death be not one stroke, as I supposed,
Bereaving sense, but endless misery
From this day onward, which I feel begun
Both in me, and without me, and so last
To perpetuity; — ay me! that fear
Comes thundering back with dreadful revolution
On my defenceless head: both Death and I
Am found eternal, and incorporate both;
Not I on my part single, in me all
Posterity stands cursed: — fair patrimony
That I must leave ye, sons! Oh! were I able
To waste it all myself, and leave ye none!
So disinherited how would ye bless
Me, now your curse! Ah! why should all mankind
For one man's fault thus guiltless be condemned,
If guiltless? But from me what can proceed,
But all corrupt, both mind and will depraved,
Not to do only, but to will the same
With me? How can they then acquitted stand
In sight of God? Him, after all disputes,
Forced, I absolve: all my evasions vain,
And reasoning, though through mazes, lead me still
But to my own conviction: first and last
On me, me only, as the source and spring
Of all corruption, all the blame lights due;

So might the wrath! Fond wish! Couldst thou support
That burden heavier than the earth to bear,
Than all the world much heavier, though divided
With that bad woman? Thus what thou desirest,
And what thou fear'st, alike destroys all hope
Of refuge, and concludes thee miserable
Beyond all past example and future,—
To Satan only like both crime and doom—
O conscience, into what abyss of fears
And horrors hast thou driven me; out of which
I find no way, from deep to deeper plunged!"

"Expression" as before.

The Sinner expiring in conscious Guilt and Horror — Massillon.

"Alas! the dying man had lived as if the body had formed his only being and treasure; he had even tried to persuade himself that his soul was nothing: that man is only a composition of flesh and blood, and that everything perishes with us. He is now informed that it is his body which is nothing but a morsel of clay, now on the point of crumbling into pieces; and that his only immortal being is that soul, that image of the Divinity, that intelligence, alone capable of knowing and loving its Creator, which now prepares to quit its earthly mansion, and appear before his awful tribunal.

"Then, the expiring sinner, no longer finding in the remembrance of the past, but regrets which overwhelm him; in all which takes place around him, but images which afflict him; in the thoughts of futurity, but horrors which appal him; no longer knowing to whom to have recourse; neither to created beings, who now leave him; nor to the world, which vanishes; nor to men, who cannot save him from death; nor to the just God, whom he looks upon as a declared enemy, and from whom he has no indulgence to expect: a thousand horrors occupy his thoughts; he torments, he agitates himself, in order to fly from death which grasps him, or at least to fly from himself. From his expiring eyes issues something, I know not what, of dark and gloomy, which expresses the fury of his soul; in his anguish, he utters words interrupted by sobs, which are unintelligible, and to which others know not whether repentance or despair gives birth. He is seized with convulsions, which they are ignorant whether to ascribe to the actual dissolution of his body, or to the soul which feels the approach of its Judge. He deeply sighs; and they know not whether the remembrance of his past crimes, or the despair at quitting life, forces from him such groans of anguish. At last, in the midst of these melancholy exertions, his eyes fix, his features change, his countenance becomes disfigured, his livid lips convulsively separate; his whole frame quivers; and, by this last effort, his miserable soul tears itself reluctantly from that body of clay, falls into the hands of its God, and finds itself alone at the foot of the awful tribunal."

Joy.

" Orotund Quality," Full Force, rising to " Empassioned,"—" Expulsive Radical Stress," Pitch, from " Middle " to " High,"— Prevalent ' Falling Inflection," " Lively Movement," Pauses short, Emphasis bold.

Isaiah XII.

V. 1. " O Lord, I will praise thee: though thou wast angry with me, thine anger is turned away, and thou comfortedst me. 2. Behold, God is my salvation; I will trust, and not be afraid; for the Lord Jehovah is my strength and my song; he also is become my salvation. 3. Therefore with joy shall ye draw water out of the wells of salvation. 4. And in that day shall ye say, ' Praise the Lord, call upon his name, declare his doings among the people, make mention that his name is exalted. 5. Sing unto the Lord; for he hath done excellent things: this is known in all the earth. 6. Cry out and shout, thou inhabitant of Zion; for great is the Holy One of Israel in the midst of thee.'"

"Expression" as before, but moderated.

Hymn. — Watts.

"Joy to the world — the Lord is come!
    Let earth receive her King;
Let every heart prepare him room,
    And heaven and nature sing.

"Joy to the world — the Saviour reigns:
    Let men their songs employ;
While fields and floods — rocks, hills, and plains
    Repeat the sounding joy.

"No more let sin and sorrow grow,
    Nor thorns infest the ground;
He comes to make his blessings flow
    Far as the curse is found.

"He rules the world with truth and grace,
    And makes the nations prove
The glories of his righteousness,
    And wonders of his love."

"Expression" as before, but moderated.

The Dying Believer. — Buckminster.

"Oh! that I could open to you the recesses of the dying believer's soul; that I could reveal to you the light which darts into the chambers of his understanding. He approaches the world which he has so long seen in faith. The imagination now collects its diminished strength; and the eye of faith opens wide.

"Friends! do not stand, thus fixed in sorrow, around this bed of death. Why are you so still and silent? Fear not to move — you cannot disturb the last visions which entrance this holy spirit. Your lamentations break not in upon the songs of seraphs, which enwrap his hearing in ecstasy. Crowd, if you choose, around his couch — he heeds you not — already he sees the spirits of the just advancing together, to receive a kindred soul. Press him not with importunities; urge him not with alleviations. Think you he wants now these tones of mortal voices, — these material, these gross consolations? No! He is going to add another to the myriads of the just, that are every moment crowding into the portals of heaven!"

Happiness.

"Quality" rising from "Pure Tone" to "Orotund," — Force "Moderate," "Median Stress," gently expulsive, — Pitch, "Middle" to "High," — Varied but moderate Inflection, — Movement, Pauses, and Emphasis, Moderate.

Stanzas. — Watts.

"There is a stream, whose gentle flow
Supplies the city of our God:
Life, love, and joy, still gliding through,
And watering our divine abode.

"That sacred stream — thy holy word, —
Supports our faith, — our fear controls:
Sweet peace thy promises afford,
And give new strength to fainting souls."

"Expression" as in the preceding example, but fuller, deeper, and stronger in degree.

Extract from Psalms XXXVI. *and* LXV.

V. 5. Thy mercy, O Lord, is in the heavens; and thy faithfulness reacheth unto the clouds. 6. Thy righteousness is like the great mountains; thy judgments are a great deep: O Lord, thou preservest man and beast. 7. How excellent is thy loving-kindness, O God! therefore the children of men put their trust under the shadow of thy wings. 8. They shall be abundantly satisfied with the fatness of thy house; and thou shalt make them drink of the river of thy pleasures."

V. 9. "Thou visitest the earth, and waterest it: thou greatly enrichest it with the river of God, which is full of water: thou preparest them corn, when thou hast so provided for it. 10. Thou waterest the ridges thereof abundantly: thou settlest the furrows thereof: thou makest it soft with showers: thou blessest the springing thereof. 11. Thou crownest the year with thy goodness; and thy paths drop fatness. 12. They drop upon the pastures of the wilderness: and the little hills rejoice on every side. 13. The pastures are clothed with flocks; the valleys also are covered over with corn; they shout for joy, they also sing."

Extract from Isaiah 11.

V. 2. "And it shall come to pass in the last days, that the mountain of the Lord's house shall be established in the top of the mountains, and shall be exalted above the hills; and all nations shall flow unto it. 3. And many people shall go and say, ' Come ye, and let us go up to the mountain of the Lord, to the house of the God of Jacob; and he will teach us of his ways, and we will walk in his paths:' for out of Zion shall go forth the law, and the word of the Lord from Jerusalem. 4. And he shall judge among the nations, and shall rebuke many people: and they shall beat their swords into plough-shares, and their spears into pruning-hooks: nation shall not lift up sword against nation, neither shall they learn war any more. 5. O house of Jacob, come ye, and let us walk in the light of the Lord."

"Expression" as before.

The Pleasures of Youthful Piety. — Alison.

"In every part of Scripture, it is remarkable with what singular tenderness the season of youth is always mentioned, and what hopes are afforded to the devotion of the young."

"If these, then, are the effects and promises of youthful piety, rejoice, O young man, in thy youth! — rejoice in those days which are never to return, when religion comes to thee in all its charms, and when the God of nature reveals himself to thy soul, like the mild radiance of the morning sun, when he rises amid the blessings of a grateful world. If already Devotion hath taught thee her secret pleasures; — if, when Nature meets thee in all its magnificence or beauty, thy heart humbleth itself in adoration before the Hand which made it, and rejoiceth in the contemplation of the wisdom by which it is maintained; if, when Revelation unveils her mercies, and the Son of God comes forth to give peace and hope to fallen man, thine eye follows with astonishment the glories of his path, and pours at last over his cross those pious tears which it is a delight to shed; — if thy soul accompanieth him in his triumph over the grave, and entereth on the wings of faith into that heaven 'where he sat down at the right hand of the Majesty on high,' and seeth the 'society of angels and of the spirits of just men made perfect,' and listeneth to the 'everlasting song which is sung before the throne:' — If such are the meditations in which thy youthful hours are passed, renounce not, for all that life can offer thee in exchange, these solitary joys. The world which is before thee, — the world which thine imagination paints in such brightness, — has no pleasures to bestow which can compare with these. And all that its boasted wisdom can produce, has nothing so acceptable in the sight of Heaven, as this pure offering of thy youthful soul."

"Expression" as before, but moderated.

The Enjoyments of the Poor, in Spring — Duncan.

"This is truly the glad season of the year. Wherever we turn our eyes, Nature wears a smile of joy, as if, freed from the storms and the cold of winter, she revelled in the well enhanced luxury of spring. The lengthening day, the increasing warmth of the air, and the gradually deepening green of the awakened earth, excite in every breast a lively sense of gratitude, and pleasingly affect the imagination. A walk among the woods or fields, in a calm spring day, when the trees are bursting forth into beauty, and all the land is echoing with song, may well soothe the stormiest passions, and inspire that 'vernal delight,' which is 'able to drive away all sadness but despair.' The mind sympathizes with the joy of inanimate Nature, and rejoices to behold the reviving beauty of the earth, as if itself had escaped from a period of gloom, to bask in the sunshine of hope and enjoyment.

"We are familiar with the joys of spring, as felt or sung by poets and other ardent lovers of Nature. They form the burden of many a poetic strain, and excite to many a meditative reverie. They have inspired enthusiasm and deep delight, ever since there was an eye to witness, or a mind to feel, the harmony and loveliness of this gorgeously arrayed and breathing world. They are the source of exquisite emotion to every mind, in which dwells a sense of beauty and creative design. They also light the brow of care, and bring back the flush of health and hope to the pale and wasted cheek. And not only by the rich and the enlightened, — by the children of luxury and mental refinement, — are the fine and indescribable delights of this season deeply felt and valued; spring is also a time of increased enjoyment to the poor. It fills the inmates of many an humble dwelling with gladness, and makes even desponding poverty smile, and hope for better days.

"There is something in the flowery sweetness and genial warmth of spring, that kindles in the rudest bosom feelings of gratitude and pleasure. The contrast to the cold and desolation of winter, is so striking and agreeable, that every heart, unless it be hardened by the direst ignorance and crime, is melted to love and pious emotion; and breathings of deep-felt adoration escape from the most untutored lips. The carols of the ploughman, as he traverses the field, the live-long day, and turns up the fresh soil, seem to bespeak a lightsome heart, and evince the joyousness of labor. The shepherd, as he sits upon the hill-side and surveys his quiet flock with its sportive companies of lambs, — those sweetest emblems of innocent mirth, — feels a joy and calm satisfaction, that is heightened by the recollection of the vanished snow-storms of recent winter, and of all the anxieties and toils attending his peculiar charge. Even the hard-working mechanic of the village or town, shares the general gladness of the season. As he strolls in sweet relaxation into the glittering fields, or along the blossoming hedgerows and lanes, haply supporting with his hand the tottering footsteps of his child, or carrying the tender infant in his arms, he breathes the freshning air, treads the reviving turf beneath his feet, and inhales the first faint perfumes, and listens to the first melodies of the year, with an enjoyment that his untaught powers of expression cannot describe."

Composure, Serenity, and Complacency.

"Pure Tone" swelling to "Orotund," "Moderate" Force, "Median Stress," "Middle" Pitch, "Moderate" Inflection "Moderate Movement," Pauses, and Emphasis.

Hymn. — Mrs. Steele.

"Father, whate'er of earthly bliss
 Thy sovereign will denies,
Accepted at thy throne of grace
 Let this petition rise: —

"'Give me a calm, a thankful heart,
  From every murmur free ;
The blessings of thy grace impart,
  And make me live to thee.'

"Oh! let the hope that thou art mine,
  My life and death attend —
Thy presence through my journey shine,
  And crown my journey's end."

"Expression" as before, but carried nearer to that of Joy, by a slight increase of Force, rise of Pitch, and quickening of "Movement."

Extract from Isaiah XI.

V 1. "And there shall come forth a rod out of the stem of Jesse, and a branch shall grow out of his roots: 2. And the Spirit of the Lord shall rest upon him, the spirit of wisdom and understanding, the spirit of counsel and might, the spirit of knowledge and of the fear of the Lord; 3. and shall make him of quick understanding in the fear of the Lord: and he shall not judge after the sight of his eyes, neither reprove after the hearing of his ears; 4. but with righteousness shall he judge the poor, and reprove with equity for the meek of the earth: and he shall smite the earth with the rod of his mouth, and with the breath of his lips shall he slay the wicked. 5. And righteousness shall be the girdle of his loins, and faithfulness the girdle of his reins. 6. The wolf also shall dwell with the lamb, and the leopard shall lie down with the kid; and the calf and the young lion and the fatling together; and a little child shall lead them. 7. And the cow and the bear shall feed; their young ones shall lie down together: and the lion shall eat straw like the ox. 8. And the sucking child shall play on the hole of the asp, and the weaned child shall put his hand on the cockatrice's den. 9. They shall **not hurt nor destroy** in all my holy mountain : for the earth shall be full of the knowledge of the Lord, as the waters cover the sea."

"Expression" as before, but softened and levelled by the influence of Tranquility.

Religious Retirement. — Logan.

"Religious retirement takes off the impression which the neighborhood of evil example has a tendency to make upon the mind. The world, my friends, is not in general a school of virtue, it is often the scene of vanity and vice. Corrupted manners, vicious deeds, evil communications, surround us on every side.

"To avoid the pollution with which the world is infected, to keep off the intrusion of vain and sinful thoughts, enter into thy chamber, and shut thy doors around thee. There the wicked cease from troubling, there the man who is wearied of the world is at rest. There the glare of external objects disappears, and the chains that bound you to the world, are broken. There you shut out the strife of tongues, the impertinences of the idle, the lies of the vain, the scandal of the malicious, the slanders of the defamer, and all that world of iniquity which proceeds from the tongue. In this asylum thy safety dwells. To thy holy retreat, an impure guest dares not approach. Enjoying the blessed calm and serenity of thy own mind, thou hearest the tempest raging around thee, and spending its strength; the objects of sense being removed, the appetites which they excited, depart along with them. The scene being shifted, and the actors gone, the passions which they raised, die away."

"Expression" as before, but deepened by the mood of Contemplation.

Evening. — Alison.

"There is an even-tide in the day, — an hour when the sun retires, and the shadows fall, and when nature assumes the appearance of soberness and silence. It is an hour from which everywhere the thoughtless fly, as peopled only in their imagination with images of gloom: — it is the hour, on the other hand, which, in every age, the wise have loved, as bringing with it sentiments and affections more valuable than all the splendors of the day.

"Its first impression is to still all the turbulence of thought or passion which the day may have brought forth. We follow, with our eye, the descending sun, — we listen to the decaying sounds of labor and of toil, — and, when all the fields are silent around us, we feel a kindred stillness to breathe upon our souls, and to calm them from the agitations of society.

"From this first impression, there is a second which naturally follows it; — in the day we are living with men, — in the eventide we begin to live with nature; — we see the world withdrawn from us, — the shades of night darken over the habitations of men; and we feel ourselves alone. It is an hour fitted, as it would seem, by Him who made us, to still, but with gentle hand, the throb of every unruly passion, and the ardor of every impure desire; and while it veils for a time the world that misleads us, to awaken in our hearts those legitimate affections which the heat of the day may have dissolved.

"There is yet a farther scene it presents to us: — While the world withdraws from us, and while the shades of the evening darken upon our dwellings, the splendors of the firmament come forward to our view. In the moments when earth is overshadowed, heaven opens to our eyes the radiance of a sublimer Being; our hearts follow the successive splendors of the scene; and while we forget, for a time, the obscurity of earthly concerns, we feel that there are 'yet greater things than these.'"

"Expression" as before, but enlivened by Cheerfulness.

A Cheerful Mind. — Addison.

"I cannot but look upon a cheerful state of mind as a constant habitual gratitude to the great Author of nature. An inward cheerfulness is an implicit praise and thanksgiving to Providence, under all its dispensations. It is a kind of acquiescence in the state wherein we are placed, and a secret approbation of the Divine will in his conduct towards man.

"A man who uses his best endeavors to live according to the dictates of virtue and right reason, has two perpetual sources of cheerfulness, — in the consideration of his own nature, and of that Being on whom he has a dependence. If he looks into himself, he cannot but rejoice in that existence, which is so lately bestowed upon him, and which, after millions of ages, will be still new, and still in its beginning. How many self-congratulations naturally arise on the mind, when it reflects on this its entrance into eternity, when it takes a view of those improvable faculties, which in a few years, and even at its first setting out, have made so considerable a progress, and which will be still receiving an increase of perfection, and consequently an increase of happiness! The consciousness of such a being spreads a perpetual diffusion of joy through the soul of a virtuous man, and makes him look upon himself, every moment, as more happy than he knows how to conceive.

"The second source of cheerfulness to a good mind, is, its consideration of that Being on whom we have our dependence, and in whom, though we behold him as yet but in the first faint discoveries of his perfections, we see everything that we can imagine as great, glorious, or amiable. We find ourselves everywhere upheld by his goodness, and surrounded with an immensity of love and mercy. In short, we depend upon a Being, whose power qualifies him to make us happy by an infinity of means, whose goodness and truth engage him to make those happy who desire it of him, and whose unchangeableness will secure us in this happiness to all eternity.

"Such considerations, which every one should perpetually cherish in his thoughts, will banish from us all that secret heaviness of heart which unthinking men are subject to when they lie under no real affliction,— all that anguish which we may feel from any evil that actually oppresses us,— to which I may likewise add those little cracklings of mirth and folly, that are apter to betray virtue than support it; and establish in us such an even and cheerful temper, as makes us pleasing to ourselves, to those with whom we converse, and to Him whom we are made to please."

EXERCISES IN "VARIATION."

The term "variation," in its relations to elocution, is used as a convenient designation for the change of "expression," which occurs in passing from the utterance of one emotion to that of another, in successive reading or speaking. It is, in reality, nothing else than true expression, adapted to the variations of feeling, in consecutive passages. The term "modulation" is in popular language often employed,— though incorrectly, as regards musical nomenclature, — to designate the changes of voice which arise from change of feeling.

The actual variation, however, by whatever name it may be called, is felt, by all hearers, to be an essential point in elocution, as the only means of rendering sentiment natural or impressive to the ear. An unvaried voice, as contrasted with one which gives a change of effect to every new turn of thought or feeling, is, relatively, as the dead body contrasted with the living man. The student cannot be too careful to repeat exercises such as the following, till his voice has acquired perfect flexibility, and **the full power of instant change of effect, from the style** of one emotion to that of another. Some passages require frequent and entire changes of every trait of voice, to keep up with the perpetually shifting effect of sentiment and expression, in the language of the composition. — The following are but a few specimens of the requisite exercises in this department of elocution; but they may suffice to suggest the mode in which practice should be conducted.

INVOCATION OF LIGHT. — Milton.

Sublimity.

"Orotund Quality," Full Force, "Median Stress," "Low" Pitch, Prevalent "Falling Inflection," and "Monotone," "Slow Movement," Long Pauses, Moderate Emphasis, Powerful "Expression."

" Hail holy Light! offspring of Heaven first-born,
Or of the Eternal co-eternal beam
May I express thee unblamed? Since God is Light,
And never but in unapproached light
Dwelt from eternity; dwelt then in thee,
Bright effluence of bright essence increate!
Or hear'st thou, rather, pure ethereal stream
Whose fountain who shall tell? Before the sun
Before the heavens thou wert, and, at the voice
Of God, as with a mantle didst invest
The rising world of waters, dark and deep,
Won from the void and formless infinite.
Thee I revisit now with bolder wing,
Escaped the Stygian pool, though long detained
In that obscure sojourn, while on my flight
Through utter and through middle darkness borne,
With other notes than to the Orphean lyre
I sung of chaos and eternal night,
Taught by the heavenly Muse to venture down
The dark descent, and up to re-ascend,
Though hard and rare. — Thee I revisit safe,
And feel thy sovereign vital lamp.

Deep Pathos.

"Quality" as before, Force "Subdued," "Stress" as before, "Lowest" Pitch, "Semitone" and plaintive effect of "minor" intervals, "Slowest Movement," Pauses as before, Tender and subdued "Expression."

"But thou
Revisit'st not these eyes, that roll in vain
To find thy piercing ray, and find no dawn;
So thick a drop serene hath quenched their orbs,
Or dim suffusion veiled.

Tranquility, Solemnity, and Sublimity.

"Quality" as before, Force "Moderate," "Stress" as before, "Middle" Pitch, "Inflection" varied, "Movement" and Pauses "Moderate," "Expression" moderate.

"Yet not the more
Cease I to wander where the muses haunt
Clear spring, or shady grove, or sunny hill;
Smit with the love of sacred song. But chief
Thee Zion, and the flowery brooks beneath,
That wash thy hallowed feet, and warbling flow,
Nightly I visit; nor sometimes forget
Those other two, equalled with me in fate,
(So were I equalled with them in renown,)
Blind Thamyris and blind Mæonides,
And Tiresias and Phineus, prophets old;

Beauty, — added to the preceding emotions.

"Quality" as before, Force softened, "Stress" as before, Pitch deepened, Prevalent "Monotone," "Movement" slower, Pauses longer, "Expression" ardent but gentle.

"Then feed on thoughts that voluntary move
Harmonious numbers; as the wakeful bird
Sings darkling, and in shadiest covert hid
Tunes her nocturnal note. Thus with the year
Seasons return.

Deep Pathos.

"Quality" as before, Force "Subdued," " Stress" as before, Pitch "Low," Prevalent " Semitone " and occasional "Minor Thirds," "Movement Slow," Pauses long, " Expression " deeply plaintive

" But not to me returns
Day, or the sweet approach of even or morn,
Or sight of vernal bloom, or summer's rose,
Or flocks or herds, or human face divine ;

Deep Grief and Melancholy.

" Aspirated Orotund Quality," Force " Suppressed,"* " Vanishing Stress," " Lowest " Pitch, Prevalent " Falling Inflection," " Slowest Movement," Long Pauses, Strong Emphasis, Intense " Expression."

" But cloud, instead, and ever during dark
Surround me, from the cheerful ways of men
Cut off; and, for the book of knowledge fair,
Presented with a universal blank
Of Nature's works, to me expunged and rased ;
And wisdom at one entrance quite shut out.

Sublime and Devout Aspiration.

" Pure Orotund Quality," Earnest and " Empassioned " Force " Median Stress," " Middle " Pitch, Prevalent " Falling Inflection," " Moderate Movement," Moderate Pauses, Strong Emphasis, Intense " Expression."

" So much the rather, thou, celestial Light,
Shine inward, and the mind through all her powers
Irradiate ; there plant eyes ; all mists from thence
Purge and disperse, that I may see and tell
Of things invisible to mortal sight !"

---

* The distinction between "suppressed" and "subdued" force, is that the latter is "pure," the former "aspirated." " Subdued " force merges the breath wholly in sound: "suppressed" force merges, partially, sound in breath, — and causes a slightly hoarse or whispering effect to the ear.

SOLILOQUY OF SATAN.—Milton.

Hatred.

"Aspirated Orotund Quality," Intense Force, "Thorough Stress," Pitch varying from "Low" to "Middle," Prevalent "Falling Inflection," "Movement" varying from "Slow" to "Moderate," and thence to "Rapid," Pauses varying in length with the rate of the "Movement," Intense Emphasis, and Fierce "Expression."

" O thou, that with surpassing glory crowned,
Look'st from thy sole dominion like the god
Of this new world, at whose sight all the stars
Hid their diminished heads, to thee I call,
But with no friendly voice, and add thy name
O sun ! to tell thee how I hate thy beams,

Regret.

"Pure Orotund Quality," Softened Force, "Median Stress," "Low" Pitch, Prevalent "Falling Inflection" of "Minor Third," "Slow Movement," Long Pauses, Subdued "Expression."

" That bring to my remembrance from what state
I fell, how glorious once ! — above thy sphere,
Till pride and worse ambition threw me down,
Warring in heaven against heaven's matchless king.—

Remorse.

Style, in all respects, as before, but "Expression" deepened in every trait.

"Ah ! wherefore ? He deserved no such return
Of me, whom he created what I was
In that bright eminence, and with his good
Upbraided none. Nor was his service hard.
What could be less than to afford him praise,
The easiest recompense, and pay him thanks
How due !—

Self-Reproach.

Style, as before, but deepened, and rendered more intense, throughout.

"Yet all his good proved ill in me,
And wrought but malice; lifted up so high,
I 'sdained subjection, and thought one step higher
Would set me highest, and in a moment quit
The debt immense of endless gratitude
So burdensome, still paying, still to owe:
Forgetful what from him I still received;
And understood not that a grateful mind
By owing owes not, but still pays, at once
Indebted and discharged. — What burden then?

Grief and Regret.

"Pure Orotund Quality," Intense but "Subdued" Force, "Vanishing" and tremulous "Stress," Pitch varying from "High" to "Middle," "Plaintive Inflection" of "Minor Third," "Slow Movement," Long Pauses, "Expression" intense, but plaintive and subdued.

"Oh! had his powerful destiny ordained
Me some inferior angel, I had stood
Then happy; no unbounded hope had raised
Ambition!

Hesitation.

"Aspirated Orotund Quality," "Suppressed" Force, "Radical Stress," "High" Pitch, Prevalent "Falling Inflection," "Moderate Movement," Pauses Long, Earnest "Expression."

"Yet why not? — some other power
As great might have aspired, and me, though mean,
Drawn to his part.

Envy.

"Aspirated Pectoral and Guttural Quality," "Empassioned" Force, "Explosive Radical Stress," "Low" Pitch, "Falling Inflection,"

"Rapid Movement," Brief Pauses, Intense Emphasis, Fierce "Expression."

"But other powers as great
Fell not, but stand unshaken, — from within
Or from without, — to all temptation armed.

Self-Reproach.

"Aspirated Orotund Quality," Intense Force, "Explosive Radical" and "Vanishing Stress," High Pitch, Varied inflection, "Movement" varying from "Rapid" to "Slow," Pauses varying from brief to long, Earnest Emphasis, Strong "Expression."

"Hadst thou the same free will and power to stand?
Thou hadst: whom hast thou, then, or what to accuse,
But heaven's free love, dealt equally to all?

Imprecation.

"Aspirated Pectoral and Guttural Quality," Utmost "Empassioned Force," "Explosive Radical Stress," "Low" Pitch, Deep "Falling Inflection," "Movement" varying from "Rapid" to "Slow," Pauses varying from brief to long, Strongest Emphasis, "Expression" varying from fierceness to grief.

"Be then his love accursed! since love or hate
To me alike it deals eternal wo:
Nay cursed be thou; since against his thy will
Chose freely what it now so justly rues.

Distraction, Agony, Horror, and Despair.

"Quality" varying from "Aspirated Orotund" to harshest Guttural and Pectoral Utterance, Force varying from the utmost intensity to suppression, "Vanishing Stress," Pitch varying from "High" to "Lowest," Deep "Falling Inflection," "Movement" varying from "Slow" to "Rapid," Pauses varying from long to brief, Intensest Emphasis and "Expression."

"Me miserable! — which way shall I fly
Infinite wrath and infinite despair?
Which way I fly is hell; myself am hell;
And in the lowest deep a lower deep

Still threatening to devour me opens wide;
To which the hell I suffer seems a heaven.

Contrition.

"Pure Orotund Quality," "Subdued" Force, Gentle "Vanishing and tremulous Stress," "High Pitch," Plaintive "Inflection" of "Minor Third," "Slowest Movement," Pauses extremely long, Softened and tender "Expression."

"Oh! then at last relent. — Is there no place
Left for repentance, none for pardon left?

Scorn.

"Aspirated Orotund Quality," "Empassioned" Force, "Explosive Radical Stress," "Middle" Pitch, Prevalent "Falling Inflection," "Brisk Movement," Pauses short, Vehement Emphasis, Abrupt "Expression."

"None left but by submission; and that word
Disdain forbids me, and my dread of shame
Among the spirits beneath, whom I seduced
With other promises and other vaunts
Than to submit, boasting I could subdue
The Omnipotent.

Deep Regret and Despair.

"Aspirated Pectoral Quality," "Empassioned" Force, "Vanishing Stress," "Low" Pitch, Prevalent "Falling Inflection" of the "Fifth," "Slow Movement," Long Pauses, Intense Emphasis and "Expression."

"Ay me! they little know
How dearly I abide that boast so vain,
Under what torments inwardly I groan,
While they adore me on the throne of hell;
With diadem and sceptre high advanced,
The lower still I fall, only supreme
In misery: such joy ambition finds.

Reflection and Deliberation.

"Pure Orotund Quality," "Moderate" Force, "Radical Stress," "Middle" Pitch, Prevalent "Falling Inflection," "Movement" varying from "Moderate" to "Animated," Pauses varying from moderate to brief, Emphasis and "Expression" increasing in intensity from moderate to fierce.

" But say I could repent, and could obtain
By act of grace my former state; how soon
Would height recall high thoughts, how soon unsay
What feigned submission swore! Ease would recant
Vows made in pain, as violent and void.
For never can true reconcilement grow
Where wounds of deadly hate have pierced so deep;
Which would but lead me to a worse relapse
And heavier fall; so should I purchase dear
Short intermission bought with double smart.
This knows my Punisher; therefore as far
From granting he as I from begging peace.

Malice.

"Aspirated Pectoral and Guttural Quality," "Empassioned" Force, "Vanishing Stress," "Low" Pitch, Prevalent "Falling Inflection" of the "Fifth," "Slow Movement," Long Pauses, Emphasis and "Expression" intense.

" All hope excluded thus, behold, instead
Of us outcast, exiled, his new delight
Mankind created, and for him this world.

Defiance and Revenge.

"Quality" varying from "Aspirated Pectoral" to "Pure Orotund," and reverting to the former, — "Empassioned" Force, of the utmost intensity, — "Thorough Stress," Pitch varying from "Low" to "High," and reverting to the former, — "Movement" varying from "Slow" to "Rapid," reverting to "Slow" and again to "Rapid," and closing with "Slow," — Pauses varying with the rate of "Movement," Emphasis and "Expression" of the deepest and fiercest character.

" So farewell hope; and with hope, farewell fear,
Farewell remorse: all good to me is lost;
Evil, be thou my good; by thee at least
Divided empire with heaven's king I hold,

By thee; and more than half perhaps will reign,
As man ere long, and this new world shall know."

THE DYING CHRISTIAN.— Pope.
Awe.
Gently " Aspirated Pectoral Quality," " Suppressed Force," " Median Stress," " Lowest Pitch," " Monotone," " Slowest Movement," Long Pauses, " Expression " intensely earnest but subdued.

" Vital spark of heavenly flame,

Longing.
" Pure Tone," Earnest but " Subdued " Force, " Vanishing Stress," " High " Pitch, Plaintive " Semitone," " Slow Movement," Long Pauses, " Expression " as before.

" Quit, oh! quit this mortal frame!

Fear.
" Aspirated Quality," " Suppressed " Force, Tremulous " Stress," " High " Pitch, " Semitone," " Slowest Movement," Very long Pause preceding and following, " Expression " soft but extremely vivid.

" Trembling,

Joy.
" Pure Tone," " Empassioned " Force, " Median Stress," " Highest " Pitch, " Falling Inflection," Lively " Movement," Intense " Expression."

hoping,

Languor.
" Pure Tone," " Subdued " Force, " Median Stress," " High " Pitch, " Semitone," " Slowest Movement," Feeble and Plaintive " Expression."

lingering,

Ardor.
" Aspirated Orotund," " Empassioned " Force, " Thorough Stress," " Middle " Pitch, " Falling Inflection," " Rapid Movement," Vivid " Expression."

flying. —

Anguish.

"Aspirated Orotund," "Empassioned" Force, "Median Stress," "Highest" Pitch, Plaintive Double Inflection,* "Slowest Movement," Intense "Expression."

    "Oh! the pain, —

Rapture.

"Pure Orotund Quality," Intense "Empassioned" Force, "Radical Stress," "High" Pitch, "Falling Inflection" of the "Fifth," "Lively Movement," Vivid "Expression."

    the bliss of dying!

Entreaty.

Slightly "Aspirated Quality," Earnest but "Subdued" Force, "Tremulous Stress," "High" Pitch, "Falling Inflection" of "Semitone" and "Minor Third," "Slow" Movement, Feeble Emphasis, Long Pauses, Plaintive and languid "Expression."

    "Cease, fond Nature, cease thy strife,
    And let me languish into life!

Extreme Earnestness.

Half-whisper, "Suppressed" Force, "Explosive Radical Stress," "High" Pitch, Prevalent "Falling Inflection," "Animated Movement," Earnest Emphasis, Brief Pauses, Intense "Expression."

    "Hark! they whisper — angels say,
    'Sister spirit, come away.'

Awe and Astonishment.

"Aspirated Pectoral Quality," "Suppressed" Force, "Explosive Radical Stress," "Low" Pitch gradually descending to "Lowest," "Poetic Inflection" of "Upward Second," "Slowest Movement," Exhausted Emphasis, Long Pauses, "Expression" suppressed.

    "What is this absorbs me quite?
    Steals my senses, shuts my sight,

---

* "Falling Circumflex," or "Direct Wave" with "Minor Third." The former designation is presented for the convenience of students of Walker's system. The latter is the more exact and the true scientific distinction, as in the analysis of Dr. Rush.

Drowns my spirits, draws my breath? —
Tell me, my soul, can this be — death? —

Wonder.

"Aspirated Orotund," Intense "Empassioned" Force, "Explosive Radical Stress," "High" Pitch, "Falling Inflection," "Rapid Movement," Brief Pauses, Intense Emphasis and "Expression."

"The world recedes! it disappears!

Rapture, Exultation, and Triumph.

"Pure Orotund Quality," "Empassioned" Force, approaching to Shouting, "Thorough Stress," "High" Pitch, Prevalent "Falling Inflection" of the "Fifth," "Movement" "Rapid" and constantly accelerating in the first three of the following lines, then retarded by the full and prolonged swell of triumph, in the last two lines, — Pauses corresponding to the rate of "Movement," Emphasis intense, "Expression" ecstatic.

"Heaven opens to mine eyes! — mine ears
With sounds seraphic ring!
Lend, lend your wings! — I mount! I fly!
O grave! where is thy victory?
O death! where is thy sting?"*

THE ENTERPRISE OF THE PILGRIM FATHERS OF NEW ENGLAND. — Edward Everett.

Didactic Sentiment.

"Pure Orotund Quality," "Moderate" Force, Unempassioned "Radical Stress," "Middle" Pitch, Varied "Inflection,"—"Moderate" "Movement," Pauses, and Emphasis,—"Expression" rising from moderate to animated.

"As in private character, adversity is often requisite to give a proper direction and temper to strong qualities; so the noblest traits of national character, even under the

---

* The above example was selected intentionally, as an impressive lesson on the extent to which lyric poetry, — and, particularly, sacred lyrics, — carry the variation of vocal expression. The hymn quoted is the highest flight of the human soul, in this form; and the utterance is necessarily carried to ecstasy, in its effect, — if the spirit of the poetry is thrown into the voice.

freest and most independent of hereditary governments, are commonly to be sought in the ranks of a protesting minority, or of a dissenting sect. Never was this truth more clearly illustrated than in the settlement of New England.

"Could a common calculation of policy have dictated the terms of that settlement, no doubt our foundations would have been laid beneath the royal smile. Convoys and navies would have been solicited to waft our fathers to the coast; armies, to defend the infant communities; and the flattering patronage of princes and lords, to espouse their interests in the councils of the mother country.

Oratorical Sentiment.

"Pure Orotund Quality," "Declamatory" Force, "Thorough Stress" of moderate energy, "Middle" Pitch, — Varied "Inflection," but prevalent "Downward Slide" of the "Fifth" and "Third," — "Moderate" "Movement" and Pauses, Energetic Emphasis, Vivid "Expression."

"Happy, that our fathers enjoyed no such patronage happy, that they fell into no such protecting hands; happy, that our foundations were silently and deeply cast in quiet insignificance, beneath a charter of banishment, persecution, and contempt; so that when the royal arm was at length outstretched against us, instead of a submissive child, tied down by former graces, it found a youthful giant in the land, born amidst hardships, and nourished on the rocks, indebted for no favors, and owing no duty. From the dark portals of the star-chamber, and in the stern text of the acts of uniformity, the pilgrims received a commission, more efficient, than any that ever bore the royal seal. Their banishment to Holland was fortunate; the decline of their little company in the strange land, was fortunate; the difficulties which they experienced in getting the royal consent to banish themselves to this wilderness, were fortunate; all the tears and heart-breakings of that ever memorable parting at Delfthaven, had the happiest influence on the rising destinies of New England. All this purified the ranks of the settlers. These rough touches of fortune brushed off the light, uncertain, selfish spirits. They made it a grave, solemn, self-denying expedition, and required of those who engaged in it, to be so too. They cast a broad shadow of thought and seriousness over the cause;* and if this sometimes deepened into melancholy and bitterness, can we find no apology for such a human weakness?

Pathetic Description.

" Pure Orotund Quality," " Subdued " Force, " Median Stress," " Low " Pitch, Prevalent " Falling Inflection " of " Minor Third," " Slow Movement, Long Pauses, Softened Emphasis, Grave and plaintive " Expression."

" It is sad indeed to reflect on the disasters, which the little band of pilgrims encountered. Sad to see a portion of them, the prey of unrelenting cupidity, treacherously embarked in an unsound, unseaworthy ship, which they are soon obliged to abandon, and crowd themselves into one vessel; one hundred persons, besides the ship's company, in a vessel of one hundred and sixty tons. One is touched at the story of the long, cold, and weary autumnal passage; of the landing on the inhospitable rocks at this dismal season; where they are deserted before long by the ship, which had brought them, and which seemed their only hold upon the world of fellow-men, a prey to the elements and to want, and fearfully ignorant of the numbers, the power, and the temper of the savage tribes, that filled the unexplored continent, upon whose verge they had ventured.

Energetic Declamation.

" Orotund Quality," " Declamatory " Force, Moderate " Thorough Stress," " Middle " Pitch, Prevalent " Falling Inflection," " Mod-

---
* Here the expression varies suddenly to the style of subdued and

erate" "Movement" and Pauses, Energetic Emphasis, Strong "Expression."

"But all this wrought together for good. These trials of wandering and exile, of the ocean, the winter, the wilderness, and the savage foe, were the final assurance of success. It was these that put far away from our fathers' cause, all patrician softness, all hereditary claims to preëminence. No effeminate nobility crowded into the dark and austere ranks of the pilgrims. No Carr or Villiers would lead on the ill-provided band of despised puritans. No well-endowed clergy were on the alert, to quit their cathedrals, and set up a pompous hierarchy in the frozen wilderness. No craving governors were anxious to be sent over to our cheerless El Dorado of ice and snow. No, they could not say they had encouraged, patronized, or helped the pilgrims: their own cares, their own labors, their own councils, their own blood, contrived all, achieved all, bore all, sealed all. They could not afterwards fairly pretend to reap where they had not strown; and as our fathers reared this broad and solid fabric with pains and watchfulness, unaided, barely tolerated, it did not fall when the favor which had always been withholden, was changed into wrath; when the arm which had never supported, was raised to destroy.

Pathetic Description.

Style of *elocution*, as in the example of the same species of *rhetorical* style, on the preceding page.

"Methinks I see it now, that one solitary, adventurous vessel, the Mayflower of a forlorn hope, freighted with the prospects of a future state, and bound across the unknown sea. I behold it pursuing, with a thousand misgivings, the uncertain, the tedious voyage. Suns rise and set, and weeks and months pass, and winter surprises them on the deep, but brings them not the sight of the wished-for shore. I see them now scantily supplied with provisions, crowded almost to suffocation in their ill-stored prison, delayed by calms, pursuing a circuitous route;— and now driven in fury before the raging tempest, on the high and giddy waves.

Awe and Horror.

Partially "Aspirated Quality," "Empassioned" Force, "Thorough Stress," "Low" Pitch, Prevalent "Falling Inflection" of the "Fifth," "Slow Movement," Long Pauses, Intense Emphasis, and "Expression."

"The awful voice of the storm howls through the rigging. The laboring masts seem strained from their base; the dismal sound of the pumps is heard;— the ship leaps, as it were, madly, from billow to billow:— the ocean breaks, and settles with engulfing floods over the floating deck, and beats with deadening, shivering weight, against the staggered vessel.

Pathetic Description.
Style, as before.

"I see them, escaped from these perils, pursuing their all but desperate undertaking, and landed at last, after a five months' passage, on the ice-clad rocks of Plymouth, — weak and weary from the voyage,— poorly armed, scantily provisioned, depending on the charity of their ship-master for a draught of beer on board, drinking nothing but water on shore,— without shelter,— without means,— surrounded by hostile tribes.

Oratorical Apostrophe.

"Orotund Quality," "Declamatory" Force. "Thorough Stress," "Middle" Pitch, Prevalent "Falling Inflection," of the "Fifth," "Moderate" "Movement," and Pauses, Energetic Emphasis, and bold "Expression."

"Shut now the volume of history; and tell me, on any principle of human probability, what shall be the fate of this handful of adventurers.— Tell me, man of military science, in how many months were they all swept off by the thirty savage tribes, enumerated within the early limits of New England? Tell me, politician, how long did this shadow of a colony, on which your conventions and treaties had not smiled, languish on the distant coast? Student of history, compare for me the baffled projects, the deserted settlements, the abandoned adventures of other times, and find the parallel of this.

Earnest Interrogation.

" Quality " and Force, as before, — " Radical Stress," " High " Pitch, " Rising Inflection " of the " Third," " Moderate Movement," Long Pauses, Earnest Emphasis and " Expression."

" Was it the winter's storm, beating upon the houseless heads of women and children; was it hard labor and spare meals; — was it disease, — was it the tomahawk, — was it the deep malady of a blighted hope, a ruined enterprise, and a broken heart, aching in its last moments, at the recollection of the loved and left, beyond the sea: was it some, or all of these united, that hurried this forsaken company to their melancholy fate? —

Astonishment

Slightly " Aspirated Quality," " Declamatory " Force, " Compound Stress," " Highest " Pitch, " Rising Inflection," of the " Fifth '» and " Octave," " Slow Movement," Long Pauses, Intense Emphasis and " Expression."

" And is it possible that neither of these causes, that not all combined, were able to blast this bud of hope? — * Is it possible, that from a beginning so feeble, so frail, so worthy, not so much of admiration as of pity, there has gone forth a progress so steady, a growth so wonderful, an expansion so ample, a reality so important, a promise, yet to be fulfilled, so glorious?"

---

* The effect of increasing astonishment is to produce "empassioned" force, " vanishing stress," and " falling inflections " of the " fifth," in the last sentence.

READING OF THE SCRIPTURES.

The mechanical and unmeaning style of reading, which arises from prevalent defects in early education, is nowhere more perceptible or more injurious in effect, than when exemplified in a passage of Scripture. With the language of the sacred volume are associated all the highest thoughts and profoundest emotions of which the soul is susceptible; and our utterance, in the reading of its pages, ought to be the expression of such states of mind. But no book, generally speaking, is read with less of appropriate feeling or expressive sense.

The Scriptures are not unfrequently read with tones which do not indicate any personal interest, on the part of the reader, in the sentiments which he is uttering. The effect of the cold, dry style, commonly adopted in reading the Bible, is often, indeed, rendered utterly absurd, when the attention happens, for a moment, to fall on the oriental fervor and sublimity of the style of language, in contrast with the meagre and shabby effect of the readers' voice. The words, in such cases, speak of God and of eternity, in strains which the undebased mind associates with the vastness of the overhanging firmament, and the grandeur of the reverberating thunder; but the reader's tone is that of the coolest indifference, or of an affair ordinary and trivial. The fault of a cold, inexpressive voice, is often the result of an anxiety to shun all appearance of assumed and imposing style, and to allow the hearer to feel for himself, the solemnity of the subject. But as it is destitute of the natural indication of earnestness, in the reader, it deadens the sympathy of the hearer.

Another error in the style of reading, is that of loading the words of Scripture with a formal, unwieldly, and unmeaning tone, which aims at a certain solemn dignity of effect, but only reaches a very unmusical song.

Sometimes, a third fault is incurred, by a desire to break through the trammels of conventional restraint, and produce a lively impression on the mind, by familiar and vivid tone, which savors too much of ordinary talk by the fireside. But coldness and familiarity are alike forbidden, on subjects which appeal to the deepest susceptibilities of the heart.

The monotonous solemnity of tone, which is exemplified by many readers of the sacred volume, defeats its own purpose, by a dull uniformity of effect; as a painter would spoil a picture by the exclusive use of one sombre tint, applied indiscriminately to scenes of evening, morning, and midday. The cold, indifferent reader seems to forget the vivid interest which appropriately belongs to every subject introduced in the pages of Scripture; the lively reader seems, by his familiar and anecdotic style, to overlook the majesty of the sacred volume; but the formal reader seems blind to all the varied beauties of language, and the natural and simple expression, which pervade, and so peculiarly characterize, both the Old Testament and the New.

The dignity of the subject, the sublimity of the style, the simplicity of the language, demand, in every passage of Scripture, the mingling effects of grave, full, and vivid expression. To the reading of the sacred page should be brought every aid arising from the deepest impressions on the heart, the most vivid effects of poetic imagination, the most refining influences of the highest intellectual culture. All the treasures of knowledge, gathered by excursive thought from the fields of science and literature, all the richer and truer wealth of life and experience, which an individual possesses, — and which never fails to modify the qualities and expression of the voice, — should be made tributary to the exercise of reading the sacred Scriptures, in the offices of devotion. The spiritual and the intellectual nature of man is then, if ever, at its maximum of experience and of power, when permitted to mingle its workings with those of the Divine mind in revelation.

The defectiveness and poverty of our modes of education, together with the deadening effects of habit and routine, convert the reading of the most impressive of all books into an ineffectual ceremony. A living and a genuine culture in early life, — a culture which should cherish the expressive powers of man, would effectually prevent these and similar results. That such would be the general issue, no one can doubt, who has observed the effects of faithful self-culture, in a single instance. Who can ever forget the impressions left on his mind by hearing, even once, a passage of Scripture read by the late Dr. Nettleton, with that characteristic depth and vividness of effect, which seemed to bespeak a soul communing, face to face, with the Invisible? Who, that was ever present on such an occasion, can forget the hushed and profound attention with which a congregation would listen to the deep and quiet, but thrilling tones of Channing, in the exercise of reading the sacred volume?

The mindless and heartless style in which the Bible is read, at school, when it is made a part of the requisite exercises for acquiring a merely mechanical facility in the process of reading, fastens itself upon the ear, as an unconscious standard of manner, for life; so much so, that the majority of readers in the pulpit, seem never to imagine, that they can ever so far identify themselves with what they read, as to render it the common justice of a single true or natural tone of the voice.*

---

* The weekly reading of the Bible, as a Saturday exercise, in the parish schools of **Scotland**, is usually accompanied by **oral explanations**

Could we, for a moment, divest ourselves of the influence of association, and,—standing aloof from "things as they are," in the "second nature" of habit,—fasten our minds on the great thought, that the world contains a volume stamped with the legible impress of Revelation, would not our just expectation be that those whose duty it is to minister at the altar, would covet, above all acquisitions, the ability to read it worthily and impressively? At present, the thing is not even thought of. The very idea startles the theological student, as something odd. But when you come to inquire into the case, you find that he has, all along, had his mind on a certain shabby, dingy-looking, much worn volume, out of which, in common with others of his age, he had, in the days of his boyhood, to learn to read, at school; or from which he had to read a single detached verse, in the daily routine of family devotion; or which, in the long, weary, warm, summer sabbaths, he used to hear droned over in the pulpit.

Mere animation, or a rhetorical style, in reading the Scriptures, is unquestionably offensive, both to just sentiment and good taste, and to be as carefully avoided as the other faults which have been enumerated. But while all artificial and fancied excellence, is, in the utterance of the words of sacred truth, a thing that only disgusts or shocks a sober mind, it is not less true, that genuine cultivation and diligent practice, are as successful in this, as in any other form of human effort, and that when the occupants of our pulpits shall have acquitted themselves in this as in other parts of their public duties, the power and authority, and the daily influence of the sacred volume, will penetrate society to an extent corresponding to the difference between a dormant and an active life,—a latent and an operative power.

---

from the teacher, and thus rendered an aid to good reading as well as to religious instruction

Classification of the Parts of Scripture.

The Bible, regarded for the moment, as a volume which may be used for the purposes of audible reading, may be classified, in rhetorical arrangement, as follows:

1. Narrative passages, varying in style, with their subjects, from the familiar to the sublime, — as in the historical books of the Old Testament, and the Gospels, in the New.

2. Didactic and doctrinal passages, — as in the Epistles, which, being addressed to the understanding and the reason, require modifications of voice in the forms, chiefly, of inflection, emphasis, and pause, — the *intellectual* instruments of effect in elocution.

3. Prophetic and Descriptive passages, — marked by the language of strong epic and dramatic emotion, and requiring a bold, vivid, and expressive style of voice.

4. Lyric passages, — requiring intense expression, in strains of joy, pathos, triumph, grief, adoration, supplication.

NARRATIVE PASSAGES.

The ancient rhetorical arrangement of "low," or familiar, "middle," and "sublime," or elevated styles, may be practically serviceable in arranging the narrative portions of Scripture, for the purposes of elocution. The first division, ("the low,") would comprise all simple and familiar narrations; the last, ("the sublime,") narrative passages of great elevation of style; the second, ("the middle,") would include whatever forms of narrative were neither so familiar as the first, nor so elevated as the third.

Passages which exemplify the style of *familiar* narration, demand attention to the due observance of two opposite principles of expression in elocution, — *grandeur* and *simplicity;* the former being inseparable from sacred *subjects*, — the latter, from the peculiar style of *language*, in the Scriptures. The former mode of expression in elocution, unmodified by the latter, would assume the form of deep "pectoral," and full "orotund" utterance,— a grave, round, ample, and swelling effect of voice. The latter mode of expression, on the contrary, would incline to "oral" quality, — a higher, thinner, and softer utterance, approaching to that of colloquial style. The mild effect of this style of utterance, blending with that of "orotund" grandeur, softens and chastens it to a gentle expression, but does not impair its dignity. The effect on the ear is similar to that produced on the eye and the mind, by a noble deportment softened by condescension.

The common faults in the style of reading the familiar narrative passages of Scripture, are dry monotony, undue vivacity, pompous solemnity, rhetorical and forced variation. The analysis of the appropriate tone for such passages, would suggest that the familiar narratives of the books of Scripture, should be read with a *deeper, softer,* and *slower* voice, than similar compositions in other works; the whole style *vivid, earnest,* but *subdued,* — indicating, at the same time, the *interest* awakened by the *events* which are related, and the *chastening effect* of the *reverence* due to the sacred volume.

EXAMPLES IN FAMILIAR STYLE.

Abraham offering up Isaac. — Gen. xxii. 1—13.

V. 1. "And it came to pass after these things, that God did tempt Abraham, and said unto him, 'Abraham:' And he said, 'Behold, here I am.' 2. And he said, 'Take now thy son, thine only son Isaac, whom thou lovest, and get thee into the land of Moriah; and offer him there for a burnt-offering upon one of the mountains which I will tell thee of.'

3. "And Abraham rose up early in the morning, and saddled his ass, and took two of his young men with him,

and Isaac his son, and clave the wood for the burnt-offering, and rose up, and went unto the place of which God had told him.

4. "Then, on the third day, Abraham lifted up his eyes and saw the place afar off. 5. And Abraham said unto his young men, 'Abide ye here with the ass, and I and the lad will go yonder and worship, and come again to you.' 6. And Abraham took the wood of the burnt-offering, and laid it upon Isaac his son; and he took the fire in his hand and a knife; and they went both of them together.

7. "And Isaac spake unto Abraham his father, and said, 'My father:' and he said, 'Here am I, my son.' And he said, 'Behold the fire and the wood: but where is the lamb for a burnt-offering?' 8. And Abraham said, 'My son, God will provide himself a lamb for a burnt-offering:' so they went both of them together.

9. "And they came to the place which God had told him of; and Abraham built an altar there, and laid the wood in order; and bound Isaac his son, and laid him on the altar upon the wood. 10. And Abraham stretched forth his hand, and took the knife to slay his son. 11. And the angel of the Lord called unto him out of heaven, and said, 'Abraham, Abraham!' And he said, 'Here am I.' 12. And he said, 'Lay not thine hand upon the lad, neither do thou anything unto him: for now I know that thou fearest God, seeing thou hast not withheld thy son, thine only son, from me.'

13. "And Abraham lifted up his eyes, and looked, and behold, behind him a ram caught in a thicket by his horns: And Abraham went and took the ram, and offered him up for a burnt-offering in the stead of his son."

Additional examples of familiar narrative may be found as follows: the Betrothing of Rebekah, Gen. xxiv.; Judah's Appeal to Joseph, Gen. xliv.; Samuel's Report to Eli, 1 Sam. iii. 1—18; the Blind Man restored to Sight, John ix.; the Prodigal Son, Luke xv. 11—32.

EXAMPLES IN "MIDDLE" STYLE.

Narrative passages which, according to rhetorical arrangement, may be classed under the head of "middle" style, require, in reading, a tone of voice which is *deeper, firmer, and more uniformly sustained*, than that of simple and familiar narration, as exemplified in the preceding extracts.

A homely, anecdotic turn of voice, is decidedly objectionable, even in the reading of ordinary historical incidents, as utterly incompatible with the appropriate dignity and elevation of the subject; and the objection to such tones becomes insuperable, when the themes are those of sacred history. The effect of fireside, colloquial intonation, applied to the pages of the Bible, is similar, in its effect, to that of parody on elevated composition. It suggests degrading and ridiculous associations.

A formal and mechanical solemnity of tone, however, can never comport with the reading of a book so remarkable for perfect simplicity of style and natural turns of expression, as the sacred volume. Nor is it claiming too much for the appropriate reading of the Scriptures, to say that it demands the deepest sensibility of soul to revealed truth, united to the quickest and keenest perception of the varying effects of language.

The Death of Abel. — Gen. iv. 3—14.

V. 3. "And in process of time it came to pass, that Cain brought of the fruit of the ground an offering unto the Lord. 4. And Abel, he also brought of the firstlings of his flock, and of the fat thereof. And the Lord had respect unto Abel, and to his offering: 5. but unto Cain, and to his offering, he had not respect. And Cain was very wroth, and his countenance fell. 6. And the Lord said unto Cain, 'Why art thou wroth? and why is thy countenance fallen? 7. If thou doest well, shalt thou not be accepted? and if thou doest not well, sin lieth at the door. And unto thee shall be his desire, and thou shalt rule over him.' 8. And Cain talked with Abel his brother: and it came to pass when they were in the field, that Cain rose up against Abel his brother, and slew him.

9. "And the Lord said unto Cain, 'Where is Abel thy brother?' And he said, 'I know not: Am I my brother's keeper?' 10. And he said, 'What hast thou done? the voice of thy brother's blood crieth unto me from the ground. 11. and now art thou cursed from the earth, which hath opened her mouth to receive thy brother's blood from thy hand. 12. When thou tillest the ground, it shall not henceforth yield unto thee her strength: A fugitive and a vagabond shalt thou be in the earth.' 13. And Cain said unto the Lord, 'My punishment is greater than I can bear. 14. Behold, thou hast driven me out this day from the face of the earth; and from thy face shall I be hid; and I shall be a fugitive and a vagabond in the earth; and it shall come to pass, that every one that findeth me shall slay me.'"

Additional Examples. — Jephthah's Vow, Judges xi. 2—40; the Curse of Jotham, Judges ix.; the Death of Eli, 1 Sam iv. 1—18; the Rejection of Saul, 1 Sam. xv.; David's Encounter with Goliah, 1 Sam. xvii. 1—54; the Reign of Josiah, 2 Kings, xxiii. 1—30; the Raising of Lazarus, Gospel of John, xi. 1—44.

EXAMPLES IN ELEVATED STYLE.

Narration, when characterized by *sublimity*, or by marked elevation, requires a *deeper, fuller, slower, more forcible* and *impressive manner*, than that which is exemplified in the preceding passages.

The common fault in the reading of such parts of Scripture, consists in the absence of an impressive and commanding effect of voice, correspondent to the peculiar character of the subject. The mode of utterance, in such passages as the following, should not only be deep-toned and energetic, but warm and glowing. Fervor is a prominent element in the expression of sublimity and grandeur.

While the voice, however, is rendered full and resonant, in the reading of the loftier and bolder portions of Scripture narrative, correct taste and chastened judgment alike forbid all rhetorical display and inflation of manner, as utterly inconsistent with the genuine utterance of the language of the sacred records. The voice, though glowing with emotion, is, in such circumstances, to be subdued to the mood of reverence and hallowed association. No true heart can tolerate the idea of using the word of God as a theatre for the exhibition of vocal effect and artistic accomplishment.

While the reader shrinks, however, from such results, he can derive from this just repugnance to desecration no plea for the cold, lifeless, and heartless style of mechanical reading, which is so prevalent in the pulpit, and which effectually paralyzes the power of the Bible over the human heart.

Creation. — Gen. i. and ii. 1.

V. 1. " In the beginning God created the heaven and the earth. 2. And the earth was without form, and void; and darkness was upon the face of the deep: and the Spirit of God moved upon the face of the waters. 3. And God said, ' Let there be light:' and there was light. 4. And God saw the light that it was good: and God divided the light from the darkness. 5. And God called the light Day, and the darkness he called Night: and the evening and the morning were the first day.

6. " And God said, 'Let there be a firmament in the midst of the waters, and let it divide the waters from the waters.' 7. And God made the firmament, and divided the waters which were under the firmament from the waters which were above the firmament: and it was so. 8. And God called the firmament Heaven: and the evening and the morning were the second day.

9. "And God said, 'Let the waters under the heaven be gathered together unto one place, and let the dry land appear:' and it was so. 10. And God called the dry land Earth; and the gathering together of the waters called he Seas: and God saw that it was good. 11. And God said, 'Let the earth bring forth grass, the herb yielding seed, and the fruit-tree yielding fruit after his kind, whose seed is in itself, upon the earth:' and it was so. 12. And the earth brought forth grass, and herb yielding seed after his kind, and the tree yielding fruit, whose seed was in itself, after his kind: and God saw that it was good. 13. And the evening and the morning were the third day.

14. "And God said, 'Let there be lights in the firmament of the heaven, to divide the day from the night; and let them be for signs, and for seasons, and for days, and years. 15. And let them be for lights in the firmament of the heaven, to give light upon the earth:' and it was so. 16. And God made two great lights; the greater light to rule the day, and the lesser light to rule the night: he made the stars also. 17. And God set them in the firmament of the heaven to give light upon the earth, 18. and to rule over the day, and over the night, and to divide the light from the darkness: and God saw that it was good. 19. And the evening and the morning were the fourth day.

20. "And God said, 'Let the waters bring forth abundantly the moving creature that hath life, and fowl that may fly above the earth, in the open firmament of heaven.' 21. And God created great whales, and every living creature that moveth, which the waters brought forth abundantly after their kind, and every winged fowl after his kind: and God saw that it was good. 22. And God blessed them, saying, 'Be fruitful, and multiply, and fill the waters in the seas, and let fowl multiply in the earth.' 23. And the evening and the morning were the fifth day.

24. "And God said, 'Let the earth bring forth the living creature after his kind, cattle, and creeping thing, and

beast of the earth after his kind:' and it was so. 25. And God made the beast of the earth after his kind, and cattle after their kind, and everything that creepeth upon the earth after his kind: and God saw that it was good.

26. "And God said, 'Let us make man in our image, after our likeness: and let them have dominion over the fish of the sea, and over the fowl of the air, and over the cattle, and over all the earth, and over every creeping thing that creepeth upon the earth.' 27. So God created man in his own image, in the image of God created he him; male and female created he them. 28. And God blessed them, and God said unto them, 'Be fruitful, and multiply, and replenish the earth, and subdue it: and have dominion over the fish of the sea, and over the fowl of the air, and over every living thing that moveth upon the earth.'

29. "And God said, 'Behold, I have given you every herb bearing seed, which is upon the face of all the earth, and every tree, in the which is the fruit of a tree yielding seed; to you it shall be for meat. 30. And to every beast of the earth, and to every fowl of the air, and to everything that creepeth upon the earth, wherein there is life, I have given every green herb for meat:' and it was so. 31. And God saw everything that he had made, and behold, it was very good. And the evening and the morning were the sixth day. CH. II. V. 1. Thus the heavens and the earth were finished, and all the host of them."

Additional Examples. — The Flood, Gen. vii. 11—24, and viii. 1—22; Abraham's Vision, Gen. xv. 1—18; Jacob's Dream, Gen. xxviii. 10—22; the Mission of Moses, Exod. iii. 1—20; the Passage of the Red Sea, Exod. xiv. 5—31; Dedication of the Temple, 1 Kings viii. 1—63; the Day of Penticost, Acts ii.; Paul's Defence before Agrippa, Acts xxvi. 1—29

DIDACTIC PASSAGES.

The peculiar mode of voice which characterizes appropriate didactic reading, in ordinary composition, as differing from that which belongs to narrative or descriptive style, holds good, also, in the reading of the Scriptures. Narration and description address themselves, in many instances, to feeling and imagination, for their chief effect; while didactic subjects are usually directed exclusively, or nearly so, to the reason and judgment, through the understanding.

Narrative and descriptive reading, accordingly, abound, comparatively, in vivid and varied tones, associated with the different moods of sympathy and emotion. Didactic reading holds a more steady, uniform, and regulated course of utterance, adapted to a clear, distinct conveyance of thought to the intellect. It depends less on empassioned variation of voice, and more on correct and exact articulation, — less on vivid tone and strong expression, more on true inflection, just emphasis, and appropriate pauses, as aids to the effect of clear apprehension and precise discrimination.

The common faults in the reading of didactic portions of Scripture, are a mechanical and inexpressive tone, the lifeless result of mere habit; a heavy, solemn, grandiose style, destitute of spirit and effect; a formal, sermonizing manner, utterly unsuited to the simple and vivid style of Scripture instruction; an over familiar, flippant utterance, which divests the language of the sacred volume of its dignity and authority, and its proper power over the soul.

The doctrinal parts of the Bible, require, in reading, a firm, energetic, spirited, authoritative, but quiet and steady voice; perfectly clear and distinct in enunciation, free from any dryness or formality, and breathing a tone of conscious dignity and power, blended with that of mildness, condescension, gentleness, and affectionate interest.

EXAMPLES IN ORAL AND PARABOLIC STYLE.

From the Sermon on the Mount. — Matthew VI.

V. 1. "Take heed that ye do not your alms before men, to be seen of them: otherwise ye have no reward of your Father which is in heaven. 2. Therefore, when thou doest thine alms, do not sound a trumpet before thee, as the hypocrites do, in the synagogues, and in the streets, that they may have glory of men. Verily, I say unto you, They have their reward. 3. But when thou doest alms, let not thy left hand know what thy right hand doeth; 4. That thine alms may be in secret: and thy Father which seeth in secret, himself shall reward thee openly.

5. "And when thou prayest, thou shalt not be as the hypocrites are; for they love to pray standing in the synagogues, and in the corners of the streets, that they may be seen of men. Verily, I say unto you, They have their reward. 6. But thou, when thou prayest, enter into thy closet; and when thou hast shut thy door, pray to thy Father which is in secret; and thy Father which seeth in secret, shall reward thee openly.

7. "But when ye pray, use not vain repetitions, as the heathen do: for they think that they shall be heard for their much speaking. 8. Be not ye therefore like unto them: for your Father knoweth what things ye have need of before ye ask him. 9. After this manner therefore pray ye: Our Father which art in heaven, hallowed be thy name. 10. Thy kingdom come. Thy will be done in earth as it is in heaven. 11. Give us this day our daily bread. 12. And forgive us our debts, as we forgive our debtors. 13. And lead us not into temptation, but deliver us from evil. For thine is the kingdom, and the power, and the glory, forever. Amen. 14. For, if ye forgive men their trespasses, your heavenly Father will also forgive you: 15. But, if ye forgive not men

their trespasses, neither will your Father forgive your trespasses.

16. "Moreover, when ye fast, be not as the hypocrites, of a sad countenance: for they disfigure their faces, that they may appear unto men to fast. Verily, I say unto you, They have their reward. 17. But thou, when thou fastest, anoint thy head, and wash thy face; 18. That thou appear not unto men, to fast, but unto thy Father, which is in secret: and thy Father, which seeth in secret, shall reward thee openly.

19. "Lay not up for yourselves treasures upon earth where moth and rust doth corrupt, and where thieves break through and steal: 20. But lay up for yourselves treasures in heaven, where neither moth nor rust doth corrupt, and where thieves do not break through nor steal. 21. For where your treasure is, there will your heart be also. 22. The light of the body is the eye: if therefore thine eye be single, thy whole body shall be full of light. 23. But if thine eye be evil, thy whole body shall be full of darkness. If therefore the light that is in thee be darkness, how great is that darkness!

24. "No man can serve two masters; for either he will hate the one, and love the other; or else he will hold to the one, and despise the other. Ye cannot serve God and mammon. 25. Therefore I say unto you, Take no thought for your life, what ye shall eat, or what ye shall drink; nor yet for your body, what ye shall put on. Is not the life more than meat, and the body than raiment? 26. Behold the fowls of the air: for they sow not, neither do they reap, nor gather into barns; yet your heavenly Father feedeth them. Are ye not much better than they? 27. Which of you by taking thought can add one cubit unto his stature? 28. And why take ye thought for raiment? Consider the lilies of the field how they grow; they toil not, neither do they spin; 29. And yet I say unto you, that even Solomon in all his glory was not arrayed like one of these. 30. Wherefore, if God so clothe

the grass of the field, which to-day is, and to-morrow is cast into the oven, shall he not much more clothe you, O ye of little faith? 31. Therefore take no thought, saying, What shall we eat? or, what shall we drink? or, wherewithal shall we be clothed? 32. (For after all these things do the Gentiles seek:) for your heavenly Father knoweth that ye have need of all these things. 33. But seek ye first the kingdom of God, and his righteousness, and all these things shall be added unto you. 34. Take therefore no thought for the morrow: for the morrow shall take thought for the things of itself. Sufficient unto the day is the evil thereof."

Additional Examples. — The Parable of the Sower, Matthew xiii. 1—43; The Parable of the Talents, Matthew xxv. 14—46; Rebuke of Covetousness, Luke xii. 13—40; Regeneration, John iii. 1—21: Parting Words of Jesus to his Disciples, John xiv.

EXAMPLES FROM THE EPISTLES.

Equality of Jew and Gentile. — Rom. III.

V. 1. "What advantage then hath the Jew? or what profit is there of circumcision? 2. Much every way: chiefly, because that unto them were committed the oracles of God. 3. For what if some did not believe? shall their unbelief make the faith of God without effect? 4. God forbid: yea, let God be true, but every man a liar; as it is written, 'That thou mightest be justified in thy sayings, and mightest overcome when thou art judged.' 5. But if our unrighteousness commend the righteousness of God, what shall we say? Is God unrighteous who taketh vengeance? (I speak as a man,) 6. God forbid: for then how shall God judge the world? 7. For if the truth of God hath more abounded through my lie unto his glory; why yet am I also judged as a sinner? 8. And not rather, (as we be slanderously reported, and as some affirm that we say,) Let us do evil, that good may come? whose damnation is just. 9. What then?

are we better than they? No, in no wise: for we have before proved both Jews and Gentiles, that they are all under sin; 10. As it is written, There is none righteous, no, not one: 11. There is none that understandeth, there is none that seeketh after God. 12. They are all gone out of the way, they are together become unprofitable: there is none that doeth good, no, not one 13. Their throat is an open sepulchre; with their tongues they have used deceit; the poison of asps is under their lips: 14. Whose mouth is full of cursing and bitterness. 15. Their feet are swift to shed blood. 16. Destruction and misery are in their ways: 17. And the way of peace have they not known. 18. There is no fear of God before their eyes.

19. " Now we know that what things soever the law saith, it saith to them who are under the law: that every mouth may be stopped, and all the world may become guilty before God. 20. Therefore by the deeds of the law, there shall no flesh be justified in his sight; for by the law is the knowledge of sin. 21. But now the righteousness of God without the law is manifested, being witnessed by the law and the prophets; 22. Even the righteousness of God, which is by faith of Jesus Christ unto all, and upon all them that believe: for there is no difference: 23. For all have sinned, and come short of the glory of God; 24. Being justified freely by his grace, through the redemption that is in Christ Jesus: 25. Whom God hath set forth to be a propitiation, through faith in his blood, to declare his righteousness for the remission of sins that are past, through the forbearance of God; 26. To declare, I say, at this time his righteousness: that he might be just, and the justifier of him which believeth in Jesus.

27. " Where is boasting then? It is excluded. By what law? of works? Nay: but by the law of faith. 28. Therefore we conclude, that a man is justified by faith without the deeds of the law. 29. Is he the God of the

Jews only? is he not also of the Gentiles? Yes, of the Gentiles also: 30. Seeing it is one God which shall justify the circumcision by faith, and uncircumcision through faith. 31. Do we then make void the law through faith? God forbid: yea, we establish the law."

Additional Examples. — Justification by Faith, Rom. v.; The carnal State and the spiritual, Rom. viii.; Charity, 1 Cor. xiii.; The Resurrection, 1 Cor. xv.

PASSAGES FROM THE PROPHETIC WRITINGS.

The prophets are distinguished, among the sacred writers, for poetic beauty and grandeur of thought, and for graphic and dramatic effect of style. The prophetic books embody more descriptive power and vivid expression, than any other writings whatever. They require, accordingly, more intensity and variety of tone, in reading, — a nobler majesty of utterance, a fuller, deeper, stronger, character of voice, — a perfect "*orotund quality.*"

The oriental fervor of emotion, and the poetic and imaginative language which characterize the prophets, taken in connection with their sublime force of thought, naturally call for a higher degree of *energy* in the voice, than is required for ordinary reading, or even for the style of the other writers of the sacred volume. The appropriate reading of most portions of the prophetic books, requires, likewise, a more marked and peculiar "*stress,*" than occurs in forms of writing less expressive and peculiar. The style of prophetic language, in the Sacred Scriptures, is not less striking in regard to its effect on the *pitch* of the voice. It abounds in the solemn and majestic tones of the epic, in the transports of joy and the bursts of grief peculiar to the lyric ode, and in the abrupt conversational turns of dramatic dialogue. Its variety and range of pitch, therefore, are remarkable; and to the same causes are owing its frequent use of special "*inflections,*" as the "*wave,*" the "*monotone,*" the bold "*downward slide*" of exclamation and command, and the acute "*rising inflection*" of eager and stern interrogation. The "*movement*" of the voice, too, in the appropriate reading of passages from the prophets, is strikingly marked in every degree required by intense and varied emotion, from the slowest style of awe, gloom, and horror; to the rapid rate of haste, joy, and triumph. The whole style of elocution, in this department of Scripture reading, is marked by the peculiar force of its *emphasis*, the occasional brevity, and the occasional impressive length, of its *pauses*, the intensity of its "*expression*," and the abruptness and extent of its "variation."

The Doom of Babylon.— Isaiah XIII.

V. 1. "The burden of Babylon, which Isaiah the son of Amoz did see. — 2. Lift ye up a banner upon the high mountain, exalt the voice unto them, shake the hand, that they may go into the gates of the nobles. 3. I have commanded my sanctified ones, I have also called my mighty ones for mine anger, even them that rejoice in my highness. 4. The noise of a multitude in the mountains, like as of a great people; a tumultuous noise of the kingdoms of nations gathered together: the Lord of hosts mustereth the host of the battle. 5. They come from a far country, from the end of heaven, even the Lord, and the weapons of his indignation, to destroy the whole land.

6. "Howl ye: for the day of the Lord is at hand; it shall come as a destruction from the Almighty. 7. Therefore shall all hands be faint, and every man's heart shall melt: 8. And they shall be afraid: pangs and sorrows shall take hold of them; they shall be in pain as a woman that travaileth: they shall be amazed one at another; their faces shall be as flames. 9. Behold, the day of the Lord cometh, cruel both with wrath and fierce anger, to lay the land desolate: and he shall destroy the sinners thereof out of it. 10. For the stars of heaven and the constellations thereof shall not give their light: the sun

shall be darkened in his going forth, and the moon shall not cause her light to shine. 11. And I will punish the world for their evil, and the wicked for their iniquity; and I will cause the arrogancy of the proud to cease, and will lay low the haughtiness of the terrible. 12. I will make a man more precious than fine gold; even a man than the golden wedge of Ophir. 13. Therefore I will shake the heavens; and the earth shall remove out of her place, in the wrath of the Lord of hosts, and in the day of his fierce anger. 14. And it shall be as the chased roe, and as a sheep that no man taketh up: they shall every man turn to his own people, and flee every one into his own land. 15. Every one that is found shall be thrust through; and every one that is joined unto them shall fall by the sword. 16. Their children also shall be dashed to pieces before their eyes; their houses shall be spoiled, and their wives ravished. 17. Behold, I will stir up the Medes against them, which shall not regard silver; and as for gold, they shall not delight in it. 18. Their bows also shall dash the young men to pieces; and they shall have no pity on the fruit of the womb; their eye shall not spare children.

19. "And Babylon, the glory of kingdoms, the beauty of the Chaldees' excellency, shall be as when God overthrew Sodom and Gomorrah. 20. It shall never be inhabited, neither shall it be dwelt in from generation to generation; neither shall the Arabian pitch tent there; neither shall the shepherds make their fold there. 21. But wild beasts of the desert shall lie there; and their houses shall be full of doleful creatures; and owls shall dwell there, and satyrs shall dance there. 22. And the wild beasts of the islands shall cry in their desolate houses, and dragons in their pleasant palaces: and 'her time is near to come, and her days shall not be prolonged."

Additional Examples.—Israel's Triumph over Babylon, Isaiah xiv.; the Restoration of Jerusalem, Isaiah xl.; the Restoration of the Holy City and Temple, Isaiah xliv.; the Exaltation of Cyrus, dna the Restoration of Israel, Isaiah xlv. 1—23; the Promise of a Redeemer, Isaiah liii.; Assurance of the Return of Divine Favor to Israel, Isaiah liv. lv.; the Debasement and Self-reproach of Israel, Isaiah lix. 1—15; Assurances of Divine Favor to Israel, Isaiah lx. lxi.; Earnest Entreaty, Isaiah lxiv.; Divine Retribution, Isaiah lxv.; Denunciations against Israel, Jeremiah iv., vi., vii., viii.; Grief and Prostration of Judah, Jeremiah xiv.; Denunciation against the King of Judah, Jeremiah xxii.; Denunciations against False Prophets, Jeremiah xxiii. 9—40; the Restoration of Israel, Jeremiah xxxi., xxxiii.; Denunciation against Babylon, Jeremiah l., li.; Calamities of Judah and Jerusalem, Lamentations i., ii., iv. 1—20.

LYRIC PASSAGES.

The Book of Psalms, and the devotional strains interspersed with the narratives of the sacred volume, may be conveniently classified for the purposes of elocution, according to the character of their predominant emotions, as indicating their prevalent tones of expression in reading, in the following manner.

1. *Examples of Solemnity, Sublimity, and Awe.*

* Psalm lxxvii. 11—20; lxxxix. 2—14; xc., civ., cxxxix. 1—18.

2. *Grandeur, Majesty, and Power.*

Psalm xviii., xix., xxix., lxv., xcvii.

3. *Tranquility and Serenity.*

Psalm viii., xxiii.

4. *Joy, Praise, and Triumph.*

Psalm xxx., lxiii., lxv., lxvi., lxvii., lxviii., xcv., xcvi., xcvii., xcviii., c., ciii., civ., cvii., cxiii., cxiv., cxlv., cxlvi., cxlvii., cxlviii., cl.

5. *Pathos, Entreaty, and Supplication.*

Psalm vi., xxxviii., xxxix., lxxxviii., cxlii., cxliii.

---

* Examples extracted from the above and similar passages, have been presented as exercises under various emotions, and need not, therefore, be repeated here. They may be repeated orally if necessary, by referring to the pages in which they occur.

6. *Varied Expression.*

Psalm xxii., xxxi., xxxvi., xl., xli., xlii., xliii., li., lxix., lxxi., lxxxix., cii., cxxx.

7. *Didactic Sentiment.*

Psalm i., xxxvii.

THE READING OF HYMNS.

This department of pulpit elocution is one which requires, more than any other, the closest attention of the student. Our existing modes of education are so generally imperfect, as regards the early training of the voice, that habit is, in most cases, formed to defective and erroneous modes of reading, long before an individual has arrived at maturity. Few persons, comparatively, seem to possess the power of uttering the words of a lyric stanza, in the spirit of poetic feeling; and few, indeed, seem capable of reading verse without a false intonation, which, when applied to the beautiful language of the poet, makes it fall on the ear

"Like sweet bells jangled, — out of tune and harsh."

Many pulpit readers are actually so little moulded, either by nature or art, for the exercise of devotional reading, that the loftiest inspirations of the sacred muse, become, in their hands, absolute doggerel to the ear. The associations of devotion are thus thrust out of the mind of the hearer, to make room for those of ludicrous incongruity. — No reformation in the modes of public or of private life, is more urgently demanded by general sentiment, than a change, as regards the power of the Christian ministry to render the services of the pulpit appropriate and impressive in manner. In no respect is present deficiency so deeply and so generally felt, as in the preparatory act of reading the hymn, which should be, — in the reading not less than the singing of it, — the living voice of assembled hearts lifted to the throne of Infinite Majesty. The reading of the hymn should be the prelude by which both congregation and choir have their souls attuned to the sentiment of the sacred song, before entering on the performance of the accompanying strains of music. The best security for the appropriate and truly expressive singing of a psalm or hymn, is that just and impressive reading of it, which imparts its spirit to heart and ear. But to fulfil the apostolic injunction of "making melody in the heart," after a dull, cold, prosaic, or see-saw reading of the hymn, is a task next to impracticable. An attentive eye may, in fact, see that, in such circumstances, the youthful and the thoughtless among a congregation, have, sometimes, as much as they can do, to preserve decorum.

The situation of the student of theology, is by no means favorable to the acquisition of a command over the voice, such as the appropriate utterance of poetic sentiment, and, especially, in the lyric form, necessarily requires. He shares, in early years, in all the common disadvantages of imperfect cultivation of the vocal organs; and the sedentary and secluded life of his boyhood and youth, tends directly to reduce his power of organic action and expression. His daily life is one of intense cerebral action, in which the vital energies are withdrawn, to a great extent, from the muscular and nervous systems, which are the special apparatus of expressive action. As a student, he loses energy, and vivacity, and susceptibility, which are the necessary measures of his expressive power. The passive capacity of impression, which he has acquired by reading and contemplation, might, under a judicious system of proportioned culture, have been an element of vast effect; but its excess actually renders it an obstacle to expression. The receptive sensibility of the soul not being balanced by the power of utterance, oppresses rather than enlivens feeling, and quells rather than inspires the voice. Habit, and culture, and skill, are all required to render feeling tributary to expression. Passion and imagination are not less important to the reader than to the poet; and the discipline of these much neglected parts of man's constitution, is as valuable to the former as to the latter. Hence the great moment of personal cultivation and self-education in elocution, to him who would worthily occupy the pulpit, as the leader of an assembly met for the purposes of devotion.

The power over human feeling which lies in a hymn appropriately read, is indescribable. It is difficult, indeed, for the most indifferent heart to escape from the appointed influence of the sanctuary, when the minister yields his whole soul to the sentiment and spirit of a hymn, and gives these forth in tones that come fresh from the great fount of feeling, and hallow the imagination with the presence of devotional associations. Add to such effects that of the well-tuned voice which breathes life and music into sound, and thus gives presence and audible beauty to the spirit of poetry; and the result becomes a combination which no man can resist, whose heart is not seared to every good influence.*

Music is universally recognized as of divine ordination for the purposes of worship. But it is too generally forgotten that poetry is so also, and that, without the inspiration of the latter, the former is but the " sounding brass and the tinkling cymbal." The reading of the eminent servant of God referred to in the note to the preceding paragraph, ever indicated, in the tone and expression of

---

* "If I have ever been of any use, as an instrument of spiritual good, it has been, to a great extent, through the reading of sacred poetry: where I have had my choice of means, I have selected it in preference to any other. I would charge it on you, young men, to cultivate and cherish this invaluable aid to your usefulness." Such were the words of the late Dr. Nettleton to the students around his bed, during his last illness.

the hymn, a soul baptized into its inmost sentiment and its deepest effect. His low-pitched, solemn, but sweet intonation could quell and absorb every heart in an assembled multitude, and cause the very frame of the hearer to thrill with the deep-felt sense of the reality of spiritual truths. The unlettered working-man felt, then, the efficacy of a human voice hallowed by genuine devotional feeling; and the cultivated student became aware how imagination, and taste, and ear, might all be rendered tributary to the deepest spiritual impressions.

But, in addition to the usual disadvantages of imperfect culture, the clergyman, in the daily routine of life's active duties, has a host of impediments to the appropriate and impressive use of the voice, in conducting the part of public worship to which we now refer. He needs peculiar preventives to counteract unfavorable influences. He is called, not unfrequently, from the midst of active duties of a merely temporary, but, perhaps, of an exciting and absorbing character, to conduct the devotions of a weekday prayer meeting. He commences, perhaps, with the reading of a hymn, with the din and the bustle of business yet sounding in his ears, and its unavoidable cares yet lingering about his heart. Happy for him then, if his early culture had given him that instant susceptibility of feeling, by which the charm of poetry, lending its tributary aid to the spirit of devotion, the lines which he begins to read should instantly raise his soul to the height of seeing Him who is invisible, and inspire the power of uplifting the heart of the worshipping assemblage, by the utterance of a spirit attuned to the vivid tones of deep and genuine emotion! Without a degree of such effect, the reading of the hymn is but a desecration, and the meeting but a ceremony. Yet how often are such occasions found to pass unprofitably by, from, in part, this very circumstance! It were, perhaps, well worth while to inquire whether the coldness and deadness of heart which are so often lamented at such meetings, are not, in degree, owing to the absence of those appropriate *expressions* of the heart, which devotional poetry was meant to secure in the voice. Here, as elsewhere, there is a plain question of means and ends often overlooked, amidst a vain inquiry after remote rather than present sources of evil.

The student, in practising the following exercises, should fix his attention on two points mainly, — the deep feeling of the sentiment in each example, and the full expression of the heart in the tones of the voice. Next to these points ranks the correct "intonation," by means of inflection and "melody;" so as to keep the voice in tune, according to the form of poetry presented in each stanza.

The full expression of feeling, is — from our corrupted conventional habits in daily social life, which withhold the utterance of the heart, and muffle the sounds of the voice, — a thing which most students are apt to shrink from, under the very erroneous impression, that, if they give full and free vent to the emotion which a hymn inspires, they will appear affected or theatrically excessive in style, or deficient in judgment and taste. The elocutionist replies that genuine feeling can never be mistaken, and that such fears are unfounded. It is by listening to such suggestions that our prevalent coldness in hymn-reading is produced. True elocution was perfectly exemplified in the noble and beautiful and impressive reading of the eminent individual before mentioned: no one ever ventured the insinuation that his manner was artificial or theatrical. What is needed is a full heart and a natural utterance, — not labor and effort to reach a certain style or effect.

Another source of defective hymn-reading, is the want of discrimination as to the proper difference between the tones of ordinary conversation and of prose reading, — in contrast with the appropriate style of utterance, which applies to the language of poetry; more especially when the latter assumes the form of sacred lyrics, — the highest species of all verse. Many readers shrink from the full expression of feeling and imagination, in the high-wrought forms which these justly assume in the composition of psalms and hymns, because, say they, such expression is not natural or habitual to us; it seems forced and excessive: we prefer to read in a plain, unpretending style. Such is, usually, the plea offered for reading poetry, in its sublimest and most sacred forms, as if it were not only flat prose but hum-drum, or familiar talk. It is forgotten, in such cases, that the standard of conversation and of prose reading cannot apply to poetry of a lofty or a solemn character, and that the tones in which we talk of domestic incidents and ordinary affairs, can never be those in which we can properly discourse of God, eternity, and immortality.

But the prevalent fault of some readers, is, to utter every stanza of every hymn with one uniform, heavy, and unwieldly solemnity of voice, which observes no distinction of subject, style, or versification, and kills the effect of every form of sentiment by a dull monotony. The peculiar vividness and fire, the pathos and the fervor, the sublime force of lyric compositions, are thus altogether lost to heart and ear. The whole design of the composition of hymns, is thus defeated; and the soul remains uninspired, the feelings untouched.

The minor details of defective elocution in the reading of hymns, regard chiefly the application of the rules of inflection. False "intonation" commonly consists in overlooking the distinctive slide of verse, as contrasted with those of prose. The former varies but little in effect from the "monotone," and does not, in most passages, transcend the limits of the interval of the "second," or the slightest rise of voice except the plaintive "semitone." The use of the larger intervals of "thirds" and "fifths," turns poetry into prose, — so far as the ear is concerned. To persons whose ear is not trained to these distinctions in music and in elocution, it may be sufficient to say that the fault lies in raising or lowering the voice too much in a style approaching to that of question and answer, instead of keeping it nearly level.

The fault of sing-song reading is usually caused by allowing the voice to drop at the end of the second line of a stanza, instead of keeping it up till the proper cadence at the close. Thus

> "There is a land of pure delight,
> Where saints immortal rèign;
> Eternal day excludes the night,
> And pleasures banish pain."

There are two obvious reasons why the fall, or downward slide, at the word "reign," should not be used: 1st, the sense is not independently completed there, since the words *and where* are required, mentally, to fill up an ellipsis between the second and third lines of the stanza; 2d, if the word "reign" is allowed the "downward slide," the corresponding rhyming word "pain" having necessarily the same "slide" at the cadence, a painful sameness of melody is produced to the ear, as if the reader were, in the last two lines of the stanza, repeating, in a mocking tone, his own melody used in the first two.

The rule of appropriate intonation in stanza, is, Keep the voice up, at the end of the second line, unless emphasis, or independent sense, or abrupt style authorizes or requires a downward slide; and let the voice take a lower pitch, at the beginning of the third line.

But the worst of all faults,— the doggerel see-saw,— is that which is produced by throwing the voice up and down alternately in the penultimate line of a stanza,— and alternately down, up, and down again, in the last line. Thus

> "Etérnal dày exclùdes the nìght,
> And pleàsures bánish pàin."

The following exercises should be repeated till a perfect command of "**expression**" and "**melody**," is attained.

EXAMPLES OF SOLEMNITY AND AWE.*

Eternity of God. — Watts.

1. "Great God! how infinite art thou! —
   What worthless worms are we! —
   Let all the race of creatures bow,
   And pay their praise to thee.

2. "Thy throne eternal ages stood,
   Ere seas or stars were made:
   Thou art the everliving God,
   Were all the nations dead.

3. "Eternity, with all its years,
   Stands present in thy view:
   To thee there's nothing old appears;
   Great God! there's nothing new.

4. "Our lives through various scenes are drawn,
   And vexed with trifling cares;
   While thine eternal thought moves on
   Thine undisturbed affairs.

5. "Great God! how infinite art thou! —
   What worthless worms are we! —
   Let all the race of creatures bow,
   And pay their praise to thee."

"The house appointed for all living." — Anon.

1. "How still and peaceful is the grave,
   Where, life's vain tumults past,
   The appointed house, by heaven's decree,
   Receives us all at last!

---

* The classification of hymns for the purposes of elocution, is similar to that of the Book of Psalms, exemplified before. The style of reading as to "quality" of voice, force, "stress," pitch, "inflection," "movement," pauses, emphasis, and "expression," should be defined, in every instance, before commencing the reading. The examples of this elocutionary analysis which occur in previous pages, may serve as guides to the mode of performing this exercise.

2. "The wicked there from troubling cease —
　Their passions rage no more;
And there the weary pilgrim rests
　From all the toils he bore.

3. "All, levelled by the hand of death,
　Lie sleeping in the tomb,
Till God in judgment call them forth,
　To meet their final doom."

Grandeur, Majesty, and Power.

The Majesty of God. — Steele.

1. "The Lord, the God of Glory, reigns,
　In robes of majesty arrayed;
His rule Omnipotence sustains,
　And guides the worlds his hands have made.

2. "Ere rolling worlds began to move,
　Or ere the heavens were spread abroad,
Thy awful throne was fixed above;
　From everlasting thou art God.

3. "The swelling floods tumultuous rise,
　Aloud the angry tempests roar,
Lift their proud billows to the skies,
　And foam, and lash the trembling shore.

4. "The Lord, the mighty God, on high,
　Controls the fiercely raging seas;
He speaks — and noise and tempests fly,
　The waves sink down in gentle peace.

God the Creator. — Watts.

1. "Eternal Wisdom, thee we praise,
　Thee all thy creatures sing;
While with thy name, rocks, hills, and seas,
　And heaven's high palace ring.

2. "Thy hand — how wide it spread the sky!
　How glorious to behold!
Tinged with a blue of heavenly dye,
　And starred with sparkling gold.

3. "Thy glories blaze all nature round,
    And strike the gazing sight,
Through skies, and seas, and solid ground,
    With terror and delight.

4. "Almighty power, and equal skill
    Shine through the worlds abroad,
Our souls with vast amazement fill,
    And speak the builder — God.

* 5. "But still, the wonders of thy grace
    Our warmer passions move;
Here we behold our Saviour's face,
    And we adore his love."

Psalm XIX. — Addison.

1. "The spacious firmament on high,
With all the blue ethereal sky,
And spangled heavens, a shining frame,
Their great Original proclaim.

2. "The unwearied sun, from day to day,
Does his Creator's power display,
And publishes to every land
The work of an almighty hand.

3. "Soon as the evening shades prevail,
The moon takes up the wondrous tale,
And nightly, to the listening earth,
Repeats the story of her birth; —

4. "While all the stars that round her burn,
And all the planets, in their turn,
Confirm the tidings, as they roll,
And spread the truth from pole to pole.

5. "What though in solemn silence all
Move round this dark terrestrial ball —
What though nor real voice, nor sound
Amid their radiant orbs be found? —

---

* Change of expression from *awe* to *gratitude*, blending *ardor* and *tenderness*.

6. "In reason's ear they all rejoice,
And utter forth a glorious voice;
Forever singing, as they shine,
'The hand that made us is Divine.'"

Psalm XIX. — Watts.

1. "The heavens declare thy glory, Lord,
In every star thy wisdom shines;
But when our eyes behold thy word,
We read thy name in fairer lines.

2. "The rolling sun — the changing light,
And nights, and days, thy power confess;
But that blest volume thou hast writ
Reveals thy justice and thy grace.

3. "Sun, moon, and stars, convey thy praise
Round all the earth — and never stand;
So when thy truth began its race,
It touched and glanced on every land.

4. "Nor shall thy spreading gospel rest,
Till through the world thy truth has run;
Till Christ has all the nations blest,
Which see the light, or feel the sun."

Resurrection of Christ. — Scott.

1. "Awake, our drowsy souls,
And burst the slothful band;
The wonders of this day
Our noblest songs demand:
Auspicious morn! thy blissful rays
Bright Seraphs hail, in songs of praise.

2. "At thy approaching dawn,
Reluctant death resigned
The glorious Prince of life,
In dark domains confined;
The angelic host around him bends,
And midst their shouts the God ascends.

3. "All hail, triumphant Lord!
　　Heaven with hosannas rings;
　While earth, in humbler strains,
　　Thy praise responsive sings!
'Worthy art thou, who once wast slain —
Through endless years to live and reign.'

4. "Gird on, Great God, thy sword,
　　Ascend thy conquering car,
　While justice, truth, and love,
　　Maintain the glorious war:
Victorious, thou thy foes shalt tread,
And sin and hell in triumph lead."

The Final Judgment. — Oliver.

1. "Lo! he comes, with clouds descending,
　　Once for favored sinners slain!
　Thousand, thousand saints attending,
　　Swell the triumph of his train:
　　　Hallelujah!
　Jesus comes — and comes to reign.

2. "Every eye shall now behold him,
　　Robed in dreadful majesty!
　Those who set at nought and sold him,
　　Pierced, and nailed him to the tree,
　　　Deeply wailing,
　Shall the true Messiah see!

3. "When the solemn trump has sounded,
　　Heaven and earth shall flee away;
　All who hate him must, confounded,
　　Hear the summons of that day —
　　　'Come to Judgment! —
　Come to judgment! — come away.'

4. "Yea, amen! — let all adore thee,
　　High on thine eternal throne!
　Saviour, take the power and glory;
　　Make thy righteous sentence known!
　　　Oh! come quickly —
　Claim the kingdom for thine own!"

REPOSE, TRANQUILITY, AND SERENITY.

Contentment. — Steele.

1. "Father, whate'er of earthly bliss
    Thy sovereign will denies,
    Accepted at thy throne of grace
    Let this petition rise: —

2. "'Give me a calm, a thankful heart,
    From every murmur free;
    The blessings of thy grace impart,
    And make me live to thee.

3. "'Oh! let the hope that thou art mine,
    My life and death attend —
    Thy presence through my journey shine,
    And crown my journey's end.'"

Adoration, Resignation, and Trust. — H. M. Williams.

1. "While thee I seek, protecting Power!
    Be my vain wishes stilled;
    And may this consecrated hour
    With better hopes be filled.

2. "Thy love the power of thought bestowed;
    To thee my thoughts would soar:
    Thy mercy o'er my life has flowed;
    That mercy I adore.

3. "In each event of life, how clear
    Thy ruling hand I see!
    Each blessing to my soul more dear,
    Because conferred by thee.

4. "In every joy that crowns my days,
    In every pain I bear,
    My heart shall find delight in praise,
    Or seek relief in prayer.

5. "When gladness wings my favored hour,
    Thy love my thoughts shall fill;

Resigned, when storms of sorrow lower,
My soul shall meet thy will.

6. "My lifted eye, without a tear,
The gathering storm shall see;
My steadfast heart shall know no fear;
That heart will rest on thee."

Psalm XLVI. — Watts.

1. "God is the refuge of his saints,
When storms of sharp distress invade
Ere we can offer our complaints,
Behold him present with his aid!

2. "Loud may the troubled ocean roar —
In sacred peace our souls abide,
While every nation — every shore
Trembles, and dreads the swelling tide.

3. "There is a stream, whose gentle flow
Supplies the city of our God!
Life, love, and joy still gliding through,
And watering our divine abode.

4. "That sacred stream — thy holy word, —
Supports our faith, our fear controls:
Sweet peace thy promises afford,
And give new strength to fainting souls.

5. "Zion enjoys her Monarch's love,
Secure against a threatening hour;
Nor can her firm foundation move,
Built on his truth — and armed with power."

JOY, PRAISE, AND TRIUMPH.

The Seasons. — Dwight.

1. "How pleasing is the voice
Of God, our heavenly King,
Who bids the frosts retire,
And wakes the lovely spring!

Bright suns arise, | And beauty glows,
The mild wind blows, | Thro' earth and skies.

2. "The morn, with glory crowned,
   His hand arrays in smiles;
He bids the eve decline,
   Rejoicing o'er the hills:
The evening breeze | His beauty blooms
His breath perfumes; | In flowers and trees.

3. "With life he clothes the spring,
   The earth with summer warms:
He spreads the autumnal feast,
   And rides on wintry storms:
His gifts divine | And round the year
Through all appear; | His glories shine."

Praise. — Mrs. Barbauld.

1. "Praise to God! — immortal praise,
For the love that crowns our days:
Bounteous Source of every joy,
Let thy praise our tongues employ.

2. "All that spring, with bounteous hand,
Scatters o'er the smiling land;
All that liberal autumn pours
From her rich, o'erflowing stores, —

3. "These, to that dear Source we owe
Whence our sweetest comforts flow;
These, through all my happy days,
Claim my cheerful songs of praise.

4. "Lord, to thee my soul would raise
Grateful, never-ending praise;
And, when every blessing's flown,
Love thee for THYSELF alone."

Psalm C. — Watts.

1. "Before Jehovah's awful throne,
Ye nations, bow with sacred joy:

Know that the Lord is God alone;
He can create, and he destroy.

2. "His powerful word, which all things made,
Gave life to clay, and formed us men;
And, when like wandering sheep we strayed,
He brought us to his fold again.

3. "We are his people, we his care,
Our nobler and our meaner frame:
What lasting honors can we rear,
Almighty Maker, to thy name?

4. "We'll crowd thy gates with thankful songs;
High as the heavens our voices raise;
And earth, with her ten thousand tongues,
Shall fill thy courts with sounding praise.

5. "Wide as the world is thy command;
Vast as eternity thy love;
Firm as thy throne thy truth shall stand,
When rolling years shall cease to move."

Gratitude. — Addison.

1. "When all thy mercies, O my God,
    My rising soul surveys,
Transported with the view, I'm lost
    In wonder, love, and praise.

2. "Unnumbered comforts to my soul
    Thy tender care bestowed,
Before my infant heart conceived
    From whom those comforts flowed.

3. "When in the slippery paths of youth
    With heedless steps I ran,
Thine arm, unseen, conveyed me safe,
    And led me up to man.

4. "Ten thousand thousand precious gifts
    My daily thanks employ;
Nor is the least a cheerful heart,
    That tastes those gifts with joy.

5. "Through every period of my life,
    Thy goodness I'll pursue;
And after death, in distant worlds,
    The glorious theme renew.

6. "Through all eternity, to thee
    A joyful song I'll raise:
But oh! eternity's too short
    To utter all thy praise!"

Worship. — Watts.

1. "Sweet is the work, my God, my King,
To praise thy name, give thanks, and sing —
To show thy love by morning light,
And talk of all thy truth at night.

2. "Sweet is the day of sacred rest —
No mortal care shall seize my breast;
Oh! may my heart in tune be found,
Like David's harp of solemn sound.

3. "My heart shall triumph in my Lord,
And bless his works, — and bless his word: —
Thy works of grace — how bright they shine!
How deep thy counsels — how divine!

4. "Sure I shall share a glorious part,
When grace hath well refined my heart,
And fresh supplies of joy are shed,
Like holy oil, to cheer my head.

5. "Then shall I see — and hear — and know
All I desired, or wished below;
And every power find sweet employ,
In that eternal world of joy."

Worship. — Watts.

1. "Lord of the worlds above,
    How pleasant and how fair
The dwellings of thy love,
    Thine early temples are!

> To thine abode
> My heart aspires,
> With warm desires,
> To see my God.

2. "Oh! happy souls, who pray,
    Where God appoints to hear;
   Oh! happy men, who pay
    Their constant service there!
> They praise thee still!
> And happy they,
> Who love the way
> To Zion's hill.

3. "They go from strength to strength,
    Through this dark vale of tears,
   Till each arrives at length,
    Till each in heaven appears:
> Oh! glorious seat,
> When God our king
> Shall thither bring
> Our willing feet."

Design of Christ's Advent. — Doddridge.

1. "Hark! the glad sound! the Saviour comes, —
    The Saviour promised long!
   Let every heart prepare a throne,
    And every voice a song.

2. "He comes — the prisoner to release,
    In Satan's bondage held:
   The gates of brass before him burst,
    The iron fetters yield.

3. "He comes — from thickest films of vice
    To clear the mental ray;
   And on the eyes oppressed with night —
    To pour celestial day.

4. "He comes — the broken heart to bind,
    The bleeding soul to cure;
   And, with the treasures of his grace,
    To enrich the humble poor.

5. "Our glad hosannas, Prince of Peace,
    Thy welcome shall proclaim;
   And heaven's eternal arches ring
    With thy beloved name."

The Advent of the Saviour. — Watts.

1. "Joy to the world — the Lord is come!—
   Let earth receive her King;
   Let every heart prepare him room,
   And heaven and nature sing.

2. "Joy to the world — the Saviour reigns:
   Let men their songs employ;
   While fields and floods, rocks, hills, and plains,
   Repeat the sounding joy.

3. "No more let sin and sorrow grow,
   Nor thorns infest the ground:
   He comes to make his blessings flow
   Far as the curse is found.

4. "He rules the world with truth and grace,
   And makes the nations prove
   The glories of his righteousness,
   And wonders of his love."

Redemption. — Watts.

1. "Raise your triumphant songs
   To an immortal tune;
   Let all the earth resound the deeds
   Celestial grace has done.

2. "Sing how eternal Love
   Its chief beloved chose,
   And bade him raise our ruined race
   From their abyss of woes.

3. "His hand no thunder bears,
   No terror clothes his brow,
   No bolts to drive our guilty souls
   To fiercer flames below.

4. "'T was mercy filled the throne,
   And wrath stood silent by,
   When Christ was sent with pardons down
   To rebels doomed to die.

5. "Now, sinners, dry your tears,
    Let hopeless sorrow cease;
    Bow to the sceptre of his love,
    And take the offered peace."

The Resurrection of Jesus. — Anon,

1. "Christ, the Lord, has risen to-day,
    Sons of men, and angels say!
    Raise your songs of triumph high;
    Sing ye heavens — and earth, reply.

2. "Love's redeeming work is done; —
    Fought the fight — the battle won:
    Lo! our sun's eclipse is o'er —
    Lo! he sets in blood no more.

3. "Vain the stone, the watch, the seal, —
    Christ hath burst the gates of hell:
    Death in vain forbids his rise, —
    Christ hath opened paradise.

4. "Lives again our glorious King —
    Where, O Death, is now thy sting?
    Once he died our souls to save —
    Where thy victory, boasting Grave?"

The Resurrection of Jesus. — Doddridge.

1. "Yes! the Redeemer rose,
        The Saviour left the dead,
        And o'er our hellish foes
        High raised his conquering head:
In wild dismay, | Fall to the ground,
The guards around | And sink away.

2. "Behold the angelic bands
        In full assembly meet,
        To wait his high commands,
        And worship at his feet:
Joyful they come, | From realms of day
And wing their way | To Jesus' tomb.

3. "Then back to heaven they fly,
     The joyful news to bear: —
   Hark! as they soar on high,
     What music fills the air!

| Their anthems say, | Hath left the dead — |
| 'Jesus who bled | He rose to-day!' |

4. "Ye mortals, catch the sound —
     Redeemed by him from hell —
   And send the echo round
     The globe on which you dwell, —

| Transported, cry — | Hath left the dead, |
| 'Jesus who bled | No more to die!'" |

The Hope of Heaven through Christ. — Doddridge.

1. "Sing, all ye ransomed of the Lord,
     Your great deliverer sing:
   Ye pilgrims, now for Zion bound,
     Be joyful in your King.

2. "His hand divine shall lead you on,
     Through all the blissful road,
   Till to the sacred mount you rise,
     And see your gracious God.

3. "Bright garlands of immortal joy
     Shall bloom on every head;
   While sorrow, sighing, and distress,
     Like shadows, all are fled.

4. "March on, in your Redeemer's strength,
     Pursue his footsteps still;
   With joyful hope still fix your eye
     On Zion's heavenly hill."

Worthy the Lamb. — Anon.

1. "Glory to God on high!
     Let heaven and earth reply,
       'Praise ye his name!'
   Angels, his love adore,

Who all our sorrows bore;
  Saints, sing for evermore,
    'Worthy the Lamb!'

2. "Ye, who surround the throne,
  Cheerfully join in one,
    Praising his name:
  Ye, who have felt his blood
  Sealing your peace with God,
  Sound through the earth abroad,
    'Worthy the Lamb!'

3. "Join all the ransomed race,
  Our Lord and God to bless:
    Praise ye his name.
  In him we will rejoice,
  Making a cheerful noise,
  Shouting with heart and voice,
    'Worthy the Lamb!'"

PATHOS, ENTREATY, AND SUPPLICATION.

The Cross. — Steele.

1. "Stretched on the cross, the Saviour dies:
  Hark! his expiring groans arise!
  See from his hands — his feet — his side,
  Descends the sacred crimson tide!

2. "And didst thou bleed — for sinners bleed?
  And could the sun behold the deed?
  No — he withdrew his cheering ray,
  And darkness veiled the mourning day.

3. "Can I survey the scene of wo,
  Where mingling grief and mercy flow,
  And yet my heart so hard remain,
  As not to move with love or pain?

4. "Come — dearest Lord, thy grace impart,
  To warm this cold, unfeeling heart,
  Till all its powers and passions move
  In melting grief and ardent love."

Godly Sorrow. — Watts.

1. " Alas! and did my Saviour bleed,
    And did my Sovereign die?
   Would he devote that sacred head
    For such a worm as I?

2. " Was it for crimes that I had done,
    He groaned upon the tree?
   Amazing pity! — grace unknown!
    And love beyond degree!

3. " Well might the sun in darkness hide,
    And shut his glories in,
   When Christ, the almighty Saviour, died
    For man, the rebel's sin.

4. " Thus might I hide my blushing face,
    While his dear cross appears;
   Dissolve my heart in thankfulness,
    And melt my eyes to tears.

5. " But drops of grief can ne'er repay
    The debt of love I owe:
   Here, Lord, I give myself away —
    'T is all that I can do."

Pardon implored. — Stennett.

1. " Prostrate, dear Jesus, at thy feet,
    A guilty rebel lies,
   And upwards to thy mercy-seat
    Presumes to lift his eyes.

2. " If tears of sorrow would suffice
    To pay the debt I owe,
   Tears should from both my weeping eyes
    In ceaseless torrents flow.

3. " But no such sacrifice I plead
    To expiate my guilt;
   No tears, but those which thou hast shed —
    No blood, but thou hast spilt.

4. "I plead thy sorrows, dearest Lord;
   Do thou my sins forgive:
   Thy justice will approve the word,
   That bids the sinner live."

Succor implored in spiritual Conflicts. — Steele.

1. "Alas! what hourly dangers rise!
   What snares beset my way!
   To heaven, oh! let me lift mine eyes,
   And hourly watch and pray.

2. "How oft my mournful thoughts complain,
   And melt in flowing tears!
   My weak resistance! — ah! how vain!
   How strong my foes and fears!

3. "O gracious God! in whom I live,
   My feeble efforts aid;
   Help me to watch, and pray, and strive,
   Though trembling and afraid.

4. "Increase my faith — increase my hope,
   When foes and fears prevail;
   Oh! bear my fainting spirit up,
   Or soon my strength will fail.

5. "Whene'er temptations fright my heart,
   Or lure my feet aside,
   My God, thy powerful aid impart,
   My guardian and my guide.

6. "Oh! keep me in thy heavenly way,
   And bid the tempter flee;
   And let me never, never stray
   From happiness and thee.

Psalm LI *Part* I. — Watts.

1. "Show pity, Lord — O Lord, forgive, —
   Let a repenting rebel live: —
   Are not thy mercies large and free?
   May not a sinner trust in thee?

2. "My crimes are great — but can't surpass
The power and glory of thy grace;
Great God, thy nature hath no bound,
So let thy pardoning love be found!

3. "Oh! wash my soul from every sin,
And make my guilty conscience clean:
Here, on my heart, the burden lies;
And past offences pain mine eyes.

4. "My lips, with shame, my sins confess,
Against thy law — against thy grace:
Lord, should thy judgment grow severe,
I am condemned — but thou art clear.

5. "Yet, save a trembling sinner, Lord,
Whose hope, still hovering round thy word,
Would light on some sweet promise there,
Some sure support against despair."

Invocation. — Watts.

1. "Come, Holy Spirit, heavenly Dove,
With all thy quickening powers,
Kindle a flame of sacred love
In these cold hearts of ours.

2. "Look! how we grovel here below,
Fond of these trifling toys!
Our souls can neither fly nor go,
To reach eternal joys.

3. "In vain we tune our formal songs,
In vain we strive to rise;
Hosannas languish on our tongues,
And our devotion dies.

4. "Dear Lord! and shall we ever lie
In this poor dying state,
Our love so faint, so cold to thee,
And thine to us so great!

5. " Come, Holy Spirit, heavenly Dove,
   With all thy quickening powers;
   Come, shed abroad a Saviour's love,
   And that shall kindle ours."

VARIED " EXPRESSION."*

Redemption. — Watts.

1. " Plunged in a gulf of dark despair,
   We wretched sinners lay,
   Without one cheerful beam of hope,
   Or spark of glimmering day!

2. " With pitying eyes the prince of grace
   Beheld our helpless grief;
   He saw — and — oh amazing love ! —
   He ran to our relief.

3. " Down from the shining seats above
   With joyful haste he fled,
   Entered the grave in mortal flesh,
   And dwelt among the dead.

4. " Oh! for this love let rocks and hills
   .Their lasting silence break,
   And all harmonious human tongues
   The Saviour's praises speak.

5. " Angels! assist our mighty joys,
   Strike all your harps of gold;
   But when you raise your highest notes,
   His love can ne'er be told."

The Gospel. — Watts.

1. " Salvation ! oh, the joyful sound!
   'T is pleasure to our ears;
   A sovereign balm for every wound,
   A cordial for our fears.

---

* The elocutionary analysis of the style of reading, should now be applied to every change of emotion indicated in each stanza.

2. "Buried in sorrow and in sin,
 At hell's dark door we lay;—
But we arise by grace divine,
 To see a heavenly day.

3. "Salvation!—let the echo fly
 The spacious earth around;
While all the armies of the sky
 Conspire to raise the sound."

Faith. — Watts.

1. "When I can read my title clear
 To mansions in the skies,
I bid farewell to every fear,
 And wipe my weeping eyes.

2. "Should earth against my soul engage,
 And hellish darts be hurled,
Then I can smile at Satan's rage,
 And face a frowning world.

3. "Let cares, like a wild deluge, come,
 And storms of sorrow fall;
May I but safely reach my home,
 My God, my heaven, my all;—

4. "There shall I bathe my weary soul
 In seas of heavenly rest;
And not a wave of trouble roll
 Across my peaceful breast."

The heavenly Canaan. — Watts.

1. "There is a land of pure delight,
 Where saints immortal reign;
Eternal day excludes the night,
 And pleasures banish pain.

2. "There everlasting spring abides,
 And never-fading flowers;
Death, like a narrow sea, divides
 This heavenly land from ours.

3. "Sweet fields, beyond the swelling flood,
    Stand dressed in living green:
So to the Jews fair Canaan stood,
    While Jordan rolled between.

4. "But timorous mortals start and shrink,
    To cross this narrow sea;
And linger, trembling on the brink,
    And fear to launch away.

5. "Oh! could we make our doubts remove,
    Those gloomy doubts that rise,
And see the Canaan that we love
    With unbeclouded eyes;—

6. "Could we but climb where Moses stood,
    And view the landscape o'er,
Not Jordan's stream — nor death's cold flood,
    Should fright us from the shore."

The Atonement. — Cowper.

1. "There is a fountain, filled with blood
    Drawn from Immanuel's veins;
And sinners, plunged beneath that flood,
    Lose all their guilty stains.

2. "The dying thief rejoiced to see
    That fountain, in his day;
And there may I, though vile as he,
    Wash all my sins away.

3. "Thou dying Lamb! thy precious blood
    Shall never lose its power,
Till all the ransomed church of God
    Are saved, to sin no more.

4. "Since first, by faith, I saw the stream
    Thy flowing wounds supply,
Redeeming love has been my theme,
    And shall be, till I die.

5. "And when this feeble, stammering tongue
    Lies silent in the grave —

Then, in a nobler, sweeter song,
 I'll sing thy power to save."

Almighty Power and Majesty of God. — H. K. White.

1. " The Lord our God is clothed with might,
 The winds obey his will;
He speaks — and in his heavenly height
 The rolling sun stands still.

2. " Rebel, ye waves — and o'er the land
 With threatening aspect roar!
The Lord uplifts his awful hand,
 And chains you to the shore.

3. " Howl, winds of night! your force combine! —
 Without his high behest,
Ye shall not, in the mountain pine,
 Disturb the sparrow's nest.

4. " His voice sublime is heard afar,
 In distant peals it dies;
He yokes the whirlwinds to his car,
 And sweeps the howling skies.

5. " Ye nations, bend — in reverence bend;
 Ye monarchs, wait his nod,
And bid the choral song ascend
 To celebrate our God."

Diffusion of the Gospel. — Heber.

1. " From Greenland's icy mountains,
 From India's coral strand,
Where Afric's sunny fountains
 Roll down their golden sand;
From many an ancient river,
 From many a palmy plain,
They call us to deliver
 Their land from error's chain.

2. " What though the spicy breezes
 Blow soft o'er Ceylon's isle —

Though every prospect pleases,
And only man is vile?
In vain with lavish kindness,
The gifts of God are strown;
The heathen, in his blindness,
Bows down to wood and stone.

3. " Shall we, whose souls are lighted
By wisdom from on high —
Shall we to man benighted
The lamp of life deny? —
Salvation! — oh! salvation!
The joyful sound proclaim,
Till earth's remotest nation
Has learned Messiah's name.

4. " Waft — waft, ye winds, his story;
And you, ye waters, roll;
Till, like a sea of glory,
It spreads from pole to pole;
Till o'er our ransomed nature,
The Lamb for sinners slain,
Redeemer, King, Creator,
Returns in bliss to reign!"

The Final Judgment. — Newton.

1. " Day of judgment — day of wonders!
Hark! — the trumpet's awful sound,
Louder than a thousand thunders,
Shakes the vast creation round! —
How the summons
Will the sinner's heart confound!

2. " See the Judge our nature wearing,
Clothed in majesty divine!
You, who long for his appearing,
Then shall say, ' This God is mine!'
Gracious Saviour,
Own me in that day for thine!

3. " At his call the dead awaken,
   Rise to life from earth and sea;
   All the powers of nature shaken
   By his looks, prepare to flee: —
      Careless sinner,
   What will then become of thee?

4. " But to those who have confessed,
   Loved and served the Lord below!
   He will say, ' Come near, ye blessed,
   See the kingdom I bestow:
      You forever
   Shall my love and glory know.'"

DIDACTIC SENTIMENT.

Blessedness of the Righteous. — Watts.

1. " Blest are the humble souls that see
   Their emptiness and poverty:
   Treasures of grace to them are given,
   And crowns of joy laid up in heaven.

2. " Blest are the men of broken heart,
   Who mourn for sin with inward smart:
   The blood of Christ divinely flows,
   A healing balm for all their woes.

3. " Blest are the meek, who stand afar
   From rage and passion, noise and war:
   God will secure their happy state,
   And plead their cause against the great.

4. " Blest are the souls that thirst for grace,
   Hunger and long for righteousness:
   They shall be well supplied, and fed
   With living streams and living bread.

5. " Blest are the men whose mercies move
   To acts of kindness and of love:
   From Christ, the Lord, shall they obtain
   Like sympathy and love again.

6. " Blest are the pure, whose hearts are clean,
Who never tread the ways of sin :
With endless pleasure they shall see
A God of spotless purity.

7. " Blest are the men of peaceful life,
Who quench the coals of growing strife :
They shall be called the heirs of bliss,
The sons of God — the God of peace.

8. " Blest are the faithful, who partake
Of pain and shame for Jesus' sake :
Their souls shall triumph in the Lord;
Eternal life is their reward."

Christ our Example. — Anon.

1. " Behold, where, in a mortal form,
Appears each grace divine !
The virtues, all in Jesus met,
With mildest radiance shine.

2. " To spread the rays of heavenly light,
To give the mourner joy,
To preach glad tidings to the poor,
Was his divine employ.

3. " Midst keen reproach and cruel scorn,
He, meek and patient, stood ;
His foes, ungrateful, sought his life,
Who labored for their good.

4. " When in the hour of deep distress,
Before his Father's throne,
With soul resigned, he bowed, and said,
' Thy will, not mine, be done !'

5. " Be Christ our pattern, and our guide,
His image may we bear !
Oh ! may we tread his holy steps, —
His joy and glory share !"

The Life of Christ a Pattern. — Watts.

1. "My dear Redeemer, and my Lord,
    I read my duty in thy word;
    But in thy life the law appears
    Drawn out in living characters.

2. "Such was thy truth, — and such thy zeal,
    Such deference to thy Father's will,
    Such love, — and meekness so divine,
    I would transcribe and make them mine.

3. "Cold mountains and the midnight air
    Witnessed the fervor of thy prayer:
    The desert thy temptations knew,
    Thy conflict, and thy victory too.

4. "Be thou my pattern, — make me bear
    More of thy gracious image here;
    Then God, the Judge, shall own my name
    Among the followers of the Lamb."

Confidence in God. — Addison.

1. "How are thy servants blest! O Lord,
    How sure is their defence!
    Eternal wisdom is their guide,
    Their help, omnipotence.

2. "In foreign realms, and lands remote,
    Supported by thy care,
    Through burning climes they pass unhurt,
    And breathe in tainted air.

3. "When, by the dreadful tempest, borne
    High on the broken wave,
    They know thou art not slow to hear,
    Nor impotent to save.

4. "The storm is laid — the winds retire,
    Obedient to thy will;
    The sea, that roars at thy command,
    At thy command is still.

"In midst of danger, fear, and death,
Thy goodness we adore;
We'll praise thee for thy mercies past,
And humbly hope for more."

The Bible suited to the Wants of Mankind. — Steele.

1. "Father of Mercies, in thy word
What endless glory shines!
Forever be thy name adored
For these celestial lines!

2. "Here may the wretched sons of want
Exhaustless riches find;
Riches, above what earth can grant,
And lasting as the mind.

3. "Here springs of consolation rise,
To cheer the fainting mind;
And thirsty souls receive supplies,
And sweet refreshment find.

4. "Here the Redeemer's welcome voice
Spreads heavenly peace around;
And life, and everlasting joys
Attend the blissful sound!

5. "Oh! may these heavenly pages be
My ever dear delight;
And still new beauties may I see,
And still increasing light!

6. "Divine Instructor, gracious Lord,
Be thou forever near;
Teach me to love thy sacred word,
And view my Saviour there!"

PRINCIPLES OF GESTURE.

MAN, as a communicative and expressive being, naturally imparts his states of thought and feeling by visible as well as audible language. His corporeal organization is adapted to this, among the other ends of his constitution. All vivid and powerful emotions of the human breast, become legible, and are transmitted, by their effects on the features of the countenance, the attitude of the body, and the actions of the arm and hand. This fact is universally exhibited in the unconscious habits of childhood, and, with no less certainty, in those of manhood, when under the influence of earnest feeling. We read each other's inmost hearts in a glance of the eye, a quiver of the features, a change of hue in the countenance, a posture or a movement of the body, or a wave of the hand, more surely than in any tone or expression of the voice. It is but a superficial and narrow philosophy which leads to the neglect of that ordination of Divine wisdom, by which the law of language is written on man's exterior frame, as distinctly as on his organs of speech; and few among the numerous deficiencies of existing modes of education, are greater, or more unfavorable to the free and full development of the human being, than the general omission of such culture and training as might yield to every youth, and especially to those who are destined to the sacred profession, the unspeakable advantages resulting from a perfect command over all those natural and appropriate aids to expressive utterance, which arise from the cultivation of the eloquence of action.

Man expresses himself most naturally and most effectively when he obeys the law of his constitution which leads him to use his whole bodily frame as an organ of communication. He becomes impressively eloquent when the breathing thoughts come "beaming from the eye," as well as "speaking on the tongue," and "urge the *whole man* onward."

Our conventional modes of life, which quench or suppress expression, by withholding corporeal action, — the natural accompaniment of speech, — are as faulty, in point of true taste, as they are false to nature. The very condition of eloquence in address, is, that we become sufficiently exalted by thought and emotion, to rise above such habits, and to give sentiment an expression and a character to the eye, as well as to the ear. Undisciplined habit may, it is true, carry this, as any other mode of expression, to excess. But the theory which founds on this fact a sweeping objection to the use of action in speaking, is not at all more rational than would be that which should enjoin abstinence from aliment, on the ground of the tendency of ungoverned appetite to excess in eating and drinking.

Genuine culture would prescribe in this, as in other departments of expression, a strict guard against faults of excess, no less anxiously than it would solicit and cherish the power and the beauty of appropriate and proportioned action.

Another current error on this subject of gesture, is, that it is a thing not capable of being reduced to study or systematic practice, that it is a pure result of unconscious impulse, and beyond the search of the understanding. So was musical sound thought to be, till man had the patience to observe it attentively, and trace its relations and its principles. Faithful observation of phenomena and effects, was the condition on which the beautiful, the profound science of music was constructed, and in consequence of which it became a definite and intelligible art, involving processes of systematic execution.

All expressive arts have a common groundwork of principles. Patient application discovers and defines these, and embodies them in rules. Study and practice follow, in due order; and the result is a recognized form of beauty or of power. Depth, breadth, force, truth, and grace, are each the same thing, in whatever art; be it architecture, sculpture, painting, music, poetry, or oratory. The mind which submits to the requisite conditions of patient and skillful investigation, will succeed in finding, and naming, and exemplifying them.

The great impediment to effective speaking, so far as depends on action, lies in the defective character of early education. The child is originally a model and a study for the sculptor and the painter, in the spontaneous perfection of attitude and gesture. Education, as generally conducted, does nothing to secure this natural excellence; but, on the contrary, allows it to die out of use, and even displaces it by a defective routine of mechanical habit. The awkwardness of the schoolboy, and the stiffness of the student, are proverbial. The minister in the pulpit, naturally, — we might almost say necessarily, — exhibits the habitual faults of the student, to their fullest extent. His modes of life, if not counteracted by express care and due self-cultivation, lead him to a cold, reserved, ineffective, inexpressive style of action. So much so, that nothing is more frequently or more generally a subject of popular remark, than the coldness and the lifelessness of the style of speaking usually exemplified in the pulpit. In too many cases, the sacred precincts seem to be occupied by an automaton or a statue, endowed with nothing beyond the power of a mechanical articulation.

The opposite faults of excessive, redundant, or over vehement action, and of labored or fanciful gesticulation, instead of a just and manly style of gesture, are the unavoidable results of an injudicious reaction against the effects of early neglect. Judgment and taste must discharge their salutary office here as elsewhere; and for the discipline of these controlling faculties education ought to be held responsible. The present order of affairs devolves this duty on the individual; and when we advert to the fact that, in addresses from the pulpit, more than in any other form of speaking, every look and action has an immediate and, perhaps, an abiding effect of the deepest moral character, and of the utmost moment to the objects of the sacred office, the duty of self-culture in this branch of eloquence, becomes inexpressibly important to all who are already occupied in that sphere of professional usefulness, or who are expecting to be so.

The study of that branch of elocution which consists of the visible effects of attitude and action, is sometimes erroneously suffered to settle down into an analysis of the mere details of gesture, and the application of arbitrary rules for the motions and postures of the body. Such study, it is hardly necessary to say, is worse than none, as it leads to artificial and mechanical style. Empirical directions and manual exercise, may accidentally take a right shape, in some instances, and aid in breaking up awkward tendencies of habit. But they may also take a wrong shape, and lead to the worst results of glaring impropriety. Genuine cultivation can be built on no other foundation than that of principles; and, as regards gesture, the principles of effect, if they are just and true, must, as was mentioned before, be identical with those of all other forms of expressive art.

The leading characteristics of expression, in whatever form we contemplate it, are, in the first place, *perfect truth*, or correspondence to nature, as opposed to whatever is factitious. Referring to this department of the subject, the student derives the important practical lesson, that all forms of action are faulty, which are merely the various phases of national, local, or personal and constitutional habit, and do not spring from the sentiment to the utterance of which they are applied. Under this head **elocution classes the superabundant shrugs and grimaces** of French and Italian custom, the absence of action or the hammering gesture which mark the Englishman, the uncouth gestures of the Scotchman, the narrow, frigid, and angular action of the New Englander, the oratorical display of our Southern and the grotesque style of our Western speakers.

The whole array of artificial faults of studied manner, falls under the same general classification of violations of truth and nature.

The second prominent principle of oratorical action, is *force*. Weakness, in any form of attitude or action, we may pardon to woman, but we cannot to man: his prime natural attribute is *force;* and to that native trait we can pardon the absence of nearly every other quality; while its opposite can only produce a feeling of indifference or contempt. The vehemence of Chalmers, and the very violence of Irving, pass with slight censure, in the judgment of even critical observers, because the energy of soul which action such as theirs bespeaks, is irresistible. It becomes, in fact, an element of indescribable power. But faults such as these can be pardoned in such men only. The habitual athletic displays in which some of our own public speakers, even in the pulpit, allow themselves, savor too much of brute force, for any deep and permanent effect on the soul.

The third requisite in the position and movements of the body, as connected with public speaking, is entire *freedom*, — not negligence or nonchalance, not a vulgar familiarity of personal habit; all of which are so repulsive to feeling, and so inappropriate in the pulpit, — yet unfortunately too prevalent; but that exemption from constraint and embarrassment, which is inseparable from manly energy and self-possession. What a correct elocution demands, is the dignity arising from repose and serenity of manner. The posture and the motions of the body and the action of the arm, when regulated by this principle, are freed from all confining or constraining narrowness and littleness of effect; the attitude is easy and therefore graceful; the action, liberal and flowing in its style. Nothing is more indicative of the perfect mechanism of the human frame, than the ease with which its members combine to perform any movement or action, — even the most complex and apparently difficult.

The confined mode of the student's life, subjects him to a degree of muscular feebleness incompatible with freedom of action in the body and limbs. Nor do the limited forms of mechanical exercise or manual labor, even when habitually resorted to, prove an adequate preventive. The tendency of these modes of exertion, is, from the habitual reïteration of one action, which they all imply, unfavorable to the free use of the body, with that unity and wholeness of effect which an oratorical action demands, as contrasted with the style of one which is mechanical. The recreative exercises of a student whose subsequent life is to be occupied with the business of public speaking, should be free and varied, so as to impart pliancy as well as force to the body and limbs. Active and enlivening sports have in all ages, and in every community, been recognized as an important aid to man's physical culture. Health and animation demand these as an indispensable condition of their existence, and of no class more urgently than of the sedentary and the studious, but particularly of students of theology, who are so prone to subside into inactive and enfeebling habits, — the greatest of all obstacles to free and effective speaking.

Next, in importance, as an element of oratorical effect, is the principle of *adaptation*, — the moulding of external manner and action, in consistency with the character of the subject of address, the mode of thought, and the style of language. This department of elocution is that in which, as a man of cultivated mind and accordant habit, the preacher should be comparatively perfect. Yet his daily habits incline him more than other speakers, to be uniform and monotonous, and to relinquish his style to the mere mechanism of habit and routine. The power of adapting manner to matter, is one which, of course, depends on taste and judgment, and on a culture co-extensive with the whole broad field of criticism, as involving the philosophy of expression.

It is much to be regretted that this subject receives so little attention during the progress of education, and that a thoroughly æsthetic discipline is not a part of the course pursued at all our public institutions for mental culture. The best possible school of instruction, in every department of oratory, but particularly that of gesture, would be a liberal and effectual education with reference to the constituent elements of expression, on the common grounds of nature and art, but directed specifically to the forms of speech and writing. The modicum of attention assigned to such subjects, on our present plans of instruction, is utterly inadequate to the purpose of creating a sound and just taste, even in regard to language.

The student of theology needs, more than any other, the aid of such cultivation. But, at present, it must be the fruit of his own nearly unaided application; for our language furnishes but very few works of reference on such topics; and such as we have are merely elementary, and many of them extremely defective. The personal study of nature and of art, with a view to the detection and recognition of the principles of expression, has, frequently in these pages, been suggested as the student's best resort for guidance as to the formation of manner and habit in speaking; and, for the present, it may suffice to reïterate the hint. Appropriateness of manner can be learned only from those analogies which reveal themselves to faithful observation in the great schools of genuine nature and true art.

The results of such study are always legible in manner. Appropriate action carries sentiment home to the heart, with a power not second to that of the fitting word. If the study of action as a part of eloquence, has, in our day, fallen into discredit, the fact is owing to the general tendency of modern mind. We suffer our modes of mental action to be narrowed down to the standard of a taste which is usurped by the influence of man's external condition and relations. We lose, accordingly, the benefits of that wider action of the mind which should stretch beyond such limitations, and aspire to a nobler aim. Our discipline of man, as a being capable of varied action, is altogether inferior, in extent and living power, to that which was the standard of former times. The Grecian culture had a truer regard than ours, to man as a being designed to exert an influence on man. A liberal education derives no small share of its value from the light which it sheds on this fact, and on the path of the student's duty to himself in personal cultivation.

All these, and innumerable other considerations of similar tendency, become doubly impressive when we advert to the next prominent characteristic of gesture, as a part of expression,—*grace*. This trait, it is true, can be more easily dispensed with, than any of the others which have been mentioned. It is one, confessedly, of inferior moment. We may justly require, of every public speaker, a manly force and freedom in his demeanor and action; we may justly require of every speaker, even of limited opportunities, the judgment which enables him to avoid incongruities of voice and gesture. But grace is a feature of eloquence which belongs to comparatively high culture and refinement. Still, even this we have a right to expect of the man of liberal education. To what end, otherwise, were all his classical studies, with their perfect models of expressive art, their atmosphere of elegance, their presiding muses, and attendant graces?

If there is anything which more than another displays the incompetent manner in which classical culture is generally conducted, as to its effect on the mind, it is the case of a man who, as a scholar, appreciates every shade of beauty in a sentence of Cicero or a turn of Horace, who hangs with a species of idolatry over a single epithet in Homer, or a line in Euripides, who throws his whole soul into the force of an interrogation in Demosthenes, but who addresses his fellow-men on the themes of duty and immortality, with a half-stretched angular arm, which, under other circumstances, the eye would recognize as the style of paralysis or deformity, and who shortens even the proverbial step from the sublime to the ridiculous, by uttering the former with his tongue, and, at the same moment, exhibiting the latter with his hand.

A graceful style of speaking, so far as regards the visible part of oratory, resolves itself into a compliance with the natural laws of form and motion, which preserve curved and waving lines, with free and flowing movements, as contrasted with straight lines and angles, accompanied by narrow, abrupt, and jerking motions.

Every action of the arm, however, depends, for its true effect, on the condition that the body is self-balanced and reposing, not stooping, leaning, wavering, lounging, or reclining. Hence, attention is due, in the first place, to the posture of the body, that it be *firm* and *free*, *appropriate*, and, at least negatively, *graceful.* The student's first point of attention, in personal training, is, accordingly,

THE ATTITUDE OF THE BODY, REQUIRED FOR PUBLIC SPEAKING.

This point is, by some speakers, assumed as a thing that requires no special attention, and which may be safely left to nature or to accident. Hence the prevalence of those stooping, lounging, and leaning postures which are not only ungainly and awkward to the eye of observers, but injurious to the organs of the speaker, in consequence of the false position in which they place the trunk of the body, and necessarily the chest and lungs. A healthful mode of public speaking, demands an erect and open chest, for the free unembarrassed play of the lungs, and the easy action of the air-cells, the bronchial tubes, the larynx, the vocal ligaments, and the glottis. A stooping, or lounging, or bent attitude causes a partial sinking and narrowing of the chest, an unnatural and injurious position of the whole breathing and vocal apparatus, attended by a stifled and imperfect sound of the voice, a sense of exhaustion, and, perhaps, immediate pain; to all which are probably added, in due season, — as a consequence of the violation of the natural laws of vocal sound, connected with respiration, — the successive stages of bronchial disease.

A faulty attitude of body usually leads, moreover, to awkward motions of the whole frame. The speaker who stands with bent knees, necessarily inclines to a courtseying motion of the limbs, and a swaying motion of the back, which becomes peculiarly noticeable, if, as is usually the case, the courtseys and the half-bows keep time to a rhythmical gesture of the arm.

A true, firm, and easy attitude, depends on the weight of the body being supported on one foot and limb, firmly planted, while the other foot and limb are at rest, and support their own weight merely: the feet at a moderate distance;* the one† in advance of the other, and the toes pointing moderately outward.‡ This is the natural attitude of firmness and freedom combined. The common faults of attitude are standing with the feet feebly drawn *close* to each other, or the opposite error of standing *astride;* the legs *both sinking,* or *both braced,* at the knees; — the former causing a feeble, the latter, a stiff and rigid posture; while *firmness* demands that one knee be braced, and *freedom,* that the other should be slightly bent. Another error in attitude is that of a rigid, inflexible posi-

---

* About the width of the broadest part of the foot.
† The right foot, usually.
‡ Each foot would thus be placed on a line drawn diagonally from the front of the speaker's body, at an angle of forty-five degrees; so that the relative position of the two feet constitutes a right angle.

tion of the trunk, which, on the contrary, should yield and incline slightly on the side that does not, for the moment, support the weight of the body. Still another fault is that of *bending forward too much;* a gentle inclination of the speaker's body towards those whom he is addressing, being all that is requisite. The position of the *head* is often faultily submissive and *drooping*, or *haughtily erect;* propriety lying between these extremes. An awkward effect is often produced on the general attitude of the body, in consequence of placing the feet directly forward, or, perhaps, even with the toes pointing inward. The consequence of this slight error, is, that the speaker's whole attitude resembles that of a fencer in attack, rather than of one man addressing others in the spirit of amity and conciliation. Awkwardness is to be shunned, not merely because it is unseemly, but because whatever is so, is repulsive and offensive, and hinders the speaker's access to the heart. Awkwardness, it is true, is no crime; but its tendency is to provoke mirth in the thoughtless, and pity in the reflective portion of an audience. By no possibility can a speaker who has the misfortune to exhibit such a trait, produce an appropriate effect on the mind, as regards the subject of his address. Yet our national negligence as to manner, causes too general a tendency to habits of the description to which we here refer. Five minutes' instruction or direction might, in many instances, have sufficed seasonably to remove such defects from the juvenile elocution of the speaker; but habit has, perhaps, now made them inseparable parts of himself.

But it is not only early neglect that is the source of numerous errors of manner in speaking. The inadequate attention given, by teachers themselves, to this department of education, renders their instruction sometimes erroneous. The pupils of some of our academies are actually directed to cultivate the ungainly habit of speaking with the left foot advanced while the right hand is in action, — a misfortune which the Roman orator had to undergo, in consequence, partly, of the necessity of holding up on his left arm the burden of his unweildy toga, while engaged in speaking, and, partly, from the analogy of such a position to the manly attitude of the ancient soldier, with his left foot advanced, in inevitable correspondence to the act of protecting his body by advancing his left arm, on which the shield was worn. The use of such an attitude, in modern oratory, throws over the speaker's whole mien the air of an artisan at the anvil, whose object it is to bring down a blow from the greatest practicable height and distance.

The custom of some of our academic institutions prescribes to the student the habit of standing with both feet flat on the floor, and without the aid to easy and graceful attitude which comes from the slight raising of the heel of the retired foot, when the weight of the body is supported on the advanced one. The consequences of this error, slight as it may seem, are the raising of one shoulder, and the stiffening of the whole attitude of the body, — one of the most prominent and glaring faults with which our New England students are generally chargeable, in the act of declaiming.

Another very common error in the attitude of New England speakers, and one which is, in some instances, enjoined by erroneous instruction, is the habit of standing in the square attitude of the Indian, or of the English ploughman, with the feet pointing directly forward from the body. An inevitable consequence of this error, is, that whenever the speaker advances, in the animation of energetic address, his false line of position in the foot, swings round his shoulder to his audience, so that he has then the attitude, precisely, of a fencer in attack. Another bad result of this fault in position and movement, is, that it inclines the speaker to the habit of frequently turning his side to the body of his audience, and addressing now one portion, on the right, then another, on the left, to the exclusion of the majority.*

The slight attention necessary to point the toes outward, enables the speaker, by the easy and natural turn of the head, to address his whole audience, and keep them constantly in his eye, and by the law of natural sympathy, to secure their uninterrupted attention, by directing his eye to theirs,—not at intervals, but continually; not now to one part of the congregation, and then to another; but to all successively: the speaker's attention being due to the whole assembly equally. This indispensable condition of appropriate address, is necessarily dependent on the position of the foot; as on it the whole attitude of the body is founded.

The mode of changing the bodily attitude, is another of those points of practical oratory, which need much attention from the student. The bad effects of neglected habit, are very generally apparent in this particular. One speaker shifts his position with a bold stride; another, with a timid and shuffling slide; one slips or glides to one side, when he ought to advance; another points his foot directly forward, which throws him into the shouldering attitude already described; some stand as motionless as statues, through a whole address; others are perpetually shifting their place without cause; and others, again, make every change of posture a formal and laborious operation.

Changes of attitude ought to be made either for the

---

* Austin, in his elaborate and eloquent work, Chironomia, quotes, in this connection, the following apposite description of an awkward speaker, as given from personal observation, by Cresollius, in his treatise on oratory. — "When he turned himself to the left, he spoke a few words accompanied by a moderate gesture of the hand; then, bending to the right, he acted the same part over again; then, back again to the left, and presently to the right, almost at an equal and measured interval of time, he worked himself up to his usual gesture, and his one kind of movement: you could compare him only to the blindfolded Babylonian ox going forward and returning back by the same path."

effect of quietness and repose, as a natural relief, at the end of a bold passage of earnest address, or for force of emphasis in an energetic assertion or a warm appeal. The former is properly a quiet retiring movement, made at the *close* of a paragraph or head of discourse, or at the *beginning* of such a portion of an address, when the language is less intense than in the strain immediately preceding it: the latter is a spirited advance, made during the act of speaking, and in strict time with the emphasis of the voice and the gesture of the arm. In either case, the movement is not obtrusive but is merged in the general effect. The frequency of change in attitude should always be left dependent on the comparative quietness or animation of the composition to which the speaker is giving utterance: the former style requires few, the latter may require many changes;—the former, retiring; the latter, advancing movements.

THE CHARACTER OF ORATORICAL ACTION.

The prevalent neglect of speaking, as an art, causes many great errors of habit in early life, which continue unremoved in subsequent stages. Among these, the mode of using the hand is conspicuous. The analogy on which the hand is used in oratory, is that of *imparting*, *giving*, or *bestowing;* as speaking is the audible and visible impartation or communication of sentiment. The analogy, in detail, is that of delivering an object,—as, for example, a ball, into the hand of another. Such an act requires an open and sloping position of the hand, and a slight parting of the two outer fingers from the two middle ones, as the necessary condition of *giving*.

The suggestion hence arising to the student, is that every position of the hand which holds it crooked, or level, or flat, or inclined upward, or which keeps the fingers confined, is inappropriate, because inconsistent with *giving*, imparting, or communicating. The recipient holds out a hollow hand, with crooked, or bent fingers: the giver opens and slopes his hand, and partially separates the outer fingers from the others, as mentioned. The speaker who appeals to our feelings, expands his hand, as the natural expression of appeal or of entreaty, in the spirit of free and persuasive communication.

Yet how often we see the hand of the speaker held out flat and close, like a piece of board, or edgewise, like a chopping knife, or feebly hollowed, like that of a beggar, receiving alms. Sometimes, on the contrary, we see it clinched in a style which calls up the associations of " strife and debate," and " smiting with the fist of wickedness."

The palm, (the seat of the great expansion of the sympathetic nerve,) has in it a most eloquent natural language. It is to the hand what the countenance is to the head, the seat of expression. The free opening, then, of the hand, is one of the primary conditions of visible eloquence.*

The use of the arm, in oratorical action, is another practical point of great moment to the right effect of address. The confined and angular movements of the arm, which take place in the natural and appropriate gestures

---

* Manus vero, sine, quibus trunca esset actio ac debilis, vix dici potest, quot motus habeant, cum pene ipsam verborum copiam persequantur. Nam cæteræ partes loquentem adjuvant, hæ, (prope est ut dicam,) ipsæ loquuntur. An non his poscimus? pollicemur? vocamus? dimittimus? minamur? supplicamus? abominamur? timemus? interrogamus? negamus? gaudium, tristitiam, dubitationem, confessionem, pœnitentiam, modum, copiam, numerum, tempus, ostendimus? Non eædem concitant? supplicant? inhibent? probant? admirantur? verecundantur? non in demonstrandis locis atque personis adverbiorum atque pronominum obtinent vicem? ut in tanta per omnes gentes nationesque linguæ diversitate hic mihi omnium hominum communis sermo videatur.— *Quintil. l.* xi. *c.* 3.

The value attached, by the ancients, to the eloquence of the hand, as an instrument of expression, is unequivocally intimated in the fact that the whole art of elocution was comprehended under the term Χειρονομια.

of the parlor or the study, when the persons who are addressed are seated near to the speaker, are utterly inapplicable to the act of addressing a public assembly, in which the speaker's action is to be directed, (if rightly performed,) to the remotest not less than the nearest of his audience. The larger space, in the latter instance, demands larger scope for the arm in action, as certainly as it demands the full tone of voice used in public speaking, and not the comparatively slight utterance used by the fireside. The style of gesture, then, in public address, requires a free action of the arm, terminating, usually, in its full extension, in whatever line a sentiment prompts, avoiding, however, such a degree of extension as terminates in a rigidly straight line, which is always an offence to the eye, as associated with a stiff or mechanical style of action.

A prevalent fault of gesture, in the pulpit, is that of allowing it to fall habitually in a line drawn from the speaker's side. This style of action might be applicable, were all his audience placed in one long row at his right hand. But as they are actually seated in front of him, his hand, — if its action is to have any meaning, — should be presented in front, and obliquely from his own body.

A horizontal sweep or swing of the arm, is the habitual gesture of some pulpit orators. But this style belongs only to descriptive effect, or to that of negation or removal, while assertion, — the prevalent mood of speaking, — demands a downward movement of the arm, more or less direct according to the form of a sentiment. The horizontal line of action is that which properly terminates the expression of general ideas, as coincident in character with the expansive horizontal sweep of the eye, in an extensive view; for the phenomena of gesture are analogous, in their influence on imagination, to the effect of ocular action on external objects, and on visible motion: hence the energetic character of the descent of the arm, in a strong assertion, the expansive effect of a wide horizontal motion, the elevation and sublimity associated with a lofty or ascending gesture, the direct character of an action which throws the speaker's arm in front, the wider effect of an oblique line outward, the still wider of the line extended from the side, the association of remoteness in time or place, which accompanies a gesture directed obliquely backward from the body, the appealing effect of the open hand, the threatening and intimidating or the determined effect of the clinched hand, the marked significance of the pointing finger, the repellant character of the extended arm and opposing hand, the solemn or impressive effect of the upraised hand of awe, wonder, grief, joy, adoration; the supplicating effect of the clasped hands, the welcoming and appealing power of the outspread arms, the triumphant and exulting style of the wave of the hand.

A fault exhibited by some speakers, consists in a ceaseless motion of the arms. The true principle of gesture is that of applying the *ictus* of the arm along with the emphasis of the voice, and reserving the consummation of an action till that moment.

Another error is that of keeping the arms habitually down by the side, and, at long intervals, bringing them up in action, or that of perpetually raising and dropping the arms, at short intervals. The proper regulation of action is founded on the principle that the hand should remain at the point to which it was brought by the movement of the preceding gesture, till occasion call for the preparation requisite to a new action, and that the dropping of the hand should be reserved for the completion or termination of a sentiment, and should be the visible indication that a pause of considerable length is about to take place.

On the obvious fault of speaking without action, it is unnecessary to enlarge. Such a mode of address can be natural only in cases influenced by the second nature of a habit of morbid reserve, or of a constitutional coldness, which disqualifies a man for the offices of eloquence. The frequency of gesture is properly dependent on the character of sentiment and style. An essay, or a lecture, or a merely doctrinal or didactic sermon, may require comparatively little action; as the themes of such discourses address themselves to the understanding and the reason, and can derive little aid from suggestive or descriptive gesture. An argumentative discourse may, from its earnestness of feeling, require frequent and strong gesture of the direct and downward character. Poetic description and glowing appeal may need continual and varied action, in coincidence with the natural demands of feeling and imagination. The spirit of a just criticism,— that which regards eloquence, and every constituent of eloquence, as the expression of the man, and not of the mere artist, — will always permit the vexed question of the proper frequency of gesture to be decided, in part, by the temperament and tendency of the individual. The active and the ardent cannot speak earnestly without a comparative copiousness of action. Their style of language, indeed, if true to their nature, is such as to demand it: they incline to impressive moods of feeling and forms of imagination, as we perceive by their figurative modes of expression. Persons of a serene temper are naturally moderate in gesture, as they are tranquil in thought. The reflective mind rather shuns external manifestation; and the phlegmatic constitution causes it, perhaps, to seem unnecessary and superfluous. The morbid condition of any temperament, however, leads necessarily to excess and disproportion; and critical objections to action, not less than the violations of principle in modes of gesture, are not unfrequently the fruits of an unhealthy taste.

No influence is more unfriendly to a genial and appropriate development of habit, as regards action in speaking, than that arbitrary criticism which makes one constitution, or **one temperament, or one tendency,** the rule for all. One man may use but one or two gestures, in a given paragraph; and his grave and reserved habit may make his manner seem perfectly appropriate: another, of more active tendencies, may double the number of actions, without seeming unnatural. Gesture resembles emphasis: its force and frequency depend, in part, on the personal habit, as well as the momentary feeling, of the man.

A studied variety of oratorical action is an impediment rather than an aid to good effect; as it detaches the attention from the subject to the manner of the speaker, and betrays a false conception of the nature of gesture, which should ever be regarded but as a mode of giving freer and truer vent to the heart. The influence of even the profoundest study of the principles of gesture, should be a thing unsolicited at the moment of speaking,—a result on habit not a trick of art,—a thing of which the speaker is himself, at the time, unconscious, but into which he naturally falls by an intuitive and unstudied effort of his mind. The act of speaking should ever proceed without one separate thought of elocution or of gesture, or any other reference whatever to mere manner. No tone of the voice, no action of the arm, can be true, that is a distinct object of attention, apart from its prompting sentiment. Preparatory practice itself should ever be conducted in the spirit of this unquestionable fact; and such matter only should be selected for exercises, as presents thought in vivid and inspiring forms,—those which naturally prompt or suggest the appropriate modes of accompanying action.

Gestures introduced merely because they are *graceful*, constitute a class of faults which hardly requires notice, even in the form of censure; the primary object and aim of all true action being to enforce, not to decorate, sentiment. True grace is never other than incidental; it does not exist apart from genuine earnestness.

Gestures which are *mimetic*, or merely imitative of

outward effects, instead of being suggestive only, form another of the class of puerile faults, which only perverted taste or deficient judgment can prompt. Some speakers plead for such modes of action, because of their graphic and dramatic power, and their startling effect on rude and uncultivated minds. But such practices, even in the pulpit, cannot be cleared of the charge of pandering to the low and the vile in taste, and of desecrating what the human heart should ever regard as holy. The stare and the laugh of unreflecting hearers, are a poor compensation to the preacher, for the sacrifice of personal dignity, on his own part, and of reverence for truth, on that of his congregation.

The minor faults of gesture are chiefly the following:

Ill-timed action, which does not "keep time" with emphasis, but either runs before or lags after it; the frequent use of the left hand in gesture; the incessant use of both hands whether the breadth or the warmth of a sentiment authorize it or not; using one or two gestures exclusively, which are perpetually recurring to the eye; allowing gestures to cross the speaker's body, or to terminate with a rebound, in the pugnacious style of popular debate; the frequent placing of the hand on the heart, when no personal feeling of the speaker is implied.

The character of gesture, in connection with the different forms of discourse, as didactic or oratorical, was alluded to in a preceding page. Attention is due, also, to the effect produced on gesture by the different parts of the same discourse. Thus, the opening sentences, being usually of an explanatory and didactic character, may need little or no accompaniment of action; the illustrative and argumentative portions of a sermon may justly require a more animated and varied style of gesture; and the concluding application, or appeal, may properly call for the highest forms of poetic and oratorical eloquence, in action as well as in language. A well-composed discourse may not happen to be constructed on such a plan as literally to require these gradations of effect in manner. But every well-written composition, and every well-spoken address, are always progressive in character, and leave on the mind the impression of a climax of sentiment and style.

The appropriate postures of devotion, are a subject on which too little attention is commonly bestowed by the occupants of the pulpit. The clasped hands, and the shut eyes, and the bent body, are obviously not alike applicable to all points of a devotional exercise. They have nothing in common with the feelings which ought to pervade the bosom of the worshipper in the sublime and inspiring acts of adoration and praise: they do not belong to intercession: they are appropriate only in confession and supplication. Every strain of devotion has its appropriate tone, from the swelling notes of adoration and praise, to the breathings of a broken and contrite spirit: each of these, if it issues from the heart rather than from habit, has its natural expression in posture and action: the former prompts the erect attitude and the upraised vertical hands of awe, reverence, and blessing; the latter, the bent frame, the drooping head, and the folded hands of self-abasement. Supplication and entreaty raise the head and clasp the hands in earnestness; petition and intercession extend the arms in the mood and attitude of reception; thanksgiving proffers the gratitude of the heart, as a tribute at the throne of Mercy, with open hands, and downward inclination of the arms, in front of the body. — A very common error in the form of action adopted in the benediction, at the close of public religious services, makes the minister apparently solicit a favor of the congregation, instead of presenting himself as, imploring a blessing on them. The false effect arises from the hands being held supine instead of prone, in the act.

The reading of the Scriptures and of hymns, is, in the practice of some clergymen, accompanied by expressive gesture. This habit seems to be founded on a mistake.

The process of elocution is, in both these cases, one of strict reading, not of speaking. It is one which calls, therefore, for audible, not visible expression. Such, at least, is the association connected with the custom in Anglo-Saxon communities, in most parts of the world. The Oriental and the European continental style of reading, with the full effect of gesture, is, perhaps, the truer method, if we settle the question affirmatively that vivid reading comes as near as possible to vivid speaking; (and we admit the principle so far as the management of the voice is concerned;) but the prevalence of general custom, with us, associates a subdued and repressed style with the reverence due to the Bible and to the offices of worship; and nothing but a singular ardor of temperament, and a recognized peculiarity of personal habit, can render an opposite practice generally tolerable. In this, however, as in other questions of expression, the natural eloquence of strong feeling, is sometimes successful in breaking through the usual restrains of custom.

The common distinctions of gesture, implied in the terms "didactic," "declamatory," and "poetic," may suggest useful hints to the student, in connection with the different modes of action appropriate in the delivery of a discourse. "Didactic" gestures include the slight uses of the open hand and the discriminative finger, in moderate emphasis; "declamatory" action implies the wide sweep and bold descent of energetic emphasis; and "poetic" gesture includes the characteristic loftiness of *epic description*, the empassioned vividness and fervor of *lyric emotion*, and the graphic and abrupt effects of *dramatic style*. A high-toned prose composition may demand, in delivery, the use of all these forms of action; as its matter and its style may partake of all the corresponding characteristics of effect.

The genuine eloquence of inspired feeling, acknowledges no arbitrary limitations. But the subduing and chastening influences of judgment and taste, ought to mould every tone, look, and action, of sacred eloquence.

The Rudiments of Gesture, embodied in the American Elocutionist, will furnish to students more extensive instruction in the elementary details of this branch of the subject; and Austin's Chironomia, (copies of which are accessible at the libraries of some of our public institutions,) will be found to contain a fund of information upon it, enriched by every aid of learned research and graphic illustration.

MISCELLANEOUS EXERCISES

IN

READING AND SPEAKING.

ENGLISH ORATORY. — *Addison.*

[This and a few of the following pieces may be read as examples of *didactic* style. But they are introduced thus early on account, chiefly, of their suggestive character, as regards the formation of *style* in reading and speaking.]

MOST foreign writers, who have given any character of the English nation, whatever vices they ascribe to it, allow, in general, that the people are naturally modest. It proceeds, perhaps, from this our national virtue, that our orators are observed to make use of less gesture or action than those of other countries. Our preachers stand stock still in the pulpit, and will not so much as move a finger to set off the best sermons in the world. We meet with the same speaking statues at our bars, and in all public places of debate. Our words flow from us in smooth, continued stream, without those strainings of the voice, motions of the body, and majesty of the hand, which are so much celebrated in the orators of Greece and Rome. We can talk of life and death in cold blood, and keep our temper in a discourse which turns upon everything that is dear to us. Though our zeal breaks out in the finest tropes and figures, it is not able to stir a limb about us.

I have heard it observed more than once, by those who have seen Italy, that an untravelled Englishman cannot relish all the beauties of Italian pictures, because the postures which are expressed in them are often such as are peculiar to that country. One who has not seen an Italian in the pulpit, will not know what to make of that noble gesture in Raphael's picture of St. Paul preaching at Athens, where the apostle is represented as lifting up both his arms, and pouring out the thunder of his rhetoric amidst an audience of pagan philosophers.

It is certain, that proper gestures, and powerful exertions of the voice, cannot be too much studied by a public orator. They are a kind of comment to what he utters, and enforce everything he says, with weak hearers, better than the strongest argument he can make use of. They keep the audience awake, and fix their attention to what is delivered to them; at the same time that they show the speaker is in earnest, and affected himself with what he so passionately recommends to others.

We are told that the great Latin orator very much impaired his health by the vehemence of action, with which he used to deliver himself. The Greek orator was likewise so very famous for this particular in rhetoric, that one of his antagonists, whom he had banished from Athens, reading over the oration which had procured his banishment, and seeing his friends admire it, could not forbear asking them, if they were so much affected by the bare reading of it, how much more they would have been alarmed, had they heard him actually throwing out such a storm of eloquence?

How cold and dead a figure, in comparison of these two great men, does an orator often make at the British bar! The truth of it is, there is often nothing more ridiculous than the gestures of an English speaker; you see some of them running their hands into their pockets as far as ever they can thrust them, and others, looking with great attention on a piece of paper that has nothing written on it; you may see many a smart rhetorician turning his hat in his hands, moulding it into several different shapes, examining sometimes the lining of it, and sometimes the button, during the whole course of his harangue. A deaf man would think he was cheapening a beaver, when perhaps he is talking of the fate of the British nation. I remember, when I was a young man, and used to frequent Westminster Hall, there was a counsellor who never pleaded without a piece of pack-thread in his hand, which he used to twist about a thumb or a finger, all the while he was speaking: the wags of those days used to call it "the thread of his discourse;" for he was not able to utter a word without it. One of his clients, who was more merry than wise, stole it from him, one day, in the midst of his pleading; but he had better have let it alone, — for he lost his cause by his jest.

I have all along acknowledged myself to be a dumb man, and therefore may be thought a very improper person to give rules for oratory; but I believe every one will agree with me in this, that we ought either to lay aside all kinds of gesture, (which seems to be very suitable to the genius of our nation,) or at least to make use of such only as are graceful and expressive.

Pulpit Eloquence of England. — *Sydney Smith.*

We have no modern sermons in the English language that can be considered as very eloquent. The merits of Blair, (by far the most popular writer of sermons within the last century,) are plain good sense, a happy application of scriptural quotation, and a clear, harmonious style, richly tinged with scriptural language. He generally leaves his readers pleased with his judgment, and his just observations on human conduct, without ever rising so high as to touch the great passions, or kindle any enthusiasm in favor of virtue. For eloquence, we must ascend as high as the days of Barrow and Jeremy Taylor: and even there, while we are delighted with their energy, their copiousness, and their fancy, we are in danger of being suffocated by a redundance which abhors all discrimination; which compares till it perplexes, and illustrates till it confounds.

To the *oüses* of Tillotson, Sherlock, and Atterbury, we must wade through many a barren page, in which the weary Christian can descry nothing all around him but a dreary expanse of trite sentiments and languid words.

The great object of modern sermons, is to hazard nothing: their characteristic is, decent debility; which alike guards the authors from ludicrous errors, and precludes them from striking beauties. Every man of sense, in taking up an English sermon, expects to find it a tedious essay, full of common-place morality; and if the fulfilment of such expectations be meritorious, the clergy have certainly the merit of not disappointing their readers. Yet it is curious to consider, how a body of men so well educated, and so magnificently endowed as the English clergy, should distinguish themselves so little in a species of composition to which it is their peculiar duty, as well as their ordinary habit to attend.

To solve this difficulty, it should be remembered, that the eloquence of the Bar and of the Senate force themselves into notice, power, and wealth, — that the penalty which an individual client pays for choosing a bad advocate, is the loss of his cause, — that a prime minister must infallibly suffer in the estimation of the public, who neglects to conciliate the eloquent men, and trusts the defence of his measures to those who have not adequate talents for that purpose: whereas, the only evil which accrues from the promotion of a clergyman to the pulpit, which he has no ability to fill as he ought, is the fatigue of the audience, and the discredit of that species of public instruction; an evil so general, that no individual patron would dream of sacrificing to it his particular interest. The clergy are generally appointed to their situations by those who have no interest that they should please the audience before whom they speak; while the very reverse is the case in the eloquence of the Bar, and of Parliament. We by no means would be understood to say, that the clergy should owe their promotion principally to their eloquence, or that eloquence ever could, consistently with the constitution of the English church, be made out a common cause of preferment. In pointing out the total want of connection between the privilege of preaching, and the power of preaching well, we are giving no opinion as to whether it might, or might not be remedied; but merely stating a fact.

Pulpit discourses have insensibly dwindled from speaking to reading; a practice, of itself, sufficient to stifle every germ of eloquence. It is only by the fresh feelings of the heart, that mankind can be very powerfully affected. What can be more ludicrous, than an orator delivering stale indignation, and fervor of a week old; turning over whole pages of violent passions, written out in goodly text; *reading* the tropes and apostrophes into which he is hurried by the ardor of his mind; and so affected at a preconcerted line, and page, that he is unable to proceed any farther?

The prejudices of the English nation have proceeded a good deal from their hatred to the French; and because that country is the native soil of elegance, animation, and grace, a certain patriotic solidity, and loyal awkardness, have become the characteristics of this; so that an adventurous preacher is afraid of violating the ancient tranquillity of the pulpit; and the audience are commonly apt to consider the man who tires them less than usual, as a trifler, or a charlatan.

Of British Education, the study of eloquence makes little or no part. The exterior graces of a speaker are despised; and debating societies, (admirable institutions, under proper regulations,) would hardly be tolerated either at Oxford or Cambridge. It is commonly answered to any animadversions upon the eloquence of the English pulpit, that a clergyman is to recommend himself, not by his eloquence, but by the purity of his life, and the soundness of his doctrine; an objection good enough, if any connection could be pointed out between eloquence, heresy, and dissipation; but if it is possible for a man to live well, preach well, and teach well, at the same time, such objections, resting only upon a supposed incompatibility of these good qualities, are duller then the dulness they defend.

The clergy are apt to shelter themselves under the plea, that subjects so exhausted are utterly incapable of novelty; and, in the very strictest sense of the word *novelty*, — meaning that which was never said before, at any time, or in any place, this may be true enough of the first principles of morals; but the modes of expanding, illustrating, and enforcing a particular theme, are capable of infinite variety.

ELOQUENCE OF THE PULPIT. — *John Quincy Adams.*

The pulpit is especially the throne of modern eloquence. There it is, that speech is summoned to realize the fabled wonders of the orphean lyre. The preacher has no control over the will of his audience, other than the influence of his discourse. Yet, as the ambassador of Christ, it is his great and awful duty to call sinners to repentance. His only weapon is the voice; and with this, he is to appal the guilty, and to reclaim the infidel; to rouse the indifferent, and to shame the scorner. He is to inflame the lukewarm, to encourage the timid, and to cheer the desponding believer. He is to pour the healing balm of consolation, into the bleeding heart of sorrow, and to soothe, with celestial hope, the very agonies of death.

Now tell me, who is it, that will best possess and most effectually exercise these more than magic powers? Who is it, that will most effectually stem the torrent of human passions, and calm the raging waves of human vice and folly? Who is it, that with the voice of a Joshua, shall control the course of nature herself, in the perverted heart, and arrest the luminaries of wisdom and virtue, in their rapid revolutions round this little world of man? Is it the cold and languid speaker, whose words fall in such sluggish and drowsy motion from his lips, that they can promote nothing but the slumbers of his auditory, and administer opiates to the body, rather than stimulants to the soul? Is it the unlettered fanatic, without method, without reason; with incoherent raving, and vociferous ignorance, calculated to fit his hearers, not for the kingdom of heaven, but for an hospital of lunatics? Is it even the learned, ingenious, and pious minister of Christ, who, by neglect or contempt of the oratorical art, has contracted a whining, monotonous, sing-song of delivery, to exercise the patience of his flock, at the expense of their other Christian graces?

Or is it the genuine orator of heaven, with a heart sincere, upright, and fervent; a mind stored with that universal knowledge, required as the foundation of his art: with a genius for the invention, a skill for the disposition, and a voice for the elocution of every argument to convince, and of every sentiment to persuade? If then we admit, that the art of oratory qualifies the minister of the gospel to perform, in higher perfection, the duties of his station, we can no longer question whether it be proper for his cultivation. It is more than proper; it is one of his most solemn and indispensable duties.

The Fatal Falsehood. — *Mrs. Opie.*

[The following extract is designed as an example of impressive narrative reading, such as is sometimes introduced in discourses from the pulpit. "Expression" and "variation" are, in passages like this, the main objects of attention in the practice of elocution. The thrilling effect of the story requires that these should be *deep* and *subdued*, yet intensely *vivid*.]

Mrs. Opie, in her " Illustrations of Lying," gives, as an instance of what she terms " the lie of benevolence," the melancholy tale of which the following passage is the conclusion. — Vernon, is a clergyman in Westmoreland, whose youngest son, at a distance from home, had, in a moment of passion, committed murder. The youth had been condemned and executed for his crime. But his brothers had kept the cause and form of his death concealed from their father, and had informed him that their brother had been taken suddenly ill, and died on his road homeward. The father hears the awful truth under the following circumstances, when on a journey.

The coach stopped at an inn outside the city of York; and as Vernon was not disposed to eat any dinner, he strolled along the road, till he came to a small church, pleasantly situated, and entered the church-yard to read, as was his custom, the inscriptions on the tombstones. While thus engaged, he saw a man filling up a new-made grave, and entered into conversation with him. He found it was the sexton himself; and he drew from him several anecdotes of the persons interred around them.

During their conversation, they had walked over the whole of the ground, when, just as they were going to leave the spot, the sexton stopped to pluck some weeds from a grave near the corner of it, and Vernon stopped also; taking hold, as he did so, of a small willow sapling, planted near the corner itself.

As the man rose from his occupation, and saw where Vernon stood, he smiled significantly, and said, "I planted that willow; and it is on a grave, though the grave is not marked out."

"Indeed!"

"Yes; it is the grave of a murderer."

"Of a murderer!" — echoed Vernon, instinctively shuddering, and moving away from it.

"Yes," resumed he, "of a murderer who was hanged at York. Poor lad! — it was very right that he should be hanged; but he was not a hardened villain! and he died so penitent! and as I knew him when he used to visit where I was groom, I could not help planting this tree for old acquaintance' sake." — Here he drew his hand across his eyes.

"Then he was not a low-born man?"

"Oh! no; his father was a clergyman, I think."

"Indeed! poor man: was he living at the time?" said Vernon, deeply sighing.

"Oh! yes; for his poor son did so fret, lest his father should ever know what he had done: he said he was an angel upon earth; and he could not bear to think how he would grieve; for, poor lad, he loved his father and his mother too, though he did so badly."

"Is his mother living?"

"No; if she had, he would have been alive; but his evil courses broke her heart; and it was because the man he killed reproached him for having murdered his mother, that he was provoked to murder him."

"Poor, rash, mistaken youth! then he had provocation?"

"Oh! yes; the greatest: but he was very sorry for what he had done; and it would have done your heart good to hear him talk of his poor father."

"I am glad I did not hear him," said Vernon hastily, and in a faltering voice; (for he thought of Edgar.)

"And yet, sir, it would have done your heart good too."

"Then he had virtuous feelings, and loved his father, amidst all his errors?"

"Aye."

"And I dare say his father loved him, in spite of his faults."

"I dare say he did," replied the man; "for one's children are our own flesh and blood, you know, sir, after all that is said and done; and may be this young fellow was spoiled in the bringing up."

"Perhaps so," said Vernon, sighing deeply.

"However, this poor lad made a very good end."

"I am glad of that! and he lies here," continued Vernon, gazing on the spot with deeper interest, and moving nearer to it as he spoke. "Peace be to his soul! but was he not dissected?"

"Yes; but his brothers got leave to have the body after dissection. They came to me, and we buried it privately at night."

"His brothers came! and who were his brothers?"

"Merchants, in London; and it was a sad cut on them; but they took care that their father should not know it."

"No!" cried Vernon, turning sick at heart.

"Oh! no; they wrote *him* word that his son was ill; then went to Westmoreland, and —"

"Tell me," interrupted Vernon, gasping for breath, and laying his hand on his arm, "tell me the name of this poor youth!"

"Why, he was tried under a false name, for the sake of his family; but his real name was Edgar Vernon."

The agonized parent drew back, shuddered violently and repeatedly, casting up his eyes to heaven, at the same time, with a look of mingled appeal and resignation. He then rushed to the obscure spot which covered the bones of his son, threw himself upon it, and stretched his arms over it, as if embracing the unconscious deposit beneath, while his head rested on the grass, and he neither spoke nor moved. But he uttered one groan; — then all was stillness!

His terrified and astonished companion remained motionless, for a few moments, — then stooped to raise him; but the FIAT OF MERCY had gone forth, and the paternal heart, broken by the sudden shock, had suffered, and breathed its last.

MUSINGS ON THE GRAVE. — *Washington Irving.*

[An example of the *deepest pathos.*]

Oh! the grave! the grave! — It buries every error, covers every defect, extinguishes every resentment. From its peaceful bosom spring none but fond regrets and tender recollections. Who can look down, even upon the grave of an enemy, and not feel a compunctious throb that ever he should have warred with the poor handful of earth that now lies mouldering before him? But the grave of those we loved — what a place for meditation! There it is we call up, in long review, the whole history of the truth and gentleness, and the thousand endearments lavished upon us, almost unheard in the daily course of intimacy; there it is we dwell upon the tenderness of the parting scene ; the bed of death, with all its stifled grief; its noiseless attendants; its most watchful assiduities, — the last testimonial of expiring love, — the feeble, fluttering, thrilling — oh! how thrilling is the beating of the pulse! — the last fond look of the glazing eye, turning upon us from the threshold of existence, — the faint faltering accent, struggling in death to give one more assurance of affection.

Ah! go to the grave of buried love, and meditate! There settle the account, with thy conscience, of every past endearment unregarded, of that departed being, who never, never can be soothed by contrition. If thou art a child, and hast ever added a sorrow to the soul, or a furrow to the silvered brow of an affectionate parent; — if thou art a husband, and hast ever caused the fond bosom that ventured its whole happiness in thy arms, to doubt a moment of thy kindness or thy truth; — if thou art a friend, and hast injured by thought, word, or deed, the spirit that generously confided in thee; — if thou art a lover, and hast ever given one unmerited pang to the true heart that now lies cold beneath thy feet, there be sure that every unkind look, every ungracious word, every ungentle action, will come thronging back upon thy memory, and knock dolefully at thy soul; be sure that thou wilt lie down sorrowing and repenting on the grave, and utter the unheard groan, and pour the unavailing tear, — bitter, because unheard and unavailing.

THE GRAVE. — *J. Montgomery.*

[An example of vivid and varied " Expression."]

There is a calm for those who weep, —
A rest for weary pilgrims found; —
They softly lie and sweetly sleep
                Low in the ground.

The storm that rocks the winter sky,
No more disturbs their deep repose,
Than summer evening's latest sigh,
                That shuts the rose.

I long to lay this painful head
And aching heart beneath the soil,
To slumber in that dreamless bed
                From all my toil. —

" Art thou a *wretch*, of hope forlorn,
The victim of consuming care?
Is thy distracted conscience torn
                By fell despair?

" Do foul misdeeds of former times
Wring with remorse thy guilty breast?
And ghosts of unforgiven crimes
                Murder thy rest?

" Lashed by the furies of the mind,
From Wrath and Vengeance wouldst thou flee? —
Ah! think not, hope not, fool, to find
                A friend in me!

" By all the terrors of the tomb, —
Beyond the power of tongue to tell; —
By the dread secret of my womb; —
                By Death and Hell; --

" I charge thee LIVE! — repent and pray;
In dust thine infamy deplore:
There yet is mercy; — go thy way,
                And sin no more.

" Art thou a *mourner?* — Hast thou known
The joy of innocent delights,
Endearing days forever flown,
    And tranquil nights?

Oh! LIVE! and deeply cherish still
The sweet remembrance of the past:
Rely on Heaven's unchanging will
    For peace at last.

" Art thou a *wanderer?* — Hast thou seen
O'erwhelming tempests drown thy bark?
A shipwrecked sufferer, hast thou been
    Misfortune's mark?

" Though long of wind and waves the sport,
Condemned in wretchedness to roam,
LIVE! — thou shalt reach a sheltering port,
    A quiet home.

" To Friendship didst thou trust thy fame?
And was thy friend a deadly foe,
Who stole into thy breast to aim
    A surer blow?

LIVE! — and repine not o'er his loss, —
A loss unworthy to be told:
Thou hast mistaken sordid dross
    For friendship's gold.

" Seek the true treasure, — seldom found, —
Of power the fiercest griefs to calm,
And soothe the bosom's deepest wound
    With heavenly balm. —

" Whate'er thy lot — whate'er thou be, —
Confess thy folly, kiss the rod,
And in thy chastening sorrows see
    The hand of God.

" A bruised reed he will not break;
Afflictions all his children feel:
He wounds them for his mercy's sake —
    He wounds to heal.

"Humbled beneath his mighty hand,
Prostrate his providence adore:
'T is done!— Arise! He bids thee stand,
     To fall no more.

"Now, Traveller in the vale of tears,
To realms of everlasting light,
Through Time's dark wilderness of years,
     Pursue thy flight!

"There is a calm for those who weep,—
A rest for weary Pilgrims found;
And while the mouldering ashes sleep
     Low in the ground,

"The Soul, of origin divine,—
God's glorious image,— freed from clay,
In heaven's eternal sphere shall shine
     A star of day.

"The *Sun* is but a spark of fire,—
A transient meteor in the sky:
The SOUL, immortal as its Sire,
     SHALL NEVER DIE."

THE GALLICAN CHURCH, AT THE PERIOD OF THE REVOLUTION. — *Croly.*

[An example of *elevated* and *impressive narrative*, combining *depth* and *force* of expressive tone.]

It is among the most memorable facts of intellectual decline, that of the forty thousand clergy of France, not one man of conspicuous ability was roused by the imminent danger of his church. Like a flock of sheep, they relied on their numbers; and the infidel drove them before him, like a flock of sheep. While the battlements of their gigantic church were rocking in every blast, there was no sign of manly precaution, none of generous self-exposure for the common cause, and scarcely any even of that wise suspicion which is the strength of the weak.

They took it for granted that the church would last their time, and were comforted. The pride of the day was distinction in literature; but the whole ecclesiastical body of France saw the race run, without an effort for the prize. They sat wrapped in their old recollections, on the benches of the amphitheatre, and looked on, without alarm, while a new generation of mankind were trying their athletic limbs, and stimulating their young ambition, in the arena where they had once been unrivalled. Raynal, and the few clerics who distinguished themselves by authorship, were avowed deists or atheists; and ostentatious of their complete, if not contemptuous separation from the establishment.

The last light of ecclesiastical literature had glimmered from the cells of Port Royal; but, with the fall of the Jansenists, "middle and utter darkness" came. During half a century, no work of public utility, none of popular estimation, none of genius, none which evinced loftiness of spirit, vigor of understanding, or depth of knowledge, had been produced by a churchman.

The consequence was inevitable and fatal. The old awe of the church's power was changed into contempt for its understanding. Ten thousand rents were made in the fabric: still they let in no light upon the voluntary slumberers within. The revolutionary roar echoed through all its chambers; but it stirred no champion of the altar. The high ecclesiastics relied upon their connection with the court, their rank, and the formal homage of their officials;— shields of gossamer against the pike and firebrand of the people. The inferior priesthood, consigned to obscurity, shrank into their villages into cumberers of the earth, or were irritated into rebels. The feeble contracted themselves within the drowsy round of their prescribed duties; the daring brooded over the national discontents and their own, until they heard the trumpet sounding to every angry heart and form of ill in France; and came forth, a gloomy and desperate tribe, trampling their images and altars under foot, and waving the torch in the front of the grand insurrection.

NIHGT. — *J. Montgomery.*

[The following piece is peculiarly expressive in its style of elocution, as well as of sentiment and language. It exemplifies, successively, the the tones of *tranquility, wonder, joy, pathos, regret, horror, sublimity,* and *devout emotion.*]

   Night is the time for rest; —
    How sweet, when labors close,
   To gather round an aching breast
    The curtain of repose,
   Stretch the tired limbs, and lay the head
    Upon our own accustomed bed.

   Night is the time for dreams; —
    The gay romance of life,
   When truth that is, and truth that seems,
    Blend in fantastic strife : —
   Ah! visions less beguiling far
    Than waking dreams by daylight are!

   Night is the time for toil;
    To plough the classic field,
   Intent to find the buried spoil
    Its wealthy furrows yield;
   Till all is ours that sages taught,
    That poets sang, or heroes wrought.

   Night is the time to weep;
    To wet with unseen tears
   Those graves of memory, where sleep
    The joys of other years,
   Hopes that were angels in their birth,
    But perished young — like things of earth.

   Night is the time to watch;
    On ocean's dark expanse,
   To hail the Pleiades, or catch
    The full moon's earliest glance,
   That brings unto the home-sick mind
    All we have loved — and left behind.

Night is the time for care;
  Brooding on hours mis-spent,
To see the spectre of despair
  Come to our lonely tent;
Like Brutus 'mid his slumbering host,
Startled by Cæsar's stalwart ghost.

Night is the time to muse;
  Then from the eye the soul
Takes flight, and with expanding views,
  Beyond the starry pole
Descries, athwart the abyss of night,
The dawn of uncreated light.

Night is the time to pray;
  Our Saviour oft withdrew
To desert mountains far away:
  So will his followers do, —
Steal from the throng to haunts untrod,
And hold communion there with God.

Night is the time for death;
  When all around is peace,
Calmly to yield the weary breath,
  From sin and suffering cease,
Think of heaven's bliss and give the sign
To parting friends — such death be mine!

THE LAND OF BEULAH. — *G. B. Cheever.*

[The prevalent "Expression" of the following passage, is that of *admiration* rising to *rapture;* — the tone of *joy*, however, softened by that of *sacred* and *solemn* feeling.]

No other language than that of Bunyan himself, perused in the pages of his own sweet book, could be successful in portraying the beauty and glory of such a scene; for now he seems to feel that all the dangers of the pilgrimage are almost over; and he gives himself up without restraint so entirely to the sea of bliss that surrounds him, and to the gales of heaven that are wafting him on, and to the sounds of melody that float in the whole air around him, that nothing in the English language can be compared with this whole closing part of the "Pilgrim's Progress," for its entrancing splendor, yet serene and simple loveliness. The coloring is that of heaven in the soul; and Bunyan has poured his own heaven-entranced soul into it. With all its depth and power, there is nothing exaggerated; and it is made up of the simplest and most scriptural materials and images. We seem to stand in a flood of light poured on us from the open gates of Paradise. It falls on every leaf and shrub by the way-side; it is reflected from the crystal streams, that between grassy banks wind amidst groves of fruit-trees into vineyards and flower-gardens. These fields of Beulah are just below the gate of heaven; and with the light of heaven there come floating down the melodies of heaven: so that here there is almost an open revelation of the things which God hath prepared for them that love him.

During the last days of that eminent man of God, Dr. Payson, he once said, "When I formerly read Bunyan's description of the land of Beulah, where the sun shines and the birds sing day and night, I used to doubt whether there was such a place; but now my own experience has convinced me of it, and it infinitely transcends all my previous conceptions." The best possible commentary on the glowing description in Bunyan is to be found in that very remarkable letter dictated by Dr. Payson to his sister, a few weeks before his death. "Were I to adopt the figurative language of Bunyan, I might date this letter from the land of Beulah, of which I have been for weeks a happy inhabitant. The Celestial City is full in my view. Its glories beam upon me; its breezes fan me; its odors are wafted to me; its sounds strike upon my ears; and its spirit is breathed into my heart. Nothing separates me from it but the River of Death, which now appears but as an insignificant rill, that may be crossed at a single step, whenever God shall give permission. The Sun of Righteousness has been drawing nearer and nearer, appearing larger and brighter as he approached; and now he fills the whole hemisphere; pouring forth a flood of glory, in which I seem to float like an insect in the beams of the sun; exulting, yet almost trembling, while I gaze on this excessive brightness. and wondering, with unutterable wonder, why God should deign thus to shine upon a sinful worm."

There is perhaps, in all our language, no record of a Christian's happiness before death so striking as this. What is it not worth, to enjoy such consolations as these, in our pilgrimage, and especially to experience such foretastes of heaven, as we draw near to the River of Death, such revelations of God in Christ as can swallow up the fears and pains of dying, and make the soul exult in the vision of a Saviour's loveliness, the assurance of a Saviour's mercy? There is no self-denial, no toil, no suffering in this life which is worthy to be compared, for a moment, with such blessedness.

It is very remarkable that Bunyan has, as it were, attempted to lift the veil from the grave, from eternity, in the beatific closing part of the Pilgrim's Progress, and to depict what passes, or may be supposed to pass, with the souls of the righteous immediately after death. There is a very familiar verse of Watts, founded on the unsuccessful effort of the mind to conceive definitely the manner of that existence into which the immortal spirit is to be ushered.

> "In vain the fancy strives to paint
> The moment after death;
> The glories that surround the saint
> In yielding up his breath."

The old poet, Henry Vaughan, in his fragment on "Heaven in Prospect," refers to the same uncertainty, in stanzas that, though somewhat quaint, are very striking

"Dear, beauteous Death, the jewel of the just,
    Shining nowhere but in the dark,
What mysteries do lie beyond thy dust,
    Could man outlook that mark!

"He that hath found some fledged bird's nest, may know
    At first sight if the bird be flown;
But what fair field or grove he sings in now,
    That is to him unknown.

"And yet, as angels in some brighter dreams
    Call to the soul, when man doth sleep,
So some strange thoughts transcend our wonted themes,
    And into glory peep."

LIFE'S COMPANIONS. — *Charles Mackay.*

[The "Expression," in the first three stanzas of this piece, is marked by the tones of *animation, cheerfulness, composure, joy,* and *courage;* it changes in the next three, to *regret,* — in the seventh to *earnest* but *tender entreaty,* — in the eighth, to sublime *aspiration* and *triumph.*]

When I set sail on Life's young voyage,
    'T was upon a stormy sea;
But to cheer me night and day,
Through the perils of the way,
    With me went companions three;
Three companions, kind and faithful,
    Dearer far than friend or bride,
Heedless of the stormy weather,
Hand in hand they came together,
    Ever smiling at my side.

One was Health, my lusty comrade,
    Cherry-cheeked and stout of limb;
Though my board was scant of cheer,
And my drink but water clear,
    I was thankful, blessed with him.
One was mild-eyed Peace of Spirit,
    Who, though storms the welkin swept,
Waking, gave me calm reliance,
And though tempests howled defiance,
    Smoothed my pillow while I slept.

One was Hope, my dearest comrade,
    Never absent from my breast,
Brightest in the darkest days,
Kindest in the roughest ways,
    Dearer far than all the rest.
And though Wealth, nor Fame, nor Station,
    Journeyed with me o'er the sea;
Stout of heart, all danger scorning,
Nought cared I, in life's young morning,
    For their lordly company.

But, alas! ere night has darkened,
    I have lost companions twain;
And the third with tearful eyes,
Worn and wasted, often flies,
    But as oft returns again.
And, instead of those departed,
    Spectres twin around me flit;
Pointing each with shadowy finger,
Nightly at my couch they linger;
    Daily at my board they sit.

Oh! alas! that I have followed
    In the hot pursuit of Wealth;
Though I've gained the prize of gold, —
Eyes are dim, and blood is cold, —
    I have lost my comrade, Health.
Care, instead, the withered beldam,
    Steals the enjoyment from my cup,
Hugs me, that I cannot quit her;
Makes my choicest morsels bitter;
    Seals the founts of pleasure up.

Ah! alas! that Fame allured me, —
    She so false, and I so blind, —
Sweet her smiles; but in the chase
I have lost the happy face
    Of my comrade, PEACE OF MIND;
And instead, Remorse, pale phantom,
    Tracks my feet, where'er I go;
All the day I see her scowling,

In my sleep I hear her howling,
    Wildly flitting to and fro.

Last of all my dear companions,
    Hope! sweet Hope! befriend me yet!
Do not from my side depart,
Do not leave my lonely heart
    All to darkness and regret!
Short and sad is now my voyage
    O'er this gloom-encompassed sea,
But not cheerless altogether,—
Whatsoe'er the wind and weather,—
    Will it seem, if blessed with thee.

Dim thine eyes are, turning earthwards,
    Shadowy pale, and thin thy form.—
Turned to heaven thine eyes grow bright,
All thy form expands in light,
    Soft and beautiful and warm.
Look then upwards! lead me heavenwards!
    Guide me o'er this darkening sea!
Pale Remorse shall fade before me,
And the gloom shall brighten o'er me,
    If I have a friend in *Thee*.

HENRY MARTYN.—*Macaulay*.

[An exercise in the reading of *biographical* narrative, embodying all the highest qualities of sentiment and language, and a corresponding *intensity of* "*Expression*" and vividness of "*Variation*."]*

Towards the middle of the last century, John Martyn of Truro was working with his hands in the mines near that town. He was a wise man, who, knowing the right use of leisure hours, employed them so as to qualify himself for higher and more lucrative pursuits; and who, knowing the right use of money, devoted his enlarged means to procure for his four children a liberal education. Henry, the younger of his sons, was accordingly entered

---

* Passages such as the above, serve to exemplify the style of elocution in obituary discourses.

at the university at Cambridge, where, in January, 1801, he obtained the degree of bachelor of arts, with the honorary rank of senior wrangler. There also he became the disciple, and as he himself would have said, the convert of Charles Simeon. Under the counsels of that eminent teacher, the guidance of Mr. Wilberforce, and the active aid of Mr. Grant, he entered the East India Company's service, as a chaplain. After a residence in Hindostan of about five years, he returned homewards through Persia, in broken health. Pausing at Shiraz, he labored there, during twelve months, with the ardor of a man, who, distinctly perceiving the near approach of death, feared lest it should intercept the great work for which alone he desired to live. That work, (the translation of the New Testament into Persian,) at length accomplished, he resumed his way towards Constantinople, followed his Mimander, (one Hassan Aga,) at a gallop, nearly the whole distance from Tabriz to Tocat, under the rays of a burning sun, and the pressure of continual fever.

On the 6th of October, 1812, in the thirty-second year of his age, he brought the journal of his life to a premature close, by inscribing in it the following words, while he sought a momentary repose under the shadow of some trees at the foot of the Caramanian mountains: "I sat in the orchard, and thought, with sweet comfort and fear, of God, — in solitude, my company, my friend, and comforter. Oh! when shall time give place to eternity! When shall appear that new heaven and new earth, wherein dwelleth righteousness and love! There shall in nowise enter anything that defileth; none of that wickedness which has made men worse than wild beasts; none of those corruptions which add still more to the miseries of mortality, shall be seen or heard of any more." Ten days afterwards, these aspirations were fulfilled. His body was laid in the grave by the hands of strangers at Tocat; and to his disembodied spirit was revealed that awful vision, which it is given to the pure in heart, and to them alone, to contemplate.

Among the most momentous events of Martin's life, was his connection with Charles Simeon, and with such of his disciples as sought learning at Cambridge, and learned leisure at Clapham. A mind so beset by sympathies of every other kind, could not but be peculiarly susceptible to the contagion of opinion. From that circle he adopted, in all its unadorned simplicity, the system called Evangelical, — that system of which, (if Augustin, Luther, Calvin, Knox, and the writers of the English Homilies, may be credited,) Christ himself was the author, and Paul, the first and greatest interpreter.

Through shallow heads and voluble tongues, such a creed, (or indeed any creed,) filtrates so easily, that, of the multitude who maintain it, comparatively few are aware of the conflict of their faith with the natural and unaided reason of mankind. Indeed, he who makes such an avowal, will hardly escape the charge of affectation or of impiety. Yet, if any truth be clearly revealed, it is, that the apostolic doctrine was foolishness to the sages of this world. If any unrevealed truth be indisputable, it is, that such sages are at this day making, as they have ever made, ill-disguised efforts to escape the inferences with which their own admissions teem. Divine philosophy, divorced from human science, — celestial things stripped of the mitigating veils woven by man's wit and fancy to relieve them, — form an abyss as impassable at Oxford, now, as at Athens, eighteen centuries ago. To Henry Martyn the gulf was visible, the self-renunciation painful, the victory complete. His understanding embraced, and his heart reposed in, the two comprehensive and ever-germinating tenets of the school in which he studied. Regarding his own heart as corrupt, and his own reason as delusive, he exercised an unlimited affiance in the holiness and the wisdom of Him, in whose person the divine nature had been allied to the human, —

that, in the persons of his followers, the human might be allied to the divine.

Such was his religious theory, — a theory which doctors may combat, or admit, or qualify, but in which the readers of Henry Martyn's biography, letters, and journals, cannot but acknowledge that he found the resting-place of all the impetuous appetencies of his mind, the spring of all his strange powers of activity and endurance. Prostrating his soul before the real, though the hidden Presence he adored, his doubts were silenced, his anxieties soothed, and every meaner passion hushed into repose. He pursued divine truth, (as all who would succeed in that pursuit must pursue it,) by the will rather than the understanding; by sincerely and earnestly searching out the light which had come into the world, by still going after it, when perceived, — by following its slightest intimations with faith, with resignation, and with constancy, though the path it disclosed led him from the friends and the home of his youth, across wide oceans and burning deserts, amidst contumely and contention, with a wasted frame and an overburthened spirit. He rose to the sublime in character, neither by the powers of his intellect, nor by the compass of his learning, nor by the subtlety, the range, or the beauty of his conceptions, (for in all these he was surpassed by many,) but by the copiousness and the force of the living fountains by which his spiritual life was nourished. Estranged from a world once too fondly loved, his well-tutored heart learned to look back with a calm though affectionate melancholy on its most bitter privations. Insatiable in the thirst for freedom, holiness, and peace, he maintained an ardor of devotion which might pass for an erotic delirium, when contrasted with the Sadducean frigidity of other worshippers. Regarding all the members of the great human family as his kindred in sorrow and in exile, his zeal for their welfare partook more of the fervor of domestic affection, than of the kind but gentle warmth of a diffusive philanthropy. Elevated in his own esteem by the consciousness of an intimate union with the Eternal Source of all virtue, the meek missionary of the cross exhibited no obscure resemblance to the unobtrusive dignity, the unfaltering purpose, and the indestructible composure of Him by whom the cross was borne. The ill-disciplined desires of youth, now confined within one deep channel, flowed quickly onwards to one great consummation; nor was there any faculty of his soul, or any treasure of his accumulated knowledge, for which appropriate exercise was not found on the high enterprise to which he was devoted.

"Ora Atque Labora!" — *Albert Pike.*

[An example of *descriptive* and *didactic* poetry.]

Swiftly flashing, hoarsely dashing.
Onward rolls the mighty river:
Down it hurries to the sea,
Bounding on exultingly;
And still the lesson teaches ever —
Ora atque labora!

Trembling fountains on blue mountains
Murmuring and overflowing,
Through green valleys deep in hills,
Send down silver brooks and rills,
Singing, while in sunlight glowing,
Ora atque labora!

Onward flowing, ever growing,
In its beauty each rejoices;
While in Night's delighted ear,
Through the amber atmosphere,
Sounds the murmur of their voices —
Ora atque labora!

Archly glancing, lightly dancing,
Eddies chasing one the other,
Round old roots the current whirls,

Over ringing pebbles curls;
Each rill singing to its brother,
  Ora atque labora!

Hoarsely roaring, swiftly pouring,
Through tall mountains cloven asunder,
Over precipices steep,
Plunging to abysses deep,
The cataract's fierce voices thunder —
  Ora atque labora!

Sunlight shifting, white mist drifting,
On its forehead, whence it marches,
Swelled with freshets and great rains,
Shouting, where, through fertile plains,
'T is spanned by aqueducts and arches —
  Ora atque labora!

Thus Endeavor striveth ever,
For the thankless world's improvement;
Each true thought and noble word,
By the dull earth though unheard,
Making part of one great movement:
  Ora atque labora!

Work then bravely, sternly, gravely!
Life for this alone is given;
What is right, that boldly do;
Frankly speak out what is true,
Leaving the result to Heaven:
  Ora atque labora!

THE FIELD OF BATTLE. — *Hall.*

[An example of the vivid "Expression" which characterizes high-wrought *graphic* and *dramatic description.*]

Science and revelation concur in teaching that this ball of earth, which man inhabits, is not the only world; that millions of globes like ours roll in the immensity of space. The sun, the moon, "those seven nightly wandering fires," those twinkling stars, are worlds. There, doubtless, dwell other moral and intellectual natures; passing what man calls time, in one untired pursuit of truth and duty; still seeking, still exploring, ever satisfying, never satiating, the ethereal, moral, intellectual thirst; whose delightful task it is, as it should be ours, to learn the will of the Eternal Father, — to seek the good, which to that end, for them and us to seek, hides; and finding, to admire, adore, and praise, "him first, him last, him midst and without end."

Imagine one of these celestial spirits, bent on this great purpose, descending upon our globe, and led by chance, to a European plain, at the point of some great battle; on which, to human eye, reckless and blind to over-ruling Heaven, the fate of states and empires is suspended.

On a sudden, the field of combat opens on his astonished vision. It is a field, which men call "glorious." A hundred thousand warriors stand in opposed ranks. Light gleams on their burnished steel. Their plumes and banners wave. Hill echoes to hill the noise of moving rank and squadron, — the neigh and tramp of steeds, — the trumpet, drum, and bugle call. There is a momentary pause, — a silence like that which precedes the fall of a thunder-bolt, — like that awful stillness, which is precursor to the desolating rage of the whirlwind. In an instant, flash succeeding flash, pours columns of smoke along the plain. The iron tempest sweeps, heaping man, horse, and car, in undistinguished ruin. In shouts of rushing hosts, — in shock of breasting steeds, — in peals of musketry, in artillery's roar, — in sabres' clash, — in thick and gathering clouds of smoke and dust, all human eye, and ear, and sense, are lost. Man sees not, but the sign of onset. Man hears not, but the cry of — "onward."

Not so the celestial stranger. His spiritual eye, unobscured by artificial night, — his spiritual ear, unaffected by mechanic noise, — witness the real scene, naked in all its cruel horrors.

He sees lopped and bleeding limbs scattered; gashed,

dismembered trunks, outspread, gore-clothed, lifeless; — brains bursting from crushed skulls, — blood gushing from sabred necks, — severed heads, whose mouths mutter rage amidst the palsying of the last agony.

He hears the mingled cry of anguish and despair, issuing from a thousand bosoms, in which a thousand bayonets turn, — the convulsive scream of anguish from heaps of mangled, half-expiring victims, over whom the heavy artillery wheels lumber, and crush into one mass, bone and muscle and sinew, — while the fetlock of the war-horse drips with blood starting from the last palpitation of the burst heart, on which the hoof pivots.

"This is not earth" — would not such a celestial stranger exclaim? — "this is not earth" — "this is hell!" — "This is not man! but demon, tormenting demon."

Thus exclaiming, would he not speed away to the skies, — his immortal nature unable to endure the folly, the crime, and the madness of man?

"NOT ON THE BATTLE FIELD." — *John Pierpont.*
[An example of the intense "Expression" arising from *vivid delineation*, accompanied by *profound and affecting sentiment.*]

  Oh! no, no — let *me* lie
Not on a field of battle, when I die!
  Let not the iron tread
Of the mad war-horse crush my helmed head:
  Nor let the reeking knife,
That I have drawn against a brother's life,
  Be in my hand, when death
Thunders along, and tramples me beneath
  His heavy squadron's heels,
Or gory felloes of his cannon wheels.

  From such a dying bed,
Though o'er it float the stripes of white and red,
  And the bald eagle brings
The clustered stars upon his wide-spread wings,
  To sparkle in my sight,
Oh! never let my spirit take her flight!

I know that Beauty's eye
Is all the brighter where gay pennants fly,
    And brazen helmets dance,
And sunshine flashes on the lifted lance;
    I know that bards have sung,
And people shouted till the welkin rung
      In honor of the brave
Who on the battle-field have found a grave.

   *   *   *   *   *   *   *

    Such honors grace the bed,
I know, whereon the warrior lays his head,
    And hears, as life ebbs out,
The conquered flying, and the conqueror's shout.—
    But as his eye grows dim,
What is a column or a mound to him?
    What, to the parting soul,
The mellow note of bugles? What the roll
    Of drums? No: let me die
Where the blue heaven bends o'er me lovingly,
    And the soft summer air,
As it goes by me, stirs my thin white hair,
    And from my forehead dries
The death-damp as it gathers, and the skies
    Seem waiting to receive
My soul to their clear depths! Or let me leave
    The world, when round my bed
Wife, children, weeping friends, are gathered,
    And the calm voice of prayer
And holy hymning shall my soul prepare
    To go and be at rest
With kindred spirits,—spirits who have blessed
    The human brotherhood
By labors, cares, and counsels for their good.

    And in my dying hour,
When riches, fame, and honor, have no power
    To bear the spirit up,
Or from my lips to turn aside the cup
    That all must drink at last,
Oh! let me draw refreshment from the past!

>   Then let my soul run back,
> With peace and joy, along my earthly track,
>   And see that all the seeds
> That I have scattered there, in virtuous deeds,
>   Have sprung up, and have given,
> Already, fruits of which to taste in heaven!
>   And though no grassy mound
> Or granite pile say 't is heroic ground
>   Where my remains repose,
> Still will I hope — vain hope, perhaps! — that those
>   Whom I have striven to bless,
> The wanderer reclaimed, the fatherless,
>   May stand around my grave,
> With the poor prisoner, and the poorest slave,
>   And breathe an humble prayer,
> That they may die like him whose bones are mouldering there.

RELIGIOUS PRINCIPLE THE VITAL ELEMENT OF POETRY. — *Carlyle.*

[An example of "Expression" affected by *noble sentiment and elevated diction.*]*

Burns was born poor, and born also to continue poor; for he would not endeavor to be otherwise: this it had been well could he have once for all admitted, and considered as finally settled. He was poor, truly; but hundreds, even of his own class and order of mind, have been poorer, yet have suffered nothing deadly from it: nay, his own father had a far sorer battle with ungrateful destiny than his was; and he did not yield to it, but died courageously warring, and, to all moral intents, prevailing, against it.

True, Burns had little means, had even little time for poetry, his only real pursuit and vocation; but so much the more precious was what little he had. In all these

---

* Passages like the above form useful elements for practice in the appropriate style of oratory on occasions such as those of literary anniversaries and similar festivals.

external respects his case was hard; but very far from the hardest. Poverty, incessant drudgery, and much worse evils, it has often been the lot of poets and wise men to strive with, and their glory to conquer. Locke was banished as a traitor; and wrote his Essay on the Human Understanding, sheltering himself in a Dutch garret. Was Milton rich or at his ease, when he composed Paradise Lost? Not only low, but fallen; not only poor, but impoverished; "in darkness and with dangers compassed round," he sang his immortal song, and found "fit audience, though few." Did not Cervantes finish his work, a maimed soldier, and in prison? Nay, was not the *Araucana*, which Spain acknowledges as its Epic, written without even the aid of paper; on scraps of leather, as the stout fighter and voyager snatched any moment from that wild warfare?

And what then had these men, which Burns wanted? Two things; both which, it seems to us, are indispensable for such men. They had a true, religious principle of morals; and a single not a double aim in their activity. They were not self-seekers and self-worshippers; but seekers and worshippers of something far better than self. Not personal enjoyment was their object; but a high, heroic idea of religion, of patriotism, of heavenly wisdom, in one or the other form, ever hovered before them; in which cause, they neither shrunk from suffering, nor called on the earth to witness it as something wonderful; but patiently endured, counting it blessedness enough so to spend and be spent. Thus the "golden-calf of self-love," however curiously carved, was not their Deity; but the invisible goodness, which alone is man's reasonable service. This feeling was as a celestial fountain, whose streams refreshed into gladness and beauty all the provinces of their otherwise too desolate existence. In a word, they willed one thing, to which all other things were subordinated, and made subservient; and therefore they accomplished it. The wedge will rend rocks; but its edge must be sharp and single: if it be double, the wedge is bruised in pieces, and will rend nothing.

Part of this superiority these men owed to their age; in which heroism and devotedness were still practised, or, at least, not yet disbelieved in: but much of it likewise they owed to themselves. With Burns, again, it was different. His morality, in most of its practical points, is that of a mere worldly man; enjoyment, in a finer or coarser shape, is the only thing he loves and strives for. A noble instinct sometimes raises him above this; but an instinct only, and acting only for moments. He has no religion: in the shallow age where his days were cast, religion was not discriminated from the "New" and "Old Light" *forms* of religion; and was, with these, becoming obsolete in the minds of men. His heart, indeed, is alive with a trembling adoration; but there is no temple in his understanding. He lives in darkness and in the shadow of doubt. His religion, at best, is an anxious wish; like that of Rabelais, "a great Perhaps."

He loved poetry warmly, and in his heart; could he but have loved it purely and with his whole undivided heart, it had been well. For poetry, as Burns could have followed it, is but another form of wisdom, — of religion; is itself wisdom and religion. But this, also, was denied him. His poetry is a stray, vagrant gleam, which will not be extinguished within him, yet rises not to be the true light of his path, but is often a wildfire that misleads him. It was not necessary for Burns to be rich, to be, or to seem, independent; but *it was* necessary for him to be at one with his own heart; to place what was highest in his nature, highest also in his life; "to seek within himself for that consistency and sequence, which external events would forever refuse him." He was born a poet; poetry was the celestial element of his being, and should have been the soul of all his endeavors. Lifted into that serene ether, whither he had wings given him to mount, he would have needed no other elevation.

Poverty, neglect, and all evil, save the desecration of himself and his art, were a small matter to him: the pride and the passions of the world lay far beneath his feet; and he looked down alike on noble and slave, on prince and beggar, and all that wore the stamp of man, with clear recognition, with brotherly affection, with sympathy, with pity. Nay, we question whether for his culture as a poet, poverty and much suffering, for a season, were not absolutely advantageous. Great men, in looking back over their lives, have testified to that effect. " I would not for much," says Jean Paul, "that I had been born richer." And yet Paul's birth was poor enough; for, in another place, he adds: "the prisoner's allowance is bread and water; and I had often only the latter." But the gold that is refined in the hottest furnace, comes out the purest; or, as he himself has expressed it, " the canary-bird sings sweeter the longer it has been trained in a darkened cage."

A man like Burns might have divided his hours between poetry and virtuous industry; industry which all true feeling sanctions, nay, prescribes, and which has a beauty, for that cause, beyond the pomp of thrones: but to divide his hours between poetry and rich men's banquets, was an ill-starred and inauspicious attempt. How could he be at ease at such banquets? What had he to do there, mingling his music with the coarse roar of altogether earthly voices, and brightening the thick smoke of intoxication with fire lent him from heaven? Was it his aim to *enjoy* life? To-morrow he must go drudge as an Exciseman! We wonder not that Burns became moody, indignant, and at times an offender against certain rules of society; but rather that he did not grow utterly frantic, and "run a muck" against them all. How could a man, so falsely placed, by his own or others' fault, ever know contentment, or peaceable diligence, for an hour? What he did, under such perverse guidance, and what he forbore to do, alike fill us with astonishment at the natural strength and worth of his character.

Doubtless there was a remedy for his perverseness: but not in others; only in himself; least of all in simple increase of wealth and worldly respectability.

EMBLEMS. — *James Montgomery.*

[An example of "Expression" and "Variation," as produced by vivid *sentiment.* The successive stages of the style of elocution, in the reading of this piece, are those which indicate *seriousness, solemnity,* and *awe.*]

  An evening-cloud, in brief suspense,
   Was hither driven and thither;
  It came I know not whence,
   And went I knew not whither:
  I watched it changing in the wind, —
   Size, semblance, shape and hue,
  Fading and lessening, — till behind
   It left no speck in heaven's deep blue.

  Amidst the marshalled host of night,
  Shone a new star supremely bright:
   With marvelling eye, well-pleased to err,
  I hailed the prodigy; — anon,
   It fell; — it fell like Lucifer,
  A flash, a blaze, a train — 't was gone!
  And then I sought in vain its place,
  Throughout the infinite of space.

  Dew-drops, at day-spring, decked a line
  Of gossamer so frail, so fine,
  A fly's wing shook it: round and clear,
   As if by fairy-fingers strung,
  Like orient pearls, at Beauty's ear,
   In trembling brilliancy they hung
  Upon a rosy brier, whose bloom
  Shed nectar round them and perfume:

  Ere long, exhaled in limpid air,
   Some mingled with the breath of morn,

Some slid down singly, here and there,
  Like tears, by their own weight overborne;
At length the film itself collapsed; and where
  The pageant glittered, lo! a naked thorn.

What are the living? Hark! a sound
  From the grave and cradle crying,
By earth and ocean echoed round,—
  "The living are the dying!"

From infancy to utmost age,
What is man's line of pilgrimage?
  The pathway to Death's portal:
The moment we begin to be,
We enter on the agony;—
  The dead are the immortal;
They live not on expiring breath,
They only are exempt from death.

Cloud-atoms, sparkles of a falling star,
Dew-drops, or films of gossamer we are:
What can the state beyond us be?
Life?—Death?—Ah! no,—a greater mystery!—
What thought hath not conceived, ear heard, eye seen;
  Perfect existence from a point begun;
Part of what GOD'S eternity hath been:
  Whole immortality belongs to none
But HIM, the first, the last, the Only One!

THE SUN'S ECLIPSE. (July 8, 1842.) — *Horace Smith.*

[The reading of this piece calls for the successive "Expression" of *awe, terror, horror,* and *joy,* as elicited by *description,* in the form of *poetry.*]

'T is cloudless morning; but a frown misplaced,
          Cold, lurid, strange,
Her summer smile from Nature's brow hath chased:
          What fearful change,
What menacing catastrophe is thus
Ushered by such prognostics ominous?

Is it the life of day, this livid glare,
          Death's counterpart?

What means the withering coldness in the air,
    That chills my heart,
And what the gloom portentous that hath made
The glow of morning a funereal shade?

O'er the Sun's disk, a dark orb wins its slow,
    Gloom-deepening way,
Climbs,—spreads,—enshrouds,—extinguishes,—and lo!
    The god of day
Hangs in the sky, a corpse! The usurper's might
Hath stormed his throne, and quenched the life of light!

A pall is on the earth;—the screaming birds
    To covert speed,
Bewildered and aghast; the bellowing herds
    Rush o'er the mead;
While men,—pale shadows in the ghastly gloom,—
Seem spectral forms just risen from the tomb.

Transient, though total, was that drear eclipse:
    With might restored,
The Sun regladdened earth;—but human lips
    Have never poured
In mortal ears the horrors of the sight
That thrilled my soul that memorable night.

To every distant zone and fulgent star
    Mine eyes could reach,
And the wide waste was one chaotic war:
    O'er all and each,—
Above—beneath—around me—everywhere—
Was anarchy,—convulsion,—death,—despair.

'T was noon;—and yet a deep unnatural night
    Enshrouded heaven,
Save where some orb unsphered, or satellite
    Franticly driven,
Glared as it darted through the darkness dread,
Blind,—rudderless,—unchecked,—unpiloted.

A thousand simultaneous thunders crashed,
    As here and there,

Some rushing planet 'gainst another dashed,
              Shooting through air
Volleys of shattered wreck, when both, destroyed,
Foundered and sank in the engulfing void.

Others self-kindled, as they whirled and turned,
              Without a guide,
Burst into flames, and rushing as they burned
              With range more wide,
Like fire-ships that some stately fleet surprise,
Spread havoc through the constellated skies.

While stars kept falling from their spheres, — as though
              The heavens wept fire, —
Earth was a raging hell of war and woe,
              Most deep and dire;
Virtue was vice, — vice, virtue — all was strife;
Brute force was law, — justice, the assassin's knife.

From that fell scene my space-commanding eye
              Glad to withdraw,
I pierced the empyrean palace of the sky,
              And shuddering saw
A vacant throne, — a sun's extinguished sphere, —
All else a void, — dark, desolate, and drear.

"What mean," I cried, "these sights unparalleled,
              These scenes of fear?"
When lo! a voice replied; and nature held
              Her breath to hear —
"Mortal! the scroll before thine eyes unfurled
Displays a *soul-eclipse*, — an *atheist* world!"

I woke — my dream was o'er! What ecstasy
              It was to know
That God was guide and guardian of the sky,
              That man below,
Deserved the love I felt, — I could not speak
The thrilling joy whose tears were on my cheek!

On a Survey of the Heavens, before Day-Brak. — *H. K. White.*

[An example of " Expression " and " Variation " in the successive forms of *awe, adoration, reverence, self-humiliation, submission*, and *resignation.*]

Ye many twinkling stars who yet do hold
Your brilliant places in the sable vault
Of night's dominion! — Planets, and central orbs
Of other systems; — big as the burning sun
Which lights this nether globe, — yet to our eye
Small as the glow-worm's lamp! — To you I raise
My lowly orisons, while, all bewildered,
My vision strays o'er your ethereal hosts;
Too vast, too boundless for our narrow mind,
Warped with low prejudice, to unfold,
And sagely comprehend, — thence higher soaring, —
Through ye I raise my solemn thoughts to Him,
The mighty Founder of this wondrous maze,
The great Creator! Him! who now sublime,
Wrapt in the solitary amplitude
Of boundless space, above the rolling sphere
Sits on his silent throne, and meditates.

The angelic hosts, in their inferior heaven,
Hymn to the golden harps his praise sublime,
Repeating loud, " The Lord our God is great!"
In varied harmonies. — The glorious sounds
Roll o'er the air serene. — The Æolian spheres,
Harping along their viewless boundaries,
Catch the full note, and cry, " The Lord is great!"
Responding to the seraphim. — O'er all,
From orb to orb, to the remotest verge
Of the created world, the sound is borne,
Till the whole universe is full of HIM.

Oh! 'tis this heavenly harmony which now
In fancy strikes upon my listening ear,
And thrills my inmost soul. It bids me smile
On the vain world, and all its bustling cares,
And gives a shadowy glimpse of future bliss.

Oh! what is man, when at ambition's height, —
What even are kings, when balanced in the scale
Of these stupendous worlds? Almighty God!
Thou, the dread author of these wondrous works!
Say, canst thou cast on me, poor passing worm,
One look of kind benevolence? — Thou canst;
For thou art full of universal love,
And in thy boundless goodness wilt impart
Thy beams as well to me as to the proud,
The pageant insects of a glittering hour.

Oh! when reflecting on these truths sublime,
How insignificant do all the joys,
The gauds and honors of the world appear!
How vain ambition! — Why has my wakeful lamp
Outwatched the slow-paced night? — Why on the page
The schoolman's labored page, — have I employed
The hours devoted by the world to rest,
And needful to recruit exhausted nature?
Say; can the voice of narrow Fame repay
The loss of health? or can the hope of glory
Send a new throb unto my languid heart,
Cool, even now, my feverish aching brow,
Relume the fires of this deep sunken eye,
Or paint new colors on this pallid cheek?

Say, foolish one — can that unbodied fame,
For which thou barterest health and happiness,
Say, can it soothe the slumbers of the grave?
Give a new zest to bliss, or chase the pangs
Of everlasting punishment condign?
Alas! how vain are mortal man's desires!
How fruitless his pursuits! — Eternal God!
Guide thou my footsteps in the way of truth;
And oh! assist me so to live on earth,
That I may die in peace, and claim a place
In thy high dwelling. — All but this is folly, —
The vain illusions of deceitful life.

THE CROWDED STREET. — *W. C. Bryant.*

[This piece is intended to exemplify the " Expression" and " Variation" which characterize *reflective sentiment.*]

Let me move slowly through the street,
   Filled with its ever-shifting train,
Amid the sound of steps that beat
   The murmuring walk, like autumn rain.

How fast the flitting figures come!
   The mild, the fierce, the stony face;
Some bright with thoughtless smiles, and some
   Where secret tears have left their trace.

They pass — to toil, to strife, to rest,
   To halls in which the feast is spread,
To chambers where the funeral guest
   In silence sits beside the dead.

And some to happy homes repair,
   Where children, pressing cheek to cheek,
With mute caresses shall declare
   The tenderness they cannot speak.

And some, who walk in calmness here,
   Shall shudder as they reach the door
Where one who made their dwelling dear,
   Its flower, its light, is seen no more.

Youth, with pale cheek and slender frame,
   And dreams of greatness in thine eye!
Go'st thou to build an early name, —
   Or early in the task to die?

Keen son of trade, with eager brow!
   Who is now fluttering in thy snare?
Thy golden fortunes, tower they now,
   Or melt the glittering spires in air?

Who of this crowd to-night shall tread
   The dance till daylight gleam again?
Who sorrow o'er the untimely dead?
   Who writhe in throes of pain?

Some, famine-struck, shall think how long
    The cold dark hours, how slow the light!
And some, who flaunt amid the throng,
    Shall hide in dens of shame to night.

Each, where his task or pleasures call,
    They pass and heed each other not.—
There *is* who heeds, who holds them all,
    In His large love and boundless thought.

These struggling tides of life that seem
    In wayward, aimless course, to tend,
Are eddies of the mighty Stream
    That rolls to its predestined End.

ROBERT HALL.— *Anon.*

[Passages such as the following exemplify the varied "Expression" resulting from the successive effects of *narration, description,* and *didactic* sentiment.]

The services preliminary to the sermon, had been nearly gone through, and the last verse of a hymn was being sung, when Mr. Hall ascended slowly, and, I thought, wearily, the pulpit stairs. No one, looking at his somewhat unwieldy and rather ungraceful figure, would have been prepossessed in his favor; and, as he sat down in the pulpit, and looked languidly round on the congregation, I experienced, I know not why, a feeling of disappointment.

He rose, and read his text: "The Father of Lights." At first, his voice was scarcely audible, and there appeared some slight hesitation; but this soon wore off; and as he warmed with his subject, he poured forth such a continuous stream of eloquence, that it seemed as if it flowed from some inexhaustible source. His tones were. although low, beautifully modulated; but, owing to soi affection in his throat, his speech was, at short interval. interrupted by a short spasmodic cough.

During the delivery of his brilliant paragraphs, the most

breathless silence reigned throughout the vast assemblage; but his momentary cessation was the signal for general relaxation from an attention so intense that it became almost painful. It was curious to observe how every neck was stretched out, so that not a word which fell from those eloquent lips should be lost; and the suspended breathings of those around me, evinced how intently all were hanging on his charmed words.

Mr. Hall's fluency was wonderful, and his command of language unsurpassed. I will not mar the beauty of his discourse, by attempting to describe it; but, as I followed him, whilst, by his vivid imagination, he conveyed his hearers through the starry skies, and reasoned, from those lights of the universe, what the Father of Lights must be, I became lost in wonder and admiration.

But the crowning glory of his sermon was his allusion to the heavenly world, whose beatific glories he expatiated on, with almost the eloquence of an angel. He seemed like one inspired; and, as he guided us by living streams, and led us over the celestial fields, he seemed carried away by his subject, and his face beamed as if it reflected Heaven's own light. And this was the man who, but an hour before, had lain down on the ground, in the excess of his agony; and who, from his earliest years, had *constantly* endured the most excruciating torture which man can be called upon to bear! I have myself heard him say that he had never known one waking hour free from extreme pain.

Mr. Hall used very little action in the pulpit. His favorite — or, rather his usual — attitude, was, to stand, and lean his chest against the cushion; his left arm lying on the Bible, and his right hand slightly raised, with the palm towards the audience. His tones were almost uniformly low; and he rarely raised them. Ideas seemed so to accumulate, whilst he was preaching, that they flowed forth without effort on his part. Never did he hesitate; — and, so pure were his oral compositions, that the most elaborate efforts of the pen would rather have injured than improved their structure.

THE MILLENNIUM ERA.— *Coleridge.*

Return pure Faith! return meek Piety!
The kingdoms of the world are yours: each heart
Self-governed, the vast family of Love,
Raised from the common earth by common toil,
Enjoy the equal produce. Such delights
As float to earth, permitted visitants!
When in some hour of solemn jubilee
The massy gates of Paradise are thrown
Wide open, and forth come in fragments wild
Sweet echoes of unearthly melodies,
And odors snatched from beds of amaranth,
And they, that from the crystal river of life
Spring up on freshened wing, ambrosial gales!
The favored good man in his lonely walk
Perceives them, and his silent spirit drinks
Strange bliss which he shall recognize in heaven.
And such delights, such strange beatitudes
Seize on my young anticipating heart
When that blest future rushes on my view!
For in his own and in his Father's might
The Saviour comes! While as the Thousand Years
Lead up their mystic dance, the Desert shouts!
Old Ocean claps his hands!

O years! the blest preëminence of saints!
Ye sweep athwart my gaze, so heavenly bright,
The wings that veil the adoring seraph's eye,
What time they bend before the jasper Throne,
Reflect no lovelier hues!

Believe thou, O my soul,
Life is a vision shadowy of Truth;
And vice, and anguish, and the wormy grave,
Shapes of a dream! The veiling clouds retire;
And lo! the throne of the redeeming God,
Forth flashing unimaginable day,
Wraps in one blaze, earth, heaven, and deepest hell.

Contemplant spirits! ye that hover o'er,
With untired gaze, the immeasurable fount
Ebullient with creative Deity!
And ye of plastic power, that, interfused,
Roll through the grosser and material mass
In organizing surge! Holies of God!
I, haply, journeying my immortal course,
Shall sometime join your mystic choir. Till then
I discipline my young and novice thought
In ministeries of heart-stirring song;
And aye on Meditation's heaven-ward wing
Soaring aloft, I breathe the empyreal air
Of Love, omnific, omnipresent Love,
Whose day-spring rises glorious in my soul,
As the great sun, when he his influence
Sheds on the frost-bound waters:— The glad stream
Flows to the ray, and warbles as it flows.

END.

www.ingramcontent.com/pod-product-compliance
Lightning Source LLC
Chambersburg PA
CBHW050845300426
44111CB00010B/1136